'This is a beautifully written book that weaves a rich tapestry of the interplay between the personal, professional and political. Our country is seriously in need of a dose of idealism to remind ourselves of the passions and energy that drove us to confront and subdue a brutal regime paving the way to the freedom we enjoy today. Neil Aggett's life story is an essential window into the enormous sacrifices that black and white activists made despite easier alternative choices. Today's younger generations need to re-commit to the easier task of consolidating a democracy bought at a very high cost.'
– Dr Mamphela Ramphele

'This is an extraordinary work of scholarly engagement on the life and death of one of South Africa's greatest idealists. It is a vital contribution to a rediscovery of a generation that foresaw what a truly liberated South Africa could become – and, in the case of Neil Aggett, paid the ultimate sacrifice in trying to realize it.'
– Professor Edward Webster

'This is the story of a young doctor's death in custody. But it is more than that. In the sensitive hands of the acclaimed writer, Beverley Naidoo, it is the unmasking of a system where torture was allowed to operate with impunity, where national security was invoked to prevent public scrutiny, where the legal system colluded in injustice and where the Rule of Law was corrupted. There are powerful and universal lessons for all time in the telling of this story. Our collective memories require a regular jolt to remind us of the need for human rights protections the world over. We have to keep the call for justice forever on our lips.'
– Helena Kennedy QC

Death of an Idealist

In Search of Neil Aggett

Beverley Naidoo

Jonathan Ball Publishers

JOHANNESBURG & CAPE TOWN

To all those who loved Neil, and to idealists, young and old,
who strive for a just society

The author would like to acknowledge quotes from the following with grateful thanks:

William Faulkner, *Go Down, Moses*. Harmondsworth: Penguin, 1960.
Steven Friedman, *Building Tomorrow Today: African Workers in Trade Unions 1970–1984*. Johannesburg: Ravan Press, 1987.
Nikos Kazantzakis, *Zorba the Greek*. London: Faber and Faber, 1961.
Oswald Mtshali, *Sounds of a Cowhide Drum*. Johannesburg: Renoster Books, 1971.
Chris van Wyk, *It is Time to Go Home*. Johannesburg: Ad Donker, 1979.

First South African Edition published in trade paperback in 2012 by
JONATHAN BALL PUBLISHERS (PTY) LTD
PO Box 33977
Jeppestown
2043

Paperbook ISBN 978-1-86842-519-8
eBook ISBN 978-1-86842-520-4

Cover design by Michiel Botha, Cape Town
Typeset by Triple M Design, Johannesburg
Printed and bound by Paarl Media, Paarl
Typeset in 10.5/15 pt Minion Pro

Twitter: www.twitter.com/JonathanBallPub
Facebook: www.facebook.com/pages/Jonathan-Ball-Publishers/298034457992
Blog: http://jonathanball.bookslive.co.za/

Contents

Abbreviations

AFCWU	African Food and Canning Workers' Union
ANC	African National Congress
CCAWUSA	Commercial, Catering and Allied Workers' Union of South Africa
COSATU	Congress of South African Trade Unions
CUSA	Council of Unions of South Africa
DLB	Dead letter box
DPSC	Detainee Parents' Support Committee
EDA	Environment and Development Agency
FCWU	Food and Canning Workers' Union
FOSATU	Federation of South African Trade Unions
GAWU	General and Allied Workers' Union
IAS	Industrial Aid Society
ILO	International Labour Organization
KAU	Kenya African Union
KPR	Kenya Police Reserve
LKB	Langeberg Kooperasie Beperk
MAWU	Metal and Allied Workers' Union
MK	Umkhonto we Sizwe

NIS	National Intelligence Service
NUSAS	National Union of South African Students
SAAWU	South African Allied Workers' Union
SACC	South African Council of Churches
SACP	South African Communist Party
SACTU	South African Congress of Trade Unions
SAP	South African Police
SASO	South African Students' Organisation
SASPU	South African Students' Press Union
SB	Special Branch or Security Branch (South African Police)
SRC	Students' Representative Council
TRC	Truth and Reconciliation Commission

Note on terminology: South Africa's history has left us with problematic racialised language – for example, 'Coloured'. We are caught in an impossible trap when describing historical reality. But readers would be driven mad were I to put all the so-called population groups in quotation marks, so I have used none.

Foreword

The struggle of man against power is the struggle of memory against forgetting.

Milan Kundera, *The Book of Laughter and Forgetting*

The Aggett inquest was a mirror held up to reflect the unimagined depths of depravity, brutality and destruction employed by the Security Police.

Helen Joseph, Founder member Congress of Democrats,
Treason Trialist and the first person put under house arrest

The vast propaganda machine of the State creates a situation in which people do not know their own history. For instance, we have lived through the period in which Neil Aggett died. What steps have we taken to ensure that the lessons of today will be taught to our children?

Dullah Omar, first Minister of Justice in a democratic South Africa

B EVERLEY NAIDOO'S *DEATH OF AN IDEALIST* IS AN IMPORTANT contribution to the history of the struggle for freedom in South Africa. Dr Neil Aggett, who died in detention on 5 February 1982, was a socially conscious young man. His dedication to his medical and trade union work, his commitment to labour activism, his uncompromising principles and his tragic death make him a very worthy subject of the insightful tribute offered in this book.

Under the apartheid regime, those with close links to African trade unions were closely scrutinised. From the mid-1970s there was a surge of trade union activity by the African workforce. Students across the country, both black and white, became involved in what was known as the 'Wages Commission', a euphemism for trade union work used by labour activists to avoid the regime's scrutiny. The National Union of South African Students (NUSAS) was at the forefront of a campaign for the recognition of trade unions and the release of political prisoners. Charles Nupen and Karel Tip, two NUSAS presidents, Glenn Moss, the president of the Wits Students' Representative Council, Cedric de Beer, a student leader, and Eddie Webster, a Sociology lecturer at the same university, were acquitted of charges that they were furthering the objects of the ANC and the Communist Party. The trial, in which Arthur Chaskalson, Denis Kuny, Raymond Tucker, Geoff Budlender and I acted as counsel, lasted ten months.

From the perspective of the regime, certain English-speaking universities were more than a mere irritant; they were a veritable anathema. Neil Aggett was a student at the University of Cape Town, where he completed a medical degree in 1976. Aggett worked as a physician in black hospitals in Umtata and Tembisa, and later at Baragwanath Hospital in Soweto. He was appointed organiser of the Transvaal branch of the Food and Canning Workers' Union. He lived with Dr Elizabeth 'Liz' Floyd, his companion (who shunned the term 'girlfriend'), in the depressed area of Jeppe in Johannesburg. Both Neil and Liz had black friends in the trade union movement. In the eyes of the security police, what better proof did one need that they were communists, terrorists and traitors? The fact that Neil Aggett avoided reporting for the regime's military service put the matter beyond any doubt.

The catalyst for Neil Aggett's arrest followed the arrest of ANC activist Barbara Hogan, whose list of 'Close Comrades' (those sympathetic to the struggle) was intercepted by the security police (through no fault of Barbara's). Over 60 students, young graduates and others involved in trade unions were detained. Many of the detainees were white. The detentions were triumphantly announced by the regime. The parents of the detainees reacted quickly, and, under the leadership of Dr Max Coleman and his wife Audrey, an organisation called the Detainees' Parents Support Committee (DPSC) was formed. They demanded access to their children and started a release campaign. No charges were brought against most of the people detained.

Neil Aggett was on that list, as was Liz. They were both detained (but not charged with any offence) on 27 November 1981. During that time, detention without trial was an integral part of the regime's strategy. The Rabie Commission had been established to placate critics of the detention system. Chief Justice Rabie was charged with reporting on the internal security of South Africa. The biased report was published on 3 February 1982. That same day, the Minister of Police Louis le Grange, when questioned in Parliament on the treatment of detainees, said,

> ... the detainees in police cells or in prisons are being detained under the most favourable conditions possible ... All reasonable precautions are being taken to prevent any of them from injuring themselves or from being injured in some other way or from committing suicide.

Just two days later, Neil Aggett was found hanging from the bars of the steel grille in his cell in John Vorster Square. He had spent 70 days in detention. He was the 51st person, and the first white person, to die in detention. He was 28.

The death of the first white detainee was more than an embarrassment to the regime. There was an outcry among the local and international press led by the *Rand Daily Mail* in South Africa and *The New York Times*. Two outstanding reporters, Helen Zille, current leader of South Africa's opposition Democratic Alliance political party, and Joseph Lelyveld, a future Pulitzer Prize-winning journalist, who became executive director of *The New York Times,* regularly reported on the inadequacy of control over the security police who tortured detainees. The regime described the media's conduct as a 'frenzy' that was becoming too much to bear.

Neil Aggett's father retained William Lane, an attorney, who in turn asked me to handle the inquest into Neil's death. Also involved were attorneys David Dison and James Sutherland, as well as advocates Denis Kuny and Mohamed Navsa. We worked very hard to produce nearly 20 statements from former detainees. Our experience told us that if we accepted the police's version that it had been a suicide, we could open up a wider inquiry into the general treatment of Neil Aggett than if we argued it was a murder. Our hope was that we could convince the magistrate that the security police could still be held responsible for driving Neil to suicide.

It is never easy for a relative to believe that their deceased loved one committed suicide. Neil Aggett's family members were no exception. But after discussions with a medical doctor, the probabilities tended to show that suicide was a distinct possibility. There was another reason that led me to this view. On the floor of Neil Aggett's cell was Nikos Kazantzakis's *Zorba the Greek*, open at page 246, dealing with the suicide of the young man whose passionate love for the widow had been rejected:

> Every minute death was dying and being reborn, just like life. For thousands of years young girls and boys have danced beneath the tender foliage of the trees in spring – beneath the poplars, firs, oaks, planes and slender palms – and they will go on dancing for thousands more years, their faces consumed with desire. Faces change, crumble, return to earth; but others rise to take their place. There is only one dancer, but he has a thousand masks. He is always twenty. He is immortal.

Neil Aggett's loving father, mother and sister bravely agreed to put forward the case based on suicide, but understandably not without great reluctance.

The inquest lasted 42 days, extended over six months. The magistrate did not make it easy for us. He stopped our cross-examination on relevant matters and ruled half of the detainees' statements inadmissable. Despite these obstacles, the graphic accounts of the systematic torture of detainees at the hands of the security police were more than embarrassing to the regime. Our argument concluded with an appeal to the court that the rule of law be observed. We argued that 'this court's finding will clearly show that we are all subject to the law of the land and its processes which protect the dignity of human life'. It was our hope that the police were not above the law, but we were sorely and sadly disappointed. The magistrate's judgment of 187 pages took nearly two days to read. The security police were exonerated and the blame was cast on one of Neil Aggett's fellow detainees, Auret van Heerden. The magistrate found that Van Heerden was not blameless in Neil Aggett's suicide, remarking that he should have informed the police immediately when he was worried that Neil Aggett had been 'broken'. The magistrate limited the detainee's obligation to a 'moral' duty and not a legal duty.

The evidence brought to light during the inquest demonstrated the flagrant disregard for human dignity that existed in South Africa. The magistrate's decision demonstrated the state's wily ability to maintain a harsh and unjust system. The finding that Neil Aggett was not hanged by his captors may have been correct. But the decision that Neil Aggett was not tortured by the security police and driven to suicide was wrong. Liz Floyd asked the question that the police and the magistrate did not answer: 'If the Security Police treated [Neil] the way the magistrate accepted they did, why did he die and why have over 50 other people died in detention?'

Where was the blame for Neil Aggett's death to lie? The Aggett inquest had cleared the security police, but at the same time had implicitly exposed the Rabie Commission's bogus findings, and the security police's callous claim that they were concerned with the welfare of detainees. 'Who would watch the watchers?' asked a report by Lawyers for Human Rights.

South Africa's Truth and Reconciliation Commission (TRC) revealed deeply troubling circumstances surrounding not only Neil Aggett's death but also the inquest, including state-organised mock hearings in advance of the actual hearings, evidence cover-ups and conscious decisions not to change the detention system following his death. The final report of the TRC stated that 'troubling inquests', such as the one into Aggett's death, led to the regime using alternative methods of eliminating its opponents.

*   *   *

About 15 000 people attended Neil Aggett's funeral on 13 February 1982. They packed St Mary's Cathedral in Johannesburg and lined the route to West Park Cemetery. Archbishop Desmond Tutu saw the funeral as a sign of hope for South Africa, 'an incredible demonstration of affection and regard for a young white man by thousands of blacks'.

Noted anti-apartheid activist Steve Biko, who was no stranger to the state's detention tactics, said in an interview before his 12 September 1977 death in police custody,

You are either alive and proud or you are dead, and when you are dead, you can't care anyway. And your method of death can itself be a politicizing thing … So if you can overcome the personal fear of death, which is a highly irrational thing, you know, then you're on your way. And in interrogation the same sort of thing applies.

Is it possible that a hopeful and altruistic Neil Aggett had read Biko's words, as well as those of Kazantzakis, before deciding to sacrifice his own life? There is no question that the death of heroes like Steve Biko and Neil Aggett, among hundreds of others, contributed to the struggle. They did not die in vain.

Thirty years later, we still find ourselves asking: what really happened to Neil Aggett? During the Nuremberg Trials, following the defeat of Nazi Germany, Romanian-born American prosecutor Benjamin B Ferencz said: 'There can be no peace without justice, no justice without law and no meaningful law without a court to decide what is just and lawful under any given circumstances.' The magistrate at Neil Aggett's inquest had clearly never read Ferencz's wise words.

This book is an inspired tribute to one of South Africa's great freedom fighters, and captures the essence of a man whose name figures among the list of heroic detainees who died in the struggle. Beverley Naidoo has meticulously, accurately and painstakingly unearthed and recorded who Neil Aggett was – from his childhood to the brave decisions he made during his student days to his detention and, finally, his untimely death. She examines his principles, beliefs and values and how justice – one of the greatest values – was cheated when it was found that there was no one to blame for his tragic death. The information is carefully laid out for readers to decide for themselves what really happened.

This book is an important contribution to the literature on the struggle for freedom. We can never forget the injustice that emerged in the name of security, the injustice that persisted in South Africa for far too many years, the injustice that claimed the lives of so many brave and innocent men and women during the darkest time of South Africa's history. I strongly encourage all those interested in the struggle and the relevance for South Africa today to read this book. Justice may have been cheated, but if we remember the tragic story of Neil Aggett, his memory and our history will not be.

George Bizos
SENIOR COUNSEL, JOHANNESBURG BAR
April 2012

In Detention

He fell from the ninth floor

He hanged himself

He slipped on a piece of soap while washing

He hanged himself

He slipped on a piece of soap while washing

He fell from the ninth floor

He hanged himself while washing

He slipped from the ninth floor

He hung from the ninth floor

He slipped on the ninth floor while washing

He fell from a piece of soap while slipping

He hung from the ninth floor

He washed from the ninth floor while slipping

He hung from a piece of soap while washing

CHRIS VAN WYK, *It is Time to Go Home*, 1979

Prologue

A 28-year-old white trade unionist has died while in detention in South Africa. The body of Dr Neil Aggett was found hanging from the bars of his cell at security police headquarters in Johannesburg in the early hours of the morning. He was being held under the country's Terrorism Act ...

I HEARD THE NEWS ON THE RADIO IN MY KITCHEN IN WINTRY ENGLAND, on 5 February 1982. Aggett? Neil Aggett? I had a second cousin with that name. Immediately, I made a long-distance call to my mother in Johannesburg. Yes, it was my cousin Joy's son. I had been an infant in 1944 when Joy had married a Kenyan settler, Aubrey Aggett, and gone up north, from Johannesburg, to live in 'Keenya', as the English used to say in those days. Although I had never met Neil, the news felt shockingly intimate. I had no idea that the security police had detained him two months earlier.

There had been at least 50 other deaths in detention, all of them black detainees. Neil's was the first white death. The official explanation: the detainee had hanged himself.

Next day's *Guardian* carried a front-page article under the headline 'Storm of anger at South African gaol death'.[1] Across the Atlantic, *The New York Times* ran the story under the headline 'White Aide of Nonwhite South African Union Found Hanged in Cell'.[2] Special correspondent Joseph Lelyveld noted that Neil and his partner, Dr Elizabeth Floyd, had been among 17 people active in black trade unions who had been arrested in early-morning raids on 27 November under the Terrorism Act. Lelyveld, who would later win the Pulitzer Prize for his book *Move Your Shadow: South Africa, Black and White* (1986), always had an eye for the personal story. He wrote of Neil having been allowed a special visit from his mother and sister on New Year's Eve, during which he had assured them, 'Don't worry. They've got nothing on me.' Colleagues, friends and relatives insisted that Neil was a very stable person who had never shown any suicidal tendency. 'He was a person of strong character. He was perfectly prepared mentally for just such an event as detention,' said Jan Theron, General Secretary of the Food and Canning Workers' Union (FCWU), for which Neil, a medical doctor, had been working voluntarily.

When some 90 000 black workers downed tools in a half-hour national work stoppage the following week, that too made international news, as did the astonishing scenes from the funeral. Thousands of black workers, with a sprinkling of white comrades, took over the streets of 'white Johannesburg' to follow the coffin, many on foot, all the way from St Mary's Cathedral to the whites-only cemetery, some nine kilometres away. Bishop Desmond Tutu, then General Secretary of the South African Council of Churches (SACC), explained the significance to white readers of *The Star*. His tone was urgent. The funeral was still a sign of hope. Under the headline, 'Mourners' tribute to a white man was a mark of respect', his message was a plea for them to remove their blinkers:

> We get an incredible demonstration of affection and regard for a young white man by thousands of blacks. This white man gets the kind of tribute that blacks reserve for those they consider their heroes – the Bikos, the Sobukwes, the Lilian Ngoyis. Neil Aggett got the kind of salute and tribute that the black townships provide only for really special people, and he was white.[3]

White South Africa's attention, however, was largely focused on mourners who raised the green, black and gold banners of the banned African National Congress (ANC), positioning it in front of the many union flags and banners. On our television news in Britain, I glimpsed Neil's parents, with a handful of family members, sitting stunned and bemused beside the grave, just a couple of feet away from Neil in his coffin under the red flag of the African

Food and Canning Workers' Union, with its circle of linking black hands. They were surrounded by workers and activists singing songs of defiance, mourning Neil as a son of the soil while pledging to continue the struggle for freedom. It was an extraordinary scene: the small white family captured in their personal grief among thousands of mourners for whom the personal was intensely political.

The Aggetts had been a part of my childhood mental landscape in colonial Africa. I vaguely knew about fearsome Mau Mau attacks on white settlers in the 1950s, and had heard that my cousin Joy and her husband Aubrey were 'sticking it out' during the State of Emergency in Kenya. They had three children: Michael, Jill and Neil, their youngest. I had gleaned from family conversations that Aubrey, a farmer and former officer in the Second World War, was a tough, strong-minded man who was involved in 'putting down' the Mau Mau rebellion.

In January 1964, a month after Kenya gained independence from Britain, Aubrey brought his family to live in South Africa, settling after a few months in Somerset West, not far from Cape Town. He was open about not wishing to live under a black government led by some of the people he had helped to lock up. They arrived in the midst of the crackdown on the opposition to apartheid. Nelson Mandela and his co-accused, who had been arrested at Rivonia six months earlier, were in the middle of their trial. The '90-days' law, rushed through Parliament and made retrospective, provided legal cover for their earlier detention. With no need for charges, no access to lawyers, solitary confinement, and the 90 days indefinitely renewable, the security police now had unfettered power to interrogate any anti-state suspects. By January 1964, the first three deaths in detention had already occurred, with two officially explained as 'suicide by hanging'. In June that year, Joy and Aubrey would have shared the relief of most white South Africans that the Rivonia trialists were being locked away for life, the black prisoners on Robben Island, and Denis Goldberg, the sole white trialist to be convicted, in Pretoria. Indeed many would have been happy to see them hanged.

When, less than a month later, my brother Paul and I were detained in the next swoop on 'subversives', the Aggetts' sympathies were most surely with our distressed, law-abiding parents, and even more so when my brother was charged and convicted in the first Bram Fischer trial.[4] Neil was ten when his parents sought their safe haven in the Cape. Eighteen years later, he was the young man whose body was reported hanging inside the notorious John Vorster Square.

Neil's parents flew to Johannesburg. His sister Jill met them at the airport. Jill remembers how her previously robust father came off the plane, instantly aged, weeping. Even before leaving home in Somerset West, in his distressed state, Aubrey had been obliged to face a *Cape Times* reporter. He kept the interview brief, having managed to type a short statement with Joy that he handed to the reporter outside the house:

> Our son was detained on November 27 last year. We still have not been told why he was held in detention. We were informed this morning that he was found hanged in his cell at John Vorster Square in Johannesburg. That is all we know.
>
> As far as we know the last time that he was seen by either family or friends was on December 31, for 40 minutes. We intend doing our utmost to find out why this happened.[5]

Aubrey's son had died in the hands of the state. In family conversation, I had picked up intimations of a rift between father and son as their views had diverged. But Neil's death was to have the effect of setting Aubrey, then nearly seventy, on a life-changing path. He wanted to know the truth.

What had happened to Neil inside John Vorster Square? Had his interrogators tortured and killed him, then strung him up to make it look like suicide? The thousands of mourners who chanted, 'Botha is a terrorist! Botha is a murderer!' were convinced of this. The security police regularly reported detainees hanging themselves, throwing themselves out of high windows, even slipping on bars of soap. Yet even if Neil had taken his own life, what had brought him to that condition? Either way, he had died in their custody.

Aubrey used his savings to fund a top-rate legal team for the inquest, led by the formidable senior counsel, George Bizos. Despite similar fact evidence from former detainees, making this a ground-breaking inquest, the verdict was 'no one to blame'. A couple of tantalising half-hour *TV Eye* documentaries in Britain could only scrape the surface of the buried stories.

For the rest of the 1980s, South Africa remained on fire, until Nelson Mandela's release in February 1990 offered the hope of dousing the flames. Exiles could now return and I could carry out research for my writing inside the country. In 1993, I set off with Olusola Oyeleye, a theatre director colleague, to find out about South African street children. Our drama workshops took us to Cape Town, which I had last seen disappearing in a purple haze beneath Table Mountain from the deck of the ship that had carried me away twenty-eight years earlier. We were on a tight timetable, but, spurred on by Olusola, I decided to drive out to Somerset West to meet Neil's parents for the first time: 'You've been talking about them. They're obviously in your mind. So why don't you go and see them?'

The Aggetts still lived in the house that had become their home not long after arriving from Kenya. Surrounded by a tidy garden, it was one of those single-storey houses with modest rooms enclosed in dark wood, brightened by sunlit windows. I was moved by their unresolved grief and deep anger at the apartheid state. They wanted to talk about Neil, with Aubrey openly acknowledging the rift that had developed between him and his son. Their pain was vivid. Aubrey's voice simmered with fury as he spoke about the police and their lies. At 81, he was still a burly, forceful man, to whom my cousin Joy often demurred. Her voice was sad, resigned, restrained. What strength of character it must have taken for Neil to stand up to, and break away from, this powerful father. The terrible irony of the death of a son at the hands of the police state that his parents had once so admired struck me more sharply than ever. Later, I would discover a deeper irony that must have tormented Aubrey even further.

According to Aubrey, Neil's chief interrogator, Lieutenant Stephan (Steven) Peter Whitehead, a man slightly younger than Neil, 'had it in for him'. Both parents were adamant that their son had never been a member of the ANC, nor a communist, as declared by the police. I sensed their unease with the idea of a future ANC government. The country was lurching towards its first democratic elections amid 'third force' violence, then being largely portrayed as 'black on black'. Aubrey spoke of Neil's death as 'this tragedy'. There was something almost mythic in the story of this once-strapping figure of authority forced to pay such a heavy price for his personal obduracy and that of his chosen country.

I took a photograph of Joy and Aubrey sitting on their floral-print sofa beneath an oil painting of bush and thorn trees below snowcapped Mount Kenya, a scene from their old farm near Nanyuki. Olusola, who had spent most of the afternoon outside playing cricket with their grandson, took a second picture. I am smiling, Joy is trying to smile and Aubrey, standing between us outside the front door, has a grim haunted look behind his tinted glasses. I came away sad. The son whom Neil's parents spoke about seemed largely a shell, although Joy seemed to hold on to something a little more tangible. Her memories about Kenya were especially poignant. 'He was such an easy child,' she said. Such an easy child. A mother's words to soothe an unhealed wound.

A year later, I was back in South Africa to gather responses to the draft of *No Turning Back*, my novel about a street child. It was July 1994. The country had survived the pre-election violence and was in honeymoon mood after President Mandela's recent inauguration. There was an almost fairy-tale atmosphere in Cape Town. I was travelling with my husband Nandha, who had narrowly escaped being sent to Robben Island, and our daughter Maya. Despite the charmed air, it was impossible to forget the myriad ways in which apartheid had eaten into the lives of so many families. Expectations across the country soared high. A long row of bright murals along a bleak Soweto street captured the mood in bold pictures and words: STEVE BIKO, MALCOLM X, MARTIN LUTHER KING, MAHATMA GANDHI and OUR MAIN MAN ROLIHLAHLA interspersed with SAVE THE WORLD, FEED THE WORLD ... SYMPTOMS AND SIGNS OF AIDS ... and EDUCATION IS THE KEY.

I couldn't help wondering what Neil would be doing in this new South Africa, had he survived. While in Cape Town, I made a second visit to the Aggetts in Somerset West, this time meeting at the home of Neil's older brother Michael, who lived nearby with his wife and five sons. Michael, an army doctor, and Mavis, a teacher, were protective and caring towards his parents. When I told them that I felt drawn towards exploring Neil's story further, Joy and Aubrey seemed pleased. I explained that I would first have to check feasibility, as the materials and people I would need to interview would be mainly in South Africa. Joy had amassed a collection of papers, photographs and news cuttings about Neil and said that I was welcome to delve into them. They were stored in their garage. Aubrey gave me details of his attorney, David Dison, in Johannesburg, who had the inquest papers. I was glad that they were keen, yet instinct told me to be cautious. I wouldn't want to cause them more distress, but if I took on the task I would have to establish my independence from the outset. My commitment had to be to the work itself and to exploring whatever truths might be revealed. I could not do less.

In Johannesburg, I visited David Dison in his bright, spacious office in a concrete-and-glass skyscraper overlooking the city's grey-domed Supreme Court. Five thick volumes, A4 in size with green covers, frayed at the edges, and faded blue and grey binding, sat on his desk. These were the court dockets, containing a full set of the statements and affidavits presented at the inquest. Aubrey had given permission for me to take them. There was a bonus. It turned out that David had known Neil. For a while, in the late 1970s and early 1980s, there had been a commune of sorts – young white radicals living in a compound of rundown white miners' houses belonging to a disused mine. Neil and his partner Liz Floyd, also a doctor, hadn't lived there, but various friends had. Apart from offering leads to those close to Neil, David said something that particularly struck me. Of all the people he had known in the commune crowd and on the left, Neil had broken away the most completely from his family. He was uncompromising. He lived his ideals.

From the outset, I knew that this was more than a single story and that this biography would have its idiosyncrasies. I was on at least two journeys. One was to discover something about the life of this younger cousin whom I'd never met but who, in a deeply racialised society, had also striven to break through the confines of upbringing. The second was, as a former exile, to understand more about the resurgence of a new generation of activists inside the country and how Neil fitted in. I have not aimed for a comprehensive picture, but, in uncovering some of the narratives and layers, I was ready to go beyond simple political legends. When I returned in 1995, to spend a week reading the papers inside the Aggetts' garage and begin my first interviews, I knew this would be a big project, although I never imagined just how long the process would take, nor that I would need to put the work aside for ten years before resuming it. Neil's parents are both dead, as is his older brother Michael. When Joy died, I felt guilty. I had raised her hopes and she had already endured so much. Out of Neil's immediate family, only his sister Jill will read this.

Nearly everyone who spoke to me about Neil, of their memories and experiences, helped me understand something more, not just about him, but the world he inhabited. Those closest to Neil took great care to explain to me, in detail, the highly charged political context in which they – and Neil – had been operating inside the country. Soon after Neil's death, there had been approaches from writers and filmmakers seeking a simplified dramatic story of the young white trade unionist-cum-doctor killed in detention. They had not got far with their projects. I sensed that had I not shown the desire to grasp the political nuances that had mattered so much to them as young activists, our conversations would have quickly terminated. A friend of Liz Floyd's commented that I should count myself lucky that she had agreed to talk with me. It was not just that I was stirring up deeply painful memories. Liz had made a judgment on my willingness to comprehend the layers of politics behind the personal story.

Throughout my search, there has been someone whose voice I have relied on more than any other. It would be impossible to understand what happened to Neil without understanding the story of his closest of comrades, Gavin Andersson, intertwined with that of Sipho Kubeka.[6] After Neil arrived in Johannesburg, about to turn 24, they became his brothers. Both spoke to me at length about their comradeship. Visiting England for a trade union course in 1995, Sipho spent a weekend at our family home. I learned that this had been no ordinary friendship. A couple of months later, in Johannesburg, Gavin Andersson made time for a number of extensive interviews and drove me to old haunts shared with Neil, most of which he hadn't visited since 'those days'. At the end of our sixth interview, he declared that he was emotionally drained and would be glad when I was back on the plane, going home.

At the end of 1997, with the Truth and Reconciliation Commission (TRC) well under way, I wrote to Gavin, explaining eighteen months' silence. There were concrete reasons why I had not begun writing, but behind these lay something much more amorphous. It's clearer to see in retrospect that I needed more time to absorb what I was hearing and reading in order to do justice to a story – stories – containing so much pain. In my email, I commented, 'But I don't think the fundamental issues are going to disappear when the hearings come to an end. What is your view?'

Gavin's perspective was encouraging. He took a long view:

> No I don't think that the issues will be any less resonant here once the TRC hearings are over. Although those who were most involved in sustaining Apartheid (the right-wing and DP [Democratic Party] politicians AND big business) protest that we are looking back too much and we must get on with life, I think it will take decades before people really erase the pain and destruction of dignity that went with that epoch.

When I finally resumed work on the project in 2007, Gavin's encouragement remained constant. Posed a question or simply asked for a view, he would respond swiftly, often at length. Most important, I felt that he was genuinely reflecting, and that this digging-up of the past was also taking him on a journey. We are now a whole generation on, yet the questions with which Neil and his comrades grappled remain alive and pressing.

PART ONE

Beginnings
and Transformation

CHAPTER 1

From Cape to Kenya

NEIL HUDSON AGGETT

> *Born on 6th October at Nanyuki, Kenya.*
> *Youngest son of J.A.E. AGGETT residing at:*

> *P.O. Box 136,*
> *Somerset West.*

I

My father was a farmer in Nanyuki, and I had one elder brother, Michael and one older sister, Jill. I went to school when I was six at the Nanyuki primary school, where I was a weekly boarder. After that I went to the Nyeri primary school, where I was a boarder until the age of ten. In January 1964, my family and I left Kenya by ship and arrived in Durban. My father sold his farm and invested his money in South Africa ...

Neil Aggett, 1st statement, John Vorster Square[7]

THE DUSTY TOWN OF NANYUKI SITS A FEW KILOMETRES NORTH OF the equator in the Laikipia Valley at the foot of Mount Kenya – Kirinyaga to Kikuyus, whose ancestral stories spoke of Ngai the Creator, who made the first man and woman, high up in its peaks, responsible for all the land as far as they could see. When Joy gave birth to Neil on 6 October 1953 at the Nanyuki Cottage Hospital, soldiers stood guard at the entrance. African 'askaris' from the King's African Rifles provided protection against night attack from Mau Mau guerrillas slipping down from the mountain forests. The 'red hats', as they were known locally – on account of their tall, black-tasselled red fezzes, worn above khaki jackets and shorts – were themselves prime targets as 'loyalists', collaborators with the European occupiers.

Knowing that the hospital was under armed guard, Joy may well have given her personal pistol to Aubrey to keep safe during labour. Carrying her pistol in a holster on her belt or in her handbag, even around the house, was a matter of course in 1953, while Aubrey always carried a large revolver. At night they slept with the guns under their pillows. Laid up in the same hospital with a bad attack of measles some months previously, Aubrey had been called upon to help fend off an attack while still in his pyjamas. The potential horror in the family tale was mitigated with a touch of humour. Yet less than nine months before Neil was born, the murder of the Ruck family on 24 January had struck a particular terror, captured in photographs of the slaughtered couple and their six-year-old son, hacked to death in his bedroom, surrounded by his toys. It was the ultimate colonial nightmare.

The Rucks were among 32 white settlers whose murders, in all their grisly details, gripped the European imagination during the Emergency years and long afterwards. However, Neil was born into a society where the majority of brutal deaths remained largely nameless in the English-speaking world, whether of the many thousands of Mau Mau fighters and civilian suspects, or the many hundreds of African loyalists.

*   *   *

Neil's grandfather, Ted Aggett, born in the eastern Cape to a farming family from Devon, in southwestern England, dreamed of going thousands of miles up north. An uncle who had been on a shooting trip to British East Africa in 1906 had returned with a deal. The British Governor had sold him 25 farms, at £25 each, in the fertile central highlands below Mount Kenya. The condition was that Ted's uncle put European settlers on the land. With each farm covering thousands of acres, he had no difficulty selling them on to family members, including Ted, who was managing a hotel in Seymour, up in the thickly wooded Amatola Mountains. In 1911, Ted's parents and three generations of Aggetts and Smiths from Ted's mother's side, a weave of cousins and in-laws, set sail with their trunks for Mombasa aboard the SS *Adolf Woermann*. Twenty-eight-year-old Ted had recently married, indeed eloped with, 21-year-old Claire Ogilvie Hudson. With a strict magistrate stepfather, who had sent her to study at the Royal College of Music in London, she had been expected to do better than Ted, a small-town hotelier. Claire, known as Bonnie to her new Aggett family, was also pregnant.

The ship anchored in the middle of the deepwater harbour at Kilindini, to the south of Mombasa Island. The family were rowed to where they could scramble over rocks to the shore and make their way to British officials in the customs shed. From Mombasa to Nairobi, they travelled on the ten-year-old railway.[8] In Nairobi, settlers who were heading for Naivasha and Nakuru could continue up-country by train. But those travelling northeast to the foothills and plains beneath Mount Kenya bought ox-wagons and mule-drawn buckboard carts, hiring Swahili-speaking cooks and other 'boys' to accompany them.

South Africans, both English and Afrikaner, were a minority in the European population in a colony that attracted many English gentry, especially military men of officer class. However the Aggetts and Smiths were to become the largest European settler 'extended family' in Kenya. Aubrey was born in Nairobi on 21 July 1912, and his brother Hudson the following year. Soon afterwards, with war looming between Britain and Germany, and East Africa likely to become a battleground, Ted took his family back south to the eastern Cape, where they remained until Aubrey was ten.

* * *

In 1922, Ted Aggett's family returned to Kenya, leaving South Africa at the time of the white miners' rebellion on the Witwatersrand. The mine owners planned to reduce wages and bring in cheap black labour. Hundreds were injured when the rebels were quelled with military force. There were deaths, including three white miners sent to the gallows.

As it happened, 1922 also saw Kenya's first wage-related political unrest. At its centre was Harry Thuku, a 27-year-old Kikuyu man who was a clerk in the government Treasury. During the war, many thousands of Africans had served in the British Army as cooks, labourers and stretcher-bearers. Far from being rewarded for their service, they returned home to find that 'land leases' for white settlers had been increased from 99 years to 999 years. A forceful orator, Thuku used his weekends to tour rural areas speaking out against exploitation of labour, laws that prevented Africans from buying land, the hut tax and the *kipande* (pass), by which the authorities controlled the movement of Africans.

In the eyes of Europeans and the more conservative Kikuyu chiefs, Thuku was an 'agitator', and on 14 March 1922 the Governor had him arrested. Thuku's supporters gathered at the police station in central Nairobi; over the next couple of days, some 7 000 to 8 000 people, including Kikuyu women, faced a line of African colonial policemen armed with rifles and bayonets.[9] Stories differ over what led to the first shots, but a massacre followed. The first Kikuyu political song, commemorating the bravery of the women who had protested with their menfolk, dates back to these first stirrings of the trade union struggle in Kenya.

Thuku, who was detained without trial in the remote semi-arid north for the next eight years, was dangerous not just because he agitated for higher wages. His articulacy threatened the core imperial belief about innate European superiority, and that it would be hundreds of years before Africans, 'the natives', would ever be 'civilised'. Fifty years later, it would be an argument repeated between Neil and his father.

*   *   *

The little family history that exists about the years between two world wars takes the form of pioneer stories. Ted took his wife Bonnie and their two sons to the land he had acquired a few miles outside of Nanyuki. In 1971, a teen-age Neil pasted an article into his journal entitled 'Pioneers of East Africa'. The writer, Elsa Pickering, tells a story of Ted Aggett and his family being stuck in the open during heavy rains for four days in lion country when their mule-drawn buckboard cart was stranded on a bridge over the flooded Ewaso Ng'iro River. A washed-down tree had got stuck in the axle, causing the mules to panic and bolt. With only a little pork to eat, they made a fire under an umbrella. The two boys, Aubrey and Hudson, slept in the buckboard, blankets draped over them as a wet tent. Reaching home eventually, they found rain pouring through the roof of their two-roomed thatched house.

Between the wars, Ted was largely absorbed in managing the Gilgil Hotel in the Rift Valley, his clients including aristocratic members of the hedonistic Happy Valley set. When he gave that up to develop his thousands of acres of bush into profitable land, the former hotelier remained a sociable man, one who enjoyed company at the club, as well as riding and boxing. For Bonnie, life revolved more closely around her two sons and the home they called 'Glen Ogilvie'. Although the terrain bears no resemblance to a Scottish glen, the name asserted both lineage and heritage.

As a young man, Aubrey began working as a farm manager for relatives, the Bastard family, on the Sweet Waters estate along the Ewaso Ng'iro River, while Hudson was sent back to South Africa to study at Glen Agricultural College, in the Orange Free State. By the time war was declared in 1939, Hudson had returned, finding work at Kenya Creameries. The brothers were close enough to have bought a farm together at Sotik, about a hundred miles southwest of their father's farm. However, plans to develop it were put on hold as both enlisted in the Kenya Regiment, Aubrey number 222 and Hudson number 404. While Hudson rose to be in charge of a battery of African artillery, Aubrey began as an intelligence officer in Abyssinia during the East African campaign, fighting alongside Emperor Haile Selassie's Ethiopian patriots against Mussolini's occupation. With the defeat of the Italians in 1941, Aubrey, now a captain, was transferred to the livestock control division, where he was responsible for buying cattle needed to feed Allied forces in North Africa, as well as their thousands of German and Italian prisoners. At the beginning of the war, both brothers were still single.

*   *   *

How Aubrey first met Joy reflects the colonial interweaving of Kenya and South Africa. Aubrey's employer at the time was Aunt Ethel, his father's youngest sister, who had married into the Bastard family. Shortly before the war, Aunt Ethel invited a young woman related by marriage to come up from South Africa for a holiday at Sweet Waters. Who can say whether the invitation was entirely innocent? But before the young lady's visit was over, she and Aubrey, the young farm manager, were engaged and he was given leave to accompany her to South Africa to arrange their marriage.

It was during the voyage south that Aubrey met Joy Norman, who was enjoying a holiday cruise with her father. A qualified librarian who worked at Johannesburg Central Library, at 22 the glamorous Joy was five years younger than Aubrey. He invited her to the wedding. Joy was unable to attend but sent a gift. A few weeks later the package was returned to her, unopened. A note from Aubrey said that his fiancée had called the marriage off and he had returned to Kenya alone. Joy wrote back, beginning a correspondence that would continue through the war.

In January 1944, with three weeks' leave, Aubrey flew to Johannesburg to propose. Joy was a town girl who had never been to the Kenya Highlands, although, as an avid reader, she may have been familiar with Karen Blixen's exotic, romantic and aristocratic memoir, *Out of Africa*, published in 1937. Joy accepted Aubrey's proposal.

A photo taken after the wedding ceremony in Kensington, Johannesburg, on 5 February 1944 shows her smiling radiantly, with hand held tight by a uniformed Aubrey. In his Winston Churchill spectacles, he looks like the cat that got the cream. They are standing on the steps of a plain brick building in front of a closed wooden door. Joy wears a stylish, knee-length white dress with matching shoes and an elegant wide-brimmed white hat. Her younger sister Madge, in a slightly darker, equally elegant outfit, stands on her other side, with what may be a touch of a question in her eyes. They are soon to be separated by thousands of miles. In the photo, my father stands smiling next to Aubrey as 'best man', in a wide-lapelled, double-breasted, pinstriped suit. Only six years older than Joy, he was her debonair, musical uncle who had often chaperoned her to dances. Aubrey in his uniform could have personified 'There's a Boy Up North', a song my father had written for Vera Lynn, nicknamed 'the Forces' Sweetheart', better known for her 'There'll Always Be an England'. There is something very English about the wedding group on the steps, and the only clue that this wartime snapshot was not taken in England lies in the resplendent bouquets carried by the sisters, overflowing with the deep-coloured cannas of a South African summer.

Any pleasure that Aubrey's mother, Bonnie, might have taken in her son's marriage was short-lived. Within a week of the marriage, news arrived that Aubrey's younger brother Hudson was dead. He and his unit had been on their way to Burma when their ship (the SS *Khedive Ismail*) was torpedoed by a Japanese submarine off the Maldives. Almost everyone had drowned.

Aubrey returned to his post up north. Arriving in Kenya, a few months later, Joy found her mother-in-law reserved and cold. She put this down to the loss of her son. However, for the young librarian brought up in the tree-lined end of Kensington, Johannesburg, who had left behind her family, friends and urban comforts, life in Kenya must have been a challenge. She had married a man whom she had got to know through correspondence but with whom she had actually spent very little time.

CHAPTER 2

Settlers and resistance

I N THE FIRST YEAR OF THEIR MARRIAGE, THE AGGETTS LIVED IN THE small Rift Valley town of Nakuru, where Aubrey worked in government livestock control. Early European settlers in the Rift Valley had sent labour recruiters east, into the Kikuyu areas of the central highlands, to encourage Kikuyu families to become tenant labourers on European farms. In return for a prescribed number of days of labour, helping the Europeans clear and work the land, 'squatter' families were allowed to live on the farms, graze their cattle and cultivate a small *shamba* (field) for themselves. While the white farmers simply regarded them as hired hands, the Kikuyu believed they were acquiring customary rights of ownership and use of land, called *githaka*. Most were unaware that a 1925 ruling in Kenya's High Court declared that they were only 'tenants at will' who could be evicted by the European landlords without even the right of appeal.

As settler farmers began to develop high-grade dairy and beef farming, they increasingly regarded Kikuyu-owned cattle as a disease threat. They also objected to these cattle grazing on land that they now wanted for their own expanding herds. When annual tenant contracts came up for renewal, European farmers reduced the amount of land that each Kikuyu family could cultivate. By 1952, the year before Neil was born, some 100 000 Africans had been forcibly 'repatriated' from the Rift Valley. The choice for Kikuyu families was stark: either go to an overcrowded 'native reserve' in the central highlands or join the growing number of poverty-stricken squatters in the shanties on the outskirts of Nairobi.

After a year of livestock control work in Nakuru, Aubrey took Joy to start their family on the farm that he had bought with his brother before the war. Sotik was far to the west, across the Aberdares, the Mau Escarpment and beyond the Mara Forest. Here, Aubrey supervised the building of a house and threw himself into developing his farm and herds of cattle, using local Kipsigi and Kisii labourers. Their first son, Michael John, was born in 1946 and their daughter, Elizabeth Jill, three years later, in 1949. In these early years of their marriage, they could not see much of his parents at their home farm, Glen Ogilvie, near Nanyuki. While Aubrey's work as the bwana took him out on the farm and beyond, Joy's life as the young memsahib revolved mainly around the house and garden, overseeing domestic staff and, after her children were born, the children's ayah. There was the social life in the club with other settlers, including those from the tea estates around Kericho. Aubrey was a keen horseman, and polo, tennis, golf and bridge interspersed days and weeks spent on their remote farm.

Yet the central thread in Joy's later reminiscences was not isolation but her pleasure in 'country life'. She loved being surrounded by the bush, with its vast herds of zebra, wildebeest and giraffe, as well as elephant, lion, cheetah, elusive leopard and all manner of antelope and other wildlife. The settlers accorded animals their domain, and the presence of wildlife was not regarded as an intrinsic threat to the settlers' way of life. But the presence of 'undomesticated' Africans was. Like the pass system in South Africa, the *kipande*[10] controlled the lives of Africans, who, if found in the 'wrong' place, could be accused of trespass, and jailed.

*   *   *

For the settlers, the person who came to epitomise the threat presented by Africans was Jomo Kenyatta. His ability to take on the British in their own language was a source of great pride to Africans, especially other Kikuyu. After 15 years in England, where he had studied Anthropology at the London School of Economics, Kenyatta returned home in 1946 and, in the

following year, became President of the Kenya African Union (KAU). Copies
of Kenyatta's speeches were published by Henry Muoria Mwaniki, a largely
self-taught man born the same year as Aubrey, in a village barely a few hours'
walk from Nairobi. Having studied journalism through a British correspondence course, Muoria founded his own Kikuyu newspaper and published political pamphlets, including a short Kikuyu political history. Muoria wrote
with pride about the 1938 publication in Britain of Kenyatta's thesis, *Facing
Mount Kenya:*[11]

> By doing so, he exposed the lies of the white man here in Kenya who says
> that black people have very small brains and that they are like monkeys and
> that [whites] took their lands because they were not people, only monkeys.[12]

In the Central Highlands and Rift Valley, violent opposition to government
cattle-dipping campaigns and squatter evictions escalated. There were arson attacks on isolated white farms and rumours of a secret organisation, believed by
Europeans to be 'Mau Mau', which was bringing farm labourers together for
mass oath-taking, or 'oathing', ceremonies dedicated to getting rid of the settlers. Despite Mau Mau being outlawed in 1950, the resistance and violence continued. In January and February 1952, there were arson attacks on white farms in
the Nanyuki region, near the senior Aggetts' home farm. Living in the foothills
of the densely forested Mount Kenya, where the attackers could hide, Nanyuki
settlers felt particularly vulnerable. By May, assassinations of chiefs loyal to the
settlers were under way. By June, there were reports that Mau Mau supporters
were taking a 'killing oath'. Whether or not the settlers understood the meaning
of Kikuyu songs that filled the air, they sensed the growing defiance:

> *My people, we have to think whether or not this land of ours*
> *Left to us long ago by Iregi, will ever be returned.*
> Chorus: *God blessed this land of ours, we Kikuyu*
> *And said we should never abandon it.*
> *The Europeans are but guests and they will leave this land of ours*
> *Where then, will you, the traitors, go when the Kikuyu rise up?*[13]

This was one of many songs that were sung on 26 July 1952 in Nyeri Showgrounds
by a crowd of some 30 000 people at a KAU rally addressed by its president,

Jomo Kenyatta. He spoke of land, unjustly taken from Africans, that only wild game was permitted to enjoy while Africans were starving of hunger. Then he moved on to education, freedom, wages and the colour bar, his audience able to contrast the principles he elaborated with their own harsh experiences at the hands of Europeans. Many hopes were raised by Kenyatta's vision.

Around this time, in 1952, Ted Aggett, now almost 70, offered Aubrey a farm near Nanyuki, just a few miles from their home farm, Glen Ogilvie. It was more than he could cope with, Ted Aggett said. Placing a manager in charge of the farm in Sotik, Aubrey brought his family to Nanyuki, at first moving in with 'the old people'. It was clearly not just age that worried Ted. The highlands were rapidly turning into a war zone.

The settlers' fears came to a head with the murder of Chief Waruhiu, the government's Paramount Chief for the Central Province. He was a Kikuyu senior elder, a Christian and a prosperous landlord who, like European settlers, had evicted tenants and was bitterly opposed to Mau Mau. The photograph of his body, slumped across the rear seat of his dark-brown Hudson automobile, after being waylaid in broad daylight on the way to a Native Tribunal in Nairobi, sent out shock waves. The settlers demanded that a government that couldn't protect even its Paramount Chief should resort to more drastic measures against the Mau Mau.

Under this pressure, the new Governor, Sir Evelyn Baring, declared a State of Emergency, which took effect from midnight on 20 October. A battalion of the Lancashire Fusiliers arrived the next morning from Egypt, bolstering five African battalions from the King's African Rifles. Over 100 suspected Mau Mau leaders were taken into custody, wiping out the entire leadership of KAU, the only African political party in the country. Some on the wanted list had already fled, including the fearless Dedan Kimathi, who was to become a symbol of the resistance and one of the most wanted Mau Mau leaders. Kimathi harnessed the growing frustration of younger Kikuyu, who had given up on their elders being able to negotiate political freedom. Several leaders had fought in the King's African Rifles alongside British soldiers during the Second World War, learning guerrilla tactics in places like Burma. Now they were ready to set up fighting units in their own forests. Others, however, like Jomo Kenyatta, waited for the knock on the door, making no attempt to escape.

Like the majority of white settlers and the colonial government, the Aggetts misread Kenyatta and Kikuyu politics. While relying on, and supporting, the small number of conservative land-owning elders like Chief Waruhiu, who controlled the patronage of the colonial state, they blurred the distinctions between moderate and militant nationalists. Kenyatta was a constitutional nationalist; even though his speeches helped to politicise many thousands of Africans, he was not a leader of Mau Mau. However, the outcome of his trial in the far-flung northern town of Kapenguria was predetermined and, as described by the historian David Anderson, was 'a petulant and unedifying affair'.[14] Judge Ransley Thacker, regarded by the settlers as one of their own, negotiated an extraordinary payment of £20 000 through clandestine correspondence with Governor Baring. According to Anderson, the evidence in the trial was thin and the charges untrue, with Kenyatta denying them all. However, Thacker's mind was already made up, his attitudes already formed. When Kenyatta endeavoured to explain the nature of the grievances that lay behind Mau Mau, Thacker expressed exasperation, declaring, 'Grievances have nothing whatever to do with Mau Mau, and Mau Mau has nothing whatever to do with grievances.'[15] Kenyatta was found guilty and jailed for seven years in the arid north, near the border with Sudan, satisfying the white settlers, the Governor and British government. But removing Kenyatta and his co-accused did nothing to stop the growing numbers of young Kikuyu who were taking to the forests to join the Mau Mau.

After returning to Nanyuki and his parents' home farm, Glen Ogilvie, with Joy and two children, Aubrey had immediately joined the Kenya Police Reserve (KPR). The job of reservists was to support the local police and British soldiers operating from their base outside Nanyuki. With Aubrey away from home a lot, tracking Mau Mau fighters sometimes for days at a time, he taught Joy how to fire a pistol, by practising on trees. Scared of the weapon, she desperately hoped that she would never have to use it. As a toddler, Jill became used to seeing her parents always carrying their guns. To the family, the threats felt palpable.

The British journalist James Cameron, then an up-and-coming correspondent for the *Daily Mirror*, visited Kenya and sounded an alarm about the KPR a few weeks after the State of Emergency was declared. In an open letter to Sir Evelyn Baring, he wrote about 'trigger-happy settlers' in vigilante uniforms whom he accused of frequently 'over-stepping the mark'.[16] He warned that their carefree attitude to the law, and racism towards Africans, was igniting an already inflammable situation and they would undermine any notion of moral order that had been claimed by the British Empire. To the settlers, Cameron was an interfering, soft-headed liberal with no idea of what it was like to be living under siege, a view that the Aggetts most likely shared. With most European settlers not prepared to accept that there was any legitimate material basis for African grievances, Mau Mau were seen as a manifestation of Africans who were 'primitive' and 'savage' in their rejection of 'European civilisation'.

The settlers' horror mounted as evidence emerged of domestic servants involved in Mau Mau attacks, especially on isolated elderly settlers. Following the murder of the Ruck family, a frenzied mob of several hundred Europeans threatened to break into Government House in Nairobi. Sir Michael Blundell, the settlers' political leader, describes the scene vividly in his memoir, *So Rough a Wind*, and the crowd's wild reaction on catching sight of the Sultan of Zanzibar, who happened to be visiting Government House. In front of him a little woman in brown, normally a respectable shop-owner, was 'beside herself with fury and crying out … "There, there, they've given the house over to the fucking niggers, the bloody bastards" … This was my first experience of men and women who had momentarily lost all control of themselves, and had become merged together as an insensate unthinking mass.'[17]

Governor Baring got the message. Trials were hastened and legal corners cut. Under the Emergency, the death penalty had already been extended to cover a wide range of offences. Many people were subsequently sentenced to death even when the evidence against them was transparently thin. There were to be far more executions in Kenya than in any other British colonial struggle, with 1 090 Kikuyu men hanged and 30 women sentenced to life imprisonment. Collective punishment, mass detentions without trial, hooded informers and torture became common.

When Joy gave birth to Neil in Nanyuki, on 6 October 1953, she and Aubrey were still living with his parents. The Emergency was at its height, with Aubrey deeply involved with KPR operations. June had been a particularly bad month for Nanyuki settlers, with a number of attacks. At Sweet Waters, where Aubrey had been a farm manager for Aunt Ethel before the war, Mau Mau fighters murdered the Payet family. Mr Payet was an assistant farm manager from the Seychelles. While the killing of an entire Indian family, including all the children, did not feature in the news in the same way as the murder of the Ruck family, it impacted on Joy and Aubrey because of their personal connection. It was certainly enough for them to single it out over 40 years later:

> AUBREY: Why they should have been killed, I don't know.
>
> JOY: Not political in any way. Terrible thing they should be done like that.
>
> AUBREY: This is the sort of thing they used to do. Kill other tribes for no rhyme – because they weren't in the Mau Mau. Kill their own people. They killed comparatively few Europeans. It was mostly their own people who hadn't joined the gangs.
>
> JOY: It was a time when it was very nerve-wracking really. Aubrey always carried a gun and I had to too, in my bag, which I was terrified of … I had a few shots [in learning to use it] but nothing very much. We were very very careful and had a high fence put around the house. It was a wooden house and could have gone up in flames just like that.
>
> AUBREY: We had guards that were supposed to patrol at night.
>
> JOY: And Aubrey had to go out tracking with the police, tracking these chaps up the mountain too.
>
> AUBREY: That was when we were at the home farm, not when we got to the second farm.

The wooden house is 'the second farm', to which they moved when Neil was three months old, early in 1954. Given to them by Aubrey's father, it was on 6 000 acres (2 428 hectares) of land, about a mile and a quarter wide and six miles long (2.8 by 9.6 kilometres). It was about 14 miles (22.5 kilometres) from Nanyuki, further into the Laikipia plain, and along the southwestern side of the broad Ewaso Ng'iro River. Its name, 'Ol Elerai', came from the great yellow fever trees growing beside the slow muddy river, on the other side of which lay the Bastards' farm, Sweet Waters. Aubrey and Joy had wanted to move there earlier, but had delayed because of the security risks. They had been concerned about leaving Aubrey's parents on their own, but had also not been able to get anybody to work on the dilapidated farmhouse. Eventually, after they had moved into the house and were more or less camping there, Aubrey was able to persuade some Indian workmen to undertake the repairs. With a house made of wood and on stilts, they felt particularly vulnerable to it being set on fire. Particularly scary for the children was the outside toilet, a 'long drop', to which they would troop out while their father watched over them with his revolver.

As a small child, Jill had a strong sense of their isolation:

> We were on what they called VHF, an emergency radio. We had a phone,
> but it was a party line, But if there was an attack, they always cut the tele-
> phone wire, so this radio contact was all there was. One of their methods of
> attacking was hamstringing, to disable the cattle, which had to be destroyed
> the next day. But they used to bellow, and if you ever heard the cattle bel-
> lowing you would suspect something was happening, and I can remember
> it once.

One afternoon, when Neil was six months old and Jill about five, their parents took them to see their grandparents at Glen Ogilvie. There was a storm,
and on the way home their vehicle stuck in the mud by the Ewaso Ng'iro
River. Aubrey tried to drive the car out, using sacks to gain purchase. He
was soaked, but the car would not budge. He sent Neil's ayah to one of the
bomas to ask the herdsman to carry a message back to Glen Ogilvie. But the
man would not risk such a journey at night. Instead, he and Aubrey worked
until very late trying to free the car. Eventually they admitted defeat. The only
thing was to wait until morning. At first, Aubrey planned to sleep near the
car in the bush, so that if anyone attacked he could shoot them. But it was
'too ruddy cold', and he soon climbed inside. The family huddled under the
mud-encrusted sacks. Neil cried because he had no food, and everyone feared
that his persistent cries would alert a Mau Mau gang. Aubrey had collected a
box of Ugandan cigars from the post office that day, so he and Joy smoked to
pass the time and to warm themselves. As soon as it grew light, the herdsman
summoned Aubrey's father, who sent a team of oxen down to the river to pull
them out. A few days later, an encampment was found nearby, intensifying
the family's sense of a close encounter with death and a lucky escape.

Yet, looking back on their Kenya days, the Aggetts recalled enjoying 'a
good life', even though they lived in fear of attack. While living with Aubrey's
parents at the height of the Mau Mau crisis, Aubrey would stand guard with
a gun while his wife and children walked across from the main house to
their sleeping quarters. Michael was forbidden to go fishing after one of their
employees was attacked with a panga and thrown into the river. The man
pretended to be dead, later making his way up to the house to bang on the
Aggetts' door. Jill remembers seeing the bleeding apparition.

The 'good life' was dependent to a large extent on plentiful labour and servants. When the district commissioner, 'Chippy' Lewin, gained information that Ted's Kikuyu labourers were feeding Mau Mau fighters, he enlisted Aubrey's help in secretly replacing them with Nandi labourers. Even when Ted objected that 'my labour is no worse than anyone else's', the forced removal went ahead. His labourers, their families and possessions were summarily loaded onto lorries and despatched to the reserve. Later, when two replacement Nandi labourers took the cattle down to the river to drink, they were hailed by a man who disappeared through the thick Kei-apple hedge as soon as he saw that they were not the usual cowherds. Police tracked the suspect through the hedge into a field of yellow maize, where three men jumped up and ran. The police shot all of them and took the bodies in a Land Rover for Ted to see. It was clear that the dead men had been eating the yellow maize and cattle meat. Ted needed no further proof of their guilt, declaring, 'I'm satisfied'. Again, little Jill heard the shots and saw the corpses. Neil would have been too small to remember, but fear permeates. Even after the effective defeat of the Mau Mau in 1954, remaining 'on guard' remained a way of life for settler families.

Neil grew up in Kenya with guns as a regular part of life. Aubrey was very particular about their cleaning and oiling, as well as their handling. Jill's brothers each had an air gun with which they would shoot birds, although shooting game was always only for food. Sometimes, in the evening, their father would take them out to shoot impala or other gazelles. Although Michael was almost eight years older than Neil, they were not allowed to go out shooting on their own. For Aubrey, who as a child had shot himself in his finger with an air gun, it was a priority to teach his children how to handle guns safely. One occasion remained imprinted in Aubrey's mind when a Thomson's gazelle, a 'tommy', had suddenly appeared close to them in the bush. In his eagerness to take out his gun, Neil had pointed it at his father. Furious, Aubrey barred Neil from shooting until he learned how to handle his gun properly. By all accounts, Aubrey had a fierce temper. I can imagine the young boy's excitement turning to embarrassment and humiliation under his father's reprimand. *How many times have I told you …?* It's a potent image: the strapping, burly father admonishing his child for a folly that could have devastating consequences.

For Aubrey, with his experience of war, knowing how to shoot to kill, whether the target be animal or human, was a necessary state of affairs:

'In war you get cruelty on both sides.' Two of the earliest Mau Mau victims
were Ian Meiklejohn, a retired naval officer, and his wife, a doctor, who lived
near Thomson's Falls. The couple had been taken by surprise at night on 22
November 1952, as they sat reading in their sitting room, where they were left
for dead, having been cut about the head and body. Dr Meiklejohn, whose
wrist had been slashed as she stretched out for her gun in her handbag, had
regained consciousness and, in her bloodied state, managed to drive eight
miles (13 kilometres) to the police station. Her husband died from his injuries.
Aubrey was involved in questioning suspects. One at a time, the suspects were
taken outside and a 'pretend' shot fired to intimidate the others who remained
behind. The suspects' employer later complained about this inhumane
treatment. When Aubrey's superior, a colonel in the special police, arrived,
Aubrey fully expected to be in trouble. Instead, the colonel said, 'I believe you
had very little to do with this, but remember this, "Dead men tell no tales".
That was my ticking off. That kind of thing does happen, and will happen.
We thought we were doing the right thing, to save somebody's life.' Asked
whether he thought the South African security police saw themselves in a
similar kind of role, Aubrey said he doubted it: 'Their main object in these
cases [like Neil's] was to curry favour. What Whitehead [Neil's interrogator]
wanted was promotion.'

Later, I thought that it was this – his own experience in the KPR and a
former commanding officer's advice that 'dead men tell no tales' – that drove
Aubrey's intense belief that his son had died, palpably and physically, in
Whitehead's hands.

CHAPTER 3

From Kenya to the Cape: 'We'll march on'

W

HILE CONSTANTLY AWARE OF SECURITY, JOY AND AUBREY
did what they could to keep their children's lives as unaffected
as possible under the Emergency. After tea, Joy would take them
in the car with their father to see the cattle in the bomas, watch the milking
or look for game. Still a keen horseman and polo player, Aubrey kept a large
paddock with about 50 horses, many of them trained for racing on the course
at the Nanyuki Sports' Club. Aubrey also bought a little Welsh pony for the
children, and once Neil could ride he would sometimes accompany Aubrey
on the little bay called Megan. There were at least once-weekly trips into town
and the club, where the children could play with other settler children. Jill
recalls her father often having business in Nanyuki, spending what seemed
like hours waiting for him in the car. Joy and the children were never left on
their own at the farm.

When Neil was about four, following the death of both grandparents,
Aubrey inherited the home farm. Reluctantly, he sold Ol Elerai to the Ol
Pejeta estate that surrounded it.[18] The family moved back to Glen Ogilvie,
which was much nearer Nanyuki. With the easing of the Emergency, it was
also possible to leave a manager on the farm once a year and go down to the
coast at Malindi for a family holiday. It was a two-day trip to get there, and Joy

packed a great picnic in a *kikapu* (Swahili for 'basket') for the journey. On the way, they would stop at Voi to see Aubrey's second cousin, Daphne Sheldrick, and her husband David, the founder and chief warden of Tsavo National Park, a vast area of over 5 000 square miles (13 000 square kilometres). Entering Tsavo, Aubrey would offer a shilling for the first person to see an elephant, but he was always first. With the Sheldricks pioneering their animal orphanage and wildlife rehabilitation programme, there were always one or two baby elephants that would be brought for the Aggett children to pet.

Continuing on their journey, as soon as they saw baobab trees they knew they were getting near the coast. Jill recalls them arriving caked in dust. Once at Malindi, with its palm trees and market smelling of mangoes and limes, they would stay in a beachside cottage that belonged to relatives, the children sleeping on camp beds on the veranda. For the children, it was a time of swimming, surfing, playing in the sand, and enjoying being together as a family. Shorter holidays, much nearer home, were spent in the Samburu National Park, either camping or staying in rondavels at Buffalo Springs or Archers' Post.

Neil spent most of his first five years as the only child at home on the farm, since Michael and Jill were away at boarding school for much of the year. At six, he was sent to Nanyuki Primary School, which catered for the children of officers in the King's African Rifles as well as those of local white settlers. During the week, Neil lived in town with a family friend who had about six other children boarding with her, but came home at weekends. At seven, he joined Jill, who was in her last year, at Nyeri Primary School, a prep school based on the English model, for white colonial children. Michael was already in Rhodes House at the Prince of Wales School in Nairobi, a public school founded by Lord Delamere and the British Governor in 1925. Neil now came home only at half term, but every three weeks Joy and Aubrey would visit the younger children and take them out for a picnic on the golf course. With his parents at Glen Ogilvie, not too far away from Nanyuki, Neil was luckier than many other children, some of whom had to travel for long hours, even days, by train. Some of these children would at times come home with the Aggetts at half term, because of the distance from their own families.

Nights at Nyeri were spent in a dormitory of some 50 children. It was the stuff of English boarding-school stories, with smelly, prickly coir mattresses, lumpy pillows and an allocation of smelly buckets and commodes. There were large open showers and a wide Matron-height table on which 20 or so shivering children had to stand for ear inspection. Matron wielded a long stick, but most misdemeanours were punished with the offender being 'tackied' with a running shoe. Years later, Neil was to tell his partner Liz Floyd how much he had missed home. This was encapsulated in a memory of lying in the sanatorium with chronic bronchitis, longing for his mother. His sister Jill, who felt very maternal towards her rather sickly younger brother, remembered him spending weeks in the 'san'. However, Jill recollects that the sister-in-charge 'absolutely adored' Neil, quite unlike Matron. The sanatorium offered some respite.

There was one matron and one housemistress for about a hundred children. Jill had started at Nyeri Primary School before the capture of Dedan Kimathi in October 1956, after which the army halted its forest operations. The school was situated on a ridge that ran between the Aberdares and Mount Kenya, close to the Kikuyu reserve. At the height of the Emergency, RAF Harvard aircraft used to fly in daylight from their base in Mweiga, within sight of the school, on bombing raids. Later these were joined by Lincoln heavy bombers and Vampire jet fighters, and the children would watch the silver specks against the sky and smoke rising from the deep green forests as bombs detonated.

At one time, a unit of KPR askaris – mainly Wakamba men from the east, including some Burma veterans – had been assigned to the school, quartered in aluminium huts alongside the senior dormitory. Every morning they would parade on the murram pitch with their Greener police shotguns and ancient 303 Lee-Enfield rifles, weaponry that reflected the racial pecking order. When older brothers or fathers in the police or army came to visit, they brought their Sten and Patchett submachine guns, Webley revolvers and Number Four and Five sniper rifles. Legends of gun battles near the school, and stories of dead 'Micks', tied hand and foot on poles as they were carried away, would have fired the imagination of little settler boys in their games of war. Contemptuous terms like 'Mickey Mice' and 'Mickey Mouse' for Mau Mau probably persisted long after the guerrilla fighters had been blasted out of the forests. A ditty, created by some of the children, mocked both school and Mau Mau:

> Nyeri, Nyeri, wet and dreary
> How does your Mau Mau go?
> With screams and yells and filthy smells
> And dead cats all in a row.

The tone of the children's verse contrasted sharply with the anodyne jingo-ism of the unofficial settlers' anthem singing the praises of a 'land of the lion … adventure and sun'. It was little wonder that children boarding at Nyeri Primary School dreamed of going home.

*   *   *

By 1963, with Kenya's independence set for the end of the year, many settler fam-ilies had put their farms up for sale and were planning to leave. South Africa, Australia and the UK were seen as prime destinations. In preparation, Aubrey sent Michael south to Kingswood College in Grahamstown. While there were relatives in Aubrey's extensive family who chose to stay on in Kenya, he felt that he had pressing reasons to leave. As a screening officer, detecting 'those mixed up with the Mau Mau' and laying charges against them, he feared that 'these chaps weren't beyond taking revenge'. Although he appreciated Jomo Kenyatta's generosity in stating 'Let bygones be bygones', Aubrey could not countenance having 'fellows in charge of us, or in high positions, who had been our original enemies and [they had] been punished as a result of what I had done'. In partic-ular, he feared that these political prisoners-turned-state functionaries were ca-pable of taking revenge on women and children too. South Africa, by contrast, seemed to promise security. Aubrey ended these recollections and reflections with a statement that shows how his worldview changed after his son's death in detention: 'As things are now, I'm jolly sorry I ever came. I would much sooner have been there. Possibly Neil would have been alive.'

The apartheid state, under Prime Minister Hendrik Verwoerd, welcomed the white families escaping black rule. Having left the British Commonwealth and become a republic in 1961, South Africa cultivated the image of a bastion of Western civilisation in Africa. The government paid £60 for each mem-ber of the family to assist with passage costs, and, if Joy and Aubrey had so wished, it would have paid for three weeks in a hotel. Nevertheless, leaving Kenya hadn't been easy, and Joy recalled that, of the children, Neil seemed to be the most affected. Perhaps Jill, who was nearly 15, covered up her feel-ings more, although she remembers crying, heartbroken at leaving. Michael was already in South Africa, but the rest of the family had one final holiday in Malindi, just before sailing south. Joy retained a vivid image of Neil as the ship drew out of Mombasa and Kilindini harbour:

He was standing there at the railing crying. I said, 'Why, why are you crying like this?' And he said 'Just everything'. I think all the excitement and the moving. We'd spent a night in the hotel at Mombasa. I think it was just too much for this little chap but he had a whale of a time on the ship coming down. There was a hostess on the ship for the children and she looked after them. He got over it, but he just felt that things were too much for him!

Neil had spent his first ten years in Kenya, and the world he had known had gone. His days of riding beside his father through the bush were over. No more checking the humped cattle in the bomas or the Friesians in the dairy. No more tracking and shooting game, or fishing for trout in the Nanyuki River. But perhaps he also hoped that there would be no more high wire fences, no more constantly being on alert, no more fear.

In South Africa, after six months at Port Alfred, the Aggetts bought a house on a hill in the prosperous residential town of Somerset West, near Cape Town, with magnificent views down to False Bay. Aubrey had always been an energetic, sociable man, an active member of his community. He no longer had land to farm and felt that he had sold below value. He was 52 and didn't want to look for another farm in South Africa. Instead, he invested the money brought from Kenya on the South African stock market. Neil now saw his father's world contract, and with it his mother's. While the family was still comfortably off, the change in his parents' lives was dramatic.

Later, when he was a student, Neil shared with Liz Floyd an abiding, idyllic image of Kenya: of walking with his mother under palm trees along the beach. It was a memory of Malindi. To Liz, Neil was a romantic, retaining this blissful picture of himself as a young boy with his mother. However the images of his father were to fracture. It's hard to know when the first cracks began to appear, but by the time he was 17 Neil was spurred into reflecting on less romantic memories. The little boy scared of visiting the 'long drop' unless his father stood guard with his revolver would become a young man ready to examine the source of those fears.

CHAPTER 4

Kingswood College: 'avoiding evil of every kind'

K INGSWOOD COLLEGE IN GRAHAMSTOWN, ONE OF THE OLDEST
Methodist educational institutions in South Africa, was a handsomely
gabled, redbrick building, with an adjacent chapel and nearby substantial boarding houses, presiding over a wide expanse of well-manicured
grounds. Catering for white families, from as far away as Zambia and even
beyond, who could afford to send their sons to an expensive English-speaking
boarding school, its culture was modelled on that of the prestigious independent, or 'public', schools in England designed to educate and train the next
generation of male leaders and top administrators. In contrast to the white
elitism of its flagship school, the Methodist Church had appointed the first
African, the Reverend Seth Mokitimi, to serve as President of Conference
shortly before Neil entered Kingswood.

Starting life at Kingswood, in a very different environment from Nyeri
Primary School, Neil had the comfort of an older brother's presence. Michael
had one more year to go before completing his matric, after which he hoped
to go to medical school. Michael was also a prefect. It wasn't long before Neil
was nicknamed 'Doc', or, as his parents remembered, 'Little Doc', following
in the footsteps of the older brother whom, according to Joy, he 'idolised'.
Andrew Rein, also a new boy in 1964, became good friends with Neil, both

in class and in Jacques House, the hostel for juniors. Andrew recalls how Neil was immediately both popular and distinctive. Andrew and the other boys were intrigued by the black elephant-hair bracelet Neil always wore on his wrist for luck. The boys assumed that everyone in Kenya wore one. It was ingeniously constructed: two clasps, also made out of elephant hair, were moved together to loosen the bracelet or moved apart to tighten it. No one else in the school wore any kind of jewellery, and, indeed, would have been mercilessly ribbed by the other boys if they had. Yet the boys admired Neil for wearing his elephant-hair bracelet. None of the teachers made any comment about it or tried to stop him wearing it.

Neil had learned how to make animal-hair bracelets from Michael, who, having been taught the skill by one of his father's workers, used to sell them at his Nairobi school for extra pocket money. An elephant-hair bracelet was made from five or six strands, while many more strands were required to make a bracelet from finer giraffe hair. It was, says Jill, a rather 'macho thing' and a way in which the 'Kenya boys' continued to identify themselves now that they were in South Africa.

The concession in allowing Neil to wear the bracelet was surprising given the prevailing regime at the school. Everything at Kingswood was regimented – waking, sleeping, eating, washing, homework. Boys could get permission to go into town to buy a milkshake on a Wednesday afternoon, or attend church on Sunday morning, and if someone had a sister at Diocesan School for Girls, she could be visited on Sunday afternoon. In Neil's first year, Michael took him every week to visit Jill. The girls were not allowed out of school, but brothers and sisters were allowed to sit together on the front lawn. For the following two years, after Michael's departure, Neil continued to visit Jill, and during her matric year was treated to tea and cakes in the matric common room. To Jill, who hated boarding school, these sibling visits were a 'lifeline'. Having a sister at 'DSG' also allowed a Kingswood boy to enjoy the company of some girls. Neil, who had been close to his maternally minded sister, both at home and in Nyeri School, surely missed his weekly visits after Jill matriculated and left.

At Kingswood, anywhere that staff were 'off duty', the prefects or 'cops' were 'on duty'. There were 'black marks' for not polishing your shoes, socks slipping around ankles, talking or being caught reading a comic or novel during 'prep', whispering or listening to a radio through headphones after 'lights out', reading under the blanket with a torch, being late to hand in laundry, pushing into a queue, covering for a friend at roll-call by answering 'Sum' ('I am' in Latin), to name a few misdemeanours. Collective punishment was also common. If a prefect judged a dormitory to be untidy, or if no one would own up to something, every boy there would be given a black mark.

Black marks were added up after Sunday evening church and punishment meted out: extra duties for a couple of marks, with an escalating number of 'cuts' the higher the marks. Fellow classmate Brian Sandberg's recollection is that Neil, as a highly diligent student, would never have been caned for his work but was unlikely to have escaped a 'whipping' for some other offence. Most boys simply accepted the system. As Andrew Rein puts it, caning was 'just a part of our life then'. Moreover, an incident from their final year reflects the extent to which the boys sustained the system, from below as it were, with the belief that it was important to 'take your caning like a man'.

In 1969, their pre-matric year, Andrew was sent as an exchange student to the liberal Kingswood School in West Hartford, Connecticut, where there was no corporal punishment. His American peers were astonished to hear that their South African counterparts submitted to being beaten. The new culture was a revelation for Andrew, who had associated thrashing with abuse of power from the time he had been among 30 junior boys caned by prefects in a dormitory on a trumped-up charge of 'whistling at 3am'. As one of a handful of Jewish boys, experiencing the 'Jewboy' taunt in his junior years – from some prefects as well as boys – Andrew felt ready to question the system. He returned to Grahamstown for his final matriculation term with the conscious resolution never again to submit to a beating, regardless of who administered it.

Within a month, Andrew's resolve was challenged when his housemaster wanted to cane him 'for I can't remember what'. Andrew refused to submit. The master was shocked at this audacity: 'Well you must either allow me to cane you or we'll go now to the headmaster and you'll be expelled', he said. It was only a month before Andrew was due to write matric. On reflection, he decided that he had better accept the caning. The housemaster seemed relieved and, perhaps experiencing some qualms of conscience, hardly tapped him, leaving no marks. Andrew was in for a shock: nobody believed that he had been caned, and he was regarded as a coward, for which his unofficial punishment was to be ostracised for the remainder of his final term.[19] It was a horrible experience.

What was Neil's reaction? Andrew and Neil had been good school friends since their junior year, until Andrew had left for his year abroad. Did Neil break the ban on speaking with him? It seems not. By way of explanation, Andrew makes the point that Neil was by then head prefect of the junior Jacques House, where he had his own room, and which involved many duties. Regarded as a good leader and motivator, he was extremely popular among the younger boys. When he ran onto the rugby field (he was captain of the second rugby team, playing eighth man), the junior school screamed for him. However, it seems impossible that the two former friends' paths didn't cross, and suggests that Neil was still embedded within the establishment.

The culture into which Kingswood boys were inducted in the 1960s was one of obedience, duty, tradition and team spirit. There are other intriguing glimpses of Neil through his earlier years that reveal a mix of influences on a boy who was both sensitive and tough. Integral to school life was the cadet corps. Cadet training was compulsory every Friday afternoon, and young 'fags' would have to 'spit and polish' the prefects' boots. Two or three times a year, Sunday morning chapel or church in town was replaced by the whole school marching to the town centre, accompanied by cadets and bands, to commemorate those who served and died in the two world wars. Cadet Neil Hudson Aggett, who made his way to the Anglican cathedral, may well have thought of the uncle whose name he carried who had drowned in the Indian Ocean. Many of the boys would know their own family stories.

With this focus on the world wars, how aware were the young cadets that they were far more likely to be deployed closer to home, both in what they called 'South West Africa' and South Africa itself?[20] Andrew Rein remembers an occasion when 'some real army guys' addressed the cadet corps. The visiting South African Defence Force members told the boys that in a war it was better not to kill your enemy, but to maim him. That way the opposing force would have to devote far more of their resources to treating the victim, whereas if he was dead they could simply bury him.

Both Andrew and Neil belonged to the school rifle team and were selected to shoot for Kingswood in an inter-school 'Bisley', at the army firing range in Port Elizabeth. This was an open field with numbered targets erected in the distance. They were each given a number and told to fire at the target with the corresponding number. Andrew recalls how he and Neil lay down in their row on some coir matting, and waited to hear the command 'Fire!' At the marshal's call, they both started firing away. Each had to fire ten rounds. Through his telescopic sight, Andrew could see that he had scored mostly bull's eyes, worth ten points each. He had three shots left when he heard a hoarse, urgent whisper, coming from Neil on his left:

> 'Rein! For God's sake – fire one of your bullets into my target. I've shot one of mine into your target by mistake!' This was strictly against the rules, of course, and Neil's mistake should have cost him ten points – equivalent to a complete miss. That would have been a disaster for us and our school would certainly have come last in the competition. I nodded grimly. There was something in the tone of Neil's voice which compelled obedience. I shifted position, lined up my sights on his target and squeezed the trigger. It was not my best shot but I scored a nine, which meant that Neil only dropped one point instead of ten. We did not win the competition but we were very respectably placed.

The pair had also been members of Kingswood's under-14 tennis team, taking part in a successful tour of the eastern Cape. Neil's mother proudly pasted a news cutting and photo of the five smiling players, entitled 'Stars of the Future', into her album. As well as this sporting prowess, according to Brian Sandberg, the two were considered part of a foursome who made up the class 'Brains' Trust', with Neil and Andrew regarded as 'the deeper, more philosophical thinkers'.[21] However, Neil's classmates do not recall deep conversations about books or issues as a norm. Indeed an 'anti-intellectual' culture was common in white South African schools, where using intellect could lead a young mind to ask awkward social and political questions. There were unspoken boundaries to conversation, both in and out of the classroom.

While sport could always be a major topic of conversation, Andrew recollects that 'Neil was the first boy in my class to take an interest in girls' when they were still in the junior Jacques House. Nyeri Primary School had been mixed, but in this boys-only environment Neil's interest in the daughter of the kitchen staff supervisor provoked bafflement from Andrew and the other 12-year-old boys. None of them 'could understand the point of it and we regarded this as a deviant form of behaviour, attributing it to his Kenyan origins'.

A further memory of Andrew's, told with some self-deprecation, reflects Neil continuing to be at ease with girls as they advanced into the senior school. Having arranged to meet two girls in town on a Wednesday afternoon, when a visit to town was permitted, Neil asked his friend to join him. Andrew gladly accepted although he 'still could not see what he [Neil] saw in these alien creatures'. They took them to the only café in town:

> It was a dreary place with Formica tables and flypaper hanging from the ceilings. We ordered milkshakes and scones. It was not a success. Unused to the company of girls, I tried to be amusing but managed only to embarrass both Neil and myself. The girls seemed to think that I was a halfwit.
>
> Neil did not invite me again. No doubt, he found that he could pursue this interest of his more successfully on his own.

Neil's school diaries reveal that, although he only saw Michael in school holidays, when his brother came home from medical school, a close bond continued, including strong spiritual influence from Michael. Their parents were nominally Anglican but Michael, who was naturally quiet and serious, had become very religious at Kingswood. In addition to Sunday worship in their own denominations, pupils attended daily Methodist services in the school chapel, and had weekly religious instruction in class. They learned about John Wesley's evangelism and how, despite persecution from the establishment of his day, he had worked steadfastly among the poor. They encountered the Wesleyan belief that human beings are corrupted by sin, yet capable of using their God-given free will to choose salvation by Jesus Christ. As a keen reader, Neil may well have learned about Wesley's abhorrence of the 'villainy' of slavery and racism, and come across the rules that Wesley laid out for the United Societies:

> It is therefore expected of all who continue therein that they should continue to evidence their desire of salvation, First: By doing no harm, by avoiding evil of every kind ...; Secondly: ... doing good of every possible sort, and, as far as possible, to all ...; Thirdly: By attending upon all the ordinances of God ...[22]

Neil's diaries for his two final years at Kingswood are fascinating, reflecting teenage preoccupations and pleasures with progression into religious ardour and self-doubt. Each diary was a present from Michael. In January 1969, entering his pre-matriculation year, 15-year-old Neil began with two very neat lists:

PRESENTS

R10 and 200 shares from Granny

R2.50 gift token from the Allisons (pen)

R1 from the Griffs

R1 token from the Trewhelas (Mila 18) – a book

Diary from Mick

Tennis book from Jill

Microscope book from Dad

Shirt from Mom

Tennis camp from Mum and Dad

Hankies from Scots

New Year Resolutions
1 No coffee or tea
2 No eating between meals
3 Get up when I wake up
4 Not too much fruit
5 Work hard
6 Be friendly to everyone

JANUARY
WED 1

The first day of the year was a fine day with a clear sky. I got up early and had some exercises. After breakfast I wrote to the Trewhelas and read part of a book called 'The Men who made Surgery'. At the moment I am reading about William Harvey who discovered blood-circulation. After trying to clean the pool I had some tennis against the wall.

I arrived back boiling hot, so I had a quick dip and a shower ...

The entry ended with notes on share prices. For the next three weeks, until he returned to school on 27 January, he kept up his diary assiduously, with full-page entries. There are details of sport, the swimming pool, visits to and from family friends, the day 'the maid turned up drunk' and they had to fend for themselves, keeping track of his shares (presumably advised by Aubrey), working with his microscope, playing billiards with Aubrey (and winning against his father!), seeing films and reading, as well as comments on girls whom he thinks are friendly and pretty. His tone is uncomplicated, unso-phisticated and unselfconscious: 'I wish Marlene was here; we could have such a nice time.' He wrote of his concern for his Granny (Joy's mother) if her sister Gwen were to die, while on 14 January he entered, 'Tonight is a lovely night and I feel so happy'. Bigger questions intrude only once, when he mentions talking one night about God and apartheid at tennis camp. Back at Kingswood, his entries are fewer, with occasional comments on tests, marks and activities, a decision to be a vet and going to church.

In English, their pre-matric class studied *Lord of the Flies*, the Romantic poets and Yeats's 'A Prayer for my Daughter'. Brian thought that Neil might have tried to read up on Irish politics. What books he would have had access to was another matter: 'Our library was typical schoolboy stuff from that era ... nothing remotely political – you have to remember we were living in a police state at that time.' A number of the teachers had also schooled at Kingswood themselves and then taught their whole life there, 'so it was quite a "closed" thinking, in many ways'.

The following year, Neil's 1970 diary once again began with lists:

Granny R100
Dad R20
Hélène Brush + Shoehorn
Mom Wallet
Jill Tie
Mick Diary
Trewhelas Book
Allisons Book
Bastards Knife
Gwen Raymond Hankies
Scotts Hankies

Other entries included lists of clothes and savings information. Hélène had re-placed Marlene, with references to 'tennis at Hélène's' and a 'braai'. But while Neil enjoyed these typical, white middle-class South African pastimes, there were signs of change. His 16-year-old mind, although still attached to its traditional moorings, was tossing, reflected in a medley of personal notes, prayers and biblical quotations. It's unclear whether some of the prayers are his own or copied:

1. Entire abandonment
2. Absolute faith

Lord Jesus I believe that thou art willing and able to deliver me from all the care and unrest and bondage of my Christian life … I believe that thou art stronger than sin and that thou canst keep me, even me, in my extreme weakness, from falling into its snares or yielding obedience to its commands. And Lord I am going to trust thee to keep me. I have tried keeping myself and have failed, failed most grievously. I am absolutely helpless. So now I will trust thee. I give myself to thee …[23]

Over the next couple of weeks, there are yet more lists, including a roll-call of chapters and verse numbers from the Bible under the heading 'Drinking', followed by exhortations with biblical quotations:

Eph 5.18 'And do not get drunk with wine for that is debauchery, but be filled with the spirit'.

Eph 6: Children obey your parents in the lord for this is right. That it may be well with you and that you may live long on the earth.

Had Neil got drunk, and had Aubrey lectured him? Or was the lecture from Michael, who, in becoming intensely religious, had also become evangelical?

JAN 11
Great afternoon at scout camp and evening at Claxtons.
Hélène is fantastic.
When doubts come meet them not with arguments but with assertions of faith. N.B.
The Holy spirit is the Comforter not the Accuser and he never shows us our need without pointing to the divine supply.

<u>Jan 14</u>

Mick at ¼ to 10. Pool.

Film show – Hélène 7–8 o'clock.

From this day forth I will not indulge in the luxury of doubt. Father I
am very weak and fall into the snare easily, but with your help it can be
done. I will believe and eventually come to know the truth, and I will
meet each doubt with 'Jesus saves me now'.

Beneath this is a map annotated 'Baby Sitting', and beneath that 'Tennis with
Mick & Jill'. The everyday events of a summer holiday are seamlessly inte-
grated with indications of an inner struggle between doubt and belief. Was
there perhaps a connection between 'Mick at ¼ to 10' and Neil's resolution to
meet doubt with 'Jesus saves me now'? Back at school, Neil's entries were once
again less frequent. This was his matriculation year and he was occupied with
prefect duties. However, in among the lists of shooting scores, test results,
films and quotations, for the first time, a growing political awareness is briefly
intimated in a reference to Nixon and troops in Vietnam. A long reading list
of fiction and non-fiction, ranging from science and war to thrillers and romance, ends with Alan Paton's *Cry, the Beloved Country* and Robert Ruark's
novel *Something of Value*, which was set in Kenya.

It was common knowledge that Neil was keen to follow in Michael's
footsteps and study medicine. Inspired by Michael's tales of working at the
remote Moffat Mission hospital in the northern Cape, in his matriculation
year Neil wrote to the hospital to ask if he could work there during a
vacation. The reply came that they couldn't consider him until he was at
least 17, preferably 18. Like Andrew, Neil was a year younger than most of
the other matric students. However, he persevered until the hospital agreed
to accept him in his final school vacation, a month before his seventeenth
birthday.

Neil drew a diagram in his 1970 diary of the train route between
Grahamstown and Kuruman, showing the connection at Kimberley. But
there are no entries about the mission hospital, people, conversations or
what he saw and experienced. However, a memory from Brian Sandberg
throws some light on what appears to have been an influential encounter.
On Neil's return journey to Kingswood, he joined the train bringing students back from the north, including Brian from what was still Rhodesia.

The onward journey to Grahamstown took more than 24 hours, during which Brian recalls Neil talking about the 'incredible experience' of having met a doctor who had introduced him to subjects like Kennedy's assassination, the Cold War and Vietnam, and, closer to home, the Belgian role in Patrice Lumumba's murder in the Congo. Neil had been loaned a batch of books that he was going to post back one at a time after reading. He showed these briefly to Brian but 'he was almost "secretive" about them, and read them quietly on his own'.

It seems likely that among these was 'Mau Mau' Detainee by Josiah Mwangi Kariuki, a graphic insider account that Neil was to tell Liz Floyd made a big impression on him.[24] This was not a book he would have found in his school library. He would also tell his university friend Dennis Rubel about the experience of seeing an image of people being herded like cattle to be 'screened'. It had deeply shocked him. The driveway of the farm, the site of the screening camp, reminded him of Ol Elerai. Indeed, Kariuki's book contains a picture like this, among a number of photographs that could have triggered disturbing memories for a settler child brought up in 1950s Kenya.

Neil matriculated at the end of 1970 with a first-class pass and a distinction in maths, delighting his parents. Such an easy child, as Joy had said. Any temporary thoughts about being a vet had been put aside, and he was set on medicine. Forty years on, Brian Sandberg recalls an unusual 17-year-old getting ready to cut his own path. In particular, Brian remembers Neil writing far more than anyone else in the class, including poetry, and that 'a measure of his standing' was that others respected him when he took time out to write for himself rather than for an assignment. To Brian, Neil also appeared at ease in discussing moral and social values, so that 'by the time he [Neil] left Kingswood his basic philosophies and tenets and vision for a more just society were matured beyond almost anyone else I knew at that time'.

At the same time, we have the young man who did not challenge the ban on talking to his classmate and friend who had bucked the system of corporal punishment. Neil's diaries reveal the 'easy child', sociable and sensible, as well as the introspective teenager, conflicted between doubt and belief, open to tough self-scrutiny. John Wesley preached 'avoiding evil of every kind', the corruption of sin and seeking salvation through Christ. But what if the entire society was corrupted by the fundamental injustice of its architecture? Whether or not Neil had yet posed this more political question, his decision to seek further work experience in the remote mission hospital suggests that he may already have been thinking about medicine in a social context, even before his first term at medical school.

CHAPTER 5

University: 'the long-haired coterie'

THE MOFFAT MISSION HOSPITAL IN BATLHAROS LAY JUST BEYOND Kuruman in the northern Cape, in an area of blue asbestos mining on the southeastern edge of the Kalahari. It was Neil's first real experience of rural poverty and man-made disease. The mission had been founded in 1820 by Robert Moffat, a Scottish Congregationalist minister with the London Missionary Society. Moffat and his wife Mary had worked for 50 years in the remote Kuruman region, Moffat publishing the first Setswana translation of the Bible. Their daughter married David Livingstone – doctor, missionary, anti-slavery campaigner and explorer – who believed passionately in the close alliance of Christianity, commerce and civilisation, and who began his missionary career in Kuruman. By the end of the nineteenth century, commerce in Kuruman meant asbestos. The most powerful name was Cape Asbestos, founded in London in 1893.

Surface mining and a system of unwaged 'tributers' meant that whole families of African and Coloured men, women and children were involved in digging out and inhaling the dust as they sorted the fibres, which were then sold to the mining companies. By the end of the Second World War, when surface deposits were exhausted, the companies turned to industrial mining. With no trade unions to ensure basic rights to occupational health, and despite growing medical evidence of asbestosis and asbestos-related diseases, the mining companies increased production while making little or no attempts to provide for workers' safety. When Neil went to work under Dr George Nurse at the mission hospital in Batlharos in December 1970, mining for blue asbestos was still at its peak, with South Africa providing 97% of global supplies. Observers described the dust clouds and the land as blue.[25]

In addition to what Neil would have seen inside the hospital wards, Kuruman and Batlharos vividly presented the crude realities of apartheid's Bantustan policy. In their oasis of green in the midst of semi-desert, the white inhabitants of Kuruman on the Ghaap Plateau took the lion's share of the water from the Eye of Kuruman, one of the country's largest springs and the source of the Kuruman River, leaving little for the villagers in the river valley below. While Kuruman was in South Africa, the outlying villages lay across an administrative border in what was about to become the designated 'black homeland' of Bophuthatswana.

In explaining her understanding of Neil's evolution, Liz Floyd singled out the two months that Neil spent with Dr Nurse, developing an intense interest in philosophy: 'He [Dr Nurse] was the connection to existentialism. I think he's mythology and adds up to a different person from what Neil made of him. I think a lot of what he [Neil] was doing was modelling himself on Dr Nurse … a relatively isolated person combining medicine in that kind of setting with philosophy.'

But George Nurse was not mythology. Highly eccentric, he was 'a polymath and a bibliophile',[26] according to his colleague and friend, Professor Trefor Jenkins. Neil noted in his 1971 journal that the doctor spoke 'French, German, Russian, English, Norwegian, Afrikaans & native languages. Worked for 3 years on a whaling ship in Antarctica. Doctor of Anthropology. Dr of medicine …'.[27] A rebel against petty regulations, George Nurse had failed to qualify in medicine at his first attempt, having disregarded the warning from his Professor of Obstetrics and Gynaecology to shave off his beard before his practical. Having passed second time round, after shaving, he let his beard grow luxuriantly thereafter. To Neil, who, from his diary's eclectic reading list, was already familiar with Joseph Conrad, George Nurse may well have stepped out of a Conrad novel. The doctor was a voracious reader and many of his books were about Africa.[28]

Whatever questions stirred for Neil here at the mission hospital, they were to grow and take root as he followed in his brother's footsteps into the prestigious, rigidly traditional medical school at the University of Cape Town (UCT). This was also where George Nurse had trained. South Africa's oldest university presides in grand style on the slopes of Table Mountain. If you stand on its presidential steps, the eye travels upwards from the Corinthian columns fronting Jameson Memorial Hall to the heights of Devil's Peak above. Part of the Groote Schuur estate, the land was bequeathed by Cecil Rhodes to the university. Early mining magnates provided funds, alongside the government, to ensure world-class facilities for the study of mineralogy and geology. A little further down the mountain lies the teaching hospital, Groote Schuur, seat of the university's medical school – also the oldest in South Africa.

Neil obtained a room in what had been Michael's hall of residence, Driekoppen, a name recalling the site where the heads of three recaptured runaway slaves had been impaled on stakes in 1724.[29] Aubrey provided him with a second-hand car. A journal-cum-scrapbook that Neil kept between June 1971 and August 1972 reveals the beginnings of a profound change. At the back of his journal, among some longer discursive pieces, he wrote poems. These four, written in his first year, capture the quietly sensitive, reflective young man leaning to the Romantics and poetry absorbed at school.

In 'Rain at Night', still part schoolboy, the poet dreams romantically of the 'makers of history':

RAIN AT NIGHT

Glistening drops –
A fine mist wafts over the black branches.
Music floats softly in –
The whole Res is pulsating,
Vibrating – Boys sleep, men wake.
What philosopher, statesman slumbers now
Who will soon be the creed of
Unknown generations.
This is when I live!

[14 August 1971]

Another, achingly lonely, poem shows him introspective and uncertain:

> Nervous, happy words.
> There is security in words
> and smiles.
> I sit alone
> Without words I look for strength
> Without the smiles, the games.
> I look within myself;
> And what I see is hollow.
>
> [7 September 1971]

A month later, we have sensuous longing and, it seems, some fulfilment. But no sooner has he imagined a warm embrace than he dismisses it as 'illusion':

> What I see I need to take –
> I long for the warmth, the dreams,
> The unseen tingling air of love.
> When she runs, hair flying, arms outstretched.
> Yet it is an illusion
> An illusion that fades at the grasping.
> But now my head lies in her lap –
> The fire crackles – we will come through.
>
> [12 October 1971]

A few weeks later, the fragile confidence of 'we will come through' is replaced by the more desolate and sad 'Tomorrow will come'.

SAFARI

The red-gray dust clings to the barren bramble.
A lonely baobab swelters in the sun.
The thirsty ants ply aimlessly over the blistering sand.
A dust cloud!
A car-full of sleepy faces flashes by
The dust settles slowly on the bumpy road.
The sun falls steadily leaving the ants to
their fruitless world.
Tomorrow will come.
                    [28 October 1971]

The writer is not one of the 'car-full of sleepy faces', but a solitary viewer, notably detached yet observant, from a vantage point somewhere beyond. The car flashes by, its occupants reduced to temporary passengers on a dusty, relentless planet. Tomorrow will come regardless of them.

The searching meditative spirit in Neil's poems was starkly at odds with the normal interests of the typical 'middle of the road, rugby playing Res character' in a medical school that was, in Liz's view, 'desperately conventional'. Although she only arrived as Neil entered his second year – and they did not meet immediately – she sensed that by the time Neil left Res to go into lodgings, he was becoming extremely introspective. The front section of his journal during this first year includes an eclectic mixture of news cuttings, pictures, quotations, commentary and poems. Neil copies out the final lines of Keats's poem 'Written in Disgust of Vulgar Superstition' below a cutting about a couple of fellow students involved in a fatal accident, on the same date that he writes 'Rain at Night'. While we hear strains of Keats in Neil's lyricism and solitary detachment, reality increasingly intrudes.

From *Sounds of a Cowhide Drum*, the debut 1971 collection of messenger and poet Oswald Mtshali, Neil pastes in a copy of 'Pigeons at the Oppenheimer Park', about the 'insolent' birds that freely perch on 'Whites Only' benches while others make love on the crest of the park's central sculpture of jumping impala. 'Where's the sacred Immorality Act? Sies!'[30] He inserts a picture of Mtshali and a second poem, 'The Shepherd and his Flock', in which a young shepherd boy drives his master's sheep into the veld. Its lyrical rural imagery would have resonated with Neil. Yet the startling beauty is then sharply undercut as the poet enters the mind of the young boy who salutes the white farmer's children on their way to school,

> and dreamily asks,
> 'O! Wise Sun above,
> will you ever guide
> me into school?'[31]

Other quotes copied out in his first-year journal reveal a growing interest in global affairs. 'We must remember that saving men's lives is more important than saving face for governments', says Senator Edmund Muskie. 'The decision to make war is too big a decision for one mind to make ... there must be collective judgement given and a collective responsibility shared', says Senator John C Stennis. 'There is no anti-Semitism in Russia. In fact, many of my best friends are Jews', says Russian Premier Alexei Kosygin. 'Children are starving every day and they die quietly because, after all, the death of children is nothing [out] of the ordinary here', says a UN official in a Pakistani refugee camp.

The articles include the nostalgic 'Pioneers of East Africa' story about young Aubrey and Hudson stranded with their parents in lion country beside the flooded Ewaso Ng'iro River. In a markedly different vein, the political commentator Stanley Uys reviewed 1971, heading his list of significant developments with economic decline and the inability of the Nationalist government to face up to apartheid's social effects. There was the visit to South Africa of Malawi's dictator president, Hastings Banda, and installation of the first black ambassador; 13 black athletes at the Mount Nelson Hotel for Cape Town's multinational games ... while the core of apartheid remained untouched, a relentless move to Bantustans, a clash between Church and State inevitable, and Prime Minister BJ Vorster continuing to fight 'spooks'.[32] Employed during university vacations as an auxiliary ambulance driver, Neil came, perhaps for the first time, into sustained contact with white workers who were hard-core Vorster supporters. His journal gives no indication whether, or how, he tried to respond, but he notes down:

> The kaffir is mos not human beings – bloody animals.
> – Ambulance Driver – Reymeker.

Also coming at the end of 1971, in the middle of the summer holidays, was a *Cape Times* article by Hugh Montefiore, the Anglican Suffragan Bishop of Kingston-upon-Thames, entitled 'The World at Stake in 1972'. Now 18, Neil was more than ready to engage the bishop in debate over his bleak political assessment: 'There is now little room for doubt that the world is now set on a disaster course … When one thinks of strikes, national rivalries, the power of private or public capital to exploit men and resources, is there really any hope?'[33] Responding in his journal, Neil takes Montefiore to task:

> … I feel that there is a definite awareness awakening in this world – take the Vietnam war medals that were thrown away and left to rot on the Washington pavements. This is an awareness springing out of a new spiritual strength, and has nothing to do with religion.
>
> This 'spiritual strength' as I call it is a very genuine feeling felt most strongly in today's youth. I could say it is a 'God Consciousness', but it isn't even that – these people do not conceive the same God that is worshipped in apartheid South Africa or in riot-torn [Northern] Ireland, but rather a wonderful force uniting all men as fellow humans. They look for their justification in human relations, and face the world with an optimistic smile – which, unfortunately because of the pressures of our outmoded society, often turns to bitterness and frustration and then drug addiction and alcoholism.
>
> It should be clear that with this feeling sweeping the world we as citizens must take part in this action. Dr Martin Luther King once said 'We are sleeping through a revolution' and drew a comparison to Rip Van Winkle.
>
> Therefore my answer to Mr Montefiore's question 'Is there really hope?' is a positive yes!

The schoolboy's prayer of 'Jesus saves me now' to stave off doubt has been replaced by a fervent optimism of 'spiritual strength' sweeping the youth of the world. When the bishop proposes an eleventh-hour 'unprecedented effort' to change the current course, Neil immediately counters that the world can only be saved with mass action and spiritual reawakening from the grassroots: 'Only when everyone refuses to be conscripted will wars be stopped, not when a new president tries in an "unprecedented effort" to withdraw troops from a foreign land.' However, in response to the bishop's call for national agreement and international cooperation, mentioning the role of young people, Neil launches into his own manifesto for 'idealistic youth': '... for what else is going to surge through the world and change its course, but a revitalised, unhypocritic generation of idealistic youth prepared to cast away their security, and not prepared to see injustice and racialism and poverty stand as they are.' When Bishop Montefiore writes, 'It is therefore necessary that there shall be a colossal reorientation of social attitudes – a new way of living if we are to change course', Neil responds buoyantly: 'All I have to say is that the Bishop has coined in a nutshell what I have been saying.'

From here on, with minor qualifications, Neil endorses the bishop's appeal for 'not just an international popular movement with a definite and realistic political programme, but also a genuine religious reawakening', except that Neil wishes to insert 'spiritual' in place of 'religious'. Arguing for the equal acceptance of all religions, Neil concludes with a ringing endorsement of human progress: 'I am sure this age will stand up and rise to the occasion, and though not solve all the problems, continue to be one step ahead of disaster – with a great effort!'

Another long philosophical piece, entitled 'Ethical argument for the existence of God', undated but probably written either in late 1971 or early 1972, reveals Neil wrestling with the source of moral consciousness and why we do 'our duty'. Further clues to his intellectual transition are contained in a set of handwritten cards about political philosophers, including Nietzsche, and quotations such as the following from the radical theologian Harry Abbott Williams: 'Christians are often too pathologically intent on preserving as far as they can an image of themselves as Christlike, that they are totally unaware of the harm their attempted humility is doing to other people.'

Elsewhere in the journal, there are signs of his questioning. On 24 October 1971 he writes,

> I will not turn to Christianity through realisation of my 'sin' – my inadequacy. For my sin is man-fathomed – it is in relation to the thought of mere men, and has no real substance. So 'sin' is not born in man, but created by man along with his moral values.
>
> The inherent 'feeling' of sin, is merely the result of society's conditioning
> ...
>
> Paul writes – you must become holy – holy how? On the same

commandments that Moses gave us? He that taught – an eye for ... while Jesus said – if your enemy ... It is time the superstitious world realised that what they read over and over again in the testaments is man written, and fallible, and start to live true, (unhypocritical), fruitful lives.

Many of Neil's entries through 1972 revolve around morality and religion. In contrast with his extended imaginary discourse with Bishop Montefiore, the following item is exceptionally pithy:

THOUGHTS OF MICHAEL 30.4.72

1 God is source of all supply
2 Give that it may be given to you
3 Expect a miracle (a result)

Here is no dialogue with his older brother, rather the loosening of ties. If Neil had once 'idolised' Michael, it appears there is now little to say. Behind the brevity, one senses something of an epitaph on what had once been a pivotal relationship. While Neil's journal was privy to a critical ferment of ideas, it was only a matter of time before his internal transformation would become more outwardly apparent, including to his family. Dennis Rubel, a fellow medical student, recalls meeting Neil in 1972, in their second-year anatomy class, where they were 'divided into six per body'. Dennis's table was 'broadly left-wing' and long-haired. Neil was on the body next to theirs, where hair was short-cropped and the chat about rugby and religion. One of Dennis's six was Neil Andersson, 'quite an alternative character', who knew Neil from Driekoppen residence although he had since moved out to a rented room. Neil Andersson commented to Dennis, 'This guy's a helluva nice guy but he's a rugger-bugger basically'. Neil also stood out as a very diligent student. Nevertheless, Dennis observed how Neil began to drift closer to their dissecting table: 'We were all interested in politics, that's as left as we were ... So Neil really sought us out and became individually friendly with all of us and then in the next year this self-driven metamorphosis began in him. He started reading philosophy, growing his hair, and moved into a cottage in Constantia.'

Although Dennis didn't know it, the outwardly 'rugger-bugger' Neil was already deep into considering philosophical questions of morality that were to lay the foundation for his subsequent 'self-driven metamorphosis'. 'Anatomy Class', a poem written early in May 1972, reveals Neil, as in his earlier poem 'Safari', reflectively distancing himself from those around him and expressing a profound unease.

ANATOMY CLASS

The class hums;
There is unrest in my mind.
Why? What do they propose to do?
They talk of people, events, exams;
How this body looked – what was its name.
Do they not realise that –
They will be 'pieces of bone' and nerves.
They will live with laughs and smiles – for how long?
They talk of racialism; nationalism!
Old people talk of communism and hippies!
What do they matter?
A great confusion falls around my ears
A weariness fills my bones.
I long for the deep sleep,
The tingling wakefulness to an alert day,
A long silence as I lie in her lap,
With no sensations and unashamed feelings,
but no thoughts.

[8 May 1972]

Shadows of Keats ('The weariness, the fever, and the fret', from 'Ode to a Nightingale') and of Wordsworth ('the weary weight/of all this unintelligible world', from 'Tintern Abbey') are almost palpable. Yet the Romantic's desire to escape the world is contested here by sharp actuality: 'The class hums … They talk of racialism; nationalism!/Old people talk of communism and hippies!' However much Neil may have longed to lie in a lover's lap, oblivious to the cares of the world, for him this was already more likely a dream than an option. In the same week he wrote 'Anatomy Class', he inserted into his

journal a report of an African man shot by a white man passing by on a mo-
ped (4 May 1972) and a report about the World Council of Churches headed
'WCC BLAMED FOR VIETNAM WITHDRAWAL' (6 May 1972).

A week after Neil wrote his poem, Alpheus Hamilton Zulu, Bishop of
Zululand and President of the World Council of Churches, addressed
students at the University of Cape Town in the annual TB Davie Memorial
Lecture. Bishop Zulu was only the second black speaker since 1959, when
the lectures were instituted – on a theme related to academic freedom – to
commemorate a distinguished vice-chancellor.[34] The previous year, he had
been charged with failing to produce his passbook in Johannesburg. Refusing
to pay a spot fine, the bishop had insisted on being brought before a court. A
copy of Bishop Zulu's paper, 'The Dilemma of the Black South African', was
tucked into Neil's journal. Neil probably attended the lecture, perhaps for the
first time listening to a black man not only speak his mind directly but also
issue him, a young white man, a challenge. The bishop addressed his audience
as a fellow South African 'in spite of my Zulustan citizenship' and with 'the
conviction that there is a basic humanity which I share with white people
and which makes our interests in life ultimately similar, despite the white
man's rejection of me'.[35] White South Africans who imagined themselves to
be free because of the franchise are 'enslaved by their inability to recognise
the humanity of the black man and the rights of black people inherent in that
humanity'. There had never been a human relationship between white and
black because of white blindness to the effects of dispossession:

> I was told how my family lost its lands when early one morning a Dutch
> farmer was seen in our yard on horseback. With a sweeping motion of the
> hand he declared every hill nearby as his land and demanded that the young
> members of the family should go to work on his farm. And they did so until
> my father fled to live on a reservation.

Bishop Zulu rejected the white man's claim 'that he was sent by God to convert
and civilize the black man when he knows full well that he came primarily for
economic reasons'. He called for 'amicable relations … established upon the
humble acceptance of the truth of history; upon honest regret for brutality
and inhumanity in the past and a firm resolution to seek together a way
of living for the future'. Giving examples of unashamedly racist utterances

made by government ministers and officials, the bishop declared that the opportunities for black and white to get to know each other were decreasing every year. Without the possibility of 'mutual and effective communication, how do people become friends and if there may be no friendships, how do black and white come to trust one another?'

He reminded his audience that 'Everywhere in the world there is an awakening of black consciousness. All black people are in a hurry to discard the white man's shackles once and for all.' The bishop did not stop there. Everybody knows, he said, about guerrilla warfare. South Africa, he believed, was 'on the verge of war'. With very few white people committed to non-violence, the harshness of apartheid 'makes a black man look simple and naive if he continues to believe and talk of non-violence ever becoming effective'. Leaving his young white audience to imagine the implications, he offered a last-ditch hope for the future that depended on none other than themselves:

> I believe that the current cultural revolution among the white youth carries a message for the world and for South Africa ... Their revolt against the traditions and even the morals of their fathers is, to them, a destruction of barriers that separate human beings that ought to be sharing all good things in life.

The bishop's focus on youth chimed with Neil's 'revitalised, unhypocritic generation of idealistic youth' that he had extolled in engaging with Bishop Montefiore. But this South African bishop was addressing him now directly, as a black man talking to a young white man, urging him to show 'spiritual and moral courage'. Through addressing the students of the University of Cape Town, he was speaking to South Africa, he said. It was an appeal to white South Africa to accept their black compatriots as 'partners in the development of the country, investing at least as much money in their development and training as in armaments'.

Behind Bishop Zulu's exhortation was the threat of escalating violence and war. Yet he concluded with a caution. His white audience should not misunderstand his appeal as asking for charity or for white people 'to resolve the black man's problems'. Black people needed the freedom to make their own decisions and mistakes. It was the same message that 24-year-old Steve Biko had articulated far more sharply to a conference of predominantly white students at the Abe Bailey Institute for Inter-racial Studies in Cape Town in January 1971, when Neil had been in Kuruman.[36]

Less than two weeks later, Neil pasted into his journal a small printed sheet, dated 1 June 1972:

1.30 LEAVE TEACH-IN

2.10 GREEN MARKET SQUARE

2.50 MARCH TO PARLIAMENT

3.05 PHILIPPE LE ROUX ARRESTED (charged for assault)

3.30 POLICE DOG THREAT

3.50 53 ARRESTED ('ILLEGAL' PROTEST)

5.30-7 RELEASED ON BAIL

Picking up on Prime Minister Vorster's reference to student demonstrators as 'loafers', Neil added his own heading: 'VARSITY LOAFERS "THE BEGINNING!"' Another printed sheet, entitled 'WHAT NEXT?' and dated 20 June, itemised the wave of student protests across the country following the expulsion from the University of the North of Abram Onkgopotse Tiro. In April, the young black president of the Students' Representative Council (SRC) had dared to attack apartheid and its inferior Bantu Education in a speech at a graduation ceremony.[37]

The 'WHAT NEXT?' list records 53 students arrested on the first two days of June during a peaceful demonstration against inequalities in education on the steps of St George's Cathedral in Cape Town. Three days later, on Monday 5 June, the police banned a much larger demonstration outside the cathedral, just minutes before it was due to begin, dispersing the crowd of some 10 000 students and non-students with tear gas. Juhan Kuus, a 19-year-old photographer, captured the relish and grins on the faces of white policemen as they grabbed students by their long hair and lobbed tear gas into the crowd.[38] It seems that Neil was there, witness to the chaos.

A month later, Neil wrote a piece entitled 'BALANCE MAINTAINED 5.7.72 IN REPLY TO MR MITCHELL MP UNITED PARTY'. The United Party formed the feeble opposition to the ruling National Party in Parliament and was the party from which the MP Helen Suzman had broken away to form the Progressive Party, which advocated power-sharing on a qualified franchise. Following the demonstration, Mitchell must have made some bland comment about seeking 'balance' that set Neil bristling:

The balance of deceived people has been maintained – do not fear Mr Mitchell …

Colonel Crouse was 'reportedly' hit from behind, and apparently he burst his spleen – this I find a little difficult to comprehend owing to the spleen's actual position, and the manner in which he featured so prominently in the ensuing scuffles …

The way that the whole affair was explained away as the work of communist agitators and foreigners, and accepted as such indicates that the public do not realise that the people protesting against educational inequality and police brutality were ordinary South Africans with a slight sense of moral value.

May I suggest that the balance of South Africa's future may be maintained by an opposition party that does more than demand an enquiry but searches out the absolute truth – <u>always</u>.

This was probably Neil's first major demonstration and experience of seeing the police at work. Regardless of whether he actually sent his letter, what prompted him to address an MP from the United Party? Was it Biko's black consciousness message, echoed in Bishop Zulu's speech, that white people should set their own house in order? Neil doesn't hide his sarcasm. He must have known that when he next visited his parents, an event like this was bound to come up in conversation. If he had been trying to avoid political confrontation with his father, it would not be possible for much longer.

Most of the writing in his journal during his second year continues to reflect philosophical tussles with religion and religious ideas, his breadth of reading interests reflected in a series of lists, hand-written in the middle of his journal. *Suicide and Attempted Suicide*, the seminal study by Erwin Stengel, published in a Pelican paperback in 1970, uncannily heads his Science list, which spans titles in medical, physical and social science. In a list of novels, Neil includes the European greats, including Camus, Gide, Sartre, Kafka, Tolstoy, Chekhov, Turgenev, Dostoyevsky and Solzhenitsyn. Camus's *The Rebel* emerges in a third untitled list, a broad philosophy batch including Nietzsche's *The Will to Power* and *Thus Spoke Zarathustra*. Elsewhere in the journal, the influence of Nietzsche now predominates in lengthy quotations and in the tone of two poems that appear to be Neil's last entries before he put his journal aside:

THESE FOOLS

These fools!
What know they of these things.
They laugh. They scorn.
They want an explanation
Of things UNexplanatory.
And in the absence thereof they <u>laugh</u>.
Their explanation is found,
In leather book,
With Gold Script,
In oft repeated phrases, dumb cliches.
I find mine in my feelings
And turn to them for all.

[20 August 1972 After Supper]

GREATNESS

This Quality of Greatness,
It shows in some so young.
They do not try to hide it
They know it is their own
It is not great ambition
It is not force and drive
It is a quiet silence
Of contemplative POWER.

[22 August 1972]

Whatever interest Neil was taking in the politics around him, here was a young man whose critical thinking remained deeply philosophical and introspective.

In 1973, during his third year at UCT, Neil left the box-like residence to take over Neil Andersson's room in the house of an elderly man in Vredenburg Circus, a quiet cul-de-sac in Mowbray. Although not far from the campus, Michael queried the wisdom of his younger brother moving out, and Neil must have fended off questions at home. Dennis Rubel observed that while some members of their small 'long-haired coterie' slackened in their studies, Neil always continued to work diligently. Nevertheless, the increasing length of Neil's hair was the trigger for a huge row between father and son, during which Dennis suspected that Neil finally confronted his father about Kenya and the screening camp. Even if father and son did not argue over the past, there could be no way of not rowing over apartheid and politics in the present. Yet when asked about their memories of Neil changing, Joy and Aubrey recalled only his hair:

> JOY: Aubrey didn't get on with him very well at that time because he would have this long hair which went right down to his shoulders ... He wouldn't listen. Aubrey said, 'That's not the way to be when you're a doctor', and of course in those days it was more unusual than it is today.
> AUBREY: And also a beard.
> BN: So how often did he used to come back here then?
> AUBREY: He used to come every week.
> JOY: To begin with, until he didn't get on with Aubrey. Then he used to come and see me (AUBREY: he used to come and see you every week when I was out playing golf). Not every week by any means. It was only when he could get off on his Thursday afternoon. Aubrey had given him a car and he managed to get out in his third or fourth year.

Although unexpressed, it was clearly very difficult for Joy, caught between father and son. Determined to break his financial dependence on his father, Neil secured a bursary from Anglo American Corporation, the terms of which required him to work for a period as a corporation doctor on Anglo's mines – otherwise, the money would have to be paid back.[39] His sister Jill, whom Neil and his parents had seen off from Cape Town docks as she sailed away on an overseas trip in November 1971, returned in February 1973, unaware of the major falling-out at home. Only her parents were there to meet her off the boat, 'and there was no Neil ... I'd had no idea about this huge rift ... I'd been so looking forward to coming home and I came home to this awful rift. Parents had said nothing.'

In September, Jill married Paul Burger, a young university lecturer in English at the University of South Africa (UNISA), based in Pretoria. Jill, who had always felt close and protective towards her younger brother, had sent

Neil an invitation to her wedding at All Saint's Church in Somerset West, but heard nothing. She hoped that he might just turn up on her special day, but there was no sign of him. It seemed that his dispute with their father had spread, affecting their previously warm sibling relationship. It was only later, while watching a home movie of the wedding made by Paul's brother, that they identified Neil, standing at the back of the congregation. He had slipped in quietly, while they were up at the altar, but disappeared before the reception.

CHAPTER 6

Searching

B Y HIS FOURTH YEAR, NEIL HAD MOVED AGAIN, VACATING HIS room in Mowbray for an isolated farm cottage on a thickly wooded mountain slope near Eagle's Nest in Constantia. A small number of young non-conformists now lived in secluded settlements on the mountain while some of South Africa's wealthiest residents lived in the valley below in gabled Cape Dutch houses surrounded by vineyards. When Michael sought out Neil in his remote cottage, which had no electricity or running hot water, he perceived his brother as an intensely lonely figure. Set amid rocky outcrops, above dense evergreen forests and tangled undergrowth, from which arose a profusion of bird calls, this bowl of the mountain provided a retreat from the world. A few kilometres away lay Hout Bay. It was here on the beach that Neil, recognising a young woman with long fair hair as a medical student, first approached Liz Floyd.

A year behind Neil, Liz had spent a year in America as a Rotary Exchange Student. She had left Rustenburg Girls' High School politically unsophisticated, but travel had begun to open her eyes, allowing her to recognise how parochial Cape Town was. In her architect father's world, that of Bishops Diocesan College and the exclusive Kelvin Grove Club, there was 'a total inability to see that there's anything else, or that Jewish people might not like the fact that Kelvin never accepted Jews, or that if you don't wear a blazer and cravat you're not being rude'.

It wasn't long before Liz joined Neil in the cottage on the mountain, ready to put up with the cold-water shower that he had built outside and the basic cooking facilities. Summers might be idyllic, but the cold, wet and windy Cape winters required endurance. Unlike Neil, Liz had thrown herself into the cut and thrust of student politics. She soon found that Neil, while not short of friends, could be 'extremely introspective', with a capacity to withdraw into himself. Neil enjoyed the solitude, walks in the pine forest, sitting around the fire at night. He spent much of his time studying, and didn't relate a great deal to others living up there. To Liz, Neil was still 'doing quite a lot of searching and landing up with Nietzsche ... which I don't think he ever outgrew ... I suppose it was the idea of transformation, the superman idea, creating a new person'.

In the summer holidays at the end of 1974, after a short visit to Jill and Paul in Eldoraigne on the outskirts of Pretoria, Neil set off for a few weeks of solo hitchhiking. Writing to his mother 'on top of a petrol pump at about 8pm at Marendellas, just outside Salisbury, before bedding down for the night',[40] he offered vivid cameos of his journey through Botswana on bad roads, with very little traffic and almost every truck stopping to give a lift or advice. He had helped to load heavy crates at numerous stops on a three-day journey to Francistown, where he finally enjoyed 'a beautiful bath and cup of tea and washed some clothes'. In parenthesis, he explained that there were no taps, so to get water, he had asked at each village and 'someone would produce water from the well'. He commented how the education level was quite high and 'the people are very happy about the political situation' – a message to his father as much as to his mother about the newly independent African country.

Travelling in Rhodesia felt different, even though lifts had been easy:

> I haven't had a bath for three days, but was caught in some rain just outside Salisbury so that should suffice. Rhodesia is looking very green and beautiful, but is still very colonial, and there is a certain tenseness between black & white here. Bulawayo is a terribly sleepy little backwater, but Salisbury is quite a pleasant place. The whites are quite shocked that Smith should have had secret talks with Kaunda! The nights are beautiful, and sleeping under the stars, I have not yet been caught in the rain. At night I make a little fire

& heat some soup & meat – it tastes good! I go to sleep as the sun sets, and rise with it, because that is when the lifts are best.

He signed off warmly, 'Happy Xmas – I will be thinking of you. Fondly, Neil'. While making no mention of his father, his tone was one of easy conversation. Time must have tempered Neil's anger since the row, but, as Jill would tell me, all three men in her family – her father and both brothers – were uncompromising, each in their own way. Despite the similarity between Neil's keen outdoor spirit and that of Aubrey's pioneering father, Neil's difference in philosophical and political outlook, signified in the length of his hair, had brought down a screen through which Aubrey would not look. The sustained pressure on Joy, whose vision was not so blinkered, must have been extreme.

The following year, Neil prepared to set off again in his summer break, this time to Europe and his first trip abroad. Writing briefly to his mother on 7 November 1975 from Jill and Paul's house in Eldoraigne, he wrote of walks in the nearby bush to see the sun rise and declared their new baby 'medically fit', before concluding affectionately, 'Stay well, and look after your grandchildren … I will probably see you again in January. Fond love, Neil'.

A 'Dear Mom' postcard showing the Houses of Parliament arrived soon afterwards from London. Everything, including his passport and money had been stolen, but 'everything is O.K. now, so don't worry'. Neil was staying 'for free in a hotel near Kensington Gardens so have a chance to read & write on my own'. He would leave for Berlin as soon as he received his new passport. He ended, 'Stay well, Neil'. Despite the injunction to his mother not to worry, it was obvious that she would.

However, a letter headed 'London. Monday 24 Nov.', raised a problem that Joy must have felt was far more difficult, if not insoluble. Neil began, 'Dear Mom, Just a short note in the early hours of the morning …'. The note extended to four air-letter pages of closely written script, beginning with a graphic description of his accommodation in 'an old disused room that leaks and has rats'. But he could look out over the rooftops of the city, enjoying 'the privacy and silence all around', and he was optimistic about receiving his new passport and traveller's cheques so he could move on to Germany. Neil then suddenly expresses his feelings of estrangement from his family:

Mom I find it very difficult to talk to you about things that really matter when I visit, and almost feel that my presence is futile. I know I've caused you a lot of worry since I left a few years ago and I'm sorry for that. I am not angry, I don't hold anything against Dad or you, but my development is just such that a split had to come. Your constant support and love all the time has been incredible; I really appreciate it. I know your existence is not very happy, but that is the lot of the world and we grow strong in our suffering. I understand Michael's religion and do not hold it against him, but it is the easy way out, and I am grateful that you have never succumbed to those platitudes or forced them on us. I find it difficult to explain, but our situation in the world is such that there will always be misunderstanding and suffering between people who love each other, because their natures run in different directions, and they fulfill [sic] a different destiny. I feel very strongly that I have a certain destiny, or life, to fulfill (to which my writing & poetry are only secondary), and I am just sorry that this should cause such a rift between us. I am forever grateful for the amazing childhood that you gave us and the calm confidence of a warm family environment in which we grew up in. After a certain time a man must begin to follow his own path; seek out his own truth and follow that ... that is what makes a man. I admire Dad's strength and independence and his belief in himself, even though I do not agree with his values. He struggled and fought out of poverty to a certain self-realization, but children cannot just accept the whole universe of values and beliefs of their parents; they must struggle and form their own identity. Please don't misunderstand me, I don't think that I have the answer to everything, or that I am superior to my family setting. I have deep in myself a warmth and feeling for the family as it nurtured me through childhood and youth ... but now with the loss of innocence our ways diverge, and I find myself totally alienated from the family. I do not regret it, it is the way our existence takes its course; there is no justice ... starving children die in suffering before they reach self-consciousness ... a mother's love is seldom repayed [sic].

But because of this we mustn't think that there is no meaning in the world. It doesn't lie in the period after death, but in the ordinary everyday petty existence we endure. I am sure you must feel frustrated and disillusioned at the life you lead, but that is the lot of everyone, and it is just in your suffering that you gain your strength and meaning. I remember clearly about 8 years ago when you dropped a milk bottle and were very upset ... I tried to comfort you. What does it matter? We have our bodies, we are still alive, we are strong enough to walk, to hear the birds sing in the morning, to watch the sun set ... what does it matter if there is going to be a war, or if the economy is going down? Excuse all this abstract talk, but I really think it is all that really matters.

I phoned Granny while I was in Pretoria, but didn't see her. I also feel deeply estranged from Jill and her family, though they are very kind to me. Granny has also been very understanding and I feel that she has become wise through all that she has been through – though I find it difficult to talk to her.

At the moment I am busy on two short stories, and am writing a little poetry – I have sent some in for publication that may be out when I get back.

London is quite cold, though the sky is clear and I spend whole days just walking through the parks and along the roads. The grass is covered in orange leaves, and with windy gusts they blow all over. This morning I spent a long time watching some school-kids playing in the park ... so innocent and beautiful. My address in Berlin is: AMERICAN EXPRESS, 11 KEURSUER-STENSDAMN [sic], BERLIN.

Bye now, Neil

With candour, sincerity and lack of rancour, Neil separates himself from his parents. While thanking them for the warmth of his childhood nurturing, he asserts, 'but now with the loss of innocence our ways diverge'. Alienation from his family is inevitable, however sad. He understands the difficulty in his mother's position but does not criticise. Instead he clarifies his own position. This is a moral journey – although he uses neither word – that must take its own true course. In spite of his rejection of Christianity, a strong philosophical core remains of becoming stronger through suffering. Neil faces his future with equanimity and, it seems, the calmness of an existential observer.[41]

After arriving in Paris, Neil wrote two further letters. Knowing that the family would be together in Somerset West for Christmas, on 15 December he addressed a letter to them all, naming everyone, including 'Dad'. Had the frankness of his earlier letter perhaps unleashed something? This letter was even longer, full of vivid observations and commentary about life in Paris. He had cut short hiking through Germany. People hadn't been friendly; he'd been 'carrying too many books' and it had rained all the time. Now he was staying in an old hotel in a poor southeastern district of the city: 'The hotel itself is falling to pieces … I have a window-pane missing, the floor creaks, and the toilet (with no paper) is so small one can barely close the door.'

In the bitterly cold winter, lakes and fountains had iced over, the sun not even melting the frost on the grass in the Luxembourg Gardens. He had been trying to get manual work at hospitals or 'loading fruit at the market, carrying bags of cement; but there are no jobs going at all'. He seemed undaunted by not speaking French and had inquired about a houseman job at the British Hospital, which looked possible, adding that he would also be applying to Cairo. Was Neil's unspoken agenda here perhaps to find work outside South Africa and so avoid the inevitable army call-up papers that would arrive as soon as he completed his medical training?

In the meantime, with the days so short, he was often working into the night and only getting up at midday. This work was writing, reading:

> … then it is dark again by 5pm. It is too cold to walk too far outside, and I have to plan places to stop and get warm again. I spend time in the 'Shakespeare' and have been to some poetry readings there (but not much good).[42] I've also found the Nietzsche library in Paris which is worth being in. The Universities are much the same as ours though the whole of Paris is swarming with riot-police … at a place I was staying before, a crowd of them rushed in and wanted to beat us up … (thugs, not much different from the American police.)
>
> Wednesday: It has just started to snow, and from my window I watch the little flakes blown by the wind swirl around, then land and disappear. On some of the roofs the whiteness starts to stay, the flakes congregate and it gets colder and colder. Across the street a woman shakes the snow off her drying clothes and takes them inside. Down below women walk with white spots tangled in their hair, and the streets shine from the moisture. I hope it warms up a bit soon, or maybe I will try to get another room with all its windows intact … Cafes are warm but expensive so I eat mainly bread and patte [sic] with milk here in my room in the evenings and sometimes go for a cup of coffee at a Cafe.

Neil had rejected the conventional European tour so prized by many of his fellow students. For a few weeks he had become the artist, the writer, who ekes out daily life, enduring what is ordinary, everyday, 'petty', while doing his work. To conclude his six pages of conversation with the family from whom he had earlier expressed estrangement, Neil proposes that they might like to walk in the forests around Constantia, wishes Michael well in his new registrar job, and ends with a touch of irony: 'Well, have a good Xmas, eat well, (and keep warm). Yours, Neil.'

Neil's final letter from abroad, dated 'Paris. 29/12/75' begins 'Dear Mom & Dad'. News of his stolen money had prompted them to send him a cheque. Thanking them both for the trouble they had taken to get this to him, and for a letter forwarded from Berlin, he assures them that he has quite a bit of money left and he would bring the cheque back to Somerset West. He was not giving up his stubborn independence:

> I must have given you the wrong impression, though at the time I wrote it was very cold. Over the last fortnight the weather has been beautifully warm, and last night I slept with the window open. It takes a while to get used to the little contingencies of existence here so that one doesn't have to concern oneself with petty problems that crop up inevitably in a strange town with a foreign language.

Echoes of Nietzsche and Camus in the letters intimate that Neil had also come to Europe, at least in part, to understand more about the writers he admired. Separation from others was a means of freeing himself to deepen his own 'subjective experience':

> It is difficult to describe the kind of life that I am leading here; it is a solitary existence with not many external events, but rich in subjective experience. On Xmas night I stood for a while in a beautiful church listening to some singing and looking out over the lights of Paris. With all the ponds frozen one appreciates to [a] far greater extent the beauty of flowing water, its infinite variety, clarity and purity. The ice looks so dirty and coarse, though it is different when it hangs in icicles from the fountains. We only had that one period of snow (only for about 10 minutes) but now it is starting to get cold again so we may be in for another spell.

Time and again, in these letters from Europe, moments of beauty interweave with mundane, often grim, realities. In this final letter, Neil mentions amputations in young people with cancer as 'the most terrible example of the absoloute [sic] indifference and injustice of the world'. However stimulating he had found Paris, he was beginning to feel 'a little stifled' and would be 'glad to get some fresh air again, and be near the sea'. He signed himself formally, 'Yours, Neil'. On his return, he would express to Liz a sense of disappointment. If he had been searching for something in Europe, it seems that he hadn't found it.

CHAPTER 7

'We should throw stones'

A ROUND THEIR FIFTH YEAR, DENNIS RUBEL AND A GROUP OF
friends had begun reading Marx, with Neil sometimes joining them.
In Dennis's view, Neil was still far more interested in broader philosophical questions than in politics. Despite his interest in medical alternatives
developed by Che Guevara in Cuba, Neil did not join Liz in social projects in
the townships. As these were led by white NUSAS students, without any black
students – because of SASO's Black Consciousness position – Dennis and his
friends would have nothing to do with them, regarding NUSAS as 'right-wing
centrist'. Liz was more pragmatic, indeed regarding Neil's interest in Che as
rather 'romanticised'.

For most of his university years, Neil had been largely content to read and
reflect, although Dennis would sometimes 'drag' him to demonstrations. But
in their final year the violence against young black students in Soweto, beginning on 16 June 1976, unleashed a new response in Neil that took Dennis by
surprise. Following the uprising, they joined a demonstration on De Waal
Drive in which about a hundred students with placards were milling around,
slowing down traffic, with two police cars parked on the other side of the
road. When students hooted and whistled, the police made threatening
gestures back. Feeling that it was one of those dull student demonstrations

where nothing was going to happen, Dennis wanted to leave but Neil responded, 'No, we should throw stones at the police.' 'What? Are you mad? They'll shoot us!' 'No', replied Neil, 'we should throw stones.' 'OK, throw a stone then.' Whereupon Neil picked up a half-brick and bowled it some 25 to 30 metres. 'It was an astonishing good shot! This half-brick came very high up and then down, and landed on the police windshield and cracked it with a great CRRCRCRACK.' The police were flung into furious activity, but, not recognising the pair from medical school, the other students (non-medicals) panicked that they were agents provocateurs and dispersed. The ruthless killing of unarmed young black students in Soweto by the police seems to have triggered 'a personal change' in Neil.

It was, however, a romantic naivety that struck the essentially cautious and slightly older Jan Theron in his first encounters with Neil around this time, introduced by Liz. Jan had recently taken charge of the Food and Canning Workers' Union, established in the 1940s as non-racial but now, in effect, a state-registered Coloured union. The Cape Town tradition of unionism was associated with political engagement and Jan's mission included reviving old branches where, in the days before apartheid legislation, there had once been an overwhelming African membership.[43]

The politically astute Theron was all too aware of the tightrope along which the union walked. They had to operate as openly and democratically as possible in a racist, repressive state with the security police constantly on the lookout for anything that might be labelled subversive. When Jan visited Neil and Liz in their mountain cottage, the impression he gained of Neil was of an amateur radical:

> He was obviously interested in unions and organization of workers and so was Liz … it was a bit conspiratorial at that point. He used to have some publications stuffed in his sofa in Constantia, Eagle's Nest, and that sort of thing.

Although unions with a non-racial outlook offered a space for young white volunteers, it wasn't easy to 'get in'. Athalie Crawford, at the time married to Jan Theron, talks of a sense in the white left of 'incredible prestige of those who worked in a union. [There was] no money, but you were paid in love.' Neil was certainly not looking for money. However, as his interest in unions developed, the earlier impressions of the romantic amateur lingered in Cape Town circles and would lead him to sense that doors there had been closed.

Neil's first internship, from the end of 1976, alongside black interns and experienced doctors in Umtata General Hospital, was, in Liz's view, his first real shift away from a European environment and would critically redirect him into South Africa. His deep involvement with German philosophers at university had led him to consider leaving the country to study philosophy full time. That, or a housemanship abroad, would also have allowed him to escape military service. But his overseas trip had left him disillusioned with Europe, and Neil set out to learn whatever he could in Umtata (now Mthatha). While Cape Town was a predominantly white city, Umtata couldn't have been more different.

The 'small and barren' town, as Neil would describe it, was capital of the Transkei, the first Bantustan to be declared 'independent' by the regime, a status not recognised by any country other than South Africa. At the hospital, for the first time, Neil joined a community of black doctors who were his superiors, equals and highly politicised. It was, according to Liz, a 'turning point':

> ... the most powerful perception changer for white South Africans is meeting a black person who is equal if not more developed than them and particularly the ANC kind of person or Steve Biko equivalent, who is not only politically very sophisticated, but extremely democratic and all encompassing ... The Umtata guys would have been SASO people from Durban University and spent six years in same hostel ... A lot of those people then actually joined the ANC ... Neil would have been very direct and honest in response to BC [Black Consciousness] rather than working off a NUSAS pre-conceived analysis. He didn't just work with them but lived with them ... In Cape Town even though patients were black, most of staff were Coloured. So Transkei would have been Neil's first African experience.

Yet Liz sensed that Umtata was also a lonely experience, even for someone like Neil. In her view, white students who rejected apartheid in the 1970s experienced a particular alienation because the rise of Black Consciousness meant that a non-racial political struggle no longer existed. Any earlier aspiration to follow in the footsteps of a Dr Nurse in his remote mission hospital had long gone for Neil. As his political antennae developed, he saw more clearly the economic roots of apartheid. With reading philosophy no longer enough, he was looking to become connected to political change.

Three letters to his mother written while in Umtata offer a few snapshots of the place. It was a big hospital, with lawns and trees between buildings spread over a large area. Neil found moments to reflect, whether standing on the veranda to watch rain falling and puddles lit up by streetlights, or walking through the wards in the early hours of the morning when everything was quiet and peaceful. Staying in the single quarters at first felt 'cramping' after the farm cottage in Eagle's Nest. However, as Neil got to know the other doctors, cooking and eating together in the evenings, he chose to stay on rather than look for a place on his own in town. The work was demanding. At one point, he found himself running the Paediatrics ward, 120 children sharing 50 beds, on his own. On his Anaesthetics stint, by his third week he was already responsible for major operations. On duty nights, he was required to cover the whole hospital and Casualty as the only doctor on call. The result was that, by the end of his six months, the experience would leave him feeling 'quite confident'.

Liz, who had her final year to complete, was still living in the farm cottage on the mountain. She made a few visits, including coming to spend a quiet Christmas with him. Neil described for his mother how they had gone out to see friends at a little village at Viedgesville (not far from Nelson Mandela's birthplace at Qunu). A sheep had been slaughtered, 'so we all ate really lovely braaied mutton'. If Joy and Aubrey wondered who these friends were in such a remote village, the next paragraph made it clear. Their son was as socially at ease among black compatriots as he had been among villagers in Botswana. White South Africa's colour and class divisions were meaningless to him:

> Last weekend we went down to Mooiplaas, near East London to see Emma (Toli) (the woman who works for Mr Berrisford), and (it being new year), we went from house to house with a huge group of people, drinking beer, eating cakes, and finally a delicious roast chicken dish – the people were very friendly. We spent the night sleeping on the floor and returned at 4am to start duty on Sunday!

After Liz returned to Cape Town, Neil would travel to East London,

Grahamstown and Durban on some off-duty weekends. Although confirming Liz's impression about an element of loneliness, in Neil's last letter to his mother from Umtata, he wrote of having made some close friends there. His ability to listen, and his openness to understanding Black Consciousness, had been a positive starting point.

He ended his last letter from Umtata, dated 15 June 1977, by returning to the matter of his estrangement from the family. It was the eve of the first anniversary of the Soweto student uprising. Neil felt the need to clarify his future direction. His mother needed to understand that he cared for her, but the rift was unavoidable. There were 'basic contradictions that neither of us could live with':

> I am always grateful for the love & care that you gave me as a child, but at some point I had to evaluate the world from an independent perspective and make my own decisions.
>   I am sorry for all the hurt I have caused you, but I am sure you realize that I am not standing against you or the family in particular, but against the whole social order.
>   Stay well,
>   Yours,
>   Neil

The loneliness perceived by Liz was not just about having friends with whom to communicate but also reflected a very deep sense of aloneness. Approaching 24, Neil was ready to stand as an individual 'against the whole social order'.

Returning to Cape Town at the end of his six months, Neil hoped to complete his housemanship year there. Liz was still in the cottage, and they resumed their relationship, but with no internships available Neil accepted the offer of a post at Tembisa Hospital. Tembisa was an extensive township on the East Rand, created by evictions of black residents of Johannesburg in the late 1950s, with workers pushed out of the city but corralled close enough to supply their daily labour. While the view from Cape Town was that 'Jozi' was a hard, ruthless place, for Neil moving to the country's industrial heart meant new possibilities. Moreover, he expected his call-up papers from the army any day. In the big city he could make himself more difficult to trace.

PART TWO

Comrades

CHAPTER 8

Jozi: Comrades

While I was working at Tembisa, I became aware that the problems of the patients I was dealing with were not only medical problems, but were basically social problems due to the people not getting enough wages, unemployment, and the poor conditions in the townships. This meant that sometimes I would stitch up a patient, only to have him return the following week due to alcoholism, unemployment, or extreme poverty, with another assault wound. Also I was working in a neurosurgery ward where I saw many people, particularly paraplegics, who had been injured at work. Often these patients did not get their compensation, or if they did, they got very little, because the compensation is based on what the workers earnings are, and not on an absolute figure related to the extent of the injury. Even if they did get their compensation, they often lost their jobs, which meant that they could not get another job due to the disability, and them and their families were without means of support.

Neil Aggett, 1st statement,
John Vorster Square[44]

A MONTH BEFORE HIS TWENTY-FOURTH BIRTHDAY, NEIL CAME TO Johannesburg. It was where his 80-year-old 'wise' Granny lived with his mother's sister Madge and her family, the Allisons, earlier noted on his schoolboy lists of Christmas presents. But he was not going to contact any relatives. Neil knew no one else in his new city, except that he had once briefly met his university friend Neil Andersson's older brother, Gavin, at the house in Vredenburg Circus. A chance meeting, not long after Neil's arrival, brought them together. Visiting Exclusive Books in Hillbrow, Neil recognised Gavin with his rugged moustache, red-black beard and long blond hair. Warm and friendly, Gavin invited Neil to visit him at the house he shared in nearby Yeoville with his partner, Nici Aime, and Annie Smyth, a young teacher.

A 'banned person', Gavin was doing his best to dodge his restrictions. For Neil, feeling his way to political change, the offer of friendship from someone already seasoned in 'the struggle' opened the door. Gavin had been banned along with fellow trade unionist Sipho Kubeka. The personal and political development of these two young comrades, one white and one black, was to have a life-changing impact on Neil as he stepped into the intensity of post-1976 Johannesburg. He was excited by their political history and keen to learn about the fiercely polarised debates over emerging trade unions. He was undeterred that Gavin and Sipho's grouping, linked to 'the movement' and stretching back to the non-racial Congress Alliance, was marginalised by those in key union roles who were insisting on unionism without politics. Nor would he live to see, within less than a decade, South Africa's largest trade union federation, the Congress of South African Trade Unions (COSATU), openly and vibrantly embrace political unionism and the idea that union struggles are a vital part of the struggle for democracy.

In 1977, however, within the city's divided white left, perceptions of Gavin in certain union circles would, in turn, affect Neil. When Neil arrived, he was also, as Gavin affectionately describes him, 'a little wet behind the ears, not good at keeping quiet about his political positions'. To understand Neil's reception, as well as to understand what drew him to his chosen comrades, it is necessary to step back a few years.

*   *   *

Born in South Africa, Gavin Andersson had grown up in Botswana, formerly the protectorate of Bechuanaland. In contrast to the Aggetts, his parents had not wanted to bring up their children under white domination. After working for a year as a diamond prospector in the desert, Gavin came to Johannesburg in 1972 to study for a BSc at the University of the Witwatersrand. To his surprise, his fellow students at Wits regarded themselves as Europeans and saw him 'as coming from Africa, while they in South Africa didn't come from Africa at all!' Nor did they know the contemporary African history that had influenced him so powerfully ... the ongoing war in Zimbabwe, FRELIMO's armed struggle in Mozambique, the writings of Kenneth Kaunda in Zambia on humanism, Julius Nyerere in Tanzania on Ujamaa and the one-party state, or Seretse Khama in Botswana on the importance of multiparty democracy.

While Neil was in Cape Town tussling with European philosophy and writing Romantic and Nietzsche-inspired poetry and journal dialogues with bishops, Gavin immersed himself in student politics. In the early 1970s, white NUSAS students had set up the Wages Commission to investigate starvation wages and cost-of-living data. With the rise of Black Consciousness, in Gavin's words, 'it was a time when politics were getting kicked into gear again'. On one thing there was agreement: the struggle would be taken forward by black workers. Beyond this, how the white left should assist was the subject of disputes and feuds.

Within two years, Gavin started a magazine, *Africa Perspective*. Shortly after the first issue appeared, in October 1974, he was approached by Pindile Mfeti, whose uncle, Govan Mbeki, was ten years into his life sentence on Robben Island. Nights of penetrating conversation followed, first with Pindile, then with small groups of others, most of whose names Gavin wasn't given. Nor did he ask. He knew that he was being vetted. Soon afterwards, he was invited to join the Industrial Aid Society (IAS), recently set up by Pindile and a network of former South African Congress of Trade Unions (SACTU) activists and two of Gavin's university friends, Steven Friedman and Jeanette Curtis. SACTU had not been proscribed as an organisation despite its alliance with the ANC; instead, it had been disabled by the banning and imprisonment of its leaders.

The IAS office at 277 Bree Street conducted its business under the eyes of the security police. Its work was only legal as long as it stuck to 'non-political' industrial matters, something that would be a constant source of tension. A legal-aid clinic on labour issues, assisted by a few professionals, attracted workers through pamphlets handed out by students outside train stations and factories, and by word of mouth. Linked to this was a worker education group that ran discussion sessions on Saturdays.

It was at one of these that Gavin first met Sipho Kubeka. Their backgrounds were far apart. On becoming a young father, Sipho had been forced to leave school in Standard 9, finding work as a clerk at a company called Imextra. An older clerk, who had spent five years on Robben Island for ANC activity, introduced Sipho and other Imextra workers to the SACTU tradition of labour politics and the IAS.[45] In due course, when Sipho and another employee were delegated to hand in a letter asking Imextra management to recognise an elected workers' committee, both were dismissed. A weeklong strike had followed, ending with recognition of the workers' committee but no reinstatements. After sponsoring an unsuccessful legal case, *Kubheka* v *Imextra*, the IAS was to employ Sipho as an organiser in 1975.

The relationship between Gavin and Sipho quickly deepened, despite the gulf in their segregated lives. In Alexandra – 'Alex' – where Sipho lived with his wife Thandi and young family, experiencing all its hardships, life remained much more traditional than that of bohemian young white and mainly middle-class radicals. Many of the latter had broken away from their families to experiment politically, as well as with personal lifestyles and relationships, reflecting a similar cultural shift under way in Europe and the USA. But as Gavin would tell me, 'We were both being mentored by Pindile and we became best friends, learning a lot, a whole lot of cross-cultural stuff, which was important in our early twenties, and good stuff, a very meaningful relationship'. Given the growing Black Consciousness movement, Pindile's mentoring from a non-racial ANC perspective was critical in enabling a relationship of trust to develop between them that, three years later, would extend to include Neil.

*   *   *

During 1974, while Neil enjoyed reading and contemplating in the solitude of Eagle's Nest, a proposal took root among the activists of the IAS to start a union in Johannesburg. Debate was heated, lasting into 1975. What kind of union? The activists mostly divided into two camps. One side proposed the 'Durban model' of industrial unions, Durban dockers having unexpectedly initiated a series of massive strikes in 1973. Proponents of this model advocated organising the working class, industry by industry (textile, metal, chemical, transport, and so on). It was going to take a long time, many years, and in the interests of building strong shop-floor organisation, it was vital to avoid politics and a direct conflict with the state.[46]

The other side argued for the 'Cape Town model' of general unions in which workers across different industries and services were united by common concerns. These were more likely to have political implications. Gavin and Sipho felt that the general unionists were correct not to divide the experience of workers artificially. Workers didn't cease 'being' when they left the factory, and their conditions at home and in their communities could be just as crucial for organising. This led the student activists, who favoured what they saw as the more political option of starting a general union, to expect that Gavin and Sipho would vote with them.

The divisions were bitter, barbs flying both ways. Anyone in the general union camp was called 'ultra-left'. Anyone in the industrial union camp was a 'reformist'. However, when an analysis of Johannesburg's workers showed that almost 70% fell into metal and allied trades – and could thus be covered by a single industrial union – the argument finally swung in favour of establishing a Metal Wing of the IAS. In their grouping, Pindile, Gavin and Sipho supported this, having decided that the whole argument had been over a false division and labels. If they could help build strong shop-floor organisation from factory to factory, as promoted within the industrial union camp, this would surely be strengthened by political organisation of workers in their townships and outside the factory gates. It was a commonsense solution. Not so, however, to the student volunteers in the general union camp, who accused them of 'betraying the revolution'.

Things came to a head at the Annual General Meeting of the IAS, when the students assumed that Gavin would stand for the key role of IAS Secretary. They planned to vote instead for one of their own. However, they didn't take into account Pindile's political savvy. On the day before the AGM, Pindile explained to their very small group that he would stand for the IAS leadership, while Gavin should stand for Secretary of the new Metal Wing. 'It was brilliant', says Gavin. The IAS was essentially a group of white people with a few black clerks and interpreters. 'There was no way at all that they could refuse the nomination of Pindile, a young black intellectual, very well connected politically and indeed a key figure behind the formation of the IAS itself. Yet they had all assumed he would go for the Metal Wing and I would be the candidate for IAS. Classic racial thinking.'

Pindile was duly elected as Secretary of the IAS, and Gavin agreed to lead the new Metal Wing for six months only, until he could hand over to a black comrade. Even Gavin's activist university friends and former allies, Jeanette Curtis and Steven Friedman, were upset and broke off contact. Gavin recalls 'a great deal of bitterness' and the students disappearing from their work, as Pindile, Gavin and Sipho now put much more time into building a workers' organisation. With increased police attention, they became very security-conscious. In the past, especially among the students, there used to be 'quite a lot of dinner parties discussing things that shouldn't be discussed. So that stopped around that time.' Since their student days, Gavin had always enjoyed Jeanette's warmth and hospitality, but his awareness of the need to bring a halt to dinner-party talk also reflected his own maturation with experiences that were taking him well beyond the white left. In due course, the lessons that he and Sipho were learning would be passed on to Neil.

*   *   *

Early in 1975, just a few weeks after Neil had hitchhiked alone through Botswana, drinking water from village wells, Pindile arranged a secret trip to Botswana for Gavin, himself and the former SACTU administrator Miriam Sithole to meet exiled leaders Ray Alexander (former General Secretary of SACTU), John Gaetsewe (General Secretary of SACTU) and 'Uncle Dan' Thloome (ANC National Executive Committee member). Having gone all that way to meet the 'big legends', Gavin was amazed to watch a drawn-out, petty argument between Ray and Uncle Dan about whether it was an ANC or a SACTU meeting and who would lead it. Not only did they seem oblivious of the impression they might leave on a new recruit, they also appeared initially to be more caught up in their own internal politics and the historical implication of the meeting than what it might mean for the three activists returning to South Africa if they were to be questioned by the police. Attending a SACTU meeting was not technically illegal. Attending an ANC meeting, on the other hand, would land each of them with a prison sentence.

The meeting lasted five hours, with the exiled leaders keen to hear about organisation inside the country. Afterwards Pindile took Gavin and Miriam to meet some other comrades. 'So somehow in all this I became an ANC cadre', says Gavin. He remained unaware that the three ANC/SACTU leaders were all stalwarts of the South African Communist Party (SACP). Although Sipho hadn't accompanied them to Botswana, he knew about the trip. He had already made his own allegiance to the ANC some time earlier, and, without being formally recruited, he had been working with people he took to be ANC operatives. With the closest of comrades, there were still questions of what to share and what not to share. They were learning from each other, and the 'need to know' principle didn't always lay down strict boundaries. The oral history into which Neil, in turn, would be inducted would contain items meant to go no further than his ears.

Pindile continued mentoring both Sipho and Gavin, as well as staying in contact with 'outside', linking to the ANC through Swaziland. While they continued to work openly together through the IAS, each separately developed less visible networks. Through Pindile, they developed a strong sense of their particular role inside South Africa. As Gavin recalls,

> ... we saw ourselves as working to establish autonomous ANC structures within the country, with an idea that later they would link up with the external structures. Despite the fact that Pindile was well connected to the external structures, he did stress regularly that the struggle's course would be determined by vibrant internal organisation and we should always resist simply following instructions from someone outside, since these folks were not as informed as we were about what was happening on the ground and hence could make severe miscalculations.

Pindile's insight was acute.

*   *   *

With the IAS and Metal Wing offices next door to each other in Bree Street, Gavin and Pindile worked closely together. But some time after this 'capture' of positions, the security police swooped on Pindile.[47] When the police came for him, they raided the IAS offices, taking away the chequebook with the stub for petty cash that had been used on the secret Botswana trip. Gavin waited to be picked up, but the police never came. When Pindile finally emerged without charges from security police headquarters at John Vorster Square, he had a broken eardrum. During interrogation on the notorious tenth floor, he had refused to budge from his statement that the meeting in Botswana had been organised by the International Labour Organization (ILO) and had nothing to do with the ANC. Throughout the hammering, he had kept to his story that it had been SACTU-led. Gavin was to remember the strategy, and this too would be a significant item of oral history to pass on to Neil.

Within a few months of its establishment, the Metal Wing was transformed in 1975 into the Transvaal branch of the Metal and Allied Workers' Union (MAWU), with Gavin making way for Sipho as its General Secretary. Gavin's work was unpaid, so to support himself and cover his rent he gave guitar lessons one afternoon a week, as well as working as a quantity surveyor's clerk on Sundays. Friends frequently fed him. Evening meetings with workers involved travelling to townships like Daveyton, Tembisa or Alex. Often he and Sipho would be up early in the morning to catch workers before they started out for their 5am shift. It was an exciting, challenging time for the two comrades. They were doing something that had the power to effect change and they could feel themselves, in Gavin's words, 'learning every day from the workers because of the incredible wisdom that comes out of the kind of organic organisation that workers have developed to cope with their situation'. Their aim was to establish strong shop-floor organisation within a factory that linked with a network of township organisation. Tembisa and Alex were divided into sectors, with a contact point in each sector connecting to departmental organisation inside a factory. Where the bosses barred discussion at work, this meant that they could organise at night and over weekends, calling people together quickly to discuss management tactics and being ready to respond.[48]

The effectiveness of their strategy was tested to the full in March 1976 in events that would hit the headlines. They had been organising MAWU workers for the past six months at the Heinemann Electric factory in Germiston.[49] Most of Heinemann's 600-plus workers had signed up for the union, boycotting the company's persistent attempts to make them vote for a management-controlled liaison committee. Finally, the management fired 20 workers, including three MAWU shop stewards. When the protesting workers gathered outside the factory, demanding to meet the managing director, they were ignored. The following morning they arrived to find the gates locked. The managers, already there with armed police, declared that the workers were on an illegal strike and therefore fired. The workers said no, they were locked out.

Meeting over the weekend in their townships, the workers decided to return on Monday 29 March. The gates were still locked, and this time police were waiting inside the factory with dogs, pickhandles and batons. As MAWU officials, Sipho, who had just taken over as General Secretary, and Gavin, now Sipho's deputy, asked to meet the managing director but were refused. At 10am, police ordered the workers to disperse within half an hour. More police arrived and the dogs were let out. With ten minutes to go, Sipho urged the workers to leave. They were singing as they set off when the police attacked. Blows rained down on defenceless workers, including a highly pregnant woman. Gavin found himself beaten to the ground, before being lifted to his feet and led to a police truck. In Steven Friedman's view, it was 'the decade's most violent assault on unionised workers'.[50] Twenty-four workers and Gavin required hospital treatment, as did three policemen who had been part of the baton charge.[51]

Gavin's sudden appearance with a broken arm in a photograph in the *Rand Daily Mail*, at a meeting of dismissed workers in Alexandra, brought to an end his 'sellout' status among the students.[52] He and Sipho stood trial for inciting an illegal strike and with obstructing the police in the course of their duties. Through the Legal Resources Centre, they were defended by George Bizos who, 35 years later, would wryly recall how the police colonel, when giving evidence, had referred to Sipho as Gavin's '*handlanger*' (hanger-on), unable to 'believe that a black man would be the Secretary of a trade union and a white man would be his assistant'.

Fortunately there were pictures taken by a photographer from the *Rand Daily Mail* that challenged the colonel's claims to have been faced by a 'murderous mob' wielding pangas and knives. In court Bizos produced photographs of the crowd, 'and the nearest to it was a woman lifting a milk-bottle … as if to say Viva!' The photographs also showed women being sjambokked and pinned up against a fence by a police vehicle. Four workers charged under the Riotous Assemblies Act were found not guilty, but Gavin and Sipho were each fined for 'inciting the continuation of a strike': Gavin R90 and Sipho R45.

The court case took them out of action for some weeks. On 17 May, Pindile was detained, this time after returning from a visit to Swaziland, and would be kept in jail, without charges, for a full year. On 16 June, with the court case still ongoing, Soweto erupted after police fired on black students protesting against new regulations forcing them to take half their lessons in Afrikaans. While the townships were on fire, a constant stream of students arrived at the MAWU and IAS offices for advice. Printing pamphlets aimed at avoiding 'black on black' violence, Gavin and Sipho felt vindicated that in Alex and Tembisa, where MAWU had been building both union and community structures, there wasn't the same fighting between parents and students and between migrants and residents that was happening in other areas.

Down in Cape Town, Neil threw his half-brick at a police car on De Waal Drive ...

In September, the Minister of Justice and Police, James 'Jimmy' Kruger, or-dered the detention without trial of a number of Cape Town trade unionists. One of them, a 32-year-old employee of the Western Province Workers' Advice Bureau, an organisation similar to IAS, was found hanging in his police cell in central Cape Town only two hours after his arrest.[53] In November, Kruger banned 26 union officials and a handful of academics. He appeared just as determined to crush the emerging union activity among black workers as he was intent on destroying the countrywide rebellion sparked by the Soweto student uprising. The majority of banned officials were white intellectuals, suggesting that Kruger's security police believed that without them, black African organisers would not be able to function. Both Gavin and Sipho were among the banned, along with Jeanette Curtis who had been arrested for a few weeks the previous year.[54] While severely restricted, however, they had no intention of capitulating. Gavin and Sipho immediately began to devise new ways of meeting.

By the time that Gavin met Neil in the Hillbrow bookshop in the latter part of 1977, the number of detainees held under security legislation had risen dra-matically within a single year. So had deaths in detention. Steve Biko, the gift-ed and charismatic proponent of Black Consciousness who had been expelled from University of Natal Medical School, was the 46th political detainee to die in detention. Responding to a question in Parliament, Minister Kruger was forced to declare there had been 130 such deaths in general police custody in 1976 alone. Two days after Biko's death, Kruger addressed a National Party

Congress in his native Afrikaans, and made the infamous statement: 'I am not glad and I am not sorry about Mr Biko. It leaves me cold (*Dit laat my koud*). I can say nothing to you. Any person who dies ... I shall also be sorry if I die. (Laughter).'[55]

CHAPTER 9

A new brotherhood

O N THE DAY THAT BIKO DIED OF MULTIPLE HEAD INJURIES ON the floor of a cell in Pretoria Central Prison, 12 September 1977, Neil started work at Tembisa Hospital. He had found a small house to rent on the flat highveld, not far away at Halfway House (now Midrand), off the road north to Pretoria. It was a remote old Transvaal farmhouse with a tin roof that sloped down over the front stoep. Inside, there was very little furniture and, as in his mountain retreat, no electricity, although there was a coal stove. The highveld was very different to the forests above Constantia, in a small way more akin to the Kenyan bush of Neil's childhood. Whatever the practical reasons for living near to Tembisa, the little farmhouse was a lonely spot. At the same time, he clearly welcomed bumping into the older brother of his friend Neil Andersson and the chance of new relationships.

On his first visit to Neil at Halfway House, Gavin commented on a poster on the kitchen wall. It showed a Sandinista woman with a gun. His brother's medical school friend was clearly no longer just the 'helluva nice guy' and 'rugger-bugger' of those early university days. What if, Gavin asked Neil, the security police were to come checking up on the young white man living in a farmhouse by himself near Tembisa, and saw this picture? Neil took the poster down. Annie Smyth, a young teacher who lived with Gavin and his partner Nici, and who, as the only person with a car at the time, did much ferrying, recalled another picture in Neil's kitchen that initially made her suspect that Neil came from a 'tradition of real ultra-leftism'. It showed members of the Baader-Meinhof gang, who had recently been found dead in their German prison cells after the failure of a plane hijacking that was designed to secure their release. The word 'MURDERED' was written in large red letters, many people on the left rejecting the official version and believing that the prisoners had been killed. This was another picture that had to come down.

Rather than dismissing Neil as naive, Gavin warmed to his romanticism and idealism but watched to see how Neil responded to advice. Gavin had learned from seeing how core union members in a factory would carefully test out potential new recruits, in order to ensure that they weren't management informers. The prospective member would be drawn into conversation at different times, first with one core member, then another. Afterwards, their responses would be discussed and carefully analysed before a decision was taken as to whether to invite them to join the union. The process was slow but had helped to build a strong, reliable core in each factory. However much Gavin warmed to Neil, he still needed to be cautious, and he also needed Sipho to sound him out.

With banning orders forbidding contact between banned persons, Gavin and Sipho were prohibited from speaking to each other. A banned person was also not allowed to meet with more than one other person at a time. Banning orders specified the limits of where the banned person could go and what work they could do. Penalties for breaking the order were severe. Both Gavin and Sipho regarded them as a challenge in testing their ingenuity to meet once a week for a couple of hours. At the same time, they were careful.

When Sipho first met Neil at Gavin's place, what impressed Sipho immediately was that Neil did not want to go into the army. This was in contrast to white comrades who excused their army service by saying they had done office work or activity that didn't involve them in the townships or on the border. But here was a comrade who was 'actually moving around so that he is not found and deciding to lead an abnormal life'. Later, as their friendship grew, Sipho introduced Neil to his family. Like Gavin, and unlike most white South Africans, Neil was thoroughly comfortable coming into a black township, day or night. He would visit Sipho and his wife Thandi and their two daughters in Alexandra, where they shared a yard, one tap and one toilet with

more than a dozen other families. One night, while they were sitting and talking, Neil's car, parked outside the yard, was stolen. It was 'a major problem,
a white man in Alexandra township at night, no transport out'. Sipho had to
accompany his friend to the outskirts of Alex from where he was able to hitch
a lift back to town. But the experience did not deter Neil from future visits to
a family with whom he felt at home.

To Sipho, Neil was always 'strikingly humble':

> ... some comrades, more especially white comrades, you find that they are
> very sure of themselves, who'd want their presence to be felt all the time, like
> talking a lot ... where people would want to draw attention to themselves.
> Now with Neil he wasn't doing those things, like wanting to talk a lot, but
> his presence would be felt that he is there.

However, as well as being a good listener, Neil was keen to share ideas and
to debate. Sipho was especially impressed with Neil's understanding of the
origins of Black Consciousness and his willingness to engage with it, rather
than simply react to it. He was also struck by how Neil shared his medical
knowledge and how he would explain medical information without any pat-
ronising. Most importantly, Neil was very keen to get involved in union work,
from which Gavin and Sipho had been cut off by their banning orders.

In the vacuum created by Gavin's and Sipho's banning, the leadership of IAS
and MAWU had been quickly taken over by those who, according to Sipho,
characterised him and Gavin as dangerous 'populists'. In their view, 'the ANC
was a purely nationalist, petit-bourgeois organisation which was not to be
supported, in fact ... it had to be opposed'. Yet regardless of whether the new
leadership's views were strongly ideological or simply strategic, to ensure that
the union didn't fall foul of the state, Neil clearly had to be mentored before he
would have a chance of being accepted for any kind of union work.

Gavin began by helping Neil start a garden, growing potatoes beside the
rented farmhouse, combining digging and discussing. It became a tradition
they were to expand. Concurrently, Gavin also introduced Neil to more formal political discussion groups. In the early days of their friendship, these
took place in various people's houses, although never at Neil's place in
Halfway House. Gavin recognised that Neil was still 'very weak at ... understanding when you can explore an issue and when you must just let it be'. In

one instance, Neil completely blew a discussion group that Gavin had just set up with a couple who were very keen to be involved. On the first night, Neil brought up the subject of white conscripts, proposing that they should go and get their rifles and then hand them over for the struggle, 'so we could wage urban guerrilla warfare'. The couple were so freaked out that they came to see Gavin the next day to say that Neil was 'a rabid ultra-leftist' and they couldn't work with him. As Gavin wryly recollected, 'that group never got going'.

Most likely, it was grand statements like these that had gained Neil his reputation for naivety among more experienced white activists in Cape Town who, Neil told Gavin, had been excluding him from meetings. However, with their enforced exclusion from union work, Gavin and Sipho had time on their hands and could take a longer view. They responded to Neil's open spirit. It was his judgments that needed to be tempered. Neil, in turn, responded to their mentoring and welcomed their brotherhood.

When Liz came to visit Neil over Christmas at the end of 1977, before starting her first intern post back in Cape Town, she was struck by the isolated location that he had chosen. Was he repeating what she had seen him do at times in Cape Town, retreating into himself and cutting himself off socially? Meeting Neil's new comrades, like Gavin and Sipho, partially allayed that fear, indicating that he was feeling his way into new relationships. However, six months later, when she returned to Johannesburg to start her second internship, she was in for a shock. Neil had told her that he had moved into town, into a tiny house in Fuller Street in Bertrams. That had been a good sign, and Liz looked forward to making it into their home. They had been apart for most of the last 18 months. But on arriving, Liz was to find her relationship with Neil far more complicated. In Cape Town, monogamy was by and large the norm among the white left, even if it was not always practised. It soon appeared to Liz to be otherwise in the metropolis. Johannesburg, known for being fast and hard, was a hub of tensions. Under the watchful eyes of the Special Branch, it was also a hub of secrets, personal as well as political.

CHAPTER 10

Breaking the rules, making the rules

T HE YOUNG WHITE RADICALS IN JOHANNESBURG, MANY OF WHOM
had broken from their parents and from traditional middle-class
lifestyles, were breaking rules and making their own rules. Crown
Mines, southwest of the city on the way to Soweto, was an ideal place to set up
a commune of sorts in the cottages vacated by former white miners following
the closure of the mines in 1975. Situated next to Langlaagte, the farm where
gold was first discovered in 1886, Crown Mines had operated for almost 90
years. Left behind were huge sun-bleached mine dumps and long lines of
small, single-storey dwellings built for the families of white miners.

There were two distinct 'villages' and political groupings out at Crown
Mines. In 'Model Village', the houses were bigger and, although there was a
mixture of people, including some younger students like Taffy Adler, there
tended to be more settled families. Taffy's neighbours were the Bonners.
About two kilometres up the hill was the main complex at 'Top Village', which
Phil Bonner, a History lecturer at Wits involved in the IAS, recalls as 'younger,
more studentish', priding itself 'on its communal atmosphere': 'There were
awful degrees of political correctness there. It tended to align itself with the
more popular, populist camp and sort of consigned us to the dustbins really.
[They were] much more wanting to sympathise directly with the ANC.'

Attached in long straight terraces, the small houses in Top Village retained many of the original features, including their red tin roofs and even the original tin walls. Not all the ex-miners had moved out, and tensions sometimes erupted as the new community of young white middle-class professionals and 'hippies' moved in. On one occasion, Gavin's photographer friend Eddie Wes recalled them taking on some miners in a fistfight over black visitors. Gavin and Eddie had shared a house while at university, and it was not the first time they had been in a punch-up together. One memorable event had been when the Special Branch, in their bright ties, had come to the Wits campus to look for a typewriter. The SB men had been wrong-footed by a mass of angry students in the student union building, at the top of a stairwell. When the students suddenly opened up, some policemen had fallen backwards, one badly injuring his back. The name 'Cronwright' would stick in Eddie's mind. In the brawling melée that followed, Gavin and Eddie had caught a plainclothes policeman, throwing their punches and bouncing him between them.

While not as involved as Gavin, Eddie used to store papers and pamphlets for him and, when required, take photographs of workers' injuries. At Crown Mines, Eddie rented a tiny house, Peacock Cottage, with three friends, including the young musician Roger Lucey. Unbeknown to them, Roger Lucey was having his career spiked by a Special Branch man, Paul Erasmus, whose job it was to spy on him and frighten off the music companies.[56] Peacock Cottage was set apart from the rows of houses, with a good plot of land at the back. Although Gavin was still living in town during the first year of his banning order, he often spent time with friends in Crown Mines and helped to set up a vegetable growing and buying co-operative. He had begun with vegetable patches in the back garden of his house in town, but when he and Nici moved to a house with no garden, Eddie proposed that they use the land at the back of Peacock Cottage. 'The most passionate people about that vegetable growing, to kick it off, were me and Neil', recalls Gavin. They would go every Sunday and Neil loved it. There was kikuyu grass that had run riot, but if a space needed clearing with a pick and a shovel, Neil was always the 'good comrade' ready to throw himself into it and dig deep.

With Gavin exhorting others to join in the digging, weeding and tending, the Vegetable Garden took off. To Liz, who became one of the regulars, the garden was one of the ways in which this group of young white middle-class intellectuals who had disconnected themselves from their families was 'formulating some of its own culture and ... experimenting with cultural things'. In a classically posed photo taken by Eddie, with echoes of young Soviet workers, Gavin and Neil, stripped to the waist, line up with their comrades. Forks and shovels in hand, they gaze resolutely into the distance behind a row of thriving spinach. The only one to break the pose is Liz, who peers directly at the camera. A year later, sometime in 1979, Eddie photographed a much larger gathering at the garden, including three black comrades, Paulinah and Josiah Mohapi and Mam'Lydia Kompe.[57] This time they are lined up behind a large handmade wooden wheelbarrow proudly stacked with cabbages. In the time between the two photos, Gavin and Nici have had a baby daughter, who is tucked into a carrier on the back of a bare-chested, bearded young man, Clive Cope, who stares smiling towards the horizon, while Neil and the others stand with folded arms, asserting their satisfaction in a job done well.

However, the line between being cooperative and being co-opted was sometimes a fine one. Annie Smyth, who had grown up on a mine, felt none of the romance. To Annie, the miners' houses, lined up like train carriages, with netting on the front to keep out the insects, were simply dark and dreary. She did, however, join in the Vegetable Garden despite what she saw as the 'terrible moralism' over whether you were one of those who worked in the garden or one of those who didn't. 'There was a thing', says Annie, 'about how you gardened, whether with fertiliser or not ...'

Phil Bonner also remembers the vegetable co-op with little pleasure:

> That really symbolised a lot of what Crown Mines was about. You weren't allowed to buy your own vegetables independently. You had to be part of this co-op and go to the market every Friday morning. I got pulled into it for a period myself, reluctantly I have to say. And there were huge disputes between ... those who wanted to grow their own vegetables and those who wanted to just buy them from the market! I had no desire to dig. But there was that kind of atmosphere. A semi-hippy atmosphere, very politically engaged, political debate going on, a huge social scene there as well.

Enthusiasts of the garden, however, loved the physical outlet. Perhaps the physical work also brought them imaginatively closer to the Italian communist Antonio Gramsci's idea of the 'organic intellectual'. They felt connected to the soil as they discussed and debated, delighting in their motto: 'When in doubt, dig!'

While his banning order prohibited union work, Gavin had been offered a job at a quantity surveying firm and applied to the Minister of Justice and Police, Jimmy Kruger, to be allowed to do it. Kruger had replied that he could, as long as it didn't contravene the terms of the banning order. The work could have involved meeting with more than one person at a time, so the answer was 'No'. Instead, Gavin began to teach himself woodwork. Designing and making beds for friends became a speciality. Beds with drawers, beds with headboards, beds showing special corner joints, bunk beds for children ... all the time learning as he was making, and preparing to pass on the skills.

In 1978, an opportunity arose to work as an 'appropriate technology prototype developer' with a small non-governmental organisation, the Environment and Development Agency (EDA). The agency's premises, a decoratively gabled single-storey building, inscribed 'JAN OWERS 1913 BUILDINGS', on 50 Pim Street, at the back of the railway lines in Newtown, had seen better days. Despite its location, ominously close to security police headquarters at John Vorster Square, Gavin saw the potential for EDA to provide a cover for political organisation. The plan was to set up a Woodworkers' Cooperative as a separate factory at the rear of the premises. Membership of 'Woodworkers' would require involvement in some other political organisation, for example, literacy work or the unions.

There was no proper door to get into Woodworkers from EDA, only a partition through which you had to duck. Near the middle of the room was an enormous table bench saw. Along one wall was a surfacer for planing one face of rough wood to be absolutely straight and getting the edge at right angles; a huge thicknesser planed the other face of the wood exactly parallel to that done on the surfacer. A radial arm saw stood against another wall. The self-taught Woodworkers were justifiably proud of their enterprise, the pleasure still evident in Gavin's description of its defiant beginnings:

> Five of us started Woodworkers. Me, Clive Cope, Sipho Kubeka, Josiah Mohapi and Patrick Mbatha ... and once I had started up as a carpenter, I managed to get some tools to Sipho as well, and he and Pat started working from home in Alexandra. Their speciality was benches made from the wood of packing crates thrown away by one of the factories in Kew, next to

Alex. They would take the crates apart and plane the planks by hand using a very old plane that I had bought from an old mines' carpenter with failing eyesight. Neil loved the irregular surfaces that came from this hand-planing and was one of the first customers for their benches, as also their asymmetrical design, and we used to sit on them at his home in Fuller Street. He also bought a little table made from the same planks for his kitchen.

In addition to the main workroom, there was a little upstairs section for a changing room and a small basement. Gavin maintained a workbench in the back southwest corner, looking out at the railway line, a little way off from everyone else. Appropriate technology pictures and articles on a notice board behind him were part of his façade. Having made a spinning wheel and a solar crop dryer, he kept them next to the bench, dusting them down every now and again. He knew that Special Branch watched the place; when questioned, he maintained that he never met with more than one person at a time and was simply working away in his own little corner. On the couple of occasions when the police came, in dramatic raids involving seven to ten officers, the locked doors at the front of the building, and a grille at the back, gave the Woodworkers sufficient warning time. Gavin would be found alone at his workbench with ear muffs on to keep out the noise of the machines, working on a solar crop dryer or spinning wheel that would then be written up in the next issue of the journal *Link*. On the board next to his bench were pictures of other technologies.

They were never complacent. The day before Gavin started at EDA, fellow worker Cedric de Beer had alerted him to the likelihood of EDA's founder, Karl Edwards, being a police spy. Edwards was a close friend of Craig Williamson, whom both Cedric and Gavin had distrusted since their student days at Wits. While strong concerns about Williamson were discounted by some key ANC people in exile,[58] Cedric enlisted Gavin's support, and within a year had Edwards ousted from EDA on a technicality over money. After his departure, it became easier for Sipho to slip into the Woodworkers' premises, but before that Edwards would almost certainly have noted Neil's visits for a security police file. Suspecting that both EDA and Woodworkers were bugged, meetings were held in a space between the two. With a ten-horsepower electric saw going in the Woodworkers' section, they felt that it would probably throw any bug out. For top-security discussion, they would go up onto the roof, from where they could look across to John Vorster Square. Woodworkers became a place of strong bonding.

Reading groups provided another forum for political discussion. The combinations of participants varied and Neil was invited into a number of them. Soon after he had moved to Fuller Street, in the rough, run-down, white working-class area of Bertrams, Gavin suggested they meet at Neil's place to undertake Marx's *Capital*. The little tin-roofed house was sparsely furnished, had holes in the linoleum and was, at first, something of a 'hovel', according to one friend. Neil would welcome the group with tea and vetkoek made on a small primus stove. The *Capital* reading group initially included three women: Annie Smyth, Gavin's partner Nici and Pat Horn, who had been radicalised by feminism in the University Christian Movement and who was under a five-year banning order. When Liz arrived in Johannesburg, she was invited to join.

It was quickly apparent to Liz that Annie and Neil had a shared interest. Annie, who lived in the same house as Gavin and Nici, found Neil easy to talk to, and they also liked the same music. When she offered to introduce him to some music venues, nightclubs in vast warehouses, he was keen. It suited Annie because she knew that Neil was around and she could always seek him out for protection if necessary:

> It was a really fun time and we used to have a good time together in a very platonic way. A lot of disco music, Aretha Franklin and those sort of people … That is my good memory of Neil. Neil as fun, sitting round not talking about anything in particular, of Neil being a person you could sit and ease out with basically.

Still in her houseman year, Liz was working long hours at Baragwanath Hospital in Soweto. When Neil wasn't working, he was now often involved with Gavin or Sipho, study groups or activities that he wouldn't discuss with Liz. In Cape Town, it had been the reverse, with Liz being the one who was more politically involved. Now it was Liz who felt very much the outsider. Moreover, she began to feel that Neil was having an affair. Annie, his night-clubbing partner, seemed the most likely suspect.

Annie felt Liz's hostility, but was in an awkward position, although her relationship with Neil was platonic. When Liz was living in Cape Town, Neil had sometimes asked her to drop him off at his house with a pleasant young woman who worked at one of the nightclubs. Annie's discomfort had increased after Liz came to work in Johannesburg and Neil continued the same pattern while Liz was on night duty at the hospital. Annie had not, however, said anything to Liz, feeling that it was not her business but something that the couple had to resolve on their own.

Things came to a head one day when Liz arrived at Annie's house and tearfully apologised for having been so hostile. Having confronted Neil, he had admitted to having an affair. Annie then admitted her own embarrassment at knowing of Neil's relationship with the young woman from the nightclub. This compounded Liz's dismay, for Neil had acknowledged having an affair with someone else. The sympathy that developed between the women led to Liz moving out of the house in Bertrams and coming to stay with Annie. The responses of other friends tended to divide along gender lines. To many of the men, the question of multiple relationships was not an issue, Liz and Annie being seen as overly moralistic.

After a while, the *Capital* reading group split along gender lines, with a women's study group now emerging to study texts from a feminist perspective. Liz stayed in the women's reading group but was not included in others to which Neil belonged. Instead she began developing her own connections and political work. Aside from their medical work, in many ways they increasingly lived their subterranean lives in separate compartments. But despite his other relationships, Neil kept coming back to Liz. They shared a history. Liz Thomson, another Vegetable Gardener who was also doing her medical internship at Baragwanath Hospital, remembers Neil telling how he had met 'this girl with this wonderful hair',

> ... and there was a lot of romance. They'd lived in this terrible or wonderful place, depending on how you looked at it. So Liz embodied a lot of the romantic side of his life. I don't think he wanted to lose her but like many men he couldn't keep his pants on and ja, he didn't feel like coming home and scrubbing the floors. And Liz always felt that he was excluding her ... and being treated as a second-class citizen and she used to resent it.

CHAPTER 11

Arguments, debates and stepping stones

It seemed absurd to suggest that these young romantics, bickering about the final goals of a tiny embattled movement whose very survival was in doubt, would one day help form strong worker organisations ... But the debates were important for all that. For almost a decade, they shaped the divisions between emerging unions and determined how they would react to government reforms and events in the factories ... Decisions affecting thousands of organised workers would hang on these esoteric academic arguments ... As they grew, organised workers began to inject their own, more practical, perspectives into the debate.

Steven Friedman,
Building Tomorrow Today[59]

WHEN NEIL APPROACHED THE IAS, TAFFY ADLER PROBABLY had misgivings, given Neil's association with the banned pair of 'populists'. But as a doctor he had skills that could be useful. Liz Thomson, who had been one of a small number of radical students at Wits Medical School, along with Jenny Cunningham and Ian Kitai, recalls how all were keen to make a contribution beyond their purely medical duties: 'Those were the days when you had to get in to the unions. You couldn't just arrive.

We spent a lot of time discussing – also about workers' clinics and then we became quite friendly with Neil.' So it was within this wider alliance of medical activists that Neil found his first point of entry into the IAS, offering medical advice regarding workers' injuries and related compensation. Entry into an actual union like MAWU would be more difficult.

When Neil started assisting at the IAS, he also began working three nights a week at Baragwanath Hospital, a pattern he was to continue and intensify. Liz Thomson recalls how the young doctors would 'work all night and then beaver off on our afternoons to go and work at the IAS'. It was mostly the non-union, unemployed, dismissed and unorganised workers who lined the corridor, waiting to be seen and looking for help. There was a complaints system, and a complaints book to be filled in, before issues could be taken up with the Department of Labour or an employer. Workers would be interviewed, and the doctors would be brought in on cases with medical problems. In hospital, the most they could do was to patch patients up while the system perpetuated itself. In the IAS, they hoped to assist workers in seeking some small redress for injuries and ill health sustained at work. Neil knew that this could only make a minimal contribution towards solving the bigger problems, but it was a stepping stone towards his goal of working in a union.

Once in the IAS, it wasn't long before Neil came up with the idea of a medical scheme for MAWU, in which he and like-minded doctors could run sessions for workers on first aid and basic health problems, as well as training worker leaders. Another idea was to establish medical centres in the townships, run by local people. He envisaged that the IAS could buy medicines in bulk and employ doctors who would be prepared to work for very little pay. Gavin and Sipho were supportive, as were the other members of a special, carefully selected discussion group to which Neil had been introduced, in effect a political reference group. With Neil, there were seven, their secret sign for calling a meeting being to flick thumb against forefinger, making a '7'. Three others were workers at Heinemann, from where Sipho had been fired, and MAWU members: Mam'Lydia Kompe, Baba K Makama and Andrew Shabangu. The seventh member was David Dison, then a young trainee lawyer doing work for the IAS and also a member of Gavin's *Capital* reading group.

The 'Group of 7' was a place where political ideas could be checked out among like-minded comrades. Having clarified a political line, when the time was right they would energise debate within the open unions. It was a way of

Gavin and Sipho continuing to play a role despite what they saw as their double exclusion, first by the state and then by those leading the IAS and MAWU,
intent on developing the union without being drawn into struggle politics.
As Gavin put it, 'there was no point for someone like Baba K or Mam'Lydia
to speak their minds in the open [union] because then they'd just get closed
down'. It was much better to go along with the general line in meetings while
focusing on building awareness of issues in their conversations with shop
stewards and seeing where links could be made between factory and township organisation. They regarded their strategy as one of 'reformist face and
revolutionary practice'. In the meantime, despite their banning orders, Gavin
and Sipho would make secret trips to Durban and Cape Town, building links
further afield in the emerging labour movement.

While Neil threw himself into learning about union issues, he probably
pushed to the back of his mind questions about his relationship with Liz. Also
pushed to the back must have been the matter of his impending conscription.
He expected the papers to be sent to his parents' house. In the first letter to
his mother after starting at Tembisa Hospital, dated 25 October 1977, thanking
her for a birthday card and money with which he had bought a pair of shoes,
he had given a Cape Town post-box address, saying he was briefly down 'on
the farm' with Liz. He had heard that Joy had experienced a fall and hoped
that she had recovered. He was not sure what he would be doing the following year, 'but I may go overseas'. He concluded his short letter with affection.
There was even a message for his father: 'Stay well Mom, and please don't
worry about me. Please give my regards to Dad. Fond love, Neil.'

Despite his proximity to Somerset West, however, Neil had not dropped
in to see her. He made no enquiry about call-up papers, but had they arrived
his mother would have felt obliged to hand them to him. Whether or not Joy
suspected why he hadn't come to see her, his 'please don't worry about me'
was unlikely to reduce a mother's hurt and misgivings of what could lie ahead.

Eight months later, in June 1978, Neil wrote to Joy announcing that he was
leaving 'for Europe and perhaps America tomorrow'. He was sorry that he
hadn't seen her before his departure, but would keep in contact. He asked to
have his regards passed on to Jill and Michael. Giving his address as 'P.O. Box
46376, Orange Grove, Johannesburg', he requested that his mother send his
mail there, so a friend could send it on. Neil clearly hoped that when his army
papers arrived, Aubrey would pass this news on to the authorities, even if his

father thought that going overseas was cowardly.

The postbox was one that he had asked Liz to hire, and he had no intention of going overseas. But when his call-up arrived, at least he would have some warning, and the military police still wouldn't know where exactly he was living. However, his plan went awry when he bumped into his brother on the steps at Wits. Michael, who happened to be visiting Johannesburg, was also taken aback. Always defensive of their parents, he was accusing: 'I thought you were overseas!' Whatever explanation Neil gave, the encounter was soon relayed and his overseas cover story was finished. The military police now only had to check with various hospitals to find out where he was working. As time went on, the matter would become more pressing. How should he respond when they caught up with him?

*   *   *

Working in the IAS, in the office next door to MAWU, Neil must have felt tantalisingly close to union work. The over-arching union-related debate throughout 1978 was around the issue of registration. In May the previous year, Professor Nicolaas Wiehahn, a former railway worker and now advisor to the Minister of Labour, had been appointed chairman of a commission to examine all labour laws. By the end of 1977, the vast majority of job reservation orders had been suspended. After decades of African workers being suppressed and denied rights, activists were further galvanised and bitterly divided over how to respond to the changes that the Wiehahn Commission was expected to recommend in its eventual report. African unions would now be allowed to 'register'. However, the clawback was that a registered union was not permitted to link with any political group. The new plans also allowed for multiracial committees that would effectively put a brake on the growing strength of registered black unions, enabling white unions to control them.[60]

The anti-registration arguments were perceived as the 'political' and 'populist' SACTU and ANC-aligned position. Despite Neil having been mentored into 'reformist face, revolutionary practice' by Gavin and Sipho, he allowed himself to get into an argument about registration with Taffy Adler in the IAS office. It took Gavin to point out that he had just scuppered his hopes of MAWU, now led by Bernie Fanaroff, taking on his medical scheme: 'Yes, you won the argument, but they're now going to sideline you!' Neil had revealed that he stood with a militant unionism linked with political struggle and would be 'flushed out as a 'leftist'. Gavin's prediction came true. Having set his sights on getting into MAWU, Neil had blown his chance. Plans for a medical scheme came to a halt, and instead of action he was confined to talk.

Prevented from getting closer to union work, it seems that Neil's earlier fascination with clandestine operations led him to contemplate the idea of 'underground unions'. Gavin would have none of it. When Neil came up with the phrase 'the underground union', Gavin had laughed saying it was 'a contradiction in terms'. But although Neil smiled back, at that stage he was entirely serious as he quietly explained that underground organisation was the way to keep the political line in the open unions. He had probably read about underground unions in the SACTU publication *Workers' Unity*, as well as in the writings of Santiago Carrillo, General Secretary of the Spanish Communist Party.[61] But SACTU's leaders were outside the country and, as Gavin knew, out of touch. It was against the very nature of democratic unionism to be reporting to an underground leadership instead of the executive being answerable to the members. Holding secret meetings in their Group of 7, to discuss and decide on what political line to take forward into open union debate, was not the same thing as an underground union. Gradually, Neil's more romantic ideas were being challenged by comrades he trusted.

*   *   *

In the middle of 1978, Jan Theron, some two years into his post as General Secretary of the Food and Canning Workers' Union, travelled up to Johannesburg with a union delegation. Their project was to try and re-establish a Transvaal branch of Food and Canning, as a parallel union, to organise African workers. Neil happily accommodated everyone at his house in Bertrams. Although Jan appreciated Neil's enthusiasm, the memory of the amateur stuffing of clandestine pamphlets under the sofa still lingered. The job of organising African workers in an unregistered parallel African Food and Canning Workers' Union (AFCWU) required not only solid work but solid judgment for walking a fine line. One of the Cape Town delegates was Oscar Mpetha, a veteran unionist who had been active, alongside Ray Alexander, as a Food and Canning organiser in the 1940s and who had recently come back to work with the union. A SACTU man, Oscar had been president of the Cape ANC until its banning in 1960. Banned and jailed, some of his early union exploits were legendary. But it was one thing to have the veteran Oscar working to revive the AFCWU. It would be quite another thing to appoint a young white man who, however sincere, Jan remembered as having his head somewhere in the clouds. So while Neil enjoyed the company, he remained simply their host, at the margins.

In the latter part of 1978, intense discussions among the emerging black unions about forming a federation led to a draft constitution being approved at the end of October, with agreement to launch the new Federation of South African Trade Unions (FOSATU) by Easter 1979. It was to be a 'tight' federation, with only those unions that shared its aims, including worker leadership, being allowed to join. It would accept registered and non-registered unions but intended to exclude any political links. Its purpose, as announced by its first General Secretary, Alec Erwin, was 'to build a strong labour movement – and that's all'.[62] Significantly, FOSATU was committed to non-racialism and to a strong education programme for shop stewards.

With his personal relationship with Liz on the rocks, and with the doors to union work closed to him, Neil's friendships within the Group of 7, Woodworkers and the Vegetable Garden, but above all with Gavin and Sipho, must have helped sustain him. Despite Liz having left him and still being very angry, he would visit the house where she was staying with Annie. They had friends in common and would meet at the Vegetable Garden as well as at 'Bara' Hospital, where they both worked. They were part of a small white left community that hung out together. But it was not just happenstance. Neil wanted Liz to come back.

Nevertheless, when a friend from Cape Town days, Bridget King, came up to Johannesburg, Neil offered her accommodation. He had room to spare in his little house. Bridget's father was the Anglican Dean of Cape Town, who had vigorously defended the students against the police in their 1972 protest on the steps of St George's Cathedral. Although Liz had made the Bertrams cottage a little more homely, Bridget's memory suggests that, after Liz's departure, it had returned to its earlier state. It was 'amazingly spartan'. There was no hot water, so Bridget would shower at a neighbour's. Neil was, however, delighted when she sewed cushions to brighten up the place. Their relationship was platonic, with Bridget finding in Neil a supportive friend. In her words, she was 'a wild party girl, recently escaped from my first relationship with a very possessive man, and rather than disapprove of my frivolous lifestyle, he enjoyed my freedom and enjoyment of it'. When Bridget left for England with a new boyfriend, she felt Neil was sorry to see her go. It was not just that he would miss the companionship. Bridget had begun going to Marxist reading groups at Wits where she was working as a university librarian, and felt that Neil had wanted to see her develop her 'political interest'.

Perhaps Neil's medical work also sustained him more than he acknowledged, despite the fact that he was now working just enough to cover his basic financial needs. He would describe to friends, in the most matter-of-fact terms, gruelling scenes from the Casualty department, where he saw himself as simply a medical worker. After weekend night duty at Bara, he would stop over in Crown Mines with David Dison, who recollects how Neil would pop in for breakfast on Sunday morning and say, 'Oh, I took about four axes out of people's heads last night ...'. Neil was not only 'strong stomached', he was highly effective as a doctor, developing a speciality in resuscitation. When someone arrives almost dead, and the doctor has to get a tube down the throat, it is a problem if the patient is still conscious and fighting. The skill is in doing it very quickly, without the conditions of an operating theatre and an anaesthetist. Neil was gaining a reputation for 'cut downs' and getting a drip up when a patient had already lost a lot of blood, was in shock and their veins had collapsed. With no vein or blood to see, the doctor has to cut the skin, dissect down, find the vein and put the knife in to attach the line. Dramatic and demanding, a successful procedure gave immediate satisfaction.

At the end of 1978, like many others, Neil escaped the heat of the city for a holiday. I gathered two versions of where he went – from Gavin Andersson and from David Dison – a salutary reminder of the fragility of memory. Each narrative added to my sense of Neil, and I am sure that both took place, though at different times. A photograph of a rugged-looking Neil with com-panions on a beach supports Gavin's recollection of the December in which he broke his banning order, having refused on principle to ask the authori-ties for permission to leave the city. Nici was pregnant and they had slipped away to stay at a little farmhouse in the south of Natal belonging to Kathy Satchwell's family. On a trip to a Wild Coast beach, Gavin was astonished to bump into Neil and Brian Cutler, another Vegetable Gardener, who were stay-ing in a tent: 'We played rounders ... it took away all my paranoia of being a banned man being with friends.' They all stopped in Durban to have a meal on the way back. Neil Young's 'After the Gold Rush' was playing, the singer's high voice telling of the end of the world from a nuclear disaster, with people gathering to watch the silver ships being loaded. They delayed their return by 'playing some game and a lot of laughter' until it was late and time for Gavin and Nici to drive back to Johannesburg, so he could 'sign in' at Hillbrow police station without being missed.

David Dison also recalls a holiday with Neil around the same time at the end of 1978. Whatever the date, the memory of driving to the eastern Cape gives us a vivid glimpse of Neil:

> We buggered up my mother's car. He [Neil] had strong connections in the Transkei – again he had stronger black connections than someone like myself had. He had doctors that he had met. He wasn't sealed off. We were far more suburban. Going down to the Transkei with him, he had his toolbox. I mean he didn't have a proper doctor's bag okay. A toolbox with his medical instrument in the back of the car! That symbolised him, and he'd stolen all the medicines and stuff, he'd appropriated from Baragwanath Hospital. He couldn't afford his own medical kit and we would treat people on the way down. It was the mad South African end-of-year rush. We were coming across scenes of accidents and he was treating people at scenes of accidents. That's how South Africa is at the end of the year. People get onto these roads and they slaughter each other. It's a different form of violence. So you know he was prepared.

Even on holiday, Neil sought purpose.

CHAPTER 12

Into the union

BY THE BEGINNING OF 1979, NEIL HAD, IN SIPHO'S WORDS, BEEN more or less 'elbowed out' of any meaningful work in the IAS. He was also feeling low about his messed-up relationship with Liz. He decided to take a break from the city by working as a locum in the Transkei. Perhaps this was when Dave Dison drove him down to Umtata. From here a friend of Neil's, Dr Mtshembla, took him up to Mount Fletcher, where Neil stood in for a doctor who was having an operation. In this remote mountainous area, many families had missing members, forced by circumstance into being migrant workers. For about six weeks, Neil took over the running of a private practice in town, as well as acting as superintendent at the small Taylor Bequest Hospital and visiting rural clinics in the afternoons. With his hopes of getting 'into the union' looking so slim, was he taking stock? Did he, I wonder, consider reverting to full-time medicine? Despite his capacity to isolate himself, which Liz believed to be a trait deep within him, after the intensity of Johannesburg and the closeness of comrades like Gavin and Sipho, who engaged so passionately in the struggle, perhaps he was also considering whether he could ever re-embrace the isolation of life as a rural doctor.

Neil returned after his six weeks, back to weekend shifts at Baragwanath and volunteering at the IAS. By now, Liz and Annie had moved from Gavin and Nici's to 451 Fox Street in Jeppestown, a white working-class area from where you could see straight down to the city's skyscrapers. Unlike in nearby Bertrams, there were patches of garden and trees here. The house had high ceilings and large rooms, and they were able to accommodate Eddie Wes after he had given up Peacock Cottage and been abroad for a few months. A curtain separated Eddie's room from Liz's. The small, intertwining, white left community shifted constantly into new combinations. Eddie Wes believes that an element of their experimentation was that they had very few role models on the left, so many people having disappeared in the 1960s, into prison or overseas or into silence. He recalled his own dad, a Lithuanian Jewish socialist, burning some of his books in those days out of fear, although there was one that he could not bring himself to destroy. It was a copy of Jules Verne's *Twenty Thousand Leagues Under the Sea*, inside which was Lenin's *Imperialism*. Eddie showed it to Neil. 'Nobody could tell us what was right', says Eddie. 'Once you realised everything was crazy, everything went.'

In this period, when Neil was still trying to get 'into the unions', there was time for long discussions. Eddie enjoyed Neil's meditative style of conversation and his 'ability to get into other people's space, to understand the parameters of where they were working from'. Many on the left pushed their position emotively, but Neil's manner was to listen and build on what his interlocutor said, exploring and trying to understand people 'and how they sat within a political context ... it wasn't an imposing kind of politics. It was a revealing kind of politics.' While Camus and Nietzsche might occasionally come into the conversation, to Eddie, Neil was 'a fundamental Marxist' rather than the kind of communist who would be accepting of down-the-line party doctrine. His influence, Eddie felt, was all the more powerful.

With two older sisters giving him some insight into feminist ideas on discourse, Eddie also noted how women especially related to this soft, sensitive listening. Occupying the other half of the house to which Annie and Liz had moved was Jane Bailie, a single parent of two small boys who was studying for her BA. As a frequent visitor to the house, Neil established a friendship with the family that was to continue after her marriage to David Rosenthal and their move to Crown Mines. While most of Neil's friendships were essentially political, Jane consciously avoided knowing too much. While trying to break out of her conditioning and learn from those more politically involved, she understood the dangers and was honest about her limits. On one occasion, however, hearing someone knocking next door and seeing a military policeman, Jane went to speak to him. He was looking for Neil. She told him that Neil didn't live there. 'That was probably the most useful thing that I did.'

Jane was aware that lack of involvement made her and David 'political nonentities' for some people, although not for Neil, who knew that she was basically sympathetic, and seemed to enjoy simply coming over to relax:

> You know people were in and out of each other's houses all the time ... He'd come over to our side of the house to have a cup of tea or something, but he was very good to my kids. This is perhaps an aspect of Neil that other people wouldn't have noticed because none of them had kids. He used to take them out into the road and play soccer and he lent Brendan his micro-scope, his proper microscope, an incredibly generous thing to do. He also lent him a bag of bones!

As an observer, Jane was aware of an 'element of competition' among those who were 'involved'. But this was absent in Neil, and she didn't feel Neil judging her. Instead, he introduced her to political ideas and books, such as a biography of Tito, the non-aligned communist leader of Yugoslavia, explaining things 'in a totally unpatronising way'.

Neil also shared an interest in philosophy with David Rosenthal, who was impressed by how Neil would listen quietly to his interpretations of the liberal philosopher Karl Popper. They were both impressed, too, at Neil's capacity to get on with Jane's very conservative father, and how Neil was quite willing to talk and find points of contact with him. He never, however, spoke about his own father.

While Neil's visits to his sister Jill and her husband Paul in Pretoria were sporadic, his enjoyment of their children was evident. A letter to his father in February 1979, the first Neil had written since their rift seven years previously, suggests he had spent an evening with the family in Pretoria at the same time as his mother had been there: 'It was good to see her again after so long ...' Although the letter began with thanks for money sent at Christmas, used to repair his motorbike, the main purpose of the letter appears to have been to repair an element of 'human friendship' between father and son, whatever their differences:

Despite all that has happened between us I do not feel any enmity as long as we realize that we have differences and we cannot impose our view of things on the other person. We are both adults with the right to choose for ourselves what we want and I don't feel that that should stand between the relationship a father should have with his son. We have both done stupid things in the past but I think that time has healed those wounds to a certain extent, although there will always be differences between us. We are living in troubled times and I think we must realize that human friendship must stand above any petty differences we have with people.

Neil ends by saying that he has heard his father had given up smoking, and hopes that he is well and active: 'I hope to see you in the coming months. Yours faithfully, Neil.' This reaching out towards a deeply authoritarian father to put their relationship on a new footing suggests a personal maturation. The calmness that Neil could now show to his father was an essential asset for a union organiser.

*   *   *

On 21 April, Oscar Mpetha arrived in Johannesburg to assist the recently established Food and Canning branch office. The two organisers who had been appointed were out of their depth and floundering. Seventy-year-old Oscar had decided to take on the task.

Neil was delighted to have Baba – 'Father' – Mpetha come to stay with him for several weeks. Sipho recalls the first time he saw Oscar in Neil's house. He didn't know who he was and Neil made no introduction, leaving Sipho curious about the 'old African man ... walking up and down in the room. He had a book of Marx ... moving up and down, reading.' Later, when Sipho asked Neil who it was, Neil told him. Neil was not one to show off, although Baba Mpetha was regarded as something of a father figure of 'the movement' by young members of the white left, who revered the commitment of a man reputed to be always willing to go to jail, indeed to have his toothbrush ready in his pocket.[63] Even someone on the fringes, like Jane Rosenthal, was pleased when Neil asked if she could lend him a blanket for his guest.

Oscar would get up early in the morning and read *Capital* and other Marxist texts that Neil kept in the house before setting off for work. Meeting

Neil's friends, including Gavin, Oscar would ask searching questions and listen very attentively to the replies. In retrospect, it was apparent that, beyond his immediate tasks, he was assessing Neil and his milieu as part of a bigger plan.

Oscar's organising strategy was to go to factories where the union had once been strong. His diary-cum-report to head office briefly notes his visits to factories and meetings, sparsely interspersed with comments on occasional successes and, more often, obstacles:

> MONDAY 23 April 1979
> Visited I & J. George Goch got into difficulties and contacted two workers made arrangements to meet them at their homes in Shawel [Soweto] on Saturday afternoon. This meeting did not materialise. After roaming the streets of Soweto we found these young chaps but they pretended never to have seen us.
> TUESDAY 24 April visited H. Jones & Co for lunch hour meeting.
> THURSDAY 26 April visited LKB for a lunch hour meetings.
> At both these meetings I emphasized the necessity of a strong executive. I pointed out that constitutionally the majority of both factories members were not in compliance with the constitution.
> FRIDAY 27 April Collected subs at H. Jones.
> SATURDAY 28th April visited the homes of I & J members at Shawel Sowetho [sic] with very bad results.[64]

Oscar's reputation in the Cape didn't count for much among Transvaal workers, who must have challenged him with questions like, 'What has your union done for us?' Back at head office, Jan Theron was aware of Neil assisting when he could, driving Oscar to factories. During the six weeks, a bond developed between the two, along with a mentoring relationship of teacher and student.

Neil also had the opportunity to learn about Food and Canning's history from one of its principal actors. From its beginnings in 1941, it had set out as a non-racial union to represent workers of all backgrounds in the food industries until forced by legislation to split into a registered union for Coloureds and an unregistered union for Africans. Nevertheless, Food and Canning continued to believe that workers were best served by a single non-racial union open to all, and, in spite of their formal separation, the two unions had tried to operate as far as possible as one. Severely weakened by bannings, imprisonment and exile of key personnel, the union had just about survived. It was only since the appointments of Jan Theron and Oscar Mpetha, in a changing economic and political climate, that it was beginning to revive.

Through accompanying Oscar, Neil glimpsed something of the arduous practicalities of union work. In mid-May, after a couple of weeks of slogging away at collecting subs and getting new committees properly elected at two or three factories, Oscar was able to report a small victory over a dismissal:

> MONDAY 14 May – Visited Renown where we received a good reception from some workers we contacted, but they were not prepared to take the initiative.
> TUESDAY 15 May – Attended a meeting after which we met the management re employee that was dismissed. We came to an agreement with the factory forman [sic], who promised to see the assistant manager there and then. But after we left the Committee was told that the factory assistant manager refused to re-instate the worker.
> THURSDAY 24 May – We met the assistant manager. After a long argument he re-instated that worker and undertook to rectify.

Meanwhile, as Oscar was struggling to gain a credible foothold for the Johannesburg branch, in Cape Town the dismissal of five Coloured workers at a milling factory of Fatti's & Moni's in Bellville unexpectedly began escalating into events that would not only make trade union history but illustrate the impossibility of isolating an economic struggle from a political one. With Oscar getting news direct from Cape Town, Neil was well placed to hear the inside story.

The union's strategy in the Cape, as now in Johannesburg, was to return to the factories where it had once been prominent. One of these was Fatti's & Moni's, a family-owned company that milled wheat for the United Macaroni group. In 1978, both Coloured and African workers within the milling section had asked Food and Canning to take up their complaints. Refusing to recognise the African Food and Canning Workers' Union, the company had ignored the union's letters. Then, in March 1979, Coloured and African workers signed a joint petition authorising the union to negotiate on their behalf an increase of the basic wage to R40 a week, instead of the current R17 for women and R19 for men. It was this petition that was to trigger the sackings.[65]

When no reply arrived by 12 April, the union wrote to the Minister of Labour, asking him to appoint a Conciliation Board. Although the board only dealt with Coloured workers, this action would at least force Fatti's & Moni's management to meet the union. Instead, Mr Terblanche, the milling manager, assembled the workers and told them that before the end of the day they must choose between the union and a liaison committee that he had recently started with his own appointees. Choose the union, warned Terblanche, and there would be 'moelike tye' (difficult times). Refusing to go along with the manager, the milling workers rang the union. On 23 April, five active Coloured supporters of the union were dismissed, with no reasons given. Two of the five had organised the signing of the petition. The following day, when the workers demanded to know the reasons, five more Coloured workers were dismissed. On 25 April, all the workers, Coloured and African, asked to see the manager. The intransigent Terblanche refused to discuss anything, calling the Department of Labour instead. Both Terblanche and the department officials now attempted to separate the Coloured and African workers. When they refused to budge, they were all told to get out and collect their pay on Friday. Eighty-eight in all had by now been dismissed.

Fatti's & Moni's had poured oil on a fire. The workers refused to go and collect their pay because at that point they would be officially signed off. The timing was fortuitous, however, as the long-awaited report of the Wiehahn Commission was published on 1 May, only a week after the dismissals. What might have passed off as business as usual now drew unusual press interest, especially this unexpected solidarity between Coloured and African workers in defiance of apartheid divisions. A mass meeting of students called for a boycott of Fatti's & Moni's products. A wide range of organisations and individuals soon backed the move. Although initially only in force in the western Cape, the boycott meant that communities were being mobilised.

Up in Johannesburg, Oscar tried to make contact with Fatti's & Moni's workers in Isando, but faced obstacles. Workers were not allowed out of the gate at lunch hour. He managed to make contact after work, and, having set up a Sunday meeting in Tembisa, simply wrote: 'This meeting was not successful.' With 88 workers dismissed in Cape Town and the company refusing to talk to the union, the reaction was not surprising. But Oscar was persistent. Before leaving Johannesburg early in June, he helped to draft a leaflet in isiZulu and Sesotho for another meeting with Fatti's & Moni's workers, to be held later in the month, hoping the union would send him to help organise and attend.

Ever the strategist, Oscar returned to Cape Town with a further plan. He concluded his report on the Transvaal situation with recommendations of the order in which factories should be organised, and then a final paragraph:

> With a sub head-office in Johannesburg. I further suggest that I be permitted to go back to Transvaal immediately to organise more factories and bring Transvaal to its potential so as to employ another person more responsible than the two organisers. They lack initiative and responsibility and also the experience to do such mighty work.

This 'another person' was Neil. Before leaving for Cape Town, Oscar had already asked him if he would be prepared to work for the union. While Neil had said that he would, he knew that the offer would have to be confirmed by head office. Jan still had to be persuaded that Neil had become more grounded and could be trusted. To be a union organiser meant that all activity had to be above board and openly accountable to the workers. Did Oscar mention Neil's banned comrades, Gavin and Sipho? Surely not. Yet he knew that through their links Neil would have access to Tembisa, the residential area for the workers whom Food and Canning hoped to organise. Perhaps Oscar simply told Jan that Neil had developed useful contacts through his IAS work, and that he had his feet well on the ground. Furthermore, Neil was so committed that he was prepared to work without pay. How many candidates would apply on those terms? Jan had one final practical reservation. Neil had not yet done his army service and was liable to be called up at any time. Oscar must have said that they would face that when the problem arose. In the meantime this committed, unassuming young man was the right person. With Oscar's recommendation, Jan offered Neil the job.

Oscar's return to Cape Town coincided with the boycott receiving a boost from an unexpected quarter. The Western Province African Chamber of Commerce had decided to support the dismissed workers, with African traders now refusing to stock bread from the Good Hope bakery, a subsidiary of Fatti's & Moni's. Sales began to be seriously affected, and the company's share price fell. It seemed to be a turning point.

Suddenly the management wanted to talk – not with the workers but with the African traders and businessmen. The latter agreed to meet, on condition that the union was present. Meetings took place at the Bellville Holiday Inn, at the company's expense. However, it was soon clear that Fatti's & Moni's still felt that it could hold out against the union's main demands; as the African workers' contract periods expired, they would be arrested for not holding valid passes and sent back to the Ciskei. It was a vivid illustration that the union struggle was not purely economic, but inextricably political.

As weeks turned to months, the union faced the problem of keeping up worker morale and resistance. There were police raids and some arrests. Thanks to a donation from abroad, Food and Canning was managing to give each striker R15 a week, but insisted that the workers meet daily for a roll call, discussion and songs, with deductions being made for absence or drunkenness. Community support and press coverage around the boycott helped to keep spirits up, giving hope that the management might be forced to negotiate seriously. To the union, the outcome was far from certain.

Then, in the middle of July, the death of the three-month-old daughter of a striker who could not afford a doctor catapulted the campaign to national attention. The Moni family had originally come from Italy to set up a tiny grocery shop in the gold-rush town of Johannesburg, and the company's products, from pasta to ice-cream cones, were meant to conjure up happy family settings. The Catholic Students' Society at the University of the Witwatersrand issued a leaflet headed 'WHAT CAN WE DO? FATTIS AND MONIS STRIKE':

> On the 14th of July, one of the workers lost his 3 month old daughter. He had delayed sending her to the doctor because he had so little money and refused to go to the factory to collect his pay. To collect pay would mean workers were no longer on Fattis and Monis books and that their passes would be endorsed, and they would be sent back to the homeland and face slow starvation.[66]

The leaflet went on to ask 'Why must we, as Christians, respond?', with the answer quoting liberally from the proceedings of the Second Vatican Council. The Moni family could not have been happy, especially fearing the spread of the boycott of Fatti's & Moni's products overseas.

Oscar returned to Johannesburg, this time with Jan, to discuss both widening the boycott and to offer Neil the job of organiser of the African Food and Canning Workers' Transvaal branch. Neil was elated. He resigned from the IAS, handing over his workman's compensation cases to three other doctors: Liz Floyd, Liz Thomson and Jenny Cunningham. At last, he was 'in the unions'.

CHAPTER 13

Learning the ropes

... it was my feeling that the laws governing employment in South Africa were inadequate to protect the workers. I felt that if I worked in a trade union I could at least contribute towards seeing these things gradually changed. It is no use giving people things or doing things for them, as this is charity, and it degrades the person. I felt that it was important that people should learn about their rights, learn to have self respect, and therefore get rid of injustices themselves. This latter happened in some of our factories, where the management now treat the workers with respect, not because of myself or other trade union officials, but because the workers have stood together and demanded their rights. In these factories, even the management seems happy now because there is a relationship of mutual respect and not that of master-servant with its mistrust. I felt that if people learnt this in all spheres of life, changes would gradually come about in South Africa for the better. That is also why it is so important that organizations work democratically so that people learn to be masters of their own lives ...

Neil Aggett, 1st statement,
John Vorster Square[67]

NEIL TRAVELLED TO CAPE TOWN, ONE OF FOUR DELEGATES TO
the union's annual conference in Paarl, where they slept on
the floor in a hall full of workers some 40 minutes away from
his parents' home in Somerset West. Joy's favourite photograph of Neil
showed her three-year-old son in rubber boots beside the flooded Ewaso
Ng'iro River, staring towards the camera in the shadow of his round
broad-brimmed hat. He stands stockily beside one of his father's workers. The worker, in overalls, averts his gaze from the camera, keeping
it fixed on the small child. It's a classic portrait of *bwana kidogo* (little
master). Twenty or so years later, Neil had finally freed himself from
the entrapments of that tight colonial world and was ready to serve the
workers.

On returning to Johannesburg, one of Neil's first tasks in the branch was
to organise the workers at Fatti's & Moni's and assist with the boycott campaign, working closely with Barbara Hogan, the campaign's coordinator in
Johannesburg. Time would reveal the terrible irony. As Neil stepped whole-
heartedly into his new role of working for an open, democratic union, he was
also entering the web of the predatory Bureau of State Security – BOSS – soon
to become the National Intelligence Service (NIS).

Politicised by Black Consciousness as a student at Wits in the early 1970s,
Barbara had joined the ANC late in 1977 via its 'forward area' in Swaziland (a
conduit for information and people), transferring within a year to its Botswana
equivalent. Here, her ANC contacts were her friends Jeanette (Curtis) and
Marius Schoon.[68] The banned pair had fallen in love after Marius's release
from jail in 1976, secretly married and escaped into Botswana. The newly-
weds used the 'escape route' offered by Craig Williamson, whom Jeanette still
regarded as a friend from university days. Despite the Schoons being well
known to the security police, they were established as key members of the
ANC's forward area, dealing with highly sensitive contact between internal
activists and the exiled leadership.

Barbara's reasons for joining the ANC included a strong sense of contributing as a white activist. She felt that the exiled leaders 'were not in touch with
the political realities of the day ... They were totally unaware of the hostility
towards the ANC within certain elements of the trade union movement. So it
was almost this thing of being a facilitator, trying to keep in touch.' Although
an ANC operative, Barbara was not taking direct instructions on every course

of action, which would have been impossible, but she saw herself as generally working within a broad ANC-oriented political framework.

By the time that Neil began to work with Barbara on the Fatti's & Moni's campaign in the latter part of 1979, a secret NIS report, compiled the following year 'for Capt. WILLIAMSON' in the Special Branch, shows that they had linked her to the ANC for some time. The report's author was none other than Karl Edwards, whom Cedric de Beer had flushed out of EDA the previous year:

> BARBAR [sic] HOGAN made a number of visits to BOTSWANA, quite definitely to see the SCHOON's [sic] and on one occasion she may even have met MAC MAHARAJ. Her known visits to BOTSWANA include 13-14/8/77, 21-23 July 1978 and 22nd January 1979 (other details of visits are on file in Operation Daisy reports). On 9.9.1978 HOGAN also made a mysterious trip to SWAZILAND on her own.
>
> By way of background it is worth noting that BARBARA HOGAN has been involved in Literacy training and has employed the PAULO FREIRE method. In addition she has been prominent at a number of seminars and her ideological line is well worked out and is identical with the ANC line on social change within Southern Africa. Furthermore, there is no doubt that this woman is a brilliant tactition [sic] and organizer. Time and time again one can see the role which BARBARA HOGAN is playing in the literacy and in particular the labour field. She is capable of giving profound ideological advice from a leftist standpoint. In addition she has the ability to follow up with practical advice on how to organize. It is the combination of the ideological and practical skills which make this woman dangerous.[69]

After his years of hanging around with white activists, Karl Edwards must have prided himself on his ability to 'interpret' the ideological meaning of all their activities to his masters, including his direct superior Craig Williamson.[70] He could ad lib on the subversive and revolutionary nature of literacy projects based on Paulo Freire's banned *Pedagogy of the Oppressed* and the process of 'conscientisation'. His report enumerates a number of Barbara's other activities, including her responsibility for the production and distribution of some 10 000 copies of the general background pamphlet on the strike at Fatti's & Moni's for the boycott campaign. Without providing any evidence on the origins of the campaign, Edwards attributes it to the ANC: 'The Fatti's and Monis campaign is considered to be initiated and directed by the ANC controlled by SACTU, which JEANETTE SCHOON is actively co-ordinating in the R.S.A.' The external ANC would surely have been very pleased to have, in reality, such power to organise the workers inside the country.

A little further on, under his 'COMMENTS AND SUGGESTIONS', Edwards shifts from 'considered to be' to the authoritative assertion that 'it is evident':

> There is no doubt that BARBARA HOGAN is deeply involved with the ANC, specifically in the labour fields. From the files it is evident that the Fatti's and Monis strike was orchestrated by the ANC and was uded [sic] by the ANC as a 'propaganda victory'. HOGAN and a dozen or so other people involved with her have close ANC connections and they were responsible for organizing against Fatti's and Monis in the Transvaal on a most successful basis.

However confidently Edwards asserts what 'is evident', it would still have to be tested in court, and he does not conclude that Barbara should be arrested and charged. Instead he ends with an ominously loose recommendation: 'She could either be banned or detained for questioning. If special attention was paid to her, perhaps a case could develop.' His report provides a glimpse of the hovering mesh of security police and National Intelligence agents. Their theories had no room for a successful boycott campaign, let alone a union movement, generated within the country without orders from the external ANC.

There were those who felt disquiet at Barbara's open networking, combined with visits to Botswana, where she was moving around in 'known circles'. While finding Barbara very supportive at a time when she needed it, Liz Floyd was among those who were concerned, recalling that 'what was risky about Barbara was the way she networked. Even as someone working above ground you actually limited your connections'. Neil's own wariness, however, came from Gavin.

While assisting in the boycott campaign, Neil's prime task was to organise and sign up workers for the union. Even before Jan and Oscar returned to Johannesburg to promote the boycott, Neil had approached Gavin and the Group of 7 for help in organising the Transvaal workers of Fatti's & Moni's. Mam'Lydia, who had been at Heinemann, was still in touch with MaMinki, the shop steward for whom she had been a deputy and one of the fired

Heinemann workers. After being dismissed, MaMinki had managed to find a job at Fatti's & Moni's. Neil was very quickly connected to Mam'Lydia's old contact. They went out to Tembisa and visited MaMinki, who said, 'Ah, there's not only me!' and pointed to some other people. Within a week, Neil was able to go back to Jan and say, 'Look, I think we've got the beginnings of an organisation here'.

To their surprise, Fatti's & Moni's management suddenly found that, despite the dismissals at Bellville, other workers elsewhere were prepared to join the union. By October, with the majority of strikers having held out for an extraordinary five months, management was ready to talk, and Food and Canning asked the South African Council of Churches (SACC) to play a mediating role. It was still to be more than a month before the breakthrough came, with the signing of an agreement on 8 November. The significance was that Fatti's & Moni's had signed a contract with an unregistered union, and both the registered FCWU and unregistered AFCWU were referred to jointly as 'the union'. Peter Moni, the company's managing director, was to comment afterwards: 'We made one fatal mistake and that was to believe we could ignore organised labour'.[71] Neil must have felt extremely pleased to have been able to contribute towards this small but important victory.

But mostly the work was slow and laborious. When first accompanying Oscar to a factory, Neil had been taken aback at the time spent on form-filling and administration, rather than taking 'opportunities to address the masses about the most important issues of the day'.[72] Oscar's attitude was, 'If [you are] not interested in membership cards and keeping forms properly, you will never keep the workers' trust'.[73] An organiser couldn't be casual about anything. Neil, too, would soon become a meticulous administrator of union business.

*   *   *

While the minutes of the Branch Executive Committee meeting held at Lekton House on Friday 16 November reveal that the union was slowly getting a grip in a number of factories, things were not going smoothly internally. This was linked to two recurring problems: the lack of regular subscriptions from workers and a lack of reliable transport to visit factories. The minutes are in Neil's handwriting, as neither of the two secretaries, Monica

Mokoena and Connie Bogatsu, was present for most of the meeting. Monica had given apologies, but Connie had not. Nor had Mr Phale, the absent chairman. Under 'Matters Arising' it states the decision that, as Mr Phale 'was no longer supporting the union as he was not collecting subs in the factory, not attending committee meetings and not co-operating in organizing meetings for the Langeberg Kooperasie Beperk (LKB) workers', the committee should accept his resignation as chairman of the branch and a new chairman would be elected at the next general meeting. Workers from another factory had also complained that their representative, who was also not present without apologies, had to do better. In addition, it was noted that 'Branch Secretary, C Bogatsu had now missed her second Branch Executive Committee meeting without apology and this irresponsible attitude was condemned'.[74]

However, Connie did arrive before the end of the meeting, in time to read a personal report she had written of her complaints. The nub was that since July there had not been enough money to pay for two secretaries, and one would have to go. Connie, however, had suggested that she and Monica would share the R100 between them, and they had promised 'to pull up our socks' in collecting subs. It was the subs that paid their wages. But, she continued, there were 'some people at LKB' who no longer want to collect subs, 'even the Chairman himself'. Ever since Neil had come to help them, there was not a single day that they didn't go out organising and hiring transport to hold evening meetings, 'but it seems nobody cares about what we are doing'.

'Nobody' was the union's head office. Connie complained that she was having to 'donate' for her own transport and was intending to look for another job. While they were fighting for higher wages and better conditions for the workers, 'there is nobody who cares for us'. Describing the branch in terms of sorrow, mist and rain, Connie stated that she needed money and cooperation 'but not stones'. She even felt 'pity for Agget who … is helping us a lot but we are unable to help him at this stage, and we are still earning half of our pay'.[75]

In the minutes, Neil summarised these complaints as lack of pay and cooperation 'between the executive and the secretary' rather than Connie's broader reference to the 'officials of our Branch'. He noted the subsequent decision that, as there was not enough money to support two secretaries, the executive would decide next time who should remain on the full R100 per month.

Less than three weeks later, in a lengthy typed letter to Oscar, after updating him on developments in each of the factories, Neil came to concerns over the functioning of their Branch. Finances were slowly improving, although they were not collecting much at LKB (where the former chairman, Mr Phale, had stopped collecting subs while retaining the books) and there was still a lot of work and training needed to develop attendance and running of committee meetings. Neil then raised the issue of transport, one of Connie's bones of contention. They had been distressed to hear that the union's Management Committee at head office had turned down the Branch's request to take over head office's old kombi. They were prepared to raise as much money as they could for it, although they might 'require some help in the full payment'.[76]

A week later, Neil was writing again. This time it was a joint letter with Connie and Monica, addressed to the Management Committee. They came straight to the point and the letter gives a vivid glimpse of some of the difficulties they faced:

Johannesburg Branch,

African Food and Canning Workers Union,

816, Lekton House,

5, Wanderers Street,

Johannesburg,

12 December 1979.

The Management Committee,
African Food and Canning Workers Union.

Dear Comrades,

We were very upset to read the last minutes of the management committee in which the decision was taken to trade in the old vehicle for a new one. We support the principle that the Branch must build itself up and not always rely on help from the rest of the Union, however, we feel that in order for us to build the branch up we must have our own transport. In only two factories are we allowed to have meetings inside the factory, and in addition the workers in Johannesburg live far apart, so that it is not easy for them all to attend meetings together over the weekend in the townships. So we have been forced to hire transport regularly and have evening meetings. This is very expensive and in addition there was a breakdown in one of the vehicles the other day and the branch will have to pay the expenses. Our finances are very low, and this is a severe strain on the organization up here. In addition we have to rely on other people for the time when their transport is available so that we often have to cancel meetings and this discourages the workers.

During the day, we have to rely on private transport as the factories are very far apart and the closest factory is about five miles away.

We have been working very hard the last few months, organizing new factories and feel now that the branch can develop well if only we had our own transport. When a new branch is started, we feel that it is necessary to give them the basic tools of organizing such as a telephone, an office and transport if they are situated so far from the head office and then the Branch has the possibility of expanding and growing.

We were planning to take this matter to the executive, but as the Branch Executive is only meeting this Sunday, we are forced to write before the Management Committee meets.

So finally, we feel (and we must still put this to the executive for their opinion) that this Branch be allowed to buy the vehicle from the Head Office at a reasonable price and that it will repay the loan by raising money here and with subscription money when we are organized in more factories.

We trust that you will realize that it is a better investment for the Union to invest its money in the tools of organizing than in the bank.

Best wishes.

Yours sincerely,

C. Bogatsu M. Mokoena N. Aggett.

Neil seems to be the leading author here, the final barbed comment suggesting his growing confidence.

Just over two months later, the minutes of the Branch Executive meeting, 24 February 1980, indicate that a number of compromises had been reached. Phale was still chairman, and there were still two secretaries. The meeting, recorded in Connie's handwriting, began with the chairman asking one of the committee members to lead them in prayer. There followed a rather opaque explanation by the chairman about why he had failed to attend two Executive meetings, stating also that he had stopped collecting subs largely because he did not get his travelling expenses back. Connie endorsed this, adding in the minutes that 'it seems to us that we are the only ones who are battling on this struggle'. Neil's response was that money had been drawn to reimburse all those attending meetings, and that when the union collected more money previous debts could be paid. Backing this up, the prayer leader put forward a motion that 'the Chairman should know that "Rome was not built on a day"'. It was necessary to hold regular meetings, added Neil, to build up understanding of the union and its rules. With the tensions now aired, a motion was passed in agreement with Neil's statement. The meeting could now move on to review the situation in individual factories.

The matter of transport and the letter to head office came up as a separate item. A reply had been received that 'our branch should donate something in order for them to help us'. Workers at the South African Dried Fruit plant in Benoni had already agreed to increase their subs from 20 cents to 25 cents, and meetings were to be held in other factories about this. Finally, Connie and Monica, who were continuing to share the Secretary's wage, asked if they could have Saturdays off but agreed to alternate their 'days off'. Thus the internal crisis that threatened the Branch at the end of 1979 was averted and Neil, honing his skills in the art of compromise in the midst of conflict, had successfully survived his first six months.

CHAPTER 14

Personal relationships

FOR MONTHS, NEIL HAD BEEN HOPING TO GET BACK TOGETHER with Liz and had been a regular visitor to the house shared with Annie in Fox Street. Before working for the union, when he had more time, he would come around to chat when Liz was off-duty. Given what had happened the previous year, Annie still felt constrained in her relationship with Neil. But after a two-month holiday in London, she returned to find Neil and Liz getting back together again, although it was still rather 'on-off, on-off'. Annie had been increasingly fed up with what she saw as the 'lifestyle politics' of the white left in Johannesburg, including the behaviour in what a number of women called 'The Boys' Club' and the constant friction in the women's reading group. She was pleased to see a cheerful Neil and Liz in their new home together at 420A Fox Street, which Liz had made cosy and homely.

Jane and David Rosenthal were also glad to see the couple together again that Christmas. Liz came back to number 451 to use Jane's oven to bake lots of little Christmas cakes in jam tins. The tiny kitchen at the back of number 420A was very basic: a gas cylinder, two hotplates, a sink and two tables that took up most of the space. A little bathroom was also at the rear of the narrow house, with the bedroom in the front and a lounge in between. Although the rooms were small, the ceilings were high, with an entire wall in the middle room covered by an extraordinary wallpaper photograph of leafy autumn trees. In the back there were steps down into a garden, filled with asters, stocks, lavender, shrubs and roses, which Liz particularly liked. Occasionally Liz and Neil would attack the wild, unkempt lawn. Although not quite as shabby as Fuller Street in Bertrams, this was still a fairly poor, white working-class area. Jane recalls Neil and Liz getting on well in the neighbourhood, being 'exceptionally polite and respectful to people whom ordinary white middle-class South Africans are generally scornful of'. People would come and knock on the door if sick, and Neil would treat them. 'He was quite unpretentious and egalitarian … He lived his principles, not only vis-à-vis people of colour but working-class whites as well.' Many of their neighbours were Afrikaners, from the class that provided the majority of police recruits. But while getting on well with neighbours, Neil and Liz were under no illusions about being targeted by the security police.

The Rosenthals clearly remembered Liz and Neil pointing out a van that had aroused their suspicions, parked in the road beyond the back garden. They were convinced it contained security policemen who were making tape recordings from vibrations on the window of their bathroom or toilet at the back of the house. Having heard a story about some Americans caught picking up vibrations off some windows in Moscow, they were sure that the South African Police would have the technology. It was a nagging concern, and to upset any such recording they would have a radio on near the windows. They would also close the doors when friends like the Rosenthals came, and have conversations in their living room at the front. While those were social occasions, they had a stricter political rule. 'We didn't have a telephone, didn't talk in the house', said Liz. Yet, as she would discover, her interrogators had 'internal information on us'.

Neil and Liz worked on the 'need to know' principle, agreeing not to discuss their separate activities with each other. While this was politically sensible, such secrecy nevertheless carried the seeds of corrosion for a personal relationship. Neil had watched Gavin's marriage to Nici break up after the birth of their daughter Tamsin, with the pressure of living under a banning order and police surveillance taking its toll. In addition, there was the stress of simply surviving such a high level of political commitment. Each of them would leave the house by seven, Neil sometimes earlier to be at the factory gates before workers began their morning shift, and often not return before eleven at night. On the nights when he worked at the hospital, he would finish in the early hours of the morning, then call in to see Gavin or other friends for breakfast at Crown Mines before going straight on to the union office to do a day's work. The strain on Neil was, inevitably, going to affect Liz as well:

> It was also the kind of value system of a union, and I think particularly so in Food and Canning, of ultimate altruism, that the union's needs are the only needs, that you're not entitled to have personal needs and especially if you are a white intellectual. So I think there was that kind of value system around, which I think is a fairly Marxist one ... I'm not sure how much of that was self-imposed and how much of it was externally imposed. I think there was some of that off the union, but I think a lot of it was self-imposed and imposed on me, so any kind of personal demand was construed as undermining the union.

Working for the union without pay, Neil's only income came from his couple of nights each week at Baragwanath. Liz, who found herself supporting him financially, believed that their personal relationship required fidelity all the more so to survive the 'incredible repression'. However, she felt that Neil would never make a relationship commitment:

> Isn't that self-destructive? You want someone then to be there with that kind of commitment to see you through all that kind of stuff. You're not prepared to make a commitment to that person, of any kind, so you're not investing in relationships. And I don't think that morality is exclusive to Neil and I think that was fairly prevalent amongst the white left in that period.

In the heat of political struggle, 'the personal' was dismissed as indulgent and evidence of weakness. Those women who raised questions about fidelity felt marginalised by the predominant male attitude that this issue was not relevant to 'the struggle'. They rejected this dismissal as a cover for macho behaviour, though Neil never came in for that accusation. It is possible that Neil told himself that, with the political risks, it was better not to make a relationship commitment. If things went wrong, only he would be affected. Yet, at the same time, he didn't want to lose Liz. Each time after he strayed, he would return and want to start again. Jane Rosenthal suggested a more basic explanation:

> JANE: Neil was just a naughty boy. He was very, very good-looking, very attractive. But the first person important to his life was Liz, I think … I think Neil was incredibly human. He had a great love of ordinary humanity. One of the reasons he came to see us was that we represented sanity, family life. You couldn't have called us a conservative, ordinary middle-class family because we were more interested in politics than the average South African. But the kids had to do their homework, the washing hung on the line …
> DAVID: He actually expressed that he felt the way we lived was the norm but it was unfortunate that people under abnormal circumstances had to live like the politicos. He actually said 'This is what we must become'.

Early in April 1980, just a few months after getting back together with Liz, Neil accompanied the Rosenthals for a few days on an Easter holiday down on Jane's father's farm near Plettenberg Bay. They were going to drive down to the Cape, setting off at night. Neil offered to drive with Jane while David and the boys slept in the back. By now, when Neil visited them, a mysterious black car would wait on the opposite side of the road. But on this trip, Neil was delighted at giving the police the slip and not being pursued. On arriving at the farm, when the tenant caretakers opened the house, Neil insisted that they have coffee with them. Although Jane and the family were at ease, the tenant caretakers were not, but Neil persisted in trying to break down the barrier. Jane thought Neil absolutely wonderful in keeping her boys 'in order' with a bribe that he would tell them about some gory incident from Baragwanath Casualty. How much blood, which scalpel he used, and every gruesome detail … the boys loved it! After two or three days, Neil had to leave, and they had left him at the side of the road, from where he hitched a lift to Cape Town.

About this time, Neil made one of his infrequent visits to Somerset West. Perhaps this was when Aubrey told his son, 'You're playing with fire and you're going to get burnt'. Certainly Joy would have done her best to ensure that tension was minimised. One thing that would have pleased both parents would be to see that Neil had cut his hair, very short and neat. As he had wryly told the Rosenthals, the workers were not impressed by untidy, shaggy-looking white men, so he had been obliged to spruce himself up.

CHAPTER 15

'Point by point by point'

He was able to come to the townships, something that surprised some of the workers. They were even calling him Black Jesus because they were saying his face was like Jesus because he used to meet with workers and advise workers. In the township he was not only dealing with worker problem things ... At night he was at the hospital and during the day he was able to meet with the workers, go and organise factories and over and above when he goes to meet in a township where you find that someone is ill, he gives them advice. Take this one to a doctor. Take this one ... Sometimes he even goes to the extent of writing a letter: 'Take your worker to this ...' That was so helpful to some of our members and that is where they started to have confidence to approach him.

Israel Mogoatlhe,
union member at Fatti's & Moni's

IN 1980, ISRAEL MOGOATLHE WAS 'FRESH FROM SCHOOL', WHERE HE had been given a 'DC ... a Don't Come Back'. There had been a student strike, and Israel, who had debated for his school, was deemed one of the ringleaders. Unable to complete his matric, he got a job at the Isando factory of Fatti's & Moni's, earning R32 a week in conditions that were 'very bad'. Israel vividly recalls that when he first saw the young white doctor freely offer his knowledge and skills, he was puzzled. 'If you are a black doctor … you are a middle class. The people are scared to come to you. So you can imagine what it was with a white doctor.' Added to this was the question: 'How can a white person come and organise us when we know that we are fighting against the whites?'

But Neil's manner and persistence were evidence that he was quite unlike the white bosses most black people encountered. Where he didn't have answers himself, he would suggest where people might go. He passed on information about the Industrial Aid Society, and, as word got around, people's confidence in him grew. Israel remembers Neil's insistence on the Cape Town agreement between the union and the workers at Fatti's & Moni's in Bellville being translated from English and isiXhosa into Sesotho and Setswana, languages more commonly spoken by the Johannesburg workers. Neil emphasised that the union official's role was to serve the workers, who should always feel that they could ask questions freely. A union official who behaved like 'a big thing' or 'a bombastic thing' would make workers scared. These were 'the tricks that the bosses like to use'.

However, things were going downhill at Fatti's & Moni's. Instead of management heeding the lessons of the previous year's national boycott and the agreement with the union in Cape Town, Peter Moni was still holding on to his non-elected liaison committee in the Isando factory. Fears that management wanted 'to split the workers' were heightened when all the workers, except those from the Macaroni department, were told to come to work an hour early on 22 April. Monica and Connie slept overnight in Tembisa so as to be at the factory gates at 5.30am singing their song, 'Amajoinile!' (come and join us). The minutes of the Branch Executive Committee meeting comment that their smiling faces and loud voices attracted people inside to join them. But after being offered a 5% increase, the workers demanded more.[77]

Peter Moni dug in his heels. While prepared to meet Neil and the other union officials at his office in town, he refused to meet them with workers inside the factory. Moreover, the officials could only meet Fatti's & Moni's workers outside the gates. Over the next few months, Neil continued discussions with the workers outside the Isando factory and in the townships where they lived. By now he was a recognisable figure, driving around in his brown

Volkswagen. On 16 June, the fourth anniversary of the Soweto uprising, the workers who met with Neil outside the gates decided it was time to draw up a petition to be handed to Moni:

PETITION.

WE, THE WORKERS OF FATTIS AND MONIS, STATE THAT WE HAVE NO CONFI-
DENCE IN THE LIASON COMMITTEE IN OUR FACTORY AND WILL NO LONGER
TAKE PART IN ITS ACTIVITIES. WE ARE MEMBERS OF THE AFRICAN FOOD
AND CANNING WORKERS UNION AND WE WANT TO BE REPRESENTED BY A
UNION COMMITTEE ELECTED INSIDE THE FACTORY BY US, IN THE PRESENCE
OF THE UNION COMMITTEE.[78]

Two months later, the petition was ready. Most workers had signed it, except for those who worked in the Macaroni section. At a meeting outside the factory on 27 August, the problem arose of how to deliver it and an accompanying letter. Anyone handing in the petition would immediately be identified as a troublemaker. Why didn't someone just 'drop' it into the personnel office when none of the office staff was looking? However, Neil raised the question, what if the bosses then did nothing and denied receiving anything? A witness was required to hand in both petition and letter personally. Young Israel volunteered as 'brave enough to take that thing – even if they dismiss me, I don't care about that'. When the white receptionist refused to accept the documents, Israel approached a manager, who agreed to take them. His story is reminiscent of Aesop's fable of the mice discussing 'Who will bell the cat?' Terror of the cat prevents any mouse coming forward. But in Isando, with the petition delivered, that terror had been broken, and the workers now waited to see what the cat would do.

Peter Moni's response was to ignore the Johannesburg Branch of AFCWU, asking instead for a meeting with Jan Theron in Cape Town. Jan agreed, on condition that a Johannesburg official and union member also be present. Neil was delegated to attend with a committee member from the Isando factory. A visit to head office would usually also have been a chance to see Oscar, but on 13 August the 71-year-old unionist had been arrested under the Terrorism Act. Neil must have been very concerned for his friend and mentor, who suffered from diabetes and whom the police intended to link to the deaths of two white people who died after their vehicle was set alight in the informal settlement at Nyanga. A founder member of the Nyanga Residents' Association, Oscar had publicly condemned the role of the police in the escalating violence.

At the meeting, Peter Moni agreed to let union officials enter the Isando factory to report back to the workers the outcome of their petition. However, since then, there had been no reply to their letter asking for a date. A phone call revealed that Peter Moni was on leave for a week, and whoever had replaced him was not willing to act. Suspecting the delay was a trick, it was decided to take a copy of the letter to another member of the family firm, John Moni, and for the union officials to come to the factory at lunchtime. If the management refused to let them enter the factory, the workers would stop work.

A classic confrontation ensued. Neil, Connie and Monica arrived, and were refused entry. The angry workers refused to leave the canteen until they were allowed to have their meeting. The management then locked the gates so that the workers couldn't go outside. Israel Mogoatlhe recalls that they even locked the tap, denying access to water, as well as stopping service in the canteen. The strike lasted for three days before the management gave in and allowed union officials to meet with the workers in the canteen. The liaison committee was rejected as a tool of management, and the workers demanded a wage agreement. Once again, Peter Moni wanted the meeting to take place in Cape Town, involving the Branch again in the expense of transport. Having proved his mettle, Israel was assigned to fly with Neil. It was his first time in an aeroplane, which he associated with 'big people and ties'. He dressed up with a tie only to find Neil 'so very simple with his Bogart [jacket] … and some other jersey there, a V-neck, very simple, with a briefcase'.

At the meeting on 20 October 1980, union officials from both the Cape and Johannesburg plants signed an agreement with Fatti's & Moni's that ensured a minimum wage of R40 a week for women and R45 for men, a R10 increase for most. It was to be paid by stop order, with the union committee recognised in both factories and its officials having the right to enter and hold meetings inside. The breakthrough agreement became the top item in the first Branch newsletter, ending with Neil's exhortation: 'it shows what can be done if the workers are well organized, united and militant'.[79]

A more intimate portrait of Neil, fuelled by adrenaline, emerges in Israel's account of their journey back to Johannesburg. Instead of returning by plane,

Neil drove a kombi, more or less non-stop from Cape Town, a journey of some 1 400 kilometres. Israel kept talking, pouring tea for him, giving him tablets to keep awake. Neil was smoking a lot. 'Neil, can I assist you?' 'No, Israel, you can't drive. You've no licence to drive.' Their only stops were to get petrol, something to drink, go to the toilet and wash their faces. 'Neil, why don't you park by the side?' 'No, Israel, as long as I'm not driving very fast, I feel awake.' Years later, Israel would tell me, 'Then I saw this man is very strong'.

For Israel, it was a defining relationship, forged with a white man, less than ten years older, who showed total dedication to the trade union struggle. Israel couldn't recall Neil ever talking to him about banned political parties, the liberation movement or, 'Release Mandela', as he put it. 'Those things were out from Neil. He would rather tell you about fighting the bosses. That is why he was there.' He tremendously admired Neil's manner in dealing with white bosses who were so used to having their own way, at times raising their voices to shouting pitch: 'But Neil was very soft. Soft-spoken man. They were making a lot of noise. He used to stay on the point, used to convince them with points, point by point by point. But the bosses were making noise. Slowly he convinced them. They were rigid.'

Neil also knew 'a lot of Acts', constantly passing on information about basic conditions of employment and rights to Israel and his fellow workers. Managers would often be infuriated when 'this stupid shop steward' contradicted them:

> They expected us to know nothing … The way the bosses used to do … Bosses choose a worker to 'advise' … They used to say, 'Can you come here. There's a hearing. Come come come.' Then Neil would say, 'Read clause what what what. It says the worker should have a shop steward *of his own choice*'. He'd say, 'Take the clause and show it to the manager.' The other thing he used to advise us was never sign something you don't understand. Some bosses would say, 'Come sign, sign. It's nothing here. Just sign.' Then that is why he said, 'Never sign anything when the shop steward is not there. Refuse to sign.'

While Israel valued this transmission of knowledge, his deep affection for Neil seemed to stem from something more, beyond even Neil's obvious dedication.

I suspect that it had to do with Neil allowing himself to be vulnerable in a society where most white people did everything possible to remain all-powerful. Israel speaks of how, during evening meetings in Tembisa, workers would be worried that Neil might be attacked on his way home. 'Leave now, Neil!' 'No Israel, we're here. Let's remain.' Others thought that he must be armed. 'Maybe he's carrying a gun. Maybe he's got a gun for him to stay. He's got a gun, so don't worry.' But Israel knew that he didn't carry any gun and that his mentor's courage lay deep within.

Israel's account of Neil's apparent lack of fear of travelling into Tembisa echoes Sipho's memories of Neil visiting him in Alexandra, another place where few white people ever set foot. As a doctor, the stethoscope in his car gave Neil a cover if stopped by the police. Israel's recollection of them being stopped at a roadblock shows Neil remaining cool, able to transform those moments of danger into another small victory. Neil did all the talking: the people with him were his patients and there were not enough ambulances. 'You must be very careful. There are crooks there', said the police. 'No no, I'll be careful. I'm not taking them too far.' Israel recalls, 'It was very nice … We drove into the township and out the other exit.'

While some white trade unionists retained a measure of division between their work and home relationships, this was not for Neil. Although Israel never became part of Gavin's and Sipho's Woodworkers or the Vegetable Garden, he would visit Neil at his house. He still remembers the first time that Neil made them spaghetti bolognese, a new dish for Israel. Their conversations went beyond work to aspects of living: 'Don't drink, Israel, because this thing is going to affect your mind and your body and how will the workers recognise you as a leader being drunk? Your dignity must be there.' The tone is reminiscent of Neil's strictures to himself in his diary as a schoolboy. Perhaps Neil was now taking on something of the older brother mentor role learned originally from Michael. Israel's admiration was for someone whom he saw living out his principles. Moreover, here was someone who had the courage to stand against the crowd when it came to corruption.

CHAPTER 16

Eating the workers' money

A T THE HEIGHT OF THE FATTI'S & MONI'S DISPUTE IN JOHANNES-
burg, the Branch was presented with a pressing internal issue.
The auditor's report had revealed that a sum of R281 was missing.
The Secretary was asked to explain. With handwriting alternating between
Connie and Monica, the Branch Minutes for September 1980 record Connie's
account of the Branch being very poor and the money being used in the last
year 'to pay the Executive and to buy tickets for themselves'.[80] Mr Phale, the
Chairman, confirmed that this was the truth and money had been given because attendance at committee meetings had been poor. Furthermore, he had
taken money from his own pocket to help out 'the poor Secretaries' who had
even gone without pay for two months. The fault was in the Secretary not
recording the money paid out. All the Committee members agreed that not
recording the money was wrong.

This was probably where the matter would have been left with an explanation sent to head office and assurances that it wouldn't happen again, had
Neil not stood up to point out that the money the Secretary said she had used
for transport was substantially less than the missing money. He had obviously done some detailed sums. He brought to the Committee's attention the
case of a previous Secretary at the Paarl branch; after being found to have

taken money, this individual was allowed to repay it, but the following year was found to have taken money again. She had ended up owing a lot more than before. Neil's view, as recorded in the minutes, was that 'if the committee keeps such persons in their organization they are adopting a very bad organization in their Branch'.

Connie denied the allegation, and another committee member suggested that 'the committee should blame itself and pay the amount of the R281 which is short'. The R281 was divided by the 25 members present and each was asked to bring R11.22. Neil was the only one to question the decision, but was told that the secretaries would also be contributing their equal share. A further complaint was raised by Mr Phale that 'there were many mistakes in this office', as the Secretary was no longer handling the account books and they were being written by Neil. Connie explained that 'from last year she was having a quiry (sic) with N. Aggett while she is supposed to write down some checks'. According to Neil, Connie had then given him the books to keep. The Committee decided that Connie should take back the books forthwith. The minutes ended in Connie's handwriting, noting that the meeting closed at 9pm and 'although N. Aggett was not satisfied' the Committee told him that the decision had been made and wouldn't change.'[81]

How can we explain the Committee's decision, which flew in the face of transparent accountability regarding use of the workers' subs? Were racial or cultural dynamics coming into play? Did some black members say among themselves that this young white man doesn't understand our way of doing things? Their Secretary had admitted her 'mistake' in taking money without recording it in the book. But when Neil had pointed out that the amount missing was greater than could be explained by travel expenses, the point was not pursued. Furthermore, Connie was told to take the books back from Neil and resume charge of the book-keeping. Although Israel was not present at this special meeting, the news must have spread among the workers. Fifteen years later, he referred to what happened with regret, expressing support for Neil's firm stance:

> He was very much against corruption. There was a case where two officials were dismissed after Neil died. How did it happen? He was saying those workers were eating the workers' money ... We said let's forget and Neil said, they are going to repeat it again, and they repeated that thing and we

remembered what Neil said. He said, 'Discipline must be taken, we must
follow the Constitution' ... He said, 'Even if I, Neil, eat the workers' money,
I must be disciplined ...'

Dealing with truculent management and an aggressive, domineering state
was one thing. At least the moral lines were clear. Dealing with the slippery
tentacles of internal corruption was something else.

*   *   *

Neil was not the only one concerned. Head office was not pleased. The Branch
Executive Minutes for 10 February 1981, almost five months later, record a
well-attended meeting in the presence of both the General Secretary and the
President of Food and Canning. Jan Theron and Comrade John Pendlani had
travelled from Cape Town. The first item on the agenda was the auditor's report. For the first time, Connie admitted that the missing money wasn't only
spent on travel expenses for herself and Monica and petty cash for some committee members. They did not mean 'to break down the Organization, the
intention was to pay it back as they were suffering. Even now they are still
prepared to pay that money back, provided the meeting allows that.'[82]

But Comrade Pendlani's view was clear. Things that were left hidden were
'very dangerous to the workers' and corrupting to the organisation. The matter should be taken to the workers at a general meeting. It was the first time
in Branch Minutes that people present were recorded as 'Comrade'. Despite
the argument from committee members that if the workers got to hear about
what had happened, 'they are going to stop paying', Jan also remained firm.
They had dealt with a similar case before, and what would other branches
think if the Constitution wasn't followed here in Johannesburg?

At noon on Sunday, President Comrade Pendlani welcomed 300 members
of the union in Tembisa's Endulwini Roman Catholic Church. The meeting
lasted four and a half hours. Jan Theron, seconded by Comrade Pendlani,
declared that 'workers should make a decision about people responsible for
their money' and that anyone 'who steals workers' money get dismissed and
that is the Policy of their Constitution'.[83] There was no disagreement about
the secretaries having done wrong. However Comrade Mohaisi of H Jones
argued that 'such problems even happens in the family and you cannot chase

out your child away or kill her because the remaining others will also fall into the same mistakes or else do worst than the first. After that you won't have a good family.' Surely an apology, with all the money paid back, and a warning would be better? Another union member inquired about the salary paid to the secretaries. When Connie said that it was R62.50 per month, the worker addressed the meeting on how impossible it was to live on so small a wage. Others also put in words of support for the secretaries, someone adding that if they were dismissed, the union would be recast in the image of the bosses!

The President noted that the views were in line with what had been decided by the Branch Committee, but warned about history repeating itself. A motion against dismissal and in favour of the secretaries paying back the money was put forward. All agreed. Comrade Pendlani stated that he wanted Neil to be responsible for receiving the money 'before 31/2/81'. Once again, 'all agreed'. In the heat of the moment it was forgotten that February only had 28 days. Neil had stayed quiet throughout the debate. In less than a year he was dead, and didn't live to see his fears, and those of Jan Theron and Comrade Pendlani, come true.

The election of Branch Chairman, Secretary and Treasurer followed the vote, and all the incumbents stayed in their posts. Three further items were hurried through; the final one concerned 14 workers laid off from South African Dried Fruit, the minutes ending 'S.A.D. is the worst factory'. It was a reminder that the union needed to get back to work. Whatever Neil thought, the workers had made their decision and it was time to move on.

CHAPTER 17

Gavin and an ANC link?

WHILE THE AFFAIR OF THE MISSING MONEY LINGERED OVER A year, this was just one thread among many in Neil's increasingly complicated life. He was interweaving his day and night union work, his nights in Baragwanath Casualty and his meetings – some open, some secret – with Gavin, Sipho and other comrades. Neil would see Gavin at least once or twice a week, usually early on a Saturday morning after his Friday night shift at the hospital before heading for the office. After splitting with Nici, who had taken their baby when she left, Gavin had moved out to Crown Mines, into a tiny outside room at Peacock Cottage. By this time, the house was rented by Joanne Yawitch, a young friend of Barbara Hogan. There was just space for a bed and a couple of shelves above the door for Gavin's clothes. But he was near to the Vegetable Garden and he threw himself into communal activities, helping to build a crèche in the old Scout Hall and a treehouse for the children. He had brought three beehives from his house in town so he could continue to distribute raw honey to everyone in the buyers' co-op.

One night, walking home in the dark on the path that led through the Vegetable Garden to his room, Gavin stumbled into a large hole. Workers from Rand Mines had come with mechanical diggers to scoop out the earth, destroying the garden. An eviction order arrived the next day. When furious protests got them nowhere, Joanne was lucky to find a house at the end of one of the rows for her and her friends. The bulldozers arrived to flatten Peacock Cottage and the outbuildings on the day they left. Only the trees where they used to sit beside the garden were left standing, with the three beehives. Before Gavin could find somewhere to move them, a felled tree had crushed one, and the others were set on fire. The scattering bees augured the end of an era.

Gavin came to rent the narrow veranda room at the front of Joanne's 'new' house. Here there was space for his bed, an old wooden armchair and a small stove with a chimney that acted as a table. This now became Neil's port of call after a night on duty. Gavin would make Neil breakfast, then lie on the bed while Neil would sit on the chair as they talked. Although it seems that Neil constantly shut himself down to Liz, he remained open to Gavin.

With Pindile's banning and subsequent banishment to the Transkei, Gavin's foremost line of contact with the ANC had been cut.[84] He had continued working within a broad ANC framework and network of activists, following Pindile's plan. However, early in 1981, Gavin was requested, via Barbara, to change the nature of his relationship with the external ANC and to link direct-ly to its forward area in Botswana. Among the trusted comrades with whom he discussed the implications were Sipho and Neil. From the beginning, Neil was 'anti links with ANC outside'. In Gavin's view, this was because 'from the ultra-left position he saw them as manipulative and … using the workers as the battering ram to get state power'. Gavin and Sipho, on the other hand, were always clear that they were building the ANC position inside the country, knowing that 'at a certain stage in history you had to mesh the internal and external machineries'. They believed that the time had come.

Neil's concern about external manipulation taking democratic control away from workers inside the country was not new. Pindile had discussed the same issue with both Gavin and Sipho, and they, in turn, had discussed it with Neil. But Neil's reservations were now grounded in his own experi-ence of working in a union, in which he had come to appreciate issues of democratic accountability in a very concrete way. Furthermore, there was the grave question of how much one could trust ANC security. Gavin knew that his link would be to the Schoons. Yet Jeanette and far more senior people in the ANC had not taken seriously his and Cedric's concerns about the now-unmasked Craig Williamson. Who knew the extent of the damage wrought by the well-fed spy as he wormed himself closer to the heart of sections of the ANC's exiled hierarchy? It was not a reassuring thought.

However, the decision was made. Gavin would make the link. It was politically necessary, and, he argued, by taking this on himself, others who were not banned and who were still able to operate in the open – like Neil – would not be compromised if the links were discovered. He was 'determined not to get bust' by being exceptionally strict about procedures, never breaking the rules about using a book code, always going to his dead letter boxes (DLBs) by a roundabout route, and making sure he was never followed. He was prepared to survey a DLB for hours before making a drop or collecting a message. But were he to be picked up by the security police, he felt confident that they would not be able to break into his networks. Sipho supported Gavin's decision, while he himself 'continued as if I am ANC and thousands of people would have worked that way without them being members of the ANC, but working for the ANC'. At the end of their discussion, Neil too had agreed that his comrade should go ahead, 'but he wasn't happy', says Gavin. He was more at ease remaining directly accountable to the union and its members, putting into practice the ANC slogan 'Power to the People'.

Gavin's formal linkage came in the wake of changes brought about by the arrival of Mac Maharaj as head of the ANC's underground political development at the beginning of 1978, including a drive to ensure that any internal political underground was more thoroughly linked and accountable to ANC leadership. Recalling that Mac had once told me that Neil had worked for the ANC, I wrote to him in 2009 to ask if he could elaborate on the information that had come through to him. I explained that, from my interviews, I had developed 'a picture of people around Neil who were working more autonomously within a broad ANC framework and network', as well as those who were 'under discipline', taking direct instructions through an ANC forward area. Mac replied that Neil had been 'organically linked' to Jenny (Jeanette) Schoon, who was on the SACTU committee focused on union organisation inside the country, and part of the ANC underground committee. He also objected vigorously to two of my phrases. His first criticism focused on the words 'working more autonomously', which, he said, 'removes any accountability to the ANC and allows the individual to claim that he/she is working "within a broad ANC framework" by picking and choosing whatever he or she agrees with in the framework'.

I had heard about the 'working more autonomously' culture from others besides Gavin and Sipho. Ismail Momoniat spoke of how activists within the Indian community in the 1970s and early 1980s were part of a wider grouping who didn't necessarily know each other but were all connected with Barbara Hogan. 'Although we saw ourselves as an explicitly ANC grouping, we didn't see the need for any formal membership. [We] saw ourselves as part of above-ground opposition, many of us coming from a Black Consciousness background, having switched. The way we operated was quite important, emerged out of years of repression … [we] would try and be smarter about how we'd link up with the outside.' This manner of fairly independent working was also reflected by Barbara in describing the first period of her relationship with the ANC, even after formal recruitment.[85] This was something that Mac had set out to rectify.

Mac was also not happy with the phrase 'under discipline' as referring to those directly linked to a forward area: 'Embedded in this is "direct instruction" which narrows down "under discipline" to reduce matters to top-down orders and instructions which the person has to carry out on pain of …' I was curious about his sharp critique of what were the perceptions of internal activists. I asked Gavin if he could explain Mac's response to me. He said he liked the rigour in Mac's letter and 'the way he makes us re-evaluate the phrase that I had easily accepted ("working more autonomously within a broad ANC framework and network"). I also chuckle at his aversion to the insinuation that "under discipline" means top-down orders and instructions, because for me this is exactly what characterised the external ANC.'

With Gavin's experience of accepting direct linkage to Botswana, his further comments on Mac's letter were revealing:

> … if you look at what constituted ANC Internal then, it was about a few comrades having connections with outside, but building up cells inside after the manner of the M plan, which linked with each other – the underground – and which fed into open organisation. So internally there were more people organising and linked to each other than were linked to the external ANC. And some individuals within this network of cells were slightly wary of the external ANC even as they celebrated and fostered its objectives and religiously listened to and punted the positions put across on Radio Freedom, because of its 'top-down' leadership style … There really

was a complete difference in cultures between external and internal, you know. Just as an example, we would take months of testing of an individual before recruiting him or her, and then would have freedom of debate within our cells where a discourse was fostered that flowed back and forth across them and eventually surfaced in open organisations.

The 'freedom of debate' maintained within their cells made it more difficult for an infiltrator to remain undetected than in a culture that strongly promoted adherence to a party line. The case of Craig Williamson was a prime example.

Williamson's conception of how the external ANC operated became a blueprint for the security police. After manufacturing his own 'escape' to Botswana, six months after the Schoons had crossed the border, he made his way to their dining table. After a discussion, Marius wrote three letters of introduction for this 'old friend of Jen's' to take to senior ANC comrades in Lusaka.[86] While working for the International University Exchange Fund in Geneva, Williamson remained in contact with Botswana comrades until his cover was broken at the end of 1979. If Williamson, or a successor, picked up a story similar to the one Mac believed – that Neil was 'organically linked' to Jenny Schoon – a note would have been inserted in Neil's security police file. But from where had this story come? The one person who could have helped to unravel this thread is no more. In 1984, Jeanette Schoon was blown up, together with her six-year-old daughter Katryn, by a parcel bomb. The parcel was addressed to Marius, who came home to find their two-year-old son Fritz wandering among the remains. The bomb had been sent by Williamson.

PART THREE

The Rising Tide

CHAPTER 18

The rising tide

T HROUGHOUT 1980, BLACK WORKERS CHALLENGED THE GOV-
ernment's attempts to control them under the guise of reforming
Wiehahn legislation, with strikes in Port Elizabeth, Cape Town,
Durban and Johannesburg. The victories of the workers at Fatti's & Moni's
in Bellville and at Ford's Cortina plant in Port Elizabeth held out hope for
change. The latter strike had occurred as the result of the dismissal of a trainee
draughtsman, Thozamile Botha.[87] Significantly, Botha was also president of
the Port Elizabeth Black Civic Organization (PEBCO) and openly addressed
large crowds on how workplace issues affected family and community life.
If a worker was underpaid or lost his job, the effect was felt well beyond the
factory.

Although not all strikes were successful, employers' hopes and government
plans for taming workers through factory liaison committees, registration and
industrial councils were in tatters. In Johannesburg, for instance, a municipal
strike involving 10 000 workers paralysed city services for a week at the end
of July. The council was only able to crush the strike 'by using methods that
left the reform plan's image in ruins'.[88] Yet, in whatever way each strike was
resolved or crushed, the message to employers was plain: deal with leaders
chosen by the workers themselves, or expect trouble. Even then, negotiating

with union leaders was no panacea. A new consciousness and confidence was rising among workers, emboldened by a battle-hardened younger generation who had experienced the resistance of 1976 and who were now joining the workforce. The ferocious assaults of the police had left them deeply angry, not cowed. A new emerging union in the eastern Cape embodied this defiant spirit. Before 1980 was over, Neil was helping its leaders establish an office in Johannesburg.

The South African Allied Workers' Union (SAAWU) had opened its doors as a non-racial union in Durban in March 1979. Within a year, its centre had moved southwest along the coast into the eastern Cape, with its East London branch, bordering the Ciskei homeland, headed by the dynamic young Thozamile Gqweta. A former OK Bazaars salesman and rugby fly-half for Winter Rose in Mdantsane, he was just 26, like Neil. Thozamile had been a Black Consciousness activist until coming into contact with Oscar Mpetha during one of Oscar's visits to organise AFCWU members in East London. As with Neil, Oscar became a mentor. The effect on Thozamile was to embrace more of an ANC outlook appropriate to a non-racial union. Seven months after SAAWU opened its East London branch in March 1980, membership had swelled from 5 000 to 15 000, encompassing almost half of the small city's African workers, and with membership still growing. The SAAWU office also organised AFCWU workers in the area, which became especially necessary after Oscar's arrest and detention in August.

SAAWU made no bones about mobilising workers around joint industrial and political issues. It was more of a union-cum-social movement. The area's geography made the politics explicit. East London, where most factories were sited, was in 'white South Africa', while Mdantsane, where black workers lived, was assigned to the Ciskei, run largely as a fiefdom of the Sebe brothers. Lennox Sebe, the homeland's chief minister, and Charles Sebe, head of Ciskei's political police, were widely regarded as profiting from the use of the Ciskei as a labour reservoir that catered for the needs of white South Africa. Thozamile's first arrest had been by Ciskei police at a rugby match in April 1980, soon after the opening of SAAWU's East London office. This initiated a brutal campaign of persecution by the Ciskei as well as the East London security police – the same unit that had been responsible for Steve Biko's death.

By October, at least ten companies had experienced strikes where management refused to recognise SAAWU, even though the union had recruited more than 60% of the workers. Employers hoped that Thozamile and the SAAWU workers would cave in under police harassment, mass arrests, detentions and torture. One East London security policeman, Captain Phillipus Olivier, became so involved in trying to suppress the work stoppages that on one occasion he even fired the strikers himself. Having appointed himself 'unofficial labour adviser', he had stern words for employers who seemed to be softening, reminding them of the part they were expected to play against the 'total onslaught' of which SAAWU was the current front line.[89]

The government was forced to revise its strategy. Open repression of trade unionists played badly in the world media and with overseas investors, who prized stability above all. In September, Labour Minister Fanie Botha signalled a change in policy away from the edifice of registration and industrial councils. All of a sudden, he urged employers to deal with 'whatever leadership group has credibility among the workers'.[90] White South Africa shouldn't fear that the onslaught was coming from all unions per se, but from those unions that moved beyond shop-floor industrial concerns into wider political issues. In other words, unions like SAAWU.

SAAWU's early spectacular success in the eastern Cape encouraged it to expand. When university graduate Sisa Njikelana joined Thozamile, Sisa quickly developed into another fiery young leader. Both were to be repeatedly arrested and tortured, although the police were to reserve their most horrific methods to destroy Thozamile. Even so, none of the charges laid against either of them in court ever stuck, probably thanks to Oscar's tutoring. In hindsight, it seems no accident that, despite the great distance between their cities, Neil's path would intertwine with theirs and that they would end up as fellow detainees at John Vorster Square. Oscar's own fate signalled that the police would stop at nothing. On 4 December, he was charged, along with 17 young people, on two counts of criminal murder and a further count under the Terrorism Act following the events at Nyanga.[91]

By the end of 1980, SAAWU had decided to expand to Johannesburg. In November, Neil welcomed SAAWU's General Secretary, Sam Kikine, to the AFCWU office and took him to a local factory to meet the workers. Both sides were happy to work 'hand in hand'.[92] SAAWU would share office space and expenses and would look for another office on the East Rand that would also be shared on an equal basis. Although the general outlook of both unions was similar, the AFCWU had established itself through solid, steady organisation while SAAWU's recent meteoric rise had more to do with catching the mood of eastern Cape workers.

A local SAAWU organiser was appointed in Johannesburg, and both Thozamile and Sisa would visit over the following months, staying with Neil and Liz. Although the relationship was to last barely a year, for Sisa it was 'one of the most unique ones, very short, very intense but extremely enriching'. Sisa was convinced that Neil must be an underground operative and a communist to be so dedicated. What other white person, he thought, would come to the union office early in the morning and doze on a bench for an hour because he was tired out from working all night at the hospital? Neil gave him Marx's *Capital* to read. Sisa found it heavy going, describing himself then as '*nog 'n laaitjie*' (just a youngster), but the fact that the security police and the state had it in for communists made him to want to understand more: 'It seemed to me this communism must be good if it can actually make whites who are privileged so dedicated.'

Neil probed the young SAAWU leaders about the political situation in East London and heard first-hand about torture and interrogation methods. Gavin and Sipho had already discussed their experiences with him, including strategies for surviving. Neil would have known that sharing the AFCWU office with SAAWU would further notch up security police attention. It's impossible to know at what point he finally began to think of detention as a real possibility. White radicals who needed to steel themselves against fear would no doubt remind themselves how their black compatriots suffered daily surveillance and could be thrown into jail on the slightest pretext. Violence hung over black South Africans, not only from the police but from brutalised fellow inhabitants who turned to criminal attacks, the results of which Neil continued to witness on his Friday and Saturday night shifts in Casualty. While Neil's calmness earned the trust of colleagues and comrades, to Liz the rising pressure by 1981 was exacting an increasing toll, hidden beneath the composed exterior of the dedicated unionist-cum-medical worker.

CHAPTER 19

Publicly and privately

P.O. Box 46376,
Orange Grove.
14/1/81

Dear Mom & Dad,

I really appreciated seeing you while I was in Cape Town, and it was good to see how well you both were. I'm sorry I've taken so long to write, but things have been quite hectic since I got back to JHB.

The trip back by train was calm and relaxing, but became a bit tedious after the second night on the train. We found C.T. so clean, fresh and quiet compared to this very tense city, and it was good to have the chance to relax for a few days. Back in the big city it has been very hot, with lots of mosquitos and an oppressive atmosphere. However my work is going well …

NEIL AND LIZ HAD MANAGED A SHORT BREAK AT THE END OF the year, and he had been over to Somerset West, where Jill and her family were also visiting, with Neil enjoying time to play with the 'lively' children. Relations had eased sufficiently for him to include his father in his letter, in which he thanks his parents for a Christmas cheque, telling them, 'I took the opportunity to buy some working clothes (jacket, pants etc) that I was in need of for the coming year, as you know JHB is quite a "smart" place and it is necessary to be dressed appropriately'.[93] But before Neil completed his letter, Jill rang to tell him that their mother had injured her foot and it was in plaster. He hoped that she would soon be on her feet again. It was 7.30pm and he was still in the office, 'having just finished a hectic day of meetings'. Adding that he would try to ring, he signed off, 'Yours fondly'. Joy added the letter to her small collection, tied together with a ribbon, which Michael would find on her death. It appears to have been Neil's last family letter.

The 'big city' was relentless. Once again, the minutes of the Branch meeting provide a glimpse into Neil's daily work and provide evidence of the ponderous but essential attention to detail, which Neil had learned from Oscar. The minutes of the well-attended Branch Executive meeting on Wednesday 18 March 1981, held at the union's office in Lekton House, are testimony to the solid mentoring of Baba Mpetha. All the factory representatives had come after a full day's work, and had been awake since four or five o'clock that morning. Neil, Connie and Monica had probably had a long day too.

Following the customary prayer and acceptance of previous minutes, under 'Matters Arising' and 'Auditor's Report', the missing-money affair involving the secretaries was finally put to rest. A single sentence noted that the money would be banked before the end of the month and proof shown to the Executive next time. Later in the meeting, a proposal for each Secretary's wage to rise to R150 received unanimous agreement. Neil, who had consistently pushed for their accountability, was also the first to support the wage increase.

A number of lengthy discussions took place that evening, including one on pensions in which Neil explained that there was widespread dissatisfaction over the government's proposals. East London and Port Elizabeth workers had gone on strike several times already over the Preservation of Pensions Bill, which would stop workers withdrawing their pension contributions when they left a job – at a time of potential need. Their money would either have to be transferred to a new pension scheme or left in the old one until the worker was 65. How many African workers ever reached that age?

The pension issue was to prove explosive in factories across the country in the coming months, with at least 27 pension strikes affecting some 30 000 workers.[94] The government said that pension funds were needed for the economy, but black workers could see no benefits. Instead their pension money would be used to boost the military and solely white interests. Such was the dissatisfaction that the Bill would finally be withdrawn early in November, just three weeks before Neil's arrest.

Another issue that took time that night involved the victimisation of union members at a factory where management was playing 'divide and rule' by continuing to back the Works Committee. There had been dismissals and canteen sit-in protests. The advice from the Branch meeting was that the union reps should not lose confidence and to 'work hard as the work of the Committee is very hard and at the end they will progress their demands'. It was a constant refrain. As the night drew on, there were yet other general items. Emma Mashinini, Secretary of the large Commercial, Catering and Allied Workers' Union of South Africa (CCAWUSA), had written to say that money had been received from overseas to build a Union Centre, and Neil was delegated to attend meetings to develop the idea. The next item was even shorter, with Neil reporting that Oscar Mpetha's trial was finally due to begin the following day. There was no discussion, but their best tribute was in getting on with the job in hand.

There were still transport matters to discuss, including reimbursing Neil for paying tax, number plate and repair costs of an old kombi donated by the firm H Jones. On the other hand, a fine that he had incurred while at a meeting with Epic Oil workers should be paid 'from his pocket as it was his fault'. However, the traffic department had damaged one of the kombi's wheels while immobilising the vehicle. Who should pay for that? Neil requested that, if the traffic department refused to reimburse them, the money should be taken from the union's transport fund. The matter was proposed, seconded and agreed.

One of the final issues was about a 'training school' on economics that Neil had attended in Cape Town. A similar school was to be started in Johannesburg at the end of the month. When the meeting finally closed, it was 10pm and everyone still had to get home. I imagine Neil driving into Tembisa, taking as many passengers as the kombi would hold, including the young Israel Mogoatlhe from Fatti's & Moni's. After making his final drop-off, Neil would drive back home on his own. As Israel observed, Neil was quite unlike most white people.

The Branch Report to the National Executive Council, which was due to meet at the end of March, revealed the steady progress made over the past year, condensed into two typewritten A4 pages. Growing subscriptions meant that the union could now afford to run their own transport and increase the secretaries' wages. A brief update on different factories showed how the union was slowly gaining strength in some while reaching new workers in others. Another item outlined progress in trying to scrap the management-controlled Sick-Pay Fund and work instead according to rules laid down in the union's agreement with each factory. 'Once this is accomplished it should be possible to establish a Union Medical Fund in the Transvaal with a Union Doctor.'[95]

A further item on the national pension funds issue indicated widespread local dissatisfaction and differing management responses, including the agreement of Fatti's & Moni's management to allow workers to withdraw their funds. Finally, the National Executive was informed that, since the beginning of the year, the Johannesburg Branch had been working closely with SAAWU, sharing offices and helping them organise. SAAWU was now planning to rent offices on the East Rand that they, in turn, would share with Food and Canning. Although the report was signed off by Branch Secretary Connie, the language throughout was Neil's.

The idea of a Union Medical Fund was Neil's special baby. On 20 May, he wrote to Jan Theron at head office to explain that members at three factories – LKB, All Gold and Irvin & Johnson – had decided that they wanted to pay their money 'to the Union so that we can start a Union Medical Fund with a Union doctor and clinics'. The technicalities and way forward still had to be worked out and 'we have no clear mandate to implement one particular type of Medical scheme, although the workers are unanimously in favour of some sort of Medical Scheme'.[96] So, his broad vision, sidelined within the IAS, had finally been presented to workers themselves and they had approved. Neil had been tasked with making it happen.

These strides within the Branch should also be seen against the backdrop of rising mass militancy. In March, the leaking of the new Labour Relations Bill provoked an outcry from across the spectrum of unions. Promising reforms, the Bill set out to tighten control over government-registered unions, while stating that unregistered unions would have to face the same political restraints as registered ones. It was, in Steven Friedman's words, a 'Velvet fist, iron glove'.[97] While the Bill must have provoked talk and debate with members, the minutes and reports show Neil systematically focusing on day-to-day building of democratic union structures and accountability. How best to harness the growing anger of workers would nevertheless have been at the heart of any discussions with trusted comrades like Gavin and Sipho.

*   *   *

Neil's outwardly calm exterior required considerable inner resources. His SAAWU connection had heightened security police attention, and there was always the possibility that the military police might knock on the door. When Jill rang to pass on family news and ask how he was, Neil would simply say that he was fine but very busy with meetings.

To Liz, with whom he continued to share the house in Fox Street, it seemed that personal time was all but squeezed out now. They had been together again since December 1979, but by the early months of 1981, she found him withdrawing into himself, increasingly shutting her out. She was Neil's connection with his past, and the person to whom he had spoken most intimately about his family. She had witnessed his transformation from the medical student who had sought isolation and read Nietzsche on the mountain to the practical unionist who saw workers as the engine for change. She had shared his vision and joined him in Johannesburg, yet was excluded from his innermost circle. The 'need to know' principle and secrecy was eroding their relationship. How do you retain normal relations with a partner in an abnormal society with a constant need for masks?

In recalling that fraught period, Liz opened up an area mostly untouched by my other interviewees, raising questions about the psychological effects of living under constant surveillance and secrecy. Whatever the dynamics of this relationship between two young people still in their twenties, the pressures were immense. For Liz, since their student days, Neil had always had a tendency to cut himself off from other people, and 'if things got tough to go very, very introspective'. She had seen his earlier 'political opening up' help enormously in taking him out of himself and giving him an external focus:

> When I met him ... he was totally, totally internally focused ... He was a
> classical outsider, and a very intense outsider. So when he moved into the
> sort of Crown Mines environment, and more into the union environment,
> it was a great personal growth. But he didn't lose that old stuff and ... prior

to the detentions he was personally extremely stressed. He had started cutting himself off from people, quite dramatically again. [By the time we were detained] he'd had six months of being followed by security police. I got followed every time I left home. He got followed by five cars everywhere he went, and when he talked to friends about it, the people who were less aware of what was going on didn't believe it. I remember one night, friends of ours came to visit, and when they got followed home, they freaked out and never visited us again.

This private withdrawal, experienced by Liz in their relationship, contrasted starkly with Neil's increasingly open political role, as mounting numbers of unionists across the country pushed their activity to a new level of militancy. The final six months of intensive surveillance to which Liz refers date back to the anti-Republic Day demonstrations in May and the surge of protests against a month of official celebrations marking the twentieth anniversary of South Africa's exit from the Commonwealth in 1961. The buoyant civil campaign involved over 50 organisations, including churches, universities, unions and political groups.[98] At the same time, there was a swell in armed attacks, with ten in May alone, making it appear as if there was prior coordination between ANC guerrillas and internal political dissent. While accounts like those of Mac Maharaj now reveal that this was far from the truth,[99] contemporary South African media and political analysts alarmed the white public. With most of the white population ready to believe that every leaflet bomb, act of sabotage, boycott and public demonstration was part of a unified 'total onslaught' directed by the underground ANC, the security police geared themselves up to uncover the links behind a mass conspiracy.

CHAPTER 20

The Anti-Republic Day Campaign, and two heady weeks

We are active and not half-active, both militarily and politically. We have launched successful campaigns within the country. The most recent one was the anti-Republic May [sic] struggles when the apartheid regime wanted to demonstrate that it has succeeded over the past 20 years to unite the people of South Africa behind its reactionary programme. We said no. South Africa is not united at all; any celebrations will be celebrations of our oppression, our exploitation, our humiliation. We called on the people to reject this insult and they responded by not only boycotting the festivities, but by going still further. They burned the so-called Republican flag, and defiantly hoisted the ANC's national flag.

Oliver Tambo, ANC President,
interviewed in New York, September 1981[100]

WHAT DID NEIL'S POLICE FILE CONTAIN BEFORE THE ANTI-Republic Day campaign, and what had first triggered the security police to open a file on him? Perhaps he had first come onto their radar in Cape Town, detected as a romantic rebel. Or had someone reported his political discussions as an intern in Umtata? Or was he first spotted with Gavin ... or Sipho? Certainly a white doctor working as an unpaid organiser of black workers, especially in a union with a history like Food and Canning's, had raised their suspicions. But was some fellow student, doctor, unionist ... also a surreptitious informer?

In August 2008, I applied with Jill, under the Promotion of Access to Information Act, to see Neil's security police file.[101] I had read what Terry Bell, with Dumisa Ntsebeza, had written about the shredding and burning of some 44 metric tonnes of records by the apartheid intelligence services before the handover of power in 1994. With the state's incinerators unable to cope, private companies, like steel manufacturer Iscor, had been enlisted to loan their furnaces: 'Into these flames disappeared the last echoes of the voices of thousands of victims. It was a paper Auschwitz, an attempt to eradicate all evidence of the nightmare memories of the tortured and the living dead ...'[102] Rationally, I knew that it would have been cleaned up. Even so, I was curious to see what we would find.

Our major surprise came up front. We couldn't have Neil's papers straight away because they contained material still classified as 'confidential'. In a Kafkaesque twist, we were informed that for his file to be 'declassified', it would have to be submitted to each department (Police, National Intelligence, Military Intelligence, etc) that had been involved in the original classification. Naively, we had assumed that all security files would have been automatically made available to the interested parties, as had happened in East Germany with the files of the Stasi. My first response was both anger and bemusement. In whose interest was it to keep files confidential until each had been scrutinised?

After seven months of repeated prodding by the coordinator of the Freedom of Information Programme at the South African History Archives, Neil's file was finally released and couriered to me in England. I looked for the earliest entry. It was a typed official letter, stamped 'DECLASSIFIED' twice, at top and bottom. Dated 8 December 1981, it was addressed to 'Die Kommissaris van die Suid-Afrikaanse Polisie' ... when Neil was already in detention. All names of people and places had been covered up or blacked out. There was nothing earlier.

In the months prior to the anti-Republic Day protests, I can only imagine that Neil's file was already beginning to grow fatter on sightings at meetings attended by others with expanding files. Thozamile Gqweta, Sisa Njikelana and Barbara Hogan were surely subjects of grubby handwritten notes, later typed up in some anonymous security police office in John Vorster Square, with carbon copies in duplicate or triplicate for cross-referencing. By 1981, those 'confidential' cabinets were engorged with files on unions and unionists.

Since the previous October, SAAWU workers had been carrying out a series of stoppages at the Wilson Rowntree factory in East London. As well as protesting about workplace issues, they were furious at the Ciskei police for working hand-in-glove with employers in detaining leaders like Thozamile and Sisa. But when workers struck again in February 1981, the Wilson Rowntree management dug in their heels, firing over 500. SAAWU officials immediately called for a national consumer boycott, with an international appeal to anti-apartheid supporters to boycott sweets made by the British parent company, Rowntree Mackintosh. Neil was asked to chair the first boycott meeting in Johannesburg at Food and Canning's offices, where a boycott committee was set up. Although he didn't have time to attend most of the meetings, people would bring the money collected for the strike fund for Neil to send to East London. As with the Fatti's & Moni's campaign, Neil's involvement once again brought him into working contact with Barbara Hogan.

While Barbara remained a friend of Liz, Neil had kept his relationship with her, as much as possible, limited to work. Barbara liked Neil, finding him 'very soft-spoken' and gentle despite striking her as sometimes 'a little bit rigid politically' in 'a western Cape tradition of being very pure'. However, as he worked with Gavin, she felt that element soften. She was very aware that Neil 'didn't want to be too closely connected', and recalls him saying to her, 'I cannot afford to be tangibly linked to the ANC because, if that is uncovered, the trade union will be smashed. It's a banned organisation.' Then he added, 'I fully support what you people are doing'.

Barbara appreciated Neil's reasons for keeping his distance. Her memories reflect his political caution. But there was also something else at work. Sisa Njikelana's recollections of Neil's enthusiasm and fervour reflect a very different dynamic in their newly established relationship. His comments seem to illustrate Liz's perception that, by this stage, Neil had moved beyond the white left. It was, Liz says, 'a fairly privileged position to get that far into an organisation that you no longer really feel like a member of the white left and that was part of Neil's alienation from the white left. Neil's peer group, in fact, was the union people, so he would relate much better to Israel than to Dave Dison.'

Or to Sisa than to Barbara. This was also a relationship between two male comrades, one white and one black, both graduates. While Neil would have readily shared any knowledge and skills with his slightly younger comrade, Sisa had access, as a young black man, to a further university of life, and Neil was equally eager to learn from him.

When Sisa made his second visit to Johannesburg to work for a couple of weeks on SAAWU's Wilson Rowntree boycott campaign, it was mid-May, with anti-Republic Day activities in full swing. He stayed at the Fox Street house with Liz and Neil, with Neil 'pulling' him immediately into a schedule of meetings that was both exhausting and exhilarating. On his previous visit, Sisa had been struck by how Neil would snatch just an hour's rest after his night at the hospital before starting work at the union. In May, however, everything was yet more intense:

> That kind of dedication began to strike me ... Here is this white... he didn't even check if it was OK with me, he just arranged meetings on Saturdays, after hours. He introduced me to all sorts of underground operatives – Gavin Andersson, Sipho Kubeka ... You know, that bloody communist, he worked a string of meetings for me for two weeks with Special Branch monitoring me. We used to joke. 'Ja, you bring me to Jo'burg and you set me up!' He used to laugh, soft laugh. He was so excited that two weeks. 'Sisa we must go and talk somewhere.'

In addition to the 'quiet meetings' with people like Gavin and Sipho, this was also his introduction to Marxist literature. Neil told Sisa that he had finished reading Volume One of *Capital*, but whenever Sisa began reading the book, he got bored. There was little time anyway in those two weeks. He recalls how he would 'Wake up in the morning, eat and rush, there's a meeting of boycott supporters somewhere, he [Neil] would drop me there, come and pick me up, leave me in the office. I was addressing a meeting in the evening, he'd rush me over there and come back.' Speaking some 14 years after those events, Sisa added that, although it was only recently that he had begun reading *Capital*, Neil was one of the people who had reinforced his commitment to Marxism. While retrospectively referring to Gavin and Sipho as 'underground operatives', at the time, 'uNeil ... never told you anything about his underground activity, never, niks. I didn't know if he was linked to the ANC or the Communist Party.' What he did know was that Neil was a totally committed comrade. The excitement around the anti-Republic Day protests buoyed them up. Although Sisa knew that they were under close police scrutiny, he believed that he could always identify 'something funny', and so they would not be intimidated.

At the end of May, as throngs of white apartheid supporters gathered near Pretoria around the Voortrekker Monument, Sisa addressed a large crowd at Johannesburg's Selborne Hall, alongside Joe Mavi from the Black Municipal Workers' Union, and Reavell Nkondo from the South African National Students' Congress. Joe Mavi, who had led the strike of some 10 000 city workers the previous year, had just emerged from jail. Initial charges of sabotage had been replaced by lesser charges of riotous assembly, and following his acquittal he had returned to the helm. An extract from a speech made by Nkondo reflects the level of anger and open defiance:

> For 350 years, the majority of the people of South Africa have been suffering
> from the ravages of colonialism, of imperialism, and from capitalist exploi
> tation. And now they want us to celebrate! Those who will be celebrating
> the twentieth anniversary of the Republic will be celebrating the massacres
> at Sharpeville. They will be celebrating the death of the children in 1976.
> On the eve of the so-called celebrations, we have roadblocks all over. We
> ask ourselves why – because freedom is knocking at our doors. Amandla!
> [Power!]
> CROWD: *Ngawethu!* [To the People!]
> REAVELL NKONDO: *Mayibuye!* [Come Back!]
> CROWD: *IAFRIKA!* [Africa!][103]

When a policeman tried to disrupt the meeting by suddenly jumping onto the stage to announce a bomb threat, the crowd, including Neil, ignored the warning. They assumed it was a hoax. It was.

Sisa's two 'rich and intense' weeks came to an abrupt end the day after the final protest meeting. Barbara Hogan had come round for supper at Liz and Neil's house in Fox Street to speak with Sisa. Her interest went beyond the Wilson Rowntree boycott campaign. Barbara, who had studied unemployment for her Master's degree, had received 'an official instruction' from her ANC forward area in Botswana to 'look towards setting up an unemployed workers' union'. Sisa could tell her of SAAWU's recent experience of trying to set up this kind of union in the eastern Cape, where thousands had been fired during the recent wave of strikes. The aim was to limit the damage of strike-breakers while building community organisation. However, with the jobless having nothing with which to bargain, let alone money for subscriptions, it was an uphill struggle.

They had been talking with the radio on, to upset police bugs, when they were interrupted by a loud knocking. Liz went to open the front door. Sisa recalls her words, 'Sisa, the police have come to fetch you'. One of the Special Branch men was Lieutenant Steven Whitehead. He probably already regarded all four in the house as his personal quarry. Barbara held Sisa, wishing him good luck. It was a strong comradely hug under the eyes of their preening future interrogator. Sisa had to control his fear. Had he been detained in East London, he would have felt psychologically within his own base. Here, in Johannesburg, he was 'shit scared'. At John Vorster Square, however, he found that he was not alone. The police had come knocking at the doors of Joe Mavi and Reavell Nkondo as well.

For Sisa, arrest was a hazard of political unionism. But Neil had under-taken not to jeopardise AFCWU's work and to walk the careful path proposed by Gavin of 'reformist face, revolutionary practice'. What had happened to that 'reformist face' during the anti-Republic Day campaign? When I posed the question to Gavin, he told me not only about Neil's rising excitement with this new wave of mass mobilisation, but how Neil was exhibiting a new con-fidence. When he had started at AFCWU, Neil had seen Jan Theron as almost an 'infallible guru'. But by now he not only had experience of organising on the factory floor and in the townships, he was also attuned to what was hap-pening well beyond his own union. To Gavin, Neil was now 'much more his own person, free to follow his own thinking, conditioned only by his vibrant everyday political interactions'.

In affirming Neil's political maturation, Gavin rejected any notion that Neil had let down his guard around the anti-Republic Day demonstrations. The excitement that he had experienced was completely in tune with that of mo-bilised and mobilising workers. Gavin still vividly remembers bumping into Sisa and Neil at the time of the Wilson Rowntree campaign, in Newtown, opposite the Market Theatre. They were eating chicken and, although a vege-tarian, Gavin thought it looked good just by the way they were relishing it:

'Neil was certainly a leader in his own right at this stage, and we met as three comrades happy to see each other and with full trust between us.'

Thus, to Gavin, Neil was by now the confident comrade and union leader, while to Liz he was the partner who was increasingly withdrawn and 'personally extremely stressed'. Perhaps both were true.

CHAPTER 21

Daily reality, 'discipline' and a relationship cracks

T HE EVERYDAY WORK OF THE UNION RETURNED NEIL TO A STEADY routine after the stirring events of May 1981. Yet Sisa's arrest suggested the distinct possibility that he too could be pulled in for questioning at any time. Were he to be arrested, he could defend all his union activity as legal. His vulnerability would lie in relation to Gavin and Sipho, and to what Sisa described as the 'quiet meetings'. It would lie in what he knew.

While ANC President Oliver Tambo, in addressing the world, suggested that all the mobilisation had been in response to the ANC's call and a planned convergence of military and political activity, Gavin's experience of working with the Botswana forward area would suggest a more haphazard reality.[104] Immediately following the success of the anti-Republic Day demonstrations, Gavin received instructions that were so out of tune with conditions of union work inside the country that he felt himself in a vice. His well-established manner of working was to consult quietly with key comrades in different cells before feeding back to Botswana. When he received an instruction to put out a call for a general strike around 16 June, he solicited opinion from trusted comrades, consulting first with Sipho and Neil. Sipho had then taken the proposal 'along his chains', and Gavin along his. A resounding 'No!' came from both. Some had rejected the idea angrily, including Neil. Workers were not yet ready for this kind of action, and it would simply risk exposing their coalescing network of cells. Gavin relayed this through his DLB, but 'got a message back saying, "Nevertheless, do it, and here's 2 000 bucks"'. The money was for pamphlets.

The external movement's insistence presented Gavin with an acute dilemma. Knowing that his closest and most trusted comrades rejected the proposal as foolhardy, it would be embarrassing to abuse his position of trust in calling what would be regarded as an 'illegitimate general strike': 'What to do? How could I honour each of them, be a disciplined cadre, when two poles of organisation that needed to come together were at such different positions about a course of action?' In the end, he produced the pamphlets by himself, using the same typewriter on which he had written previous pamphlets over the years and which he stored safely away from his home. Having prepared the stencils, he approached Alan Fine, an organiser with the National Union of Distributive Workers, saying that he needed access to Roneo machines for 'a movement printing job'. Alan agreed to leave the union's printing unit open one night so Gavin could enter clandestinely. After hours of churning out the pamphlets, Gavin cleaned up carefully to leave no trace when the office opened. The following night, by himself, he left pamphlets next to factories, bus stops and rail stations in Tembisa, Alexandra and Daveyton, to be found in the morning by workers. Cold, tired and hungry, he worked until first light, doing something that he didn't believe in, without the support of his comrades, simply to demonstrate their 'internal' discipline. He persuaded himself that maybe the external movement knew something that he and his comrades did not. Perhaps, around the country, others were doing the same thing and this was indeed going to be a 'spark' for mass action.

It wasn't, and there was no mass action. Afterwards, Gavin reassured himself that those who were pulled in for questioning by the Special Branch honestly didn't know anything and so, he hoped, couldn't get into trouble. The experience pointed to a complete difference in culture between the external and internal organisation. He and his comrades had agreed in principle that the 'two poles' of the organisation needed to come together, yet the experience illustrated the precise question that Neil and others had raised. How could one combine commitment to being accountable within the democratic political structures that they were building inside the country, and which they

saw as 'building the ANC', with being answerable to ANC structures and a hierarchy outside the country?

Gavin admits to nearly cracking under the psychological pressure. He
found a way out by carrying out the futile task alone in order to demonstrate
'internal discipline and loyalty' and show that he was a 'disciplined cadre'.
Indeed, it was probably the 'discipline' in keeping a lid on his emotions that
saw him through. Gavin also recognised that a desire for discipline was part
of Neil's make-up. However, he strongly objected when someone described
Neil disparagingly as 'a foot soldier'. How could anyone misread 'such a gentle, intelligent person with such a good sense of humour'? Nevertheless, Gavin
acknowledged that 'Neil had something of that, of really wanting to be part
of disciplined organisation … was very systematic in his questioning … then
once he arrived at decisions, quite dogged, he maintained them'.

As pressure mounted, with the security police looking for ANC links, Neil's
discipline helped to sustain him. Liz didn't know whether Neil was an ANC
operative, although she suspected that he probably wasn't because it would
have endangered his union work. Living with him, she experienced not only
the stress of surveillance but also the pain of his increasing withdrawal into
himself. She felt the effect not only on their relationship but also with friends.
She didn't think that they were 'particularly paranoid', but they endured very
intensive attention from the security police, while Neil had been dodging the
military police for years. Amazingly, the two forces never put their information together. But Liz sensed that Neil had 'cornered himself':

> To the outside world, he was a committed unionist, but on a personal level
> he was heading for a brick wall. He was certainly going down a cul-de-sac,
> and not really dealing with it, and six months before he was detained, it
> had gotten to the stage where it was really serious. He'd cut himself off from
> nearly everybody, to the point where I couldn't deal with it because … part
> of his cutting himself off was cutting me off.

Neil no longer wanted to visit friends nor wanted them coming around. To Liz,
this was something more than hunkering down as surveillance intensified. He
was becoming 'very critical of people', including her friends. As she saw Neil
'heading for a brick wall', and not prepared to talk about what was happening,
their compartmentalised relationship was strained to breaking point.

CHAPTER 22

Unions on the move

THE GOVERNMENT'S LABOUR RELATIONS BILL CONTINUED TO cause a storm of protest. Employers feared that it was inciting rather than dampening worker militancy, so much so that the Federated Chamber of Industries called for it to be withdrawn. Even some emerging FOSATU unions that shunned politics were talking about deregistering from the official system. The government's entire labour plan would then be in chaos.

On 23 June, Neil, Connie and Monica wrote to Jan. What did the union think about Food and Canning deregistering? Until now, their unregistered African branch had effectively functioned as one, with its registered parent body that served Coloured workers. While registration had helped the union maintain stability in the past, times were now changing 'with the upsurge of worker organisation and militancy':

> We therefore feel that the time may be ripe for Food and Canning Union
> to deregister, and for workers in the canning factories to rely on their own
> organization and strength in the factories to press for better conditions …
> but we are anxious not to raise the question in the factories, only to find that
> the mainstream of the Union is heading in another direction.[105]

The underlining was surely Neil's, reflecting his abiding concern for discussion and discipline.

By August, the government showed signs of partly backing down on the Labour Relations Bill. The concessions included a watering-down of the ban on political links. It was the first time that black workers had brought about a shift in legislation.[106] Although unregistered unions would continue to suffer restrictions, there was no real incentive to register since registration didn't oblige an employer to deal with a union. The divisive issue had begun to wither away. From Food and Canning's point of view, their friends were those unions, whether registered or unregistered, who rejected the present laws, unlike the 'dummy' unions that simply toed the government line. Furthermore, with overseas anti-apartheid movements ready to mount consumer boycotts and import bans, the government did not have a totally free hand. Unionists who understood the potential economic power of workers to effect change knew that they must put bitter differences aside and work towards greater unity. It was vital to meet and agree a joint strategy.

With Food and Canning undertaking one of the leading roles in setting up the first combined meeting, Neil threw himself into the task. On 8 August, in the middle of winter, over a hundred unionists from nearly 30 unions travelled from near and far to Langa, on the outskirts of Cape Town, to explore union unity. Newspapers wrote of a 'trade union summit'. Neil drove from Johannesburg with a car full of delegates, including 22-year-old Sydney Mufamadi of the General and Allied Workers' Union (GAWU). Sydney was also a member of Gavin's and Sipho's network and, although Neil would not have known, a member of the ANC who had also recently joined the South African Communist Party.[107] Jan Theron remembers them all arriving at his little cottage, where they slept on the floor, which was 'how things were done in those times'.

Five resolutions taken at Langa reflected the new spirit. Back in Johannesburg, Neil reported these to his Branch Executive. First, the unions rejected the present system of registration. Second, unions should withdraw from any industrial councils. Third, they resolved to defy the strike laws. Fourth, they rejected the homeland system and the Ciskei's harassment of unions, and would send delegations to see homeland leader Lennox Sebe. Finally, all unions would form 'solidarity committees' in order to implement the above decisions.[108]

The resolutions, especially the fourth, indicated the considerable shift for FOSATU in committing itself to working alongside unions with the political history of Food and Canning and SAAWU. With the Ciskei about to become 'independent' in December, it was recognised that this was an issue for all black workers, not simply for SAAWU. The ultimate apartheid plan was that troublesome workers anywhere in the country could have their South African citizenship removed and be 'deported' as 'foreigners' to their designated Bantustan. The Langa summit was a historic coming-together of independent, registered and unregistered, black and non-racial unions. If initially the solidarity was more in rhetoric than reality, within a few years it would be claimed as the first step on the road to the formation of a powerful national coalition, the Congress of South African Trade Unions (COSATU).

Nevertheless, old tensions and suspicions remained. 'Trade Unions today have become fashionable', Jan Theron would tell his union's delegates at their annual conference the following month. There were probably some wry smiles before he went on to say that, despite the impression of strength, 'the Unions are themselves weak, and between the Unions there is little genuine solidarity'.[109] Following the Langa summit, Jan asked Neil to arrange the setting-up of a Transvaal solidarity committee. To initiate this, Neil invited a number of unions, including those from FOSATU, to the AFCWU office, but attendance was poor. It would be November before FOSATU would call a further meeting of the solidarity committee. In the meantime, Neil would continue his own quiet discussions with unionists of opposite persuasions. It was this calm persistence that began to earn him respect from some of the unionists who would previously have dismissed him as an idealistic 'populist'.

While the tone of the Branch's August newsletter, following Langa, reflected this quality of reason and restraint, the growing militancy among workers was unmistakable. A total work stoppage at LKB had led management to agree minimum wages of R42.50, an amount higher than the minimum laid down in the government's Conciliation Board Agreement. At Irvin & Johnson (Benrose), the newsletter detailed another 'great victory' of achieving a higher-than-the-minimum settlement after 'a few meetings and lots of arguments'. At All Gold, where an abusive white foreman had been firing workers and provoked a standoff, the union had got management to take back all the workers and to give the foreman a final warning. The lesson was drawn out for the readers of the newsletter: 'A DISMISSAL TO ONE IS A DISMISSAL

TO ALL'. If Oscar Mpetha received just some of this news in his prison cell, he would have been happy at how his training in steady, solid organisation had taken root.

There was both positive and negative news about pension refunds. Some factories had returned the workers' money. However, the government was now talking of a law to make pension deductions compulsory:

> So the struggle is not over and we must be prepared for more problems over pensions. Our attitude is that the workers pay taxes, and therefore the Government should provide good State Old age [sic] pensions to all races. The workers should not have to pay for their own pensions. To win this we will have to unite with all the workers throughout South African [sic] before the Government listens to our demand.[110]

A year or two earlier, workers might have dismissed such talk as pie in the sky. But seeing management agreeing to pay even a few rands above the minimum wage gave hope that more doors could be prised open. For the first time the Transvaal Branch Newsletter ends with 'AMANDLA NGAWETHU!' Neil had reason to feel that unions were on the move.

CHAPTER 23

Conscription?

A T HEAD OFFICE, JAN WAS AWARE THAT NEIL WAS BEING
followed. The Special Branch made no attempt at concealment. For
his part, Neil was invigorated by the heightened political activity
and the first steps towards union unity. 'I think he was both excited and ap-
prehensive, as we all were', recalls Jan Theron. Nevertheless, it puzzled Jan
that the security police were picking on Neil. Two years earlier Neil had been,
in Jan's eyes, very much an outsider and 'very impressionable'. Although Neil
was a few years younger, they shared the experience of having dominant fathers from whose influence they had extracted themselves. Jan saw Neil, to
some extent, use him as a model. He noticed how Neil acquired the same kind
of tweed jacket, like adopting 'the same uniform, that sort of thing, nothing
sort of overt'. Over a couple of years, Jan witnessed Neil grow into a confident
union organiser who completely shared the union's mission of building solidly the kind of 'proper organisation' that distinguished what they were doing
from some of the ostensibly more 'political unions' that were, in Jan's view,
'basically just here today, gone tomorrow'.

The anti-Republic Day campaign had also stressed unity and solidarity. After many years, it was 'the first real articulation of a kind of ANC-
type politics' and Jan knew that any association between unions and such

activity was highly suspect. So was this why the security police were target-
ing Neil? However, he dismissed the possibility of Neil being involved in
underground work. It would have compromised the union, and that was
something Neil would surely not have risked. Moreover, where was the time
for underground activity? Union work was enormously time-consuming.
It involved hanging around outside factories, attending meetings at night,
and frequently taking people home afterwards. In addition, Neil spent two
nights every week at the hospital. Jan was convinced that Neil would simply
not have had the time.

Jan was aware of Neil evading his army call-up and had advised him that,
when the army ultimately caught up with him, he would have to go. If he
continued to resist, it would cause unnecessary controversy for the union.
Despite their respect for Jan, Gavin and Sipho counselled the very opposite.
They put the position strongly. 'Precisely because you're a young white organiser of Food and Canning, you cannot go to the army,' they told him. Neil
could dodge the military police for as long as possible, but when they caught
up with him there were only two alternatives: he could go to jail as a conscien-
tious objector, or he could leave the country, a choice that Sipho and Gavin
hoped he wouldn't make. In Gavin's words, 'But the one option that isn't there,
as someone holding your beliefs and working in the union, is to go to the
army'.

Neil had already dodged for years. That option was running out. The
'brick wall', foreseen by Liz, stood ahead. That the matter was on his mind is
evident in a conversation recalled by Sisa that took place in September 1981.
Sisa was once again out of prison. He reports Neil as saying, 'Comrade, once
again the Defence Force has approached me for conscription and, as a communist, I'm going to refuse. Some people say I should leave the country. As
a communist, I'm not going to run away ... on religious grounds. What do
you think?' Sisa replied, 'No man, make an excuse ... Take the soft option
... because your life shouldn't be in detention. It should be outside, working
with the people.' But Neil was adamant. 'Jesiss, this comrade is dedicated!'
thought Sisa. 'To an extent, I think he was also skidding towards leaving the
country. It was a short conversation, consulting me. He was worried. Who
wouldn't be?'

Neil may not, in fact, have received his call-up papers. He might, according
to Gavin, have been using the issue to let Sisa know 'where he stood politically'

and that he had clearly ruled out accepting conscription. I asked Gavin, could he imagine Neil declaring forthrightly, 'As a communist …'?

> I think Neil could have used the word. He was a radical, and would be impatient with a softer 'socialist' descriptor. And at times we tended to define ourselves as communists outside the SACP, ie not Stalinists, but more in the vein of Gramscian communists. We read *Capital* as just one of the many Marxist texts and were schooled in most of the 'classics' – Marx, Engels, Lenin, Luxemburg, Gramsci etc through to more recent writers.

Sisa, it seems, had become privy to inner political thoughts that Neil did not share with most of his union comrades. Neil, who had grown so much through his own contact with 'mentors', in books and in life, was himself now a mentor to younger comrades, although he was the kind of teacher who remains the eternal learner, excited by the exchange of ideas. He knew the danger of declaring himself 'a communist'. But recognising a kindred spirit in Sisa, I suspect that he felt impelled to communicate his understanding of an ideology that broke both racial and class barriers.

In the documentary film *Passing the Message*, it is possible to catch a glimpse of Neil that same September at the union's forty-first annual conference.[111] He had again driven down to Cape Town, this time with a delegation of eight workers. Neil and Jan appear to be the only white people in a large upstairs room, filled with delegates, in the Ray Alexander Union Centre in Paarl. A banner, behind the speakers' tables, proclaims the union's motto, 'AN INJURY TO ONE IS AN INJURY TO ALL'. On the wall is a small picture of their jailed comrade, Oscar Mpetha. The delegates open the conference with raised fists and sombre voices, singing 'Nkosi Sikelel' iAfrika'. As the legendary 80-year-old Dora Tamana speaks to the assembly, the camera pans across the room. Neil is there, bearded and wearing his tweed jacket, his head tilted, listening intently to the tiny woman in a simple knitted cap. Although she is nearly blind behind her dark glasses, her voice still retains the power of a lifetime of hardship and activism. Despite bannings and imprisonment, Aunt Dora has organised women throughout her adult life. She addresses the women in the room directly in isiXhosa. Neil's brow is furrowed, concentrating on the subsequent Afrikaans translation. Her message is clearly also for the men:

We must take action today for these are hard times. It's time the women took off their long skirts and dressed like Chinese women. You must wear trousers just like men. You must become men ... Times are bad. The workers are slaves. It's high time again we fought and if the women don't, there'll be no fight. Women unite!

The camera glances over Neil for a second time, the angle of his head suggesting that he is busy taking notes. Jan is explaining why the union cannot avoid a wider political struggle. His tone is measured, but his hands are impassioned:

We as a Trade Union are forced to confront the government's policy because the government's policy confronts us. The Ciskei is, how shall I put it, the weakest link in the chain – the chain which the government call their Bantustan policy or independent 'homeland'. Its aim is to make people foreigners in their own country ...

The Annual Report of Food and Canning's conference on that weekend of 19-20 September 1981 contains a full record of Jan seamlessly interweaving information, explanation and exhortation, his manner totally different from the pompous white managers who control the members' factories. Both Jan and Neil offer a glimmer of hope that it is possible for white people to share the same space as equals. Moreover, there is a sense of belonging to a wider world, with Jan drawing on recent events in Europe: South African workers should be inspired by the spirit of Polish workers who have swept aside officially-run unions in favour of their own union, Solidarity, and are demanding a say in running their factories. They should elect their managers. They should elect their government. It is fighting talk.[112]

Also portrayed in the film is the aspect of communal theatre, one participant saying, 'There are all kinds of songs. Singing gives us strength. When we are singing we never look backwards. We only look ahead.' Clearing away chairs, sweeping the hall, bringing in mattresses on which to sleep, union members sing as they work, weaving between each other as in a dance. Before settling down, a prayer is offered for the night. Beyond its concern with the material welfare of members, the union offers a community and shared spirit through which they will overcome adversity.

The imagery in a marching song reflects the militancy, workers transformed into soldiers, at one with those who 'are marching in':

> *Let us go to work*
> *Working for Africa*
> *The soldiers are marching in*
> *Soldiers of Africa*

How could Neil possibly accept conscription when it would mean him fighting his worker comrades? That would be betrayal.

CHAPTER 24

Close Comrades

A FTER THE CONFERENCE, NEIL REMAINED WITH A FEW
delegates in Cape Town to attend some meetings. So he was not
in Johannesburg when Gavin had a strange intuition that provoked
him into a lightning clear-out of incriminating papers stored in the house
he shared with Joanne Yawitch and others. On the evening of Monday 21
September, Gavin had run a session at Wits in the office of Fink Haysom,
then a researcher in the Department of Applied Legal Studies. Gavin had
brought together a number of trade unionists. The group included Samson
Ndou, a messenger with Anglo American and president of GAWU, who had
already been detained a couple of times, and Sydney Mufamadi, also from
GAWU. There was also a relative newcomer, H Barnabas, a worker whom Neil
had introduced to SAAWU to run its Transvaal branch, now in an office in
Kempton Park shared with AFCWU. These three unionists held an openly
political stance but had little experience of strong shop-floor organisation.
Gavin offered ways of interlinking factory with township organisation in
order to strengthen both, while also looking at open and clandestine work.
After the meeting, he was due to stay with a friend in Yeoville when he felt
'some kind of premonition' that persuaded him to go home and clean up the
house. He did this literally, by washing dishes, sweeping and mopping, but

also by burning papers and moving a couple of books to an outside hiding place. His housemates left him to it and went to bed. Gavin, finishing at about 3am, went to sleep on the small stoep.

He must have been in a deep sleep when the Special Branch began banging on the front door about an hour and a half later:

> Without any conscious decision or indeed consciousness I charged down at them, grabbed the guy around the neck with one hand while the other grabbed his gun hand and only then woke up – to see a gun (from the man behind him) pointing at me. It was all very scary because they also had a big light shining on us, and it was like waking up in the middle of a bad dream. I obviously dropped my hands and backed off and they shouted at me – I was at a bit of a disadvantage anyway since I was naked. They went into the house and I retreated to my bed, where I got some clothes on and went inside.

Despite having one hand temporarily around the throat of a security policeman, Gavin wasn't arrested. It turned out that they had come to detain Joanne. In an attempt at solidarity, he picked up his guitar and started to play Bob Marley's 'Redemption Song'. An officer grabbed it, and asked who he was. When Gavin told them, the officer in charge immediately went onto his walkie-talkie radio: 'Ons het hier Gavin Andersson.' That's when they slapped on the handcuffs.

Both Gavin and Joanne were astonished that the security police seemed not to know where he was living. Joanne had been conscious of the increasing police scrutiny in August and September. She was a close friend of Barbara Hogan, who had got her involved in politics, including 'the boycotts, strike committees, Wilson Rowntree, this committee, that committee and the next committee'. Almost everybody she knew was 'involved', although she was happy to leave things vague and didn't probe:

> As time went on, I became aware that Gavin was involved in a whole set of politics and that Neil probably was too … I then also realised that Barbara and Gavin and people like Cedric [de Beer] and Auret [van Heerden] were also meeting. Basically, through 1980, '81, a kind of political leadership was getting consolidated. The security police were kind of interested in all of us.

Joanne was only 23 and, in her words, 'fairly junior'. This was to her advantage during interrogation, where she pretended naivety. While there was much that Joanne would not have known, she had recently learned that Barbara was an ANC operative, when Barbara approached her about recruitment. She was also privy to Barbara's heightened state of anxiety over August and into September, fearing that her cover had been blown. Joanne had offered to drive her friend to the border. But it was already too late. Instead, Barbara had unwittingly fallen headlong into a police trap that would pull in an entire web of comrades and colleagues behind her. The arrests on 22 September were only the beginning of a swathe of detentions over the following weeks and months of mainly, but by no means solely, white activists. To unravel the trap we have to step back in time.

Karl Edwards's report, entitled 'An Operational Analysis of the SCHOON NETWORK, August 1980', shows that the security police had kept Barbara in their sights as an ANC link since 1977, the year in which she became an operative. For three years she had worked, in her words, somewhat 'independently, autonomously'. When her communication link had been shifted in 1978 to the ANC's forward area in Botswana, she became concerned about the security risks, but hoped that her long-standing friendship with Jeanette Schoon would provide a cover were she to be questioned. She opened a special post-box address to receive communications from the Schoons and was given a postbox address in Botswana. Barbara's role was largely to feed information back and forth. It was also decided that she should register as a Master's student at Wits, setting up voluntary work related to unemployment that could help launch a union for the unemployed.

In January 1981, however, Barbara was moved from this loose communication system into a tighter relationship involving a biweekly dead letter box and a book code. She began sending regular coded letters that were picked up and passed on by a messenger whose identity she didn't know. This lasted until one night, after the anti-Republic Day campaign, when she received a message to go to her DLB, which was in a suburban garden. The courier from Botswana, who was waiting for her there, had found her envelope split open and advised that she leave the country immediately. On her way home, she felt sure that she was being followed by a number of Special Branch cars. People like Gavin and Sipho, who had operated semi-underground in the mid-1970s, and continued as banned activists, had trained themselves in elaborate procedures to check for and to lose a 'tail'. Part of their training was not to panic. Barbara, it seems, had received little if any such training and the pressure was now full-on.

With no time to organise an underground exit, she packed her bags, and was preparing to take her chances at the border when she spotted that the envelopes that she had been using were actually all defective. Perhaps she had not been intercepted after all. Nevertheless, the Special Branch cars remained parked in her road. She managed to make her way to Alan Fine (whose union premises had been used by Gavin for his late-night printing), and asked him to get an urgent message through to Botswana. Although she had written it with her book code, her predicament persisted when Alan received no reply. She felt trapped. She couldn't leave the country legally because she was being followed everywhere and was finding it difficult constantly to give them the slip. She now wasn't sure that she was being intercepted, but why was she being followed? What should she do? She was not to know that the Schoons happened to be away for a short while and the people receiving her messages couldn't decode them, hence the lack of replies. Unable to work out what was going on, Barbara's fears increased.

Karl Edwards's report on the Schoons shows that the security police had been on to Alan Fine from at least April 1978, intercepting DLB material both before and after Marius had been instructed by Mac Maharaj to separate out Alan's network from that run by Edwards and Williamson. With no response from Botswana, a panic-stricken Barbara turned to someone else whom she knew to be an ANC operative in the white left: Rob Adam.

Like Neil, Rob had gone to a prestigious private school and to university in Cape Town, where he had been the top honours student in Chemistry. He was the great-nephew of the second Chief Justice of the Union of South Africa, Sir James Rose-Innes. In 1979, during a two-year stint working in England, Rob had been recruited into the ANC by Ronnie Kasrils, committing himself to working for the movement's armed wing, Umkhonto we Sizwe (MK), before returning to South Africa the following year and finding work in Johannesburg. His contact was through DLBs – chiefly rubbish bins in various parks – and couriers, with a post-box address in Swaziland as emergency backup. Around the middle of 1981, he was asked, through a DLB communication, to meet someone. The man, who identified himself as 'Sipho', clearly had knowledge of ANC military camps as well as individual cadres in the frontline states. 'Sipho' subsequently introduced Rob to another man, with the nom de guerre of 'Themba', who was to assist Rob in reconnaissance work. A fluent Portuguese speaker, Themba had been trained in Angola and carried a Makarov pistol.

Aware of Rob's ANC connections, Barbara approached him as a friend. Could Rob could help her now, she asked, to get out of the country using the underground? Rob relayed this to 'Sipho', who soon came back to Rob. The instructions were for Barbara to stay put for the time being. However, she should urgently send a full report because 'Lusaka' (ie, leadership at ANC headquarters) was doing an evaluation of the security of the Botswana operation. Matters were so pressing that she should not hold things up by encoding the report.

With this deviation from strict procedure failing to set off alarm bells in either comrade, Barbara immediately set about typing a report. Entitled 'Problems Arising in Internal Political Work', the focus of her 15-page paper was the relationship between the internal and external wings of the ANC, as seen from her perspective as an operative inside the country. Barbara began by urging that it was time for reassessment in view of 'possible dangers ahead', while emphasising that any criticisms should not be misconstrued as coming from 'a dissident'. Her tone was that of someone reporting to the highest authority:

> Let me stress from the outset that I still remain committed to the ANC and
> that my purpose in raising these issues is to contribute towards the better
> efficiency and success of the movement. If I have to raise criticisms it will
> be because I see them as indicative of the problems which have to be solved
> and not because I am trying to point fingers at anyone. I am speaking as a
> comrade and not as a dissident.[113]

Three pages followed, in which Barbara outlined the wide range of her political work, mainly, although not entirely, within the white left. She ended this section with concerns that her Botswana link might have been infiltrated.[114] Barbara then separated the problems of communication into two periods. In the earlier period, from 1977, she had worked 'fairly independently of outside, relying for the bulk of my political guidance and activity on comrades loyal to the ANC inside SA'. In the second period, from the beginning of 1981, she had been put into a 'much tighter relationship with the forward area'. Nevertheless, she still felt that her role was 'unclear'. More conflicts and confusions had arisen, and since July she had felt very exposed.

While the report's tone was open and honest, it also conveyed the desperation of inexperience and isolation. She spelt out the difficulties of submitting lengthy documents in code. It took her a full day to encode a report of one foolscap page in length. Apart from the laborious process, she had to find a different safe place each week to do this, after retrieving a safe typewriter from another safe place. She had to plan carefully what to communicate and, at the same time, continue with her usual work schedule for the day. Afterwards she had to return the typewriter, secretly burn material, and deposit the message in a safe place before taking it to a DLB the following day. The latter activity required at least another three hours. The alternative of sending an uncoded document required her to request permission and wait a further two weeks for a reply.

In addition to these difficulties in producing a document for the forward area, she was troubled about how it was then transmitted, and to what extent its contents would 'remain confidential and free from enemy infiltration'. There were yet other difficulties, but the rub was that they were heading for trouble with a system in which directives were being issued from a forward area when there was such poor communication:

> Although I am formally in regular contact with the forward area, I still depend on comrades inside for my political growth and development, more so than on the forward area. In this sense I would be in a schizophrenic position if the forward area were to advocate a line of action for me that was different to those advised by my comrades inside. (This has already happened as regards the question of my leaving the country.) Other comrades have also experienced the problem of different political directives coming from different forward areas.

Gavin had revealed nothing to Barbara about finding himself in just such a 'schizophrenic position', but others clearly had. Although Barbara emphasised that she was speaking 'from the vantage point of the experience of one individual – myself', it sounded as if she was relaying concerns, indeed frustrations, felt by others too. Her opening assurances about not writing as a dissident suggest that she was aware this could be tricky territory. What if the report was interpreted as showing a lack of commitment in her and, through her, the white left? With so few white comrades in the ANC, was there a psychological dimension here of feeling the need to prove her bona fides and reassert loyalty to whoever was going to read this at ANC headquarters? There are a number of insertions in parenthesis that might suggest an unspoken, perhaps even unconscious, plea not to be misconstrued as an arrogant white person: 'Please note that it is only in retrospect that I am beginning to see what the problems were, so I am not "blaming" anyone.' In another instance:

> Please do not think that I am questioning the security of your operations, they may be water-tight. All I am saying is that I am ignorant & that igno- rance breeds insecurity. Obviously I would not want to know the finer de- tails of the operation, but a general understanding of the procedure would help things considerably in that it would give guide-lines as to how much information should be detailed ... If a system is going to work well then both sides *must* have full confidence in it ...

In conclusion, Barbara once again emphasised the limitations of her opinions by saying that 'I have tried to show you how I experience the situation, instead of saying that this [is] what the situation is in reality.'

Having written so frankly, Barbara must have hoped that the ANC would act immediately to help her find a way out of country and the crisis. Instead 'Sipho' contacted Rob to say that the High Command was very pleased with Barbara's report. However, they suspected that she might be heavily infiltrated. They needed to know the names of all the people who were working with her, ANC and others, to check if any were already under suspicion in Lusaka of working for the security police. Once again, Rob passed on that the informa- tion was required as fast as possible and should be sent uncoded. Once again, neither of the young activists stopped to question the credibility of the mes- sage, nor why Barbara was not immediately advised to go to ground while an exit out of the country was arranged.

This time, without spending hours to secure her 'safe' typewriter, Barbara sat down to write, by hand, a list of names. Dividing her contacts into three sections, at the top of the page she began with the heading, 'Close Comrades (as regards above & underground work).'[115] Gavin appeared among the top three, listed with Cedric de Beer and Auret van Heerden. A note alongside explained that they were her 'Primary Reference Group' and that all three knew that she was working under discipline. While Gavin and Auret were under discipline, Cedric wasn't but did work when requested. Fink Haysom and Alan Fine followed as 'Close Comrades', with notes alongside about the nature of the relationship.

Barbara's second group was a list of people entitled 'Advisory/Reference People (only above ground work)'. Neil headed this list, his name spelt as 'Niall Aggatt', followed by Liz Floyd and four others, with three from the Indian left, including Ismail Momoniat. Barbara noted that 'None of these people know that I am under discipline, nor am I aware of any of their positions as regards outside.' Her final group of six, entitled 'People who regard me as their consultant & whom I work with closely in that capacity (potential leadership)', included Joanne Yawitch. Eight names were marked with asterisks as people who had some idea that she was 'under discipline'. Barbara placed asterisks against each of the top five 'Close Comrades', as well as three of the 'potential leadership': Joanne, Barbara Klugman and Maurice Smithers.

On 22 September, a week or so after Rob handed Barbara's list to 'Sipho', the police descended on Barbara, Rob and the asterisked eight. They were arrested and detained under Section 22(1) of the General Law Amendment Act of 1966, permitting initial detention of 'suspected terrorists' for up to 14 days of interrogation. Barbara's 'Advisory/Reference People', including Neil and Liz, had no idea that they might be next.

A few days after his arrest, Rob Adam was in a car with security police who stopped at the petrol pumps inside the John Vorster Square complex. Standing among a group of black security policemen was 'Sipho':

> This was a very traumatic moment for me, but I did not let on to my guards that I had identified him. It was clear that they wanted to keep this information from me, because my interrogation was relatively light, compared to many other detainees. Their reasoning, I assume, was that if they had questioned me in greater depth it could have become clear to me that Sipho was a double agent, and they had enough to put me in jail anyhow …

During interrogation, Rob overheard a police conversation about 'Jeffrey' and saw a note signed 'Jeffrey' on a desk. The handwriting was that of 'Sipho'.

With the compiling of the 'Close Comrades' list a tragedy had been set in motion for which Barbara and Rob would each blame themselves. When the list's provenance became known, Barbara became a particular focus for anger. People asked how could she possibly have put such sensitive material to paper, and uncoded? After Barbara gave me a copy of the document, I must have sat for hours looking at her original list, replete with doodlings, markings and comments added by her interrogators. (For instance, an arrow arcs from 'Niall Aggatt' to a note, 'Spelling? I thought it was Neil'.) Words and phrases that she had crossed out suggest the haste, and the heat of the moment, in which it was written. However, it was only after I was put in touch with Rob Adam, who filled in more of the picture, that I began to understand a little more of how the devastating error of judgment had been made. This was not an impersonal DLB instruction that Rob had been asked to convey to Barbara. It had been conveyed by the man Rob knew as 'Sipho'.

From my own reading of events, I believe two elements would have contributed. Firstly, the words 'under discipline' carry a clue to the culture into which these young comrades were operating and had committed themselves. Their understanding was that not to respond to an instruction would be an act of indiscipline. When Gavin received the instruction from his forward area to call for a general strike – an instruction that didn't 'make any kind of sense' – he nevertheless felt pressure to prove that he was a 'disciplined cadre'. His ingenuity, however, saved him, and despite the risk he found a way of satisfying the directive.

Both Barbara and Rob, I believe, felt obliged to show 'discipline'. Furthermore, neither of them had the kind of mentoring and daily experience accrued by Gavin, and subsequently Neil, within the black trade union movement. Barbara had contact with black comrades through various campaigns, but neither she nor Rob had experienced the sustained mentoring of someone like Pindile. Nor did they have the depth of links with a range of black comrades that took Gavin and Neil 'beyond the white left', an observation made by Liz. The Special Branch counted on a young white man like Rob, and through him Barbara, to trust 'Sipho', a black 'freedom fighter' who had trained in the ANC camps. It was a cruel deception.

With 'Close Comrades', the security police were convinced that they had smashed open a door to the whole underground ANC political machinery. The investigation was headed by Major Arthur Benoni Cronwright, whom

Amnesty International later named as one of South Africa's 'Chief Torturers'.[116] Cronwright enjoyed advertising himself to detainees as a relative of Hitler. Although most of his victims were black, he had pursued a special vendetta against the white left.[117] In 1979, he gave a rare hour-long interview to June Goodwin of the *Christian Science Monitor* on the ninth floor of John Vorster Square, for which she first had to undergo a thorough body search. Goodwin noted the synthetic Kelly-green suit and slick black hair with matching moustache of her brusque interviewee, who openly described himself as 'a born-again Christian' whose task was to destroy Satan by force. He assured her that the Bible said he could kill.[118] Even the head of the security police, General Johan Coetzee, to whom Cronwright was responsible, would later admit to George Bizos that the major was 'a madman'.[119] By September 1982, Barbara, and those pulled in with her, were in the hands of someone she realised was 'a raving lunatic', completely obsessed that this time his officers were going to get 'to the Satanic heart of this white left'.

CHAPTER 25

John Vorster Square

COMMISSIONER STREET RUNS STRAIGHT AS A RULER, FOR FOUR kilometres from east to west, until the road shifts at a slight angle to become Main Reef Road, heading southwest, under the M1 highway, out to Langlaagte and Crown Mines. Travelling down Commissioner Street from the east, its far western end appears to be blocked by a massive building straddling the road. You can easily count at least nine floors of windows letting through light from the other side. The glass-paned corridors connect two dark sections of the building, which each soar higher. Besides the horizontal concrete strips that mark each floor, a narrow vertical concrete strip divides the glass in two all the way down. The effect is peculiar. Pairs of translucent panes, rimmed by concrete, are transformed into giant spectacles for nine monstrous pairs of eyes, one stacked above the other. They are strangely reminiscent of the heavy spectacles worn by the building's namesake, John Vorster, or, more fully, Balthazar Johannes Vorster, Prime Minister from 1966 and State President from 1978 to 1979. Interned during the Second World War as a member of the pro-Nazi Ossewabrandwag, Vorster had belligerently declared at the building's opening ceremony, in 1968, 'The breakdown of law and order in South Africa will not be tolerated under any circumstances whatsoever.' Time and again, he spoke of the right of 'we whites' to maintain 'white identity'. As Minister of Justice in 1963, he was responsible for the original 90-days law, doing away with *habeas corpus*.

The ninth and tenth floors of John Vorster Square were exclusively reserved for the security police. A screening officer sat in the basement-cum-car park next to two dedicated lifts, allocated solely for use by the security police, leading directly up to the ninth floor. Each lift was designed to make a compulsory stop at the ninth floor where occupants would be scrutinised by an officer sitting inside a bulletproof glass cubicle. The lifts could be operated remotely by the scrutinising officer. A panoply of grilles, electronic doors and locks controlled access to the ninth and tenth floors from the floors below and above, both through the lift system and the stairs. Four other lifts served the rest of the building. These were designated as '3 Passenger for Whites, 1 Passenger/ Goods for non-Whites' and were designed not to stop at the ninth and tenth if travelling up to the eleventh or twelfth. Just in case someone tried to force a stop, the entrance points on the two security police floors were bricked up.

John Vorster Square housed the largest security police division in the country, functioning in a world of its own. While the ninth-floor 'spectacles' offered expansive views across Johannesburg, 'bugging rooms' behind electronic doors on both the ninth and tenth floors were equipped with hundreds of tape recorders and facilities for postal interceptions. A filing room contained perhaps one or two hundred thousand files. We shall never know the number, thanks to the mass incinerations in 1993. Another room stored unlicensed weaponry and kits of dirty tricks, down to typewriters and writing pads for use in forgeries in what were known as 'Stratcom' operations that extended throughout South Africa and abroad. Interrogation equipment – batteries, electric wires, pincers, broomsticks, cloth bags, water buckets, bricks and such like – must have required dedicated storerooms with easy access.

To the outside world, the Special Branch specialised in denial, so memorably captured in Chris van Wyk's poem 'In Detention'.[120] To their captives, the Special Branch revelled in their power over life and death, referring to the tenth floor as 'Timol Heights'. A 30-year-old teacher, Ahmed Timol, had been the first detainee to die at John Vorster Square, in October 1971. Dangled out of the window of Room 1026, he had plunged to his death, smashing onto a car that was parked below. The police claimed that Timol, who was more than one-and-a-half metres tall, had unexpectedly dashed past interrogator and desk, opened the narrow, one-metre-high window and dived head first, thereby committing suicide. Despite the evidence assembled by the family's lawyers indicating a very different narrative, inquest magistrate JJ de Villiers accepted the police version and concluded that no one was to blame. The verdict gave the Special Branch a green light. Three more detainees died in John Vorster Square custody between December 1976 and February 1977: Wellington Tshazibane, allegedly found hanged in his cell; Elmon Malele, who was said to have fallen unconscious and hit his head on a table; and Matthews Mojo Mabelane, who, like Ahmed Timol, 'fell' from the tenth floor.

Detainees were brought into the complex through formidably high, steel-grilled gates in Goch Street, where the adjacent elevated highway casts perpetual shadow, accentuating the gloom. Barbara, Gavin and everyone else picked up on 22 September, and in the following weeks, knew that they were entering a place of terror. Barbara recalls how Pindile used to describe the torture room: 'It was a silenced room where you couldn't hear people screaming. So you lived with that terror, from the moment you were picked up, that they would do terrible things with you ...'

While black detainees knew that their lives counted for nothing with their interrogators, white detainees were also conscious that, while they could be tortured, their connections with the white world and media generally confined interrogators to methods that would leave fewer visible marks. Whether detainees were black or white, however, interrogators aimed to terrorise the imagination. For female detainees, this was interwoven with sexual intimidation. It required considerable resolve for a detainee not to allow stories of previous horrors to unhinge and destabilise them.

From the back of the car, when Barbara heard the police say there had been no one at Alan Fine's address, she began to sense the breadth of the swoop. Once interrogation began, it became clear that the police had both the uncoded documents that she had addressed – as she thought at the time – to the exiled ANC leadership. With her 'Close Comrades' list in hand, her interrogators intended her to elaborate and explain everyone's exact role. She was at the centre of the web. Shocked and mortified to have fallen into a Special Branch trap, she now had to attempt a 'rescue job'.

Barbara had named Gavin as one of her 'Primary Reference Group'. Along with Auret van Heerden, she had noted that both knew she was 'working under discipline', as well as they themselves being 'under discipline'. How did she know that they were ANC operatives? To avoid reference to the linking request that she had carried to Gavin from Botswana in January, she went into a long story about the trip that he had made to Botswana with Pindile more than five years earlier. This was something that the police knew about already. Barbara was also familiar with Pindile's cover story about going to an ILO conference where SACTU members had been present. Barbara told her interrogators that she had always assumed that Gavin had been recruited at that time. Yes, he was someone to whom she would refer for advice, but she had no further concrete evidence that he was actually an operative. Appearing to sense that this line of questioning was a dead end, the police left it, and Barbara was confident that, under interrogation, Gavin would take the same line as Pindile and simply assert that she had got it wrong.

Early on in Gavin's interrogation up on the tenth floor, Cronwright appeared in the room. Why did Gavin think he'd been detained? Gavin replied that he guessed it was because he had given a recent talk about community support for trade unions in Lenasia. One of Cronwright's officers had caught him trying to flush his notes for the talk down the toilet on the morning of his arrest. 'No, man!' laughed Cronwright, waving a piece of paper. 'We've broken your cell. We have a list written by Barbara for the ANC which names you as one of the two most senior ANC operatives in the white left.' Gavin was genuinely astonished, 'pissed off and outraged, and showed it'. He pretended not to know Barbara well, although he had known her from IAS days and seen her regularly because of her friendship with his housemate Joanne. He reminded Cronwright that he and Barbara had been on opposite side of the bitter IAS 'general union' versus 'industrial union' conflict when she had sided with the white students. The white left had angrily rejected him and Sipho as traitors, so he had never bothered with Barbara after that:

> I struck the pose of feeling vaguely amused by and even cynical/contemptuous about her as a wannabe politician, which played nicely into their own prejudices, and I also aligned with and played into their 'machoism' and talked like we were men together gossiping about her. I don't feel proud of it at all of course, but the need was to put distance between me and her, and to get the hell out of there if at all possible.

It wasn't difficult for Gavin to sound cynical and angry about being detained because of Barbara. He was deeply upset that she had got him inside, especially when their networks didn't overlap. Seeing that he had hit a chord with Cronwright and his interrogator, Engelbrecht,[121] he held the stance, 'pretending an ever-increasing resentment and anger that this "little woman" was trying to earn her political stripes by making false claims'. When Cronwright pressed him on Barbara's description that he was 'under discipline', he replied that she knew he did yoga every day and fasted once a week. So probably that seemed incredibly disciplined to her. While it was obvious that they didn't believe such a naive explanation, Gavin hoped that he had spun enough 'false threads' by then to put them off coming to his real networks. To emphasise his yogic discipline and indignation, he embarked on a hunger strike in protest at their insistence on serving him meat.

Cronwright had assigned Gavin two interrogators. One was Warrant Officer Hendrik Pitout and the other was Engelbrecht. It looked as if Pitout was supposed to be the nice cop and Engelbrecht the tough guy, ready to beat him up at a whim. But when they took Gavin to his cell, Pitout did something that gave Gavin a chance to confuse the dynamics of the relationship. Pitout insisted on Gavin stripping and opening his bum to be inspected, to make sure he wasn't concealing anything. Gavin knew that the real intention was to humiliate him, but it gave him a clue what to do, by playing again into their prejudices. The next time Pitout joined Engelbrecht, Gavin jumped up and started trying to beat him, saying, 'This guy's a homosexual. He felt me!' Engelbrecht was startled, and Gavin refused to speak to Pitout, treating him as 'absolute dirt' and telling him not to try and seduce him. Having become so hostile to Pitout, Engelbrecht had to be the nice guy.

Another tactic Gavin used was to answer questions in Afrikaans. This helped Engelbrecht, who, with his rather poor English, became a bit warmer to him. Using Afrikaans also gained him more time to think because he'd stumble and hesitate, and they would think he was struggling with the language. However, on more than one occasion, they came close to probing a topic that could have cracked open an important network. It concerned secret trips he and Sipho had made to Durban to establish contacts, in violation of their bans. As soon as their banning orders had come to an end in August 1981, they had travelled there again, and to Cape Town. On a couple of occasions Gavin had managed to lead his interrogators away from talking about Durban, but he was worried that when trawling through the interview they would detect his evasion. The third time that they returned to this line of questioning, quite fortuitously Cronwright entered the room and changed the direction of the interrogation. Gavin believed that it saved him. After fourteen days' detention, he was released along with Joanne and a few others lower down on Barbara's list.

Auret van Heerden, the other 'close comrade' whom Barbara had noted as a key ANC operative – working 'under discipline' and aware of her own status – was not so lucky. A postgraduate student of Industrial Sociology at Wits, from an Afrikaans family, and a former president of NUSAS, Auret was a leading member of the white left. He had been detained twice before, in 1977 and 1980, and other activists had formed the impression that he was linked to the ANC. At the same time, Auret was highly critical of the setup in Botswana, and hearsay suggested that he was an enemy agent, not to be trusted. Unconvinced by these rumours, but concerned about the confusion they were causing, Barbara had consulted Gavin about going to Botswana to argue Auret's case. That had been one of the reasons for her visit in January, when she had been asked to link the forward area with Gavin. With her interrogators now demanding that she explain how she knew that Auret was 'under discipline', Barbara was at a loss, except to say it was 'an impression' she had gained. Afterwards, she was to live with the guilt of knowing, as she would tell me, that Auret 'was terrifically tortured over this'.

From the moment of her arrest, Barbara's daily interrogation was 'high-powered aggression'. She was screamed at, threatened with torture, kept up late at night, handcuffed to heaters and made to stand on one spot. When she pretended to collapse and gave them a name of someone overseas who was not due back for a long time, they thought they had broken her and became 'all sweet'. They got her Kentucky Fried Chicken and ice cream and wouldn't let her sleep in her cell, concerned that she might commit suicide because she had 'betrayed a comrade'. Shortly afterwards, however, they realised that she had duped them: 'The cop I told thought he was a great ou because he'd got the info out of me. So he had a particular hatred against me ... a bit of a maniacal guy, Prince. A madman, total maniac. Used to scream at you and show scars on his face and say, "That's what I got on the border fighting terrorists. This is what you did!"'

Barbara recognised how Cronwright's men were trying to humiliate her, but, having grown up among Afrikaners, those tactics didn't work. She felt that she was saved from what might be a culture shock for 'English-speaking northern suburbs people'. Her interrogators were, she says, 'more familiar to me culturally than to others who had perhaps never been exposed to the full-blooded racism that emerges in those situations'.

Nevertheless, the threats of torture were real, and Barbara was conscious of not wanting to drive these men into a pitch of frenzy like 'mad dogs'. She found it chilling to see 'how much brutality was a way of life for them, how they could switch it on and off at will'. It was normal for an interrogator to interrupt a beating in order to take a personal phone call from his wife, and talk about domestic matters, before resuming the assault. What she came to fear most was the crudity and lack of intelligence in most of her interrogators. However much she declared that they had everything, that she had believed she was corresponding with the High Command of the ANC and would not have lied, they always wanted to uncover more, convinced that she must be 'MK' or 'had to be a full-blooded member of the Communist Party'.

> ... you realised that you were dealing with ... very manic people ... who could not have the intelligence almost to sit down and do a proper intelligence assessment of this; whose whole experience of interrogation was torturing people to bits and pieces, and forcing confessions out of them. It wasn't based on, this is what we know, this is the probability, OK we've got a case, let's send it through.

It suddenly began to dawn on Barbara that they would 'probably go into full-scale torture' to get what she couldn't give them.

CHAPTER 26

Gavin's getaway

G AVIN HAD SPENT HIS THIRTIETH BIRTHDAY, SUNDAY 4 OCTOBER, in jail. Released two days later, he went around to all the people with whom he had worked, and who had not been arrested, in order to brief them. They included Fink Haysom, Sipho and Neil. Although Cronwright had waved the 'Close Comrades' document in front of him, he hadn't allowed Gavin to see the names. He had no inkling that Barbara had named Neil as one of her 'Advisory/Reference People'. Nor had Neil come up in his sessions. In each debriefing, Gavin went over his interrogation in detail, so everyone would know what lines the Special Branch were following and how he had dealt with their probes:

> With Sipho and Neil, and again with others like Fink we came to realise that
> I had put the SB off their thread of questioning three times, when they were
> asking about the trip that Sipho and I had made to Durban about a week
> after we were unbanned. We also realised that the Branch would go through
> the interrogation transcripts and realise the same thing, and want to know
> actually what DID happen when we went to Durban.

In Durban, Sipho and Gavin had been hosted by Pravin Gordhan and his comrades, while meeting others in the trade union movement.[122] Were the security police to return to questions on Durban, and succeed in getting the names of Durban comrades, the detentions would open up new networks beyond the damage already caused. Everyone agreed that Gavin shouldn't risk more interrogation. He should get out of the country.

However, Gavin still felt that he had a grace period and joined a couple of friends who were going for a couple of days' break down to the Drakensberg. 'Paranoid as hell' about making sure they were not being followed, he made his friends take all kinds of detours. When they hit the mountains, Gavin ran up the first one non-stop, exulting in the free space and air, until he fell down exhausted, his friends reduced to little dots below. The break also allowed him to unburden himself 'of the horror and the remorse I felt at talking my way out and talking badly about Barbara and of all sorts of other worries and remorse which I later learned affect almost everyone who has been through interrogation and solitary'.

Returning to Johannesburg, Gavin realised that he needed to get out fast. His father rang from Botswana with a warning: 'You are half a step ahead of the bastards, but don't get complacent. Get out NOW!' His father had applied to see him while he was detained. Enraged by the refusal, he had been one of the parents helping to energise the Detainee Parents' Support Committee (DPSC), which would be held together and sustained by Max and Audrey Coleman, two of whose sons were detained. In 1976, black parents had come together to protest against the detention and torture of their children. Now, white parents found themselves having to act collectively.

Gavin's father was under no illusions. He had fought against Nazism in the Second World War and regarded the apartheid regime in a similar light. Concerned that his son would be arrested at a border post, his father arranged tickets for Gavin to travel by plane with his baby daughter, Tamsin. As air travel was much more expensive, they hoped that the security police wouldn't expect him to fly out. Gavin was also extraordinarily lucky to have a valid passport. Soon after his banning, the police had demanded that he give them his passport. He had refused. The Minister of Home Affairs had issued it to him, not the Minister of Police. He would only hand it over if they brought a letter from the former. When they didn't return, Gavin assumed that it was because the passport was due to expire. Some time later, however, he had written to the Minister of Home Affairs, asking for Tamsin to be put on his passport so that she could travel to Botswana to see her grandparents. To his great surprise, the passport was returned with Tamsin's name added and an extension. Nor was there anything to indicate that it was only valid for the child!

Dressed smartly as a businessman, Gavin went through Customs carrying the toddler and a copy of the *Financial Mail*. The plane was about to taxi off when the engines suddenly shut down, the door reopened and police boarded the aircraft. Convinced that he was their target, Gavin confided urgently in the man sitting next to him. By another stroke of fortune, this was Alfred Dube, an official with Botswana's Foreign Service, later to be that country's ambassador/high commissioner to Sweden, the UK and China. Gavin asked if he would please look after his little daughter and make sure that she got to her grandparents in Botswana. Gavin handed him the passport. But the future diplomat went further. He was seated on the aisle, while Gavin looked out the window, his face hidden by his daughter, who sat on the armrest. A policeman began to walk down the aisle, looking at all the passengers. As the policeman reached their row, Alfred Dube began to chat with him in a very charming manner. Distracted by the banter, the policeman didn't even ask Gavin to show his face. After the police left, the plane departed. But later in the flight, when Gavin detected the aircraft turning, he suspected that a radio message had been received to return to Johannesburg and bring him back. His new friend patted his knee to reassure him, '*Nnya Rra*, don't worry, you are safe now. We are about to arrive home.'[123]

A matter of hours after Gavin's departure, the security police arrived at the house he had shared with Joanne in Crown Mines. She had been released a couple of days before Gavin, having maintained her stance of naivety during interrogation. This time they took the house apart, removing the ceilings and floorboards, angry and bemused that Gavin had given them the slip.

By now, news was circulating among the white left about the existence of Barbara's list of names. There was fear, anger, incomprehension and much speculation. When had this list been written – before or after her detention? Who else was on it? The latter question was answered when Barbara Klugman, listed as 'potential leadership', was released from detention and discovered a photocopy of the document among her own papers and books, confiscated by the Special Branch and now returned to her. Had the police put it there deliberately, or by mistake? Terrified, she took it immediately to Joanne Yawitch, who recalls that the two of them were 'completely freaked out'. They couldn't work out whether the document had been written by Barbara Hogan before or after she went to jail: 'We knew this thing was bloody dynamite. Barbara Klugman's parents more or less told her to go away, and I was the only one out of detention who knew about the document.'

With Gavin in Botswana and Barbara Klugman on her way to England, Joanne set about warning people who hadn't already been detained, including Neil and Liz. She knew that the couple had recently split, but started by going to the house in Fox Street, where Liz continued to live after Neil had moved out. Instead of finding Liz, she found Neil there. However, he was adamant that he wasn't in any serious danger. No, it wasn't a problem, he assured Joanne. His relationship to Barbara Hogan was an oblique one, and he had no intention of going into hiding. When Neil said that he would inform Liz, Joanne left it at that. If the security police discovered her role in alerting people to 'the bloody list', she was sure that they would come back for her a second time. Moreover, her sense of threat was growing. Notes smuggled out of jail were beginning to emerge, with news circulating through the DPSC. It was, says Joanne, 'a nightmare'.

CHAPTER 27

'Stay well bro & keep strong'

Dear Gav,

I'm sorry I missed you before you left & we never got a chance to talk about things; It would be nice to spend some time together and go through what has been going on.

Firstly, you must realise that you have our full support and trust, and what happened in detention has in no way changed that at all. It obviously worries you, but in my opinion is not important at all. The last year has been a hard one for you, and I hope that you will have time to rest & settle down in Botswana for a while.

Liz & I have separated in trying circumstances & I'm living with Doug Hinson [sic] at present – and new social relations are emerging, although I'm obviously upset about what is happening.

Union work is busy as usual & going well, but personal life is in a mess:– I envy you in Botswana in some respects.

We look forward to seeing you again, and spending some time together not just the thing about work.

Stay well bro & keep strong

Neil[124]

NICI BROUGHT THIS LETTER TO GAVIN ON A VISIT TO BOTSWANA to collect young Tamsin. She also brought news that Neil had been pleased to hear of Gavin starting a vegetable garden at his parents' place, with memories of 'When in doubt, dig!' But sadness and a sense of loss pervade Neil's reassurances of 'our full support and trust' with his exhortation to 'keep strong'.

Having left Liz in their house in Fox Street, keeping strong was what Neil was trying to do himself. He had asked Doug and Maria Hindson if he might use their flat in Hillbrow while they were travelling overseas. Their relationship with Neil was to have profound consequences for the couple. They were, in trade union circles, linked to FOSATU, branded in the earlier ideological battles as 'workerists', when Neil had been seen as a 'populist'. However, in his drive for union unity, Neil had sought to engage with Doug, who edited the *South African Labour Bulletin*, and who was interested in the sociology of work and was teaching principles of Marxist thought to workers at night. The two of them had got into intense discussions. Whatever their political differences, Doug was struck by how Neil was motivated by 'deep human values' and that he had 'an integrity that went beyond politics': 'It was a germinating friendship with the beginning of an understanding. I wasn't part of the communist movement ever, more associated with the workers' movement. At that time those things seemed so important. Neil felt safe with us … He was feeling observed and spied on. He was.'

When the Hindsons returned to their flat in Diamond Court, Neil asked if he could leave his clothes in a black plastic bag there temporarily while he sorted himself out. He also left books and a little table that he had brought from Fox Street. Although Doug sensed that Neil was battling with the breakdown of the relationship, as well as the heat from the security police, he would only learn later that the table had been an issue between Neil and Liz. The unremitting police scrutiny, having to operate a 'need to know' policy in their personal relationship, living such compartmentalised lives, had all taken their toll.

Whatever front Neil managed to maintain, his direct admission in writing to Gavin that his 'personal life is in a mess', and that he was 'obviously upset' about the split from Liz, revealed his inner vulnerability. While he concentrated on boosting Gavin's morale in his letter, the departure of his close confidant and comrade was undoubtedly a blow. Among the 'new social relations' to which he refers was a friendship with Yvette Breytenbach, a trainee architect who was part of his circle of friends in Crown Mines. Neil had known Yvette since 1979, when she had been staying with Leslie Dean and Brian Cutler from the Vegetable Garden. Neil had felt at home there, Yvette's first encounter being when he had arrived one Sunday evening, asking to have a bath after shovelling coal. She had been 'pretty scandalised' by the black rim left around the bath, showing that he had also used a lot of water. He had often called in at their house, sharing meals, conversations and lively debates, both philosophical and political:

> One big debate Leslie, Brian, Neil and I had was over whether or not a person has a soul, with Neil categorically stating the soul does not exist as he did not find one when he dissected the human body. Another ongoing heated household discussion was over why he would not cook. He point-blank stated that he couldn't and no amount of persuasion would get him to even attempt to learn … He was an all-or-nothing person.

Once Neil had begun working in the union, there was less time for social visits, but like other friends in Crown Mines Yvette had memories of Neil calling in on his journey to Baragwanath. Although she had moved on to sharing another house, Neil would call in there too. To Yvette, Neil was a 'people person' who enjoyed company and relaxed by socialising. He took pleasure in telling stories from the hospital, which he recounted with 'compassionate amusement' and a sharp eye for people's foibles. Over whisky mixed with apple juice, they shared confidences. 'He liked knowing what made people tick, what their interests and passions were.'

> Weeknights he often took a nap on my bed before going to his late-night Emergencies shift at Baragwanath Hospital. He had this little ritual where he had to page through a book no matter how tired he was or what book it was, before he could fall asleep. He would sleep while I worked at my drawing board in the same room (students of architecture worked late nights), and I would wake him in time to get there (around elevenish perhaps) and continue working once he had gone. It was a nice arrangement with a comfortable intimacy – I had company while I worked and he had company while he slept.

Over time, Yvette had got to know Liz as well, and around the middle of 1981 Neil and Liz accompanied Yvette and her boyfriend with some other friends on a short holiday down to the Drakensberg to get away from the mounting tension. They had enjoyed themselves and were planning another trip together to the Cape for early the following year. Yvette admired Neil's ability to keep calm. In the crowd at the big anti-Republic Day meeting at the end of May, when she had put her hand on his arm to get his attention, he had turned around quite composed, but later admitted that she had given him a shock. He had thought it was the touch of the security police coming to detain him.

There were, however, at least two occasions in the months before Neil's detention when Yvette suddenly saw him deeply agitated. The first was when the Volkswagen Beetle that Neil had been driving to the hospital stopped in the central street in Crown Mines. Yvette happened to be at home, and together they had tried to push-start, then tow, the car. But it wouldn't budge. Neil was running late, and was really stressed, so Yvette had driven him to the hospital. Along the way, pointing out the security police in a car parked beside the road, he spoke of how they let him know that they were watching, wherever he went. As Yvette dropped him off, Neil said he didn't know what he would have done without her help.

The second occasion must have been towards the end of October. About a month before his detention, he knocked at her door a little before midnight and asked to come in. He seemed overwrought, and needed company. No longer in Fox Street with Liz, he was staying in different locations. He had now been living under the threat of detention for months on end, working round the clock with very little respite and, in Yvette's view, always being very hard on himself in his lifestyle. She suspected that he was also a bit neglectful about eating. Relaxing over a glass of wine, they came round to talking about the struggle. Neil told Yvette that it was something for which he was prepared to give his life. 'Had he imagined what form of death this might take? I doubt it,' she writes many years later, yet he was 'quite clear and calm'.

With most of his clothes and books left with the Hindsons, leaving him unencumbered, Neil was now essentially nomadic. His unusual agitation made Yvette realise that while he had been mentally preparing himself for detention, there were actually times when he felt 'emotionally depleted', and his more familiar unruffled demeanour required effort. Yvette arranged a day out of town for a few friends, including Neil and Maurice Smithers, who had been arrested and released from detention at the same time as Gavin. They spent the day beside a swimming pool out at Fourways. Yvette, a petite brunette, wore a kikoi wrap that she had hand-tasselled 'as a sort of meditation and relaxation'. Its blue and white stripes, reflecting the light from the pool, were emboldened by narrow sunrise-colour stripes. Kikois were traditionally East African ... Kenyan. Neil was admiring. Yvette had transported them, fleetingly, to another world. But they had no illusions. The real world awaited.

CHAPTER 28

'We can use other methods'

GAVIN'S ESCAPE RAISED THE TEMPERATURE INSIDE JOHN VORSTER Square. Cronwright's men had let him get away after having him in their clutches. Angry and smarting with embarrassment, they still had their queen bee. Sensing their frustration, Barbara Hogan feared what they would do next.

During the first month of her detention, in the course of which she was transferred to Section 6 of the Terrorism Act, Barbara's almost daily interrogation had included threats of assault, shouting, screaming and abuse. The first physical assaults began after lunch on Thursday 22 October.[125] Using his hand, Warrant Officer Lawrence Prince struck her repeatedly on her back, neck and face. He made a special point of hitting her on her ears, saying he would break her eardrums; it was a pleasure to beat 'communists' and 'terrorists'. Throughout Prince's assault, Detective Warrant Officer Nicolaas Deetlefs questioned her, also striking her once across the face with his open hand. At about seven in the evening, Deetlefs waved the cord of an electric kettle. 'We can use other methods,' he declared, and then plugged the cord into a wall socket. Placing the other end on the rug under her chair, he instructed Prince to fetch a wet cloth but did not carry through the threat. Throughout the assault-cum-interrogation, various security policemen came into the room

Aubrey and Joy Aggett's wartime wedding, Johannesburg, 5 February 1944. Joy's sister, Madge Norman, was bridesmaid and their cousin, Ralph Trewhela (my father), best man. *(Courtesy of Ros Allison)*

Baby Neil on his christening day with his parents, brother Michael and sister Jill, Nanyuki Sports Club, Kenya, early 1954. *(Courtesy of UCT Special Collections)*

Three-year-old Neil with his father's mechanic at Ol Elerai beside the flooded Ewaso Ng'iro river, circa 1957. *(Courtesy of UCT Special Collections)*

Neil on his first birthday, with his mother and sister at the Aggetts' farm, Ol Elerai, Nanyuki, 6 October 1954. Neil's father Aubrey took the picture. *(Courtesy of UCT Special Collections)*

'My father sold his farm and invested his money in South Africa.' Neil, with his parents and sister Jill, outside their house in Somerset West, circa 1967. *(Courtesy of UCT Special Collections)*

'Stars of the Future' ... Neil (*near right*) and the Kingswood College under-14 tennis team after a tour of the eastern Cape, April 1967. Front: (*l to r*) Grant Dewar, Andrew Rein, Neil Aggett. Back: Peter Sole, Sydney Turner. *(Courtesy of Kingswood College)*

Cumber   Ciorovich   Staples J.   Aggett

Kirkby   Bester   Turner S.   van Niekerk C.   Friderichs C.

Head Prefect of the juniors, 16-year-old Neil (*back, far right*) stands tall in the Gane House cricket team at Kingswood College, Grahamstown, 1970. *(Courtesy of Kingswood College)*

Student Days

Neil as a first-year medical student, in the family sitting room, Somerset West, 1971. Above his brother's graduation photo is a painting of Mount Kenya, viewed from Ol Elerai. His sister Jill took the picture. *(Courtesy of UCT Special Collections)*

'At that time I had a disagreement with my father over my refusal to shave my beard, and from that time received no further assistance from him.' Neil, Cape Town, circa 1973. *(Courtesy of UCT Special Collections)*

'VARSITY LOAFERS "The Beginning!"' A policeman pulls the hair of a student demonstrator in Cape Town, June 1972. *(Juhan Kuus/Sipa Press)*

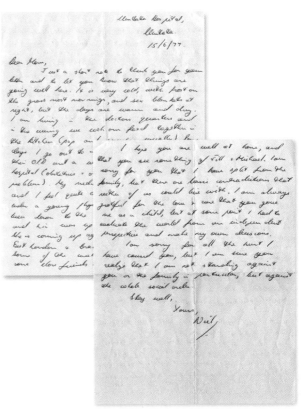

'I am sure you realize that I am not standing against you or the family in particular, but against the whole social order.' Extract from Neil's letter to his mother, Umtata General Hospital, 15 June 1977. *(Courtesy of UCT Special Collections)*

ABOVE: Police inside the Heinemann factory, Germiston, prepare to attack locked-out MAWU members, 29 March 1976. Union officials Sipho Kubeka and Gavin Andersson (*both far right*), shop stewards and workers discuss what to do. *(Photographer unknown/ Courtesy of Gavin Andersson)*

CENTRE: Police surround MAWU secretary Sipho Kubeka to prevent him talking to the workers before their baton charge. *(Photographer unknown/Courtesy of Gavin Andersson)*

BELOW: Gavin Andersson is greeted by dismissed workers in Alexandra, having been beaten, arrested and bailed. Banned a few months later, Gavin and Sipho became mentors to Neil. *(Photographer unknown/ Courtesy of Gavin Andersson)*

ABOVE: Liz and Neil in 1978. *(Photographer unknown/ Courtesy of Edwin Wes)*

CENTRE: 'When in doubt, dig!' Founding members of the Vegetable Garden Co-operative, Crown Mines, 1978. Back: (*l to r*) Gavin Andersson, Neil Aggett, Pat Horn, Roger Lucey, Liz Floyd. Front: (*l to r*) Brian Cutler, Nici Aime, Liz Thomson, Eddie Wes. *(Edwin Wes)*

BELOW: Vegetable Gardeners display their cabbages, 1979. Back: (*l to r*) Pat Horn, Rob Dyer, Nici Aime, Neil Aggett, Mam'Lydia Kompe, Paulinah Mohapi, Gavin Andersson, Clive Cope (baby Tamsin Andersson on his back), Sue Goldstein, Lisa Jacobson, Leslie Dean. Front: (*l to r*) Liz Thomson, Joanne Yawitch, Brian Cutler, Josiah Mohapi, Liz Floyd. *(Edwin Wes)*

The worker's cottage rented by Neil in Fuller Street, Bertrams, Johannesburg. Photographed in 1995, it looked much the same as it did 1978.

The end house in Crown Mines, rented by Joanne Yawitch. Gavin Andersson's stoep-cum-bedroom was a stopover for Neil after his night shift at Baragwanath Hospital. Derelict in 1995, this is where Joanne and Gavin were arrested in September 1981.

Summer getaway to a Wild Coast beach, with Gavin breaking his banning order, circa December 1978. Front: Gavin and Neil (with bat). Back: Brian Cutler (*left*) and two others. *(Photographer unknown/Courtesy of UCT Special Collections)*

Neil, at Crown Mines, around 1981.
(Photographer unknown/Courtesy of UCT Special Collections)

Oscar Mpetha recommended Neil's appointment to the AFCWU. He is shown here in 1989, aged 80, at a Soweto rally for released political prisoners. 'Baba' Oscar lost a leg to diabetes in jail. *(Joe Sefale/Avusa)*

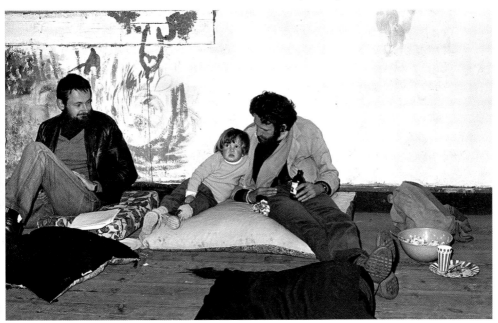

Neil with artist Steven Sack and his son Jonah at a Crown Mines May Day party, at the beginning of the 1981 anti-Republic Day campaign. *(Lesley Lawson)*

The family's last photo. Neil, on a rare weekend visit to his sister in Irene for his niece's fourth birthday, is shown here with his mother, Jill's husband Paul Burger, and Katy and Miles, July 1981. *(Jill Burger/Courtesy of UCT Special Collections)*

John Vorster Square

The mother of Cedric de Beer protests outside John Vorster Square in the week before Neil's arrest. The Detainee Parents' Support Committee kept up regular demonstrations throughout the detentions. *(Photographer unknown/MuseumAfrica/ Africa Media Online)*

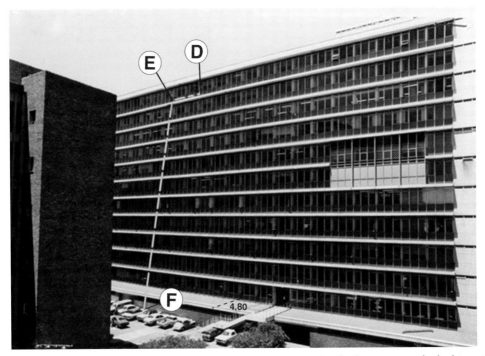

John Vorster Square, photographed from inside the complex by security police for the inquest into the death in detention of Matthews Mabelane, who 'fell' from a tenth-floor window in 1977. Neil was the next detainee to die here. *(National Archives/Sunday Times Heritage Project)*

'He was naked. He was made to do press-ups.' Maurice Smithers smuggled this tiny letter out of John Vorster Square in a matchbox the day after Neil died. Helen Suzman read out the letter in Parliament.
(Courtesy of Maurice Smithers and Frances Suzman Jowell/ UWL Historical Papers)
Transcript *(right)*.

On 25th I was at JVS (John Vorster Square) from plus minus 9.30 - 10.00 & plus minus 11.00 – 12.15.

In the first period, I saw Neil being interrogated by plus minus six guys. Then some left and three remained. Neil was standing all the time.

In the second period, he was still standing, except he was naked. He was made to do push-ups, a substantial number. He was hit either with a belt or rolled-up newspaper while doing them.

Then he had to get up and run on the spot, arms outstretched in front of him. Every so often, he was made to lift his legs up high while running and all this was interspersed with more push-ups. All the while, he was being interrogated.

The hitting with the newspaper went on all the time, especially if his arms sagged.

He was sweating profusely and, when once he nearly fell over a chair with exhaustion, he was further harassed.

When he got dressed after 12 o'clock, he was pushed around even then. It was clear that he was completely naked because he obviously drew on his underpants and then his trousers.

I can only imagine how often he had to go thru this and what worse things were done to him.

Use this info, but for the moment don't use the date or my name. But keep the note in a very safe place in case it's needed later.

Please give Yvette esp, but also everyone else all my love and strength. We must go on. I didn't know Neil well, but he was obviously a very special person. His killing mustn't be for nothing.

I'm okay. Nothing has been done to me. I don't think anything will be done. I'm not that important.

Take care

Maurice

Jane Starfield, a DPSC member, holds two placards outside John Vorster Square after Neil's death. One is for her detained boyfriend. The other, for Neil, defies the state's portrayal of detainees as traitors.
*(Photographer unknown/*Sunday Times/*Avusa)*

Funeral

As Neil's coffin emerges from St Mary's Cathedral, ANC flags appear either side in the crowd. Neil's brother Michael and his father Aubrey follow the pallbearers, with Paul Burger helping to carry the coffin at the rear.
(Courtesy of Juhan Kuus)

'A man of the people'. Union members carry Neil's pine coffin through West Park Cemetery.
(Paul Weinberg/Africa Media Online)

Neil's parents beside the grave. *(Raymond Preston/Sunday Times/Avusa)*

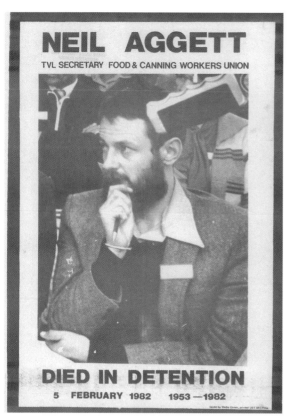

Liz Floyd greeted by Jane Rosenthal after her release from detention. *(Margot Williams/MuseumAfrica)*

This Food and Canning poster shows Neil at his union's 1981 conference. The strange object above his head is a camera handle. *(Image from the film* Passing the Message *by Cliff Bestall and Michael Gavshon/Community House)*

Inquest

Senior counsel for the family, George Bizos (*far right*), in discussion with (*l to r*) Joy and Aubrey Aggett, Liz Floyd and Neil's sister Jill. *(Juhan Kuus/Avusa)*

Aggett: bid for evidence of detainees

By ANNE SACKS

LAWYERS appearing for the family of trade unionist Dr Neil Aggett at his inquest want security detainees to give evidence when the hearing resumes on April 13.

The inquest opened in the Johannesburg Magistrate's Court yesterday.

A postponement was granted by the magistrate, Mr Lourens de Kock, to allow the family's lawyers to apply to the Minister of Police for permission to obtain "vital information" from Dr Aggett's fellow detainees.

Mr De Kock refused a request by counsel for the family, Mr George Bizos, for an immediate inspection in loco at John Vorster Square, where Dr Aggett died, because "it would surprise people".

The inquest on Dr Aggett — the 46th South African to die in detention since 1963 — began in a tiny courtroom so packed that many had to stand in the aisle and doorway.

The Press benches were crammed with representatives of local and international media.

Before the inquest, several television crews filmed a placard demonstration by the Detainees' Parents Support Committee outside.

Mr Bizos said at the outset "no useful purpose would be served as far as the family was concerned" unless their lawyers had access to

witnesses whom they believed had vital information about Dr Aggett's death.

These witnesses were detainees being held under Section 6 of the Terrorism Act at John Vorster Square, where Dr Aggett was found dead in his cell at 1.30am on February 5.

"We know access to these people is prohibited," he said. "But unless we are given access to detainees we won't be able to make a contribution to the proceedings. We intend to apply to the Minister of Police to use detainees as witnesses."

Asked by the magistrate what power he had to grant this, Mr Bizos said: "Your duty is to have the fullest possible inquiry. Any impediment to this is not a full or meaningful inquiry."

Mr Bizos said people other than police could not be precluded from giving evidence. It was "quite clear" that detainees had information about the death of Dr Aggett.

Mr Bizos also asked for an immediate inspection in loco at Dr Aggett's cell and interrogation room or rooms, saying any delay would defeat the purpose.

Mr De Kock — who may grant an inspection in terms of the Inquest Act — said it would not be fair "to surprise people" with an immediate inspection.

"We must give the authorities sufficient time to make alternative accommodation arrangements for detainees at John Vorster Square," he said.

COMFORTING TOUCH . . . Mrs Jill Burger, right, sister of trade unionist Dr Neil Aggett, with a friend at yesterday's inquest into his death in detention

Picture: JUHAN KUU

Yvette Breytenbach and Neil's sister Jill at the opening of the inquest.
(Rand Daily Mail, 3 March 1982, photo by Juhan Kuus)

Head of Johannesburg security police, Brigadier Hendrik Muller, attends the inquest to hear a nervous junior colleague attest to taking down Neil's statement on torture, the day before his death. *(Mike Herbert/Avusa)*

Petrus AJ Kotzé, a former state prosecutor in political trials, was appointed as magistrate to the inquest. *(Juhan Kuus/Avusa)*

RDM FRIDAY OCT 8th

Aggett 'an ANC sympathiser'

THE Security Police consider an ANC sympathiser to be the same as an ANC member, the Johannesburg Regional Court heard yesterday.

Giving evidence at the inquest into the death in detention of trade union leader Dr Neil Aggett, Lieutenant Steven Peter Whitehead told the court there were three kinds of ANC members — full,

card-carrying members, active supporters and sympathisers.

Dr Aggett repeatedly denied being a full member, but he was something between a sympathiser and an active supporter, Lt Whitehead said.

"Do you consider an ANC

sympathiser as a person who requires Security Police attention because his sympathy is prima facie evidence of an offence?" Mr George Bizos, SC, for the Aggett family asked.

Lt Whitehead answered in the affirmative, but added he

had had further information on Dr Aggett that led to his detention.

When Mr Bizos asked where in the Internal Security Act it says that a sympathiser is guilty of an offence, Lt Whitehead said it was not in the law but should be seen in

a wider context.

Lt Whitehead told of a meeting Dr Aggett had attended to discuss fighting for the South African Defence Force. The meeting had been chaired by Mr Gavin Anderson, whom Dr Aggett knew to be an ANC member, Lt

Whitehead said, and this showed where his sympathies lay.

He added that Dr Aggett had avoided doing his military service.

"Do you believe that if someone does something which the ANC also wants done, it is an offence?" Mr Bizos asked.

"Yes, if they are working with an ANC member," the policeman answered.

During his five-hour spell in the witness box, Lt Whitehead continually faced the magistrate, conspicuously attempting not to look at Mr Petrus Kotze, for his manner of cross-examination.

His sternest warning came when Mr Bizos told Lt Whitehead: "You have been in the witness box for three-and-a-half hours. Dr Aggett was questioned for 62 hours. You have a long way to go."

Mr Bizos asked Lt Whitehead why his affidavit had made no mention of Dr Aggett deciding to "open up his heart", as a number of other policemen had testified.

Lt Whitehead said he had gone to Dr Aggett's cell on January 28 and told him "the game was now up and he must tell the full truth". Dr Aggett had agreed to co-operate and undergo "more intensive questioning" immediately, he told the court. This was why Dr Aggett had spent the weekend in an interrogation room.

Lt Whitehead explained that "more intensive" questioning meant he was asking more pertinent questions, pinpointing areas in Dr Aggett's statement that he was not satisfied with.

Dr Aggett had made it clear in his statements that he was committed to democracy and trade unionism and was opposed to infiltration of the unions since this was contradictory to democracy in the union, Mr Bizos said.

Lt Whitehead replied that he had watched Dr Aggett for over three years and had other information that had implicated him. Dr Aggett was a Marxist and had worked to further the aims of banned organisations, he added.

Mr Bizos will continue the cross-examination of Lt Whitehead at 9am this morning.

SP detail secret search of family home

Aggett inquest told of police bribery

By ANTON HARBER
SECURITY Police sometimes find it necessary to use bribery in their work, the Johannesburg Regional Court heard yesterday.

Lieutenant Steven Peter Whitehead said this yesterday after admitting a colleague of his had pretended to be a private detective and offered a bribe to a servant in order to enter and search the house of Dr Neil Aggett's parents.

Lt Whitehead was being cross-examined by Mr George Bizos, SC, for the Aggett family during the inquest into Dr Aggett's death in detention.

He also admitted his colleague, Sergeant P Erasmus, had told the servant she would go to jail if she told anyone about the incident.

Lt Whitehead said that in March — six weeks after Dr Aggett's death — he and Sgt Erasmus had gone to the Somerset West house after being told that Mr Gavin Anderson, who he named as a suspect ANC member, was hiding there.

"I suggest that after Mr and Mrs Aggett appointed an attorney to investigate their privacy, you made up this story over Gavin Anderson," Mr Bizos said.

Lt Whitehead denied this.

Lt Whitehead, 25, who was in charge of much of Dr Aggett's interrogation, was accused of assault in a formal complaint by the detainee before his death.

He told the court he and Sgt Erasmus had gone to the Aggetts' house after being told Mr Anderson was there. He had waited in a restaurant some distance from the

Lt Steven Whitehead yesterday told the Aggett inquest of an attempt to bribe a servant.
Picture: DAVID VAN DER

house while Sgt Erasmus had spoken to the maid, Miss Sandra Isaacs.

Lt Whitehead admitted Sgt Erasmus had told Miss Isaacs he was a private detective collecting information on Dr Aggett for a book a friend of his was writing.

He had offered Miss Isaacs a bribe and told her they would both go to jail if she told anyone about it, the court heard.

Sgt Erasmus then searched the house, rifling cupboards and desks and looking through papers.

the conversation with the maid there was no mention of Mr Gavin Anderson or any inquiries about who was staying in the house.

Lt Whitehead said they were not searching for information on Dr Aggett, but such information was important to them, Sgt Erasmus may have asked questions or seen something relating to Dr Aggett while he was searching, he added.

Asked why it was necessary to search cupboards and desks, Lt Whitehead said they were looking for signs of Mr Gavin Anderson's presence.

"Are you suggesting that Mr and Mrs Aggett, in their grief soon after their son's death, would harbour a fugitive?" Mr Bizos asked.

Lt Whitehead said he had been given information and it was his duty to act on it.

He added that Brigadier Hennie Muller, head of the John Vorster Square Security Police, had known about the incident.

The head of the investigation team, Major Arthur Cronwright, told the court during his evidence he knew nothing about it.

"I am going to argue that this is yet another occasion that you showed you had no respect whatsoever for legality," Mr Bizos said. Lt Whitehead denied this.

Mr Pieter Schabort, SC, for the Minister of Law and Order, distanced himself from the incident. He put on record that it had nothing to do with the police's legal representatives and was strictly a police action.

Cross-examination of Lt Whitehead will continue on Monday morning.

While he was searching the house a neighbour was informed. He called the police and interrupted the search.

Lt Whitehead told the court he had had a warrant for the arrest of Mr Gavin Anderson, but it was in Johannesburg at the time.

Mr Bizos suggested the Security Policemen had been asked by their lawyers to gather information for a psychological report on Dr Aggett and had searched the house for information on this.

He said in the transcript of the policemen's recording of

Media interest in the drama of the inquest remained high. Neil's mother collected news cuttings, such as these about Lieutenant Steven Whitehead. When Neil's chief interrogator complained about his cross-examination, George Bizos reminded him of his interrogation of Neil.
(Rand Daily Mail, 8–9 October 1982)

Neil's parents outside the courtroom.
(Photographer unknown/Avusa)

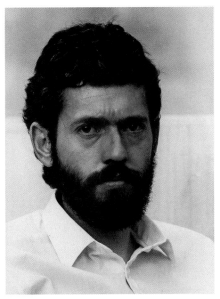

Auret van Heerden, the last detainee to see Neil alive from the opposite cell. Later, Auret sued ten police officers for torture.
(Photographer unknown/Courtesy of Simon Ratcliffe)

Sipho Kubeka at a commemoration for Neil at the University of the Witwatersrand's Great Hall, circa 1984.
(Edwin Wes)

Evidence withheld, says Floyd

By Andrew Walker

STAR December 22

"Neil Aggett 1953-1982. Died in detention. An injury to one is an injury to all."

So read the poster on a grimy Johannesburg office wall.

Beneath it friends and colleagues of Dr Aggett yesterday told the Press and TV cameramen what they thought of an inquest which exonerated security policemen of involvement in Dr Aggett's death in detention.

Other concerned groups throughout the world have spoken on his death, with Dr Aggett's name being linked with that of Steve Biko.

But for Dr Liz Floyd, Dr Aggett's girlfriend and a former detainee, the Aggett case is not just another battle lost.

In public she speaks freely and strongly against a system under which her boyfriend was detained without trial and which, she strongly believes, made him hang himself behind the closed cell doors of John Vorster Square.

But a quiet word with Dr Floyd shows she would far rather have Dr Aggett back than the memory of a man whose death resulted in the longest inquest in South African history and which put the country's security laws back in the limelight.

"Yes, the inquest was

Dr Liz Floyd addresses a Press conference after the inquest. With her is Mr Israel Mogoatlhe, chairman of the African Food and Canning Workers' Union, of which Dr Aggett was Transvaal regional secretary.

a very trying time. I never dreamt it would take so long. It has been a terrible year. Thank God the inquest is finished."

But has it helped erase the pain?

"No, it has made it worse. It will take a very long time to get over Neil."

Neil Aggett would never have taken his life had he not been driven to it, she said.

"I believe Neil was ill-treated and assaulted and I know he was not involved in any illegal organisation."

She said she had been shocked by evidence given at the

inquest by Professor Jan Plomp, a psychiatrist.

"The magistrate's decision was based mostly on the evidence of Professor Plomp and four pages of names allegedly given by Neil to Warrant-Officer Lawrence Deetlefs.

"Those four pages were not made known to the inquest proceedings. Privilege was claimed on the document but no evidence was led," she said.

"They will not get rid of the problem just because they have done away with Neil."

Liz Floyd and AFCWU chairman Israel Mogoatlhe at the press conference after the verdict.
(The Star, 22 December 1982)

'She spoke of him as a son – with a deep deep love & respect.' Mam'Lydia Kompe, trade union comrade, in her room at Crown Mines. *(Lesley Lawson)*

Neil's sister, Jill Burger, presents the first Neil Aggett Award for 'service above self' to Luyolo Sijake at Kingswood College, 23 September 2011. *(Courtesy of Kingswood College)*

Gavin Andersson and his son Somane Julian Neil at West Park Cemetery on the thirtieth anniversary of Neil's death, 5 February 2012. *(Courtesy of David Dison)*

to witness her reactions, including a laughing Lieutenant Johan van Aswegen. By the time Barbara was returned to her cell around 9pm, she was bleeding internally.

The following day, Deetlefs took her to the district surgeon, Dr Norman Jacobson, warning her that she had better not report the assault but say that she bruised easily. Barbara understood the threat. She was, in her own words, in a 'hysterical state' during her visit to the doctor, and although she made it clear that she didn't want to report an assault, when Dr Jacobson saw her bruises, he called in another doctor to note them. Before she left, he also informed her that he had just rung Colonel Muller at John Vorster Square to say that his policemen should cease assaulting her. He prescribed medication and insisted on seeing her again on Saturday 24 October, and on the following Monday. Immediately after the latter appointment, she was taken up to the tenth floor.

Warrant Officer Prince was now joined by new interrogators, including Captain Phillipus Olivier and Lieutenant Martin Johan Naude – soon to be Captain Naude – both from the eastern Cape. Olivier was the security policeman who had exhorted East London employers to stand firm against SAAWU. Naude became the main questioner, frequently screaming and shouting at her. She was now in their hands, they said, not the doctor's. By the time she was allowed to return to her cell on the second floor late in the afternoon, Barbara was in 'a state of despair'.

Before she was actually locked in her cell, without being seen, she managed to remove a packet of Syndol tablets, several Valium and two Mogadon tablets from the shelf in the room where the drugs were kept: 'I cast around for ways of committing suicide. I thought of hanging myself from the shower pipe. However, I was not sure that I would succeed in a hanging attempt as I did not know how to make a noose, or how to ensure that the hanging would kill me. I did not wish merely to maim myself.'

In her cell, she tried to pour water down her nostrils in a vain attempt to 'drown' herself. But she couldn't get her head back far enough and, with her body rejecting the water, she simply choked. Her thoughts turned to slashing her wrists. First, she tried to sharpen the bottom of a toothpaste tube against the rough brick of the wall around the toilet. However, she couldn't get it sufficiently sharp, nor could she sharpen a copper rod, the thickness of a pencil, that she extracted from her mattress. She then swallowed the two

Mogadons, three or four Valiums and about 17 Syndols, in addition to squeezing half a tube of anaesthetic cream down her throat. Knowing that these alone wouldn't kill her, she tied her dressing-gown cord around her throat, until she felt it constricting her veins. Under a blanket on her bed, she passed out, but woke up the next morning to find the cord next to her. In a semiconscious state, during the night she had torn it off.[126]

Taken once again in the morning for interrogation, and feeling terrible, Barbara asked to see the doctor. Naude, who happened to be dressed in a white safari suit, angrily claimed that he was a doctor and he would do. Later, Cronwright came to announce that he was highly dissatisfied with Barbara and was sending her away. Her possessions were brought up from her cell to the tenth floor, where he confiscated most of her clothing, toiletries, her playing cards and a Rubik's Cube. That afternoon she was transferred to a cell in Vereeniging police station and removed from Dr Jacobson's eyes.

Here, Barbara was told to complete another statement. Over two weeks later, on Saturday 14 November, interrogation resumed. Deetlefs arrived with the two East London interrogators, Captain Olivier and Lieutenant Naude, as well as a mountain of a man who towered over her. Captain Andries Struwig had made his reputation as a Koevoet (crowbar) interrogator on the border in Namibia, boasting of having thrown SWAPO guerrillas out of helicopters, sometimes attached to ropes, at other times not. Another story was of Struwig pulling out the front tooth of a comrade with a pair of pliers.[127] Whatever Barbara knew of Struwig, the four interrogators appeared to be in a very bad mood as they took her for questioning at Vanderbijlpark police station.

Again there was screaming and shouting. Deetlefs ordered her to sit under the table. She answered his questions, crouching there until it was Struwig's turn. Making her stand up, Struwig hit her across the face with his right hand and with a newspaper held in his left hand, then struck her on her hip with a piece of wood. Struwig now told her that Alan Fine was dead. Alan, he said, had committed suicide the previous night because of Barbara and what she'd told them. He was lying, but it was a while before Barbara would establish that Alan was alive. Warned that she was facing a long week ahead, she once again contemplated suicide, 'but was too exhausted and dispirited to actually do it'.

On Sunday 15 November, a new team of four arrived and subjected her to the longest and most intensive interrogation yet. Accompanied by Major Stephanus Abrie, Lieutenant van Aswegen, Warrant Officer Prince and a security policewoman, Constable Judy Knight, took her to an office in Vereeniging police station. Abrie announced that she had better cooperate because 'they were going to take me to a place where I had never ever been before in my life'. From around noon, she was interrogated in successive three-hour shifts by the three men, who frequently shouted abuse and threatened assault. There was no food and no sleep, although the officers took turns to sleep themselves, or nap on stretchers in the next office. At about seven o'clock the following morning, Barbara was given some coffee and bread. An hour later, Naude, Olivier and Deetlefs came to take over. She was finally allowed back to her cell around noon, where she found the magistrate, a Mr Killian, 'but I was too exhausted to lay any complaints'.[128]

Although Barbara's interrogation continued, the earlier assaults were not repeated, and the intensity diminished after the middle of November. However, Lieutenant Whitehead now joined Van Aswegen, introducing a distinct focus on Neil and Liz. It was Whitehead who had arrested Sisa at their house in May. Why had the couple chosen to live so simply? As doctors, they could live on a much grander scale, so why were they not interested in making money? Whitehead seemed convinced that this had to be an expression of communism. Barbara thought him obsessive, fixated with wanting to know personal details about the couple. 'He used to come to me and say, "Who wears the pants in that relationship?" It was the most appalling curiosity, almost pathological.'

By the middle of November, the security police had a problem. They had scooped up a whole crop of activists and were boasting to Barbara about their plans:

> ... they were bragging that they had smashed the whole ANC underground
> political machinery and there was going to be a massive trial. They used to
> fantasise about how many police trucks would have to come to court, how
> we were all going to stand trial, and they were basing it on Rivonia ... on the
> notion that there were cell structures and there were linkages and whatever.
> They hadn't understood that this was a very loose formation ... it led them
> to try and seek out formal organisational structures which weren't there.

Barbara's interrogators possessed what they regarded as gold-plated information from Craig Williamson, based on his years of close association with senior members of the ANC in exile. According to Williamson, as he would testify in Barbara's subsequent trial for treason, his instruction in revolutionary theory included how the National Liberation Movement encompassed both armed struggle and non-violent political struggle, including strikes, boycotts and demonstrations. Williamson also reported that it was impressed on him that it was impossible for any member of the ANC to work for the ANC without having a thorough knowledge of its strategy and tactics.[129] It was a catch-all conception in which any ANC 'member' was guilty of violent and treasonable intent.

* * *

The security police now decided to turn the screws on Auret van Heerden. Arrested on 24 September, like Barbara he had been transferred from section 22 of the General Law Amendment Act to Section 6 of the Terrorism Act. From John Vorster Square, he had been moved to Pretoria Central Prison and then to Sandton police station in Johannesburg's northern suburbs, being interrogated regularly until he had made a statement. On the afternoon of Tuesday 17 November, Auret was taken back to John Vorster Square and up to Cronwright's office on the tenth floor. Cronwright announced that his statement was very evasive and he was handing Auret over to Major Abrie, who would take him to Benoni for a thorough interrogation. It was the first time that Auret had met Abrie. Warrant Officer Lawrence Prince, the officer who had assaulted Barbara, took Auret to pack his belongings. All he could take was one change of clothing, a toothbrush and a towel. When Auret tried to slip in a Liqui-Fruit, Prince punched him in the face, knocking him across the room into a chair.

On the drive to Benoni, Abrie and Prince informed Auret that he was not going to sleep: 'They said they could break anybody. They said they didn't care if they killed me the way Biko had been killed.'[130] As Auret was booked in at the Benoni cells, Abrie spoke in a low, confidential voice. He was not going to lie. Unless Auret told them what he knew, they were going to torture him: 'Such violence would be used that I wouldn't believe it.'[131]

Auret was given until the morning to think about it. On Wednesday 18 November, around 8.30am, Prince took him from his cell to an office on the fourth floor occupied exclusively by the security police, using a lift that went only to that floor. A grilled door at either end of the passage ensured total privacy. Van Aswegen, Prince and Olivier were waiting. All three had taken turns in interrogating Barbara. Auret was told that he had a short amount of time to spell out verbally the key points that he had been concealing. When he replied that his statement was complete, Olivier informed him that the blood supply to his head 'should be improved'. Auret's right wrist was handcuffed to his left ankle, with the warning that if he sat or lay down, he would be beaten. This left him standing, bent over, on his right leg. His legs soon became numb, and he began to sway, only managing to keep his balance through various contortions. At first, a different hand would be chained to a different foot after an hour or so, but then he was left, hunched and manacled, with no interrogation for the rest of the day. Unchained at about 6.30pm in the evening, he was told to eat supper. Half an hour later, Major Abrie appeared with his team for the night: Captain Olivier, Warrant Officer Prince and a Captain Johannes Visser from John Vorster Square. A fifth man, called Hendrik, accompanied them. They all appeared to have been drinking in the police canteen and had brought a supply of brandy for the night ahead.

Abrie began. Was Auret now ready to start talking? They knew what he had left out of his statement and were waiting for him to be truthful with them. Once again, Auret said that his statement was complete. He was sat down on the floor, with his back to the wall and barefoot. A light-brown canvas bank bag was placed over his head. It was a bit too small, and Visser had to tear it at the corners so it fitted completely over Auret's head. He felt the bag becoming wet. The wetter it became, the harder it was to breathe. Then the shocks began, with electrodes applied initially to the soles of his feet, his wrists and forearms, then to the nape of his neck and the base of his spine.

He began screaming, compulsively, unable to stop himself. Panicking with the claustrophobia and shocks pulsating through his body, he couldn't breathe. When the electrodes were placed at the back of his head, blue flames and waves shot in front of his eyes. What was happening to his brain? Would there be permanent damage?

> As more and more water was applied to the bag I found myself lying on the floor in a pool of water with the current travelling up and down my body being conducted by the water and at the same time screaming and being unable to breathe. I'm not sure how they gauged how long I could actually

withstand the shocks or how long it would be before I in fact suffocated, but at a certain stage they stopped administering the shocks and took the bag off. They would then immediately being firing questions at me. The questions which were repeatedly put to me during that state were: who recruited me to the ANC, to whom in the ANC did I sent reports, where was my dead letter box? As I have never been a member of the ANC I could not answer the questions.[132]

When the answers were not what they wanted, the bag went over his head again. He felt 'absolute panic': 'The temptation to say something just in order to stop them putting the bag over my head was tremendous and I imagine that a number of people would at that point begin talking and find themselves unable to stop ...'[133] Bag and shocks were applied repeatedly. Auret prayed that he would pass out, to obliterate the pain and suffocation, but he didn't. Instinctively he tried to pull the bag off, get his fingers under the edge to lift it a little for a breath of air. But Olivier would pull his hands away, threatening to break his fingers. Finally the captain grabbed them, held them on the floor and stomped. When the bag was removed, Auret found he was coughing blood, either from the excruciating gasps for air or from some blows that had cut his gums or lips.

After the electric shocks came strangulation. The powerfully built Visser sat on a chair, with Auret between his legs. He wrapped a small white wet towel around Auret's neck, pulling his head back and twisting the towel with such intensity that Auret felt his eyes would pop out. The blood vessels were bursting. Each time Visser applied the vice, perhaps ten to fifteen times, he forced Auret to look into his eyes while shooting questions about the ANC and threatening to kill him. Auret felt that he was going to die.

Next came a battery of assaults. Held on the ground by two people, Auret was seated with his back at about 45 degrees to the floor. Visser now stood over him, pummeling Auret's head with the flat of his hand. Some of the blows were so hard that he would lose consciousness for a few seconds. Some blows forced his neck to buckle. When this happened, he was warned to keep his neck and back in a single plane, lest the neck break. The rain of blows continued.

When Prince took over, he got Auret on his hands and knees, pulling him about by his hair. Jerked forward, Auret would catapult off his hands and knees, at the same time as Prince would strike his knee into Auret's face, causing more cuts and bruises. At another point, when Auret was sitting on the floor, Prince leapt forward to slap his face while grabbing hold of Auret's beard and tugging a handful right out. At another stage, while he sat on the ground, the soles of his feet were whipped with a black sjambok, questions being fired at him between the blows. Prince stamped with his heels over the arches of Auret's feet, scraping off the skin and depositing streaks of black shoe polish below the surface.

Throughout the evening, each officer had a chance to lead. Their drinking partner, Hendrik, acted as their sidekick in their show. Introduced as a colonel, Auret suspected he was a non-commissioned officer, formerly from the Orange Free State and now stationed somewhere on the East Rand. His role included that of the joker. Afterwards, Auret recalled some 'excellent impersonations of John Vorster's speeches'. Hendrik had come along, it seemed, partly because he was fascinated that a person of Afrikaner background could be in this situation. Occasionally he would stop the torture and say, 'Look Auret, I want to have a word with you. I want to give you some advice.' Taking him into the passage with his glass of brandy in hand, he would try to get Auret to drink some. His line was, 'Look, go in and tell these guys the truth because if you don't tell them the truth, they're going to kill you, and I don't want to see you getting beaten up. We're fellow Afrikaners, we shouldn't be doing this to each other. So for goodness sake, for your sake and ours, just tell them what they want to hear.' When Auret reiterated that he was telling the truth, and that he had given all the information he could, Hendrik became angry. He would begin assaulting Auret, then throw him back into the room, and tell the others to do what they wanted. But his fascination was so extreme that he was to reappear the following evening. Auret remembered how Hendrik 'kept saying that when this was all over he would give me a plot and two "kaffirs" to farm with'.[134]

Lieutenant P Botes and Lieutenant van Aswegen took on the night shift around 10pm, ordering Auret to stand in a corner. It seems the whipping of his soles and Prince's stomping on his arches had been merely preparation. In the early hours of Thursday morning, Auret was once again manacled, ankle to wrist, and forced to continue standing in that crooked position for the next 18 hours. Apart from the terrible effect on his legs, he now found it difficult to breathe, as if he were asthmatic with a huge pain in his ribcage.

Sometime during Thursday morning, Auret heard Botes take a phone call from Cronwright. At one stage, Botes replied, '*Hy's alright maar nie te alright*' (He's alright but not that alright). A glass of water with some sugar followed, most likely on Cronwright's instructions.

Having threatened Auret with death, Major Abrie was nevertheless unhappy when, on Thursday 19 November, he came into the room and saw Auret hobbled and manacled but without a shirt. Auret had taken it off when allowed to go to the toilet, as it was still soaking wet from the earlier torture. Abrie immediately instructed the interrogators to cover Auret with his jacket, presumably so that the secretaries, who popped their heads around the door to take orders for tea, would not see the marks and bruises down his back.

Abrie returned at around 6pm to deliver a lengthy lecture while Auret continued to hover, one-legged, in aching limbo. Finally, Abrie directed that Auret be released to his cell. He would be given two hours to write down every point that he had previously concealed. Auret had until 9pm. When Abrie appeared at the cell, on time, accompanied by all his interrogators, Auret handed him a list of points. Abrie read them, declared them acceptable, and ordered that Auret should start writing his statement the next day.

For ten days, Auret was unable to walk properly. His vision clouded by burst blood vessels, he suffered a continuous headache for a week. There were so many lumps on his head that if he closed his eyes, he felt his skin tighten over his skull. Taken from his cell early each morning to the fourth floor, and returned around ten at night, he was kept out of sight. He remained in Benoni, writing his statement, until being transferred back to John Vorster Square on 3 December.

Having taken Auret to the extremes of near-death, the security police now dramatically changed tack. Visser, who had strangled him, personally massaged his back and arranged for Auret to exercise in the gym. 'It seemed as if they had come to respect me as a result of the manner in which I had withstood their interrogation,' Auret would write in an affidavit a couple of months after his release from detention the following July.[135]

Auret made it plain in his affidavit that his decision to give evidence at the inquest took 'a great deal of soul-searching and considerable anxiety'. Cronwright had warned him that he would 'suffer the consequences', but finally a sense of duty outweighed his fear of the repercussions. Twenty-seven years on, in an email dialogue with Auret, who is now President and CEO of the Fair Labor Association in Washington, DC, I asked him how, with the distance of time, he views the dynamics of his relationship with his interrogators, especially the dramatic change after he had finally made a fuller statement. In what language had he been interviewed, and did he think his Afrikaner background might have affected his treatment? It appears that it did. While his interrogators had questioned him in English, they would slip into Afrikaans among themselves and were very aware that he was Afrikaans:

> Cronwright in particular resented the fact that I was 'squandering' my cultural heritage. In my first detention in 1977 he spent most of my interrogation wrestling with that contradiction – how could an Afrikaner align himself with the blacks? In 1981 he said – 'if I had one ounce of your Afrikaner heritage in me I would die a happy man'. The other thing they could not quite understand was my sport. One of them, Lawrence Charles Prince, said to me in 1982 that they had detained something like 60 people in the course of our case but that only two of us played sport (Fink Haysom and I). This made us different somehow. The Afrikanerdom, plus the sport, made me somehow worthy of a second chance. I was redeemable, and we could have mutual respect for each other. That was a really, really important thing, that they respected me somehow and I treated them with respect as well.

Here it is again … 'respect' and 'mutual respect'. These are difficult notions to grasp in the relationship of torturer and tortured. In 1984, Auret went on to sue Cronwright and nine SB officers for his torture. In doing so, he defied what novelist and playwright Ariel Dorfman identifies as the 'silencing of what has been happening between those two bodies' and the corrupting effect of torture which 'obliges us to be deaf and blind and mute'.[136] When Auret writes of 'Afrikanerdom, plus the sport' as points of connection, he is surely talking of rugby. Did a male clan element enable Auret to suppress the political differences with his captors, and survive, in that perverted world inside John Vorster Square? Gavin engaged in a macho dynamic with his interrogators in order to survive, playing along with their homophobia and sexism, later suffering self-recrimination and disgust. In playing clever games to get out, he felt horribly compromised:

> I went through incredible anguish because I hated these bastards, I hated

them fervently and here I'd gone through this really demeaning experience, even that thing where I turned Engelbrecht round into him [Pitout], as my best buddy, to do that to someone you want to hit because he's a fascist actually, and talking … giving them anything, you hate yourself and I was, for months, terribly, terribly depressed.

Neil must have gathered this from Gavin's debriefing. Hence the reassuring words in his letter to his close comrade, now stuck in Botswana, 'It obviously worries you, but in my opinion is not important at all.' Interrogators messed with a detainee's head, and the effects could be longer-lasting and even more devastating than what they did to their bodies.

PART FOUR

Seventy Days

CHAPTER 29

Arrest

I N THOSE HIGHLY TENSE WEEKS, MOVING AROUND AND TRYING TO
escape the prying eyes of Special Branch, Neil pressed on with work.
On Sunday 22 November, the union celebrated the inaugural meeting in
Tembisa of a separate Kempton Park branch, with the office shared by SAAWU.
The union was growing. Guest speaker Popo Molefe, from GAWU, urged the
audience to extend their struggle beyond their factories into all areas of their
lives. When Israel Mogoatlhe, the young trade unionist for whom Neil had
been a mentor, was voted chairman, Neil was deeply pleased. He was running
on overdrive. On Thursday 26 November he met with Dr Benjamin Lombard,
the Director of Human Resources for the whole Premier Group, at its Epol
factory. He was due to meet Dr Lombard again, the following day, this time at
its Epic Oil plant. They were close to concluding a year-long series of meetings
during which Neil had helped to negotiate a recognition agreement in which
the union would represent the workers at Epol, Epic Oil and SA Milling. It
was to be a major step forward.

Looking for places to bed down for the night, Neil had approached Bridget
King, with whom he had once shared his little house in Bertrams. After re-
turning from England, Bridget had moved to 823 Crown Mines, in Top
Village. Her back stoep was free and she was happy for Neil to sleep there.

The arrangement was not to last long. During October and November, Special Branch officers continued to make arrests, widening their web of suspects and potential witnesses for their planned treason trial. By the last week in November, a week after Auret's interrogators had taken him to the point of death, they were ready to swoop again. On Tuesday 24 November, Maurice Smithers was re-detained. Perhaps this was a prod to Neil that he didn't have much time. Although he had known for some weeks that Liz's name was on Barbara's list, just beneath his, he hadn't yet informed her. Two nights later, Liz came out to Crown Mines to see him:

> Suddenly the night before we were detained, he mentioned it to me and I realised, hang on, this isn't a query detention – a query that this is growing in our circles and I'm looking like I'm one of the ones next in line – but that this is a definite. In some ways, it was easier. I didn't have the angst of knowing for two months that I was on the list before it happened.

But the hurt was there: 'Neil was the last person around who was able to acknowledge my organisational involvement.' In Liz's eyes, it wasn't just that Neil was pressured and terribly busy. It was that he just hadn't thought it sufficiently important, let alone a priority, to warn her so she could make her own decision. They had agreed not to discuss their work, but more fundamentally, Liz believed that Neil couldn't conceive of her involvement:

> Isn't that the classical thing? Intellectually they [men] know that women should be involved and doing things. So, for instance, my organisational involvement was tolerated provided there was food in the house and the house was clean and preferably if I wore dresses. So long as the female role was not eroded. But being able to tie up the female role, the partner role and the organisational role was impossible for him.

What they said to each other, after Neil broke the news, is not known. Recriminations at this stage wouldn't help. They needed to prepare themselves, to minimise the likelihood of being played off against each other, and to be aware that their interrogators would attempt to manipulate them. They spent the night together on the back stoep of the house, waking in the dark before dawn to banging at the front door. Bridget ran to warn them, but 'Neil quietly accepted his fate, realising there was no escape'.[137] Liz too was calm.

*   *   *

On the morning of Friday 27 November, Colonel Hendrik Muller, commander of Johannesburg security police at John Vorster Square had sent out two teams of officers. Captain Jacob Strauss had orders to arrest Neil, and Major Daniel Mahoney to arrest Liz. With no one answering the door at 420A Fox Street, they had broken in and apparently found information leading them to 823 Crown Mines.[138] The warrants for arrest under Section 22 of the General Law Amendment Act, for furthering the aims of the banned African National Congress, included a search of property. From the back stoep, the officers seized Neil's black briefcase and a Toyota logbook before driving the pair, separately, to Fox Street. Just over a year later, Liz recalled the event for Joseph Lelyveld, special correspondent of *The New York Times*:

> Elizabeth Floyd speaks with tenderness of the morning of her arrest, not simply because those moments proved to be her last with Neil Aggett, but more especially because they were brought so close together before they were parted. For two hours the police searched the house they had shared.
>
> 'We made some tea,' she recalls. 'They kept on wanting us to watch the searching but we weren't very interested. We were more interested in spending whatever time we could together.'
>
> 'It was actually very amazing,' she says, speaking of the closeness. 'There was absolutely no panic. I mean we were kind of going into it together.'[139]

While a Sergeant Michael Stephen Joubert made an inventory, from a host of ILO publications stacked on the lounge floor to Neil's passport, found in an envelope, Major Mahoney personally itemised books taken mainly from the lounge bookshelf and floor. The major topped his list with what he might have thought could be prize exhibits:

1. Theories of Karl Marx Surplus Value Part 1
2. Capital Karl Marx
3. The Social and Political Thought of Leon Trotsky

He noted 42 items, including pamphlets and papers with titles such as 'The role of the missionaries in conquest' and 'Capitalism and Cheap Labour power in SA'. In addition to 'Stencil lettering guides with pamphlet', the police seized 19 copies of 'Noise in the factory causes deafness', two copies of the *South African Labour Bulletin*, three issues of *Africa Perspective* (the journal started by Gavin) and the September issue of a radical students' newspaper, SASPU *National.* A photograph was listed 'Dr Aggett & 2 Black Women with Freedom Charter in background'. There was a copy of *The African Woman's Handbook on the Law* and Bertolt Brecht's *Mr Puntila and his Man Matti* and, finally, 'The little red Blue Book', a London Red Notes pamphlet on fighting the lay-offs at Ford. Major Mahoney must have thought he had made a good haul.[140]

From Fox Street, it was only one block north into Commissioner, then straight west towards the concrete bastion with Vorster's stacked spectacles. However, the car with Neil crossed Commissioner, heading first to the corner of Bree and Wanderers streets. Here, Neil was marched up to the union offices in Lekton House, where desks, drawers and files, with documents representing more than two years of steady work, were rifled and ransacked. An Olympia Traveller deluxe typewriter was among the items seized, along with minutes, expense, receipt and telephone books. Some 87 items in all were listed, Sergeant Joubert also recording Neil's comment in Fox Street that it would take some time to determine which books and documents had belonged to him or to Liz. Around eleven o'clock, Captain Strauss drove Neil under the shadow of the highway above Goch Street, through the iron gates and into the basement of John Vorster Square to hand him over.

CHAPTER 30

Pretoria Central Prison

F ROM THAT MOMENT, WE CAN ONLY GRASP THE REALITY OF NEIL'S final 70 days through fragments. We have odd sightings by other detainees, with a scattering of snatched conversations. We have an account from Yvette Breytenbach and another by his sister and mother of brief visits allowed in December. We have record-keeping entries for meals and medication, as well as for booking in and out times from the cells ... and we have Neil's two statements made in the interrogation room on the tenth floor, the second elaborating the first. We also have Neil's sworn affidavit, dictated to Sergeant Aletta Gertruida Blom some 14 hours before his death, in which he recorded some of the treatment meted out to him.

The Aggett legal team assembled these and much more in the evidence that they presented during the extraordinary inquest. By successfully introducing similar fact evidence from former detainees, cross-examining the interrogators and subjecting the evidence to forensic scrutiny, the family's lawyers briefly shone rays of light into the hidden world of John Vorster Square. While I have also been able to converse with some of Neil's fellow detainees, detention without trial was also intended to isolate detainees from each other. Neil was in the sole power of his interrogators, behind secured doors and mostly screened from view. However, imagination has the power to break through prison walls. In my search for what happened to my cousin, while using all the available evidence, I have also used my human liberty to imagine ...

* * *

By early afternoon on Friday 27 November, the news is out:

> More than a dozen leading trade unionists, students and labour experts were detained early today in a nationwide Security Police swoop.
>
> They were detained in terms of Section 22 of the General Laws Amendment Act which provides for a two-week period of detention with-out the detainee being brought to court.
>
> Those known to have been detained are:
>
> Mrs Emma Mashinini, General Secretary of the Commercial, Catering and Allied Workers' Union ...[141]

The first edition of *The Star* contains eight names. In the City edition, there are 12, and by the City Late, there are 14. The spelling of Neil's name has changed from 'Mr Neil Agate' to 'Mr Neil Aggut'. He is noted as 'a member of the Food and Canning Workers' Union and Miss Floyd is a member of the Industrial Aid Society in Johannesburg'. The list is diverse, with activists seized from all communities. There are people with whom Gavin has worked ... Fink Haysom, Samson Ndou and Pravin Gordhan down in Durban. There is Sam Kikine, SAAWU's General Secretary, a frequent visitor to AFCWU, with whom Neil has been working, as agreed, 'hand in hand'. *The Star*'s reporter mentions that 'further detentions' around the country have not yet been confirmed but everything points to a national swoop.

Emma Mashinini, whom Neil has been assisting daily at the CCAWUSA office in Khotso House[142] since Alan Fine's arrest, catches sight of him inside John Vorster Square. Neil appears to her calm and collected, but after the massive police raid on her Soweto home Emma is still in shock. Needing constantly to go to the toilet, she suffers the embarrassment of having to ask a policewoman each time. She is on her way there again, passing the lift when it stops. Neil walks out and greets her, 'Hello, Emma.' She wants to respond, to say hello back, but the relief of finding that she is not alone overwhelms her.

Later she will write, 'I could not bring out even that one word. I always regretted that, that I did not say hello to Neil, because I was not to see him again.'[143]

The new detainees are booked in, numbered, fingerprinted and photographed before being dispersed into isolation. Neil and Emma are taken separately to Pretoria Central Prison. (Located just off the main Johannesburg to Pretoria road, South Africa's 'Death Row' prison was where my brother Paul and I had been detained in the 1960s.) Emma is sent, without explanation, into the White Female section, which means she gets a bed. In order to keep her separated from the ordinary 'criminals', as a 'political' she is locked up in the same corridor as the white women detainees were in July 1964. With the 'condemned cell' situated at one end, Emma can overhear conversations between two black women awaiting their execution. Although it is November and midsummer, her small cell, with its tiny raised window, is very cold. For her first 14 days she has nothing to read, no visits, no interrogation. Only a plate of food, often cold, is periodically pushed through the door, on the floor. On Sundays, she listens to black prisoners singing hymns and learns one of their songs 'Simswabisile uSatan' ... 'We have disappointed the devil because he has no power over us here. We are together and the devil will never catch us again.'

Do these same plaintive tones travel across the courtyards to Neil's cell in the White Male section? Or does he, as in our time, hear black prisoners singing through the night, into the early hours of Friday morning, before a dawn execution? An email conversation with Rob Adam brings me some first-hand information. After Rob's arrest in September, through 'Sipho/Jeffrey' his interrogators soon had all they needed for their case. Rob has been sent to Pretoria Central to await the next stage. Neil is put in the same section, where even if there is singing they cannot hear it. They have been put 'in the so-called "bomb" cells, very narrow, and isolated from the other cells, used for punishment purposes usually'.

Neil is used to Spartan living, and he is no stranger to isolation but after his usual 18-hour working day, enforced solitary confinement is challenging. With no books and limited human contact, it is designed to disorient and loosen memories. However, he and Rob manage to speak regularly through the bars of their cells. To Rob, Neil's mood appears upbeat:

His interrogation had not yet begun. He was in very high spirits and did a lot to lift my spirits, which were down. I was able to tell Neil how the 'sting operation' had happened – the Sipho story and how Barbara had got sucked in … After Neil's death, which happened after I had been charged with terrorism and was awaiting trial, I took some comfort from the fact that I had been able to talk to him and to tell him how he had come to land in his predicament. But at times I still blame myself for causing his death through my carelessness and lack of attention to detail in a crisis.

So Neil now knows how he has 'come to land in his predicament'. His care in limiting his contact with Barbara was well founded. At least he can feel some reassurance that he is clearly listed among her 'Close Comrades' under 'Advisory/Reference People (only above ground work)'. He can explain that his work has been strictly legal, and he is confident that the security police have nothing on him.

Most mornings, the Adjutant Commanding Officer, Lieutenant Colonel Wessel van Niekerk, checks on Neil. Seeing a wad of cotton wool in Neil's ear on the first Monday, he learns that Neil has earache and arranges for the doctor to treat him. Lieutenant Josephus Delport, who checks on Neil at the weekends, notes that Neil is (in translation) 'a very quiet person who only speaks when spoken to'.[144]

While, with customary discipline, Neil might strive to focus on his impending interrogation, he must be worrying about the effect of his detention on the union. Of less concern is his absence at the hospital. There he can be more easily replaced. But locked in a bare cell for 23 hours every day, does his mind stray into the 'mess' of his personal relationships? Does he believe that Liz may have been arrested for her association with him rather than for activities of her own? Whichever it is, he should have warned her earlier. Their coming together only a few hours before their arrest was fortuitous. Any weakness in their relationship will be ferreted out and used against them. They need to be united.

CHAPTER 31

John Vorster Square:
'Try not to threaten them'

F OURTEEN DAYS AFTER HIS ARREST, NEIL'S TIME UNDER SECTION 22 is up. There has been no interrogation, but he is transferred to Section 6 of the Terrorism Act. When Magistrate AH Louw visits Pretoria Central to check on seven detainees on Friday 11 December, Neil is listed as 'Afwesig' (absent).[145] Detective Sergeant James van Schalkwyk has collected Neil that morning with a Constable Fleishman to drive him back to Johannesburg. 'Schalkie', as Neil and others hear Van Schalkwyk called, has only recently transferred to security police headquarters from the Railways & Harbours Police and has been assigned to work on 'Arbeids aangeleenthede' (labour matters).[146] He knows nothing about such matters from his previous work and this is his first time seeing Neil.

At the rear of John Vorster Square lies a square building with three floors of cells, built around an inaccessible inner courtyard. While some 250 'criminal' prisoners are crammed into the first- and third-floor cells, each of the 20 or so 'politicals' has to be kept in solitary confinement on the second floor. Three of the right-angled corridors are for men, with women held separately on the fourth side. However, black and white politicals are locked up alongside each other. No doubt this is due to a shortage of space, but given that they are un- der constant surveillance, with cells probably bugged, their captors are most likely looking to see who tries to be in contact with whom. While evading scrutiny is a perpetual challenge, there is no comparison in cell conditions on the different floors. Keith Coleman, whose cell faces the inner courtyard, can see up into a third-floor window. His description fits Dante's 'Inferno':

> They had the round bars going up and then the flat metal bars going across and then floor to ceiling bars in this one cell in the third floor … [The police] used to make these prisoners climb up to the top right to the roof, on these bars, and then hold on with their hands right at the top. Their heads [were] pressed against the roof and their feet quite high up as well and then they [the police] used to take a run with the whip and just run up to these guys and smack them on the back and, if you let go, you fell all the way down to the floor, and that's how they used to punish them. I used to watch. Just appalling.

During the day, Warrant Officer Walter MacPherson oversees the second floor. Classified as Coloured, MacPherson has spent 15 years as a policeman attached to the security police. The second floor has been his domain since 1977, Monday to Friday, 7.30am to 4pm. He's a strict man of few words. His job, he will tell the inquest, is to attend to complaints, check that detainees wash daily, take custody of their personal property, see to their daily exercise, and check that the magistrate and inspectors see the correct people. He keeps an 'unofficial' register of the daily wash, meals (detainees must write down items of food taken), health and any other remarks. He requires signatures from both detainees and police officials.[147]

On Friday 11 December, Auret van Heerden, who has recently been returned to John Vorster Square following his ordeal in Benoni, is coming out of one of MacPherson's rooms when he sees Neil being allocated Cell 209, directly opposite his own cell, number 215. Auret has already established contact with young Ernest Moabi Dipale, who is in 208, next to Neil. When the outer wooden doors are unlocked and opened for meal times, Auret can see Ernest, and now Neil, if they stand at their grilles. These grilles stretch from floor to ceiling and are recessed inside each cell, forming two sides of a square, so visibility is limited. However, when the doors are left open, occasionally in the evenings for as long as an hour, detainees can grab the chance to communicate across the corridor. Neil wants to know about Auret's interrogation.

Who were his interrogators, and what was the best way to handle the personal dynamics? Auret's tale of torture is not a surprise but is cause for concern. It's now two months since Barbara and her foremost 'Close Comrades' were arrested, yet the police are still pulling people in. They sense a quarry and are desperate to prove themselves right. Auret advises Neil to try and keep relations as even-tempered as possible: '... you should relate to these people in a non-antagonistic way. Try not to threaten them with your educational qualifications. Discuss issues of common interest and things like cricket, etc, be conscious of your appearance and your neatness and that kind of thing.'[148] Neil is used to approaching union negotiations in a 'non-antagonistic way'. Moreover, he has had two weeks to think about how he will defend himself and his work. He wants this interrogation over and done with.

Along the N1 highway between Pretoria and Johannesburg, Neil has glimpsed the world from which he has been extracted. A sliver of the outside world slips in with a parcel handed to him by Constable Daniel Zeelie. He signs for it. It has been waiting since the previous Friday. The DPSC doesn't know where detainees are being held, so its members deliver packages to John Vorster Square, from where they also collect dirty washing. Every item passing in and out is meticulously recorded in a makeshift register in a book that has printed columns headed, 'Name of investigator ... Name of accused ... Result ... Date and signature of Branch Commander.' Neil's first parcel entry reads:

> Friday 81/12/04 Mr L Kaplan for Neil Aggett
>
> 2 box of cheese.
>
> 1 liquifruit
>
> 1 pct. Prunes
>
> 2 box of choc creams (biscuits)
>
> 3 pcts nuts
>
> 1 fruit roll
>
> 2 pct cigarettes
>
> 1 pct cards
>
> 2 yellow tennis balls
>
> 1 cont. wet-ones
>
> 2 boxes matches
>
> 2 oranges
>
> 1 pct. games c/drink
>
> 1 pct. sweets

1 small game
1 ultra mel
1 multi coloured cloth
Handed in by: [signed L Kaplan]
Received by: [signed JE Lloyd][149]

The '1 multi coloured cloth' is a hand-tasselled kikoi of blue and white stripes with thinner reds and yellows. Yvette has sent it in to lift Neil's spirits. It's the kikoi that she wore on the day they had recently spent relaxing by her friends' pool. *It looks beautiful on you*, Neil had said. Yvette wants Neil to 'wrap it around him and feel hugged'. Someone also knows he is fond of Ultra Mel custard. It's a thoughtful parcel. Has he been allowed it because Cronwright's team hasn't got to work on him yet?

Neil is left inside his cell for a further three days. It has a toilet behind a half-wall along the same wall as the grille and door. High up on the opposite wall is a barred window. Three mats and two blankets do for a bed beneath the window and he has two concrete benches between the bed and the door. Exercise at weekends is confined to the cells, so over his first weekend in John Vorster his only chance to glimpse other detainees is when going for a shower on Sunday. Soon, however, Neil will be inducted into three specific methods of communication: 'I'll see you in United Nations!' means 'Let's shout through the windows!'; 'Lancaster House' means 'grab a chance to talk when the doors are opened for dinner!' or through the small square hatch through which the food is slung. The third method, 'conference call', requires some effort. The detainee must empty out all the water from the toilet before pulling a blanket over his head to speak through the pipes. Depending on the layout of the pipework and where curves occur, it's possible to talk with someone in the next cell or the one directly opposite. If you are lucky you can get a message down the corridor, the advantage of 'conference call' being that you speak in a normal tone of voice, allowing for more discreet conversation than 'United Nations'.[150]

There are many more detainees here than in Pretoria. Neil's SAAWU comrades from the eastern Cape, Sisa and Thozamile, have been arrested and brought to Johannesburg just a few days before his arrival. Eric Mntonga, a lab assistant at Wilson Rowntree in East London, another SAAWU comrade whom Neil knows, has also been hauled in. There are also the Johannesburg-based activists. Around the corner, in the corridor leading to the entrance gate and the showers, is Keith Coleman, a 21-year-old honours student at Wits, one of the co-founders, with Auret van Heerden, of SASPU *National*, the radical newspaper of the South African Students' Press Union (SASPU). Neil has written union stories for this journal, which carries just enough student news while publishing material never printed in the mainstream papers. The editors have been playing a cat-and-mouse game with the state by challenging every ban at the Publications Appeal Board, and quite often winning, much to the chagrin of the security police. SASPU's deeper role has been to contribute to countrywide mobilisation around common campaigns, like distributing many thousands of posters for the anti-Republic Day campaign. On the second floor, Neil finds himself among a range of comrades who have been playing various parts in a broad workers' movement, and whom the security police are determined to link into a vast treason plot. Option A for the police is to mount charges against as many co-conspirators as possible alongside Barbara. Option B is to use as many as possible as state witnesses, with those who refuse to testify being jailed for up to five years.

By now, Barbara has been returned to the women's cells at John Vorster Square, around the corner from the men. Liz remains in the police cells at Bronkhorstspruit, where she has been held since her arrest, but when she is finally brought back for interrogation at John Vorster, she will be taken to Hillbrow police station at night and on weekends. No doubt this is to reduce the chances of Neil and her meeting, even fleetingly. That way, their interrogators can spin their stories.

The detainees do their best, however, to keep as informed as possible, perfecting the art of 20- to 30-second conversations. This is usually during exercise time, running up and down the corridors, or when going to the showers, and MacPherson is suddenly called away from his observation point to attend to someone banging at the entrance gate. Sometimes there can be just enough time to push open a door that has been opened for meal time, or look through a keyhole and communicate with someone. But, as Keith Coleman recalls, you have to keep alert:

> ... you could hear Warrant Officer MacPherson – Mac as he was called – coming back, the gates closing, the keys jingling, him coming down the corridor. So I'd then pretend to be running back again, and you had to time

it, so that if I just stood there talking, he'd expect to see me running up the corridor again. So I'd sprint, then jog, then get back there and sprint again back into the cell, so you'd have very disjointed, very brief conversations with each other, and he [Neil] was too far away for me to speak to him through the toilet.

Contact is about more than passing information. It's a means of maintaining solidarity and resisting the debilitating effects of isolation.

On Tuesday 15 December at 9.53am, Detective Sergeant van Schalkwyk signs Neil out from the cells. The record shows Barbara being signed out two minutes earlier. Handcuffed, Neil is kept away as far as possible from other detainees who are being taken for interrogation. They go by lift to the ninth floor and stairs to the tenth. A wire-mesh grille above the handrail sometimes prompts the remark that it's there 'to prevent people jumping to their death'. When this is said to Liz, it will make her think of suicide, striking her with fear every time she has to walk up and down those stairs.

The tenth floor is a long corridor with offices on either side, most of them allocated to the white officers. Black policemen have a separate tea room at the opposite end of the corridor from the 'white tea room'. Cronwright's office, Room 1009, is in the middle. Captain Martin Naude has been assigned to kick off Neil's interrogation. He is the eastern Cape officer who, with his white safari suit, insisted to Barbara that he was a doctor and has since been promoted. He is known for screaming at detainees, but with Neil he takes a different tack. He will be the 'good cop'. From what Neil tells Auret, Naude's approach is non-aggressive. Neil is even led to think that Naude likes him.

For the first two sessions, five hours on Tuesday 15 December and six and a half hours on Thursday 17 December, Naude is accompanied by Van Schalkwyk, who leaves most of the questioning to Naude. Neil says to Auret that Van Schalkwyk, the railway policeman recently seconded to the security police, appears more like his guard. On Thursday, a visiting magistrate, Mr PC van der Merwe, sees Neil for the first time and asks whether he has any complaints. Most detainees say 'no'. They know about retribution. Neil, however, buoyantly asserts that his interrogation should have begun earlier. He is annoyed at the waste of time. The magistrate writes this down:

Complaints: 'I was told that I was being detained under section 22 and if I did not answer questions correctly then I would be transferred to section 6. I was only asked about 3 questions about someone I did not even know. Thereafter I was transferred to section 6.'[151]

The magistrate also reports Neil's request for 'Cigarettes and a pair of jeans and more books', that his health is 'Very good' and that he has no injuries. His official letter is sent to the Director-General of Justice, the Commissioner of Police and to the Commander of Security Police at John Vorster Square.

The following week, Naude leads only two sessions, on Monday (six hours) and Tuesday (six and a half hours), before taking his Christmas leave. Lieutenant Steven Peter Whitehead, who has a long-time interest in Neil, joins the team that week. On Wednesday 23 December, Whitehead steps into the lead, conducting a shorter session that day and on Christmas Eve. Captain Naude, who is due back at the beginning of January, is still in charge, and that must be something of a constraint on the ambitious younger officer, only recently promoted from sergeant and raring to prove himself. By most accounts, he is a few years younger than Neil, with a degree in policing and a father who is a brigadier in the South African Police (SAP), a Divisional Commander for the Witwatersrand. The clean-shaven, slightly podgy-faced officer, with schoolboyish hair neatly parted down the middle, has been in the security police at John Vorster Square for five years, assigned to look into labour matters. Having taken an interest in Neil for over two years, he needs to justify the time spent. The magistrate's report with Neil's complaint arrives after Naude has gone on his leave. It is passed down the echelons for Whitehead's eyes.

CHAPTER 32

Christmas visits: 'Don't worry'

W HITEHEAD SAYS THAT NEIL'S INTERROGATION TAKES PLACE '*altyd in 'n gemoedelike stemming*' (always in a genial mood).[152] Neil must write his life story and tell all he knows about ANC and SACTU activities. Whitehead's role is to prompt with questions.

When Yvette receives special permission to make a pre-Christmas visit on Wednesday 23 December, she is taken up to the tenth floor by a Captain Carel van Rensburg. Ushered into the interrogation room, for a moment she sees Neil before he sees her. He is sitting behind a desk, holding a pen to his mouth as if in thought, with a piece of paper in front of him. He seems taken by surprise and gives no indication that he has been expecting her. She is relieved to see that his demeanour is completely calm. Neil rises and they embrace 'in a restrained manner'. He is obviously delighted, and even teases her 'for wearing stockings and dressing up for work'.

Yvette notes that both Whitehead and Van Rensburg appear to be cordial with Neil, calling him by his first name. Whitehead stays in the room throughout the visit. When he makes out that the security police are doing them a big favour by allowing this 30-minute visit, Yvette immediately challenges this. Why is Neil only being given half an hour when other detainees have been given 45 minutes? Yvette wants Neil to know that this visit is not a special favour over other detainees. The visit will be 30 minutes, but his eyes flash approval. They sit down together, facing each other across the desk, with some knee contact. At times they hold hands. Yvette has a pen and notebook.

It's a relief to find Neil 'very calm, clear-headed and well, both physically and mentally'. He is concerned about his appearance, wanting to look 'smart'. In Yvette's eyes, he seems to be 'in complete control', showing no signs of nervousness. He repeatedly reassures her, 'Don't worry, Yvette, everything's okay.' He says that he is fitter than ever. There was a lot of time for exercise in Pretoria Central Prison. He had seen a doctor there and an ear infection has cleared. However, conditions here at John Vorster Square are much better. He is eating three meals a day, receiving parcels and sleeping well.[153]

They talk about domestic matters. Anything else is forbidden. Whitehead intervenes twice: once when Neil mentions his interrogation and a second time when Neil says it seems that this will be a big case. They are allowed to deal with Neil's car, which he says needs attention, and he is permitted to mention the agreement with Epic Oil that should have been signed on the day of his arrest. He is pleased to hear that a 'Care Group' has been set up, looking after his cats as well as the house in Fox Street. Yvette knows that he is very fond of that house and checks that he has received her handmade Christmas card: a painting of the house, with its simple red corrugated-iron roof, chimney, front door, window and a single hollyhock in the garden under a golden sky.[154]

Neil tells her that he has also received the kikoi and a shirt that she has specially sewed from anti-waste ends of fabric. It has variegated colours, which she imagines emphasise the blue of his eyes. The label says 'Yve's Boutique', and Neil has been fooled, asking her where that is. They laugh as she explains that she made it herself. She has also carried into the interrogation room a Christmas food parcel that she has packed herself. She has put it down where Neil can see it. She knows it will be checked, but it contains a surprise to cheer him. She has laced the Liqui-Fruit apple juice with whisky. It's a reminder of times gone by.

Despite Whitehead's prohibition on what they may discuss, Neil cleverly conveys how he rates his chances, telling Yvette that when he comes out of detention, he intends going back into medicine. She understands this as 'I don't expect to be charged but will be banned'. Previously, when they've spoken about how banning would force him out of union work, he has mentioned specialising in emergency surgery. He asks her now to send in a copy of Hamilton Bailey's *Emergency Surgery*. It seems to Yvette that he is already preparing himself for a transition. Nevertheless, Neil is optimistic that he will be out within weeks. Yvette asks what to do about their February holiday booking for four: Neil and Liz, herself and her boyfriend. Don't cancel, says Neil. It'll be okay.

Their time is soon over. After 30 minutes, Lieutenant Whitehead informs them that the visit is over. He stands outside the door while Neil and Yvette embrace before she leaves. Whitehead's later account of the same visit reveals, in Barbara Hogan's words, his 'appalling curiosity' and his obsession with Neil's personal relationships: 'It was clear to me that they knew each other very well and even could be lovers'; and 'After Miss Breytenbach had gone Dr Aggett made it clear to me that she was just a good friend of his'.[155] What is clear is that Whitehead pointedly probes.

Although Yvette's visit has been set up by the Detainee Parents' Support Committee, there is no one to debrief her afterwards. The DPSC and its supporters are thinly stretched. Twenty-seven years later, however, she recalls the impact of white middle-class parents who found themselves drawn into dealing with the security police through the detention of their children:

> There is nothing like the determination of parents who want to protect their offspring and who are empowered by their standing in society, ie they were white, older, respected in the community, educated, able to express themselves and their demands clearly and persuasively, and they were strategic. What the DPSC managed to do was to use the newspapers to report as much as possible, eg about the deprivations in detention, and what I think (my opinion here) needs to be understood about the success of what DPSC achieved is that it was very shocking to the white community to have so many well educated young 'respectable' whites being detained. Also possibly the fact that there were quite a lot of white women amongst them could have been shocking. Suddenly this really didn't fit white society's picture of who the Reds under the Beds were. This was very threatening to the security police and I think embarrassing and that is how the DPSC managed to negotiate the Christmas visits and parcels which were a huge deviation and 'privilege' from what usually happened for detainees who were not white.

While white middle-class power has taken the security police by surprise, the DPSC is strengthened by family members of black detainees who bring knowledge and insight into the workings of the system. Equality of treatment for all detainees is at the core of all their demands and their delegations reflect non-racial unity.[156] Neil's sister joins a delegation to General Johan Coetzee, head of the security police, at his office in Pretoria. Jill is accompanied by Max Coleman, who has two sons locked up, Auret van Heerden's father and Emma Mashinini's husband, Tom. In his heavily panelled room, on a searing mid-summer day, the general plays the 'infinite charmer'. He blithely fobs off their concerns, such as blood on detainees' clothes: 'They're absolutely fine. They're being looked after really well. Can't think what you're worrying about!' The experience is both informative and shocking for Jill.

Neil's parents, far away in Somerset West, rely on Jill for any news that she gleans through the DPSC. Neil has sent his parents a Christmas card, and received one: 'To dearest Neil with all our good wishes and fond love from Mum and Dad.' There are family greetings too from the Rosenthals: 'Dear Neil, here's hoping for a good 1982, lots of love, David, Jane and The Brats.' A second card from the Rosenthals is signed by a number of other friends, as is a card from Joanne. The cement benches in his cell are filling up with clothes, cigarettes, food (biscuits, biltong, fruit, nuts, cheese, cool drinks …), games (playing cards, chess set, jigsaws …) and, vitally, books. By Christmas, he has acquired 20 books. Friends have been sending in what they think he will enjoy. His collection is developing: Camus and Nietzsche, Orwell and Huxley, Tolstoy, Isaac Bashevis Singer, Yevgeny Zamyatin … No wonder Cronwright and his team are not amused by Colonel Muller's agreement with the DPSC.

Whitehead pulls Neil out for a morning-only session on Christmas Eve. He makes out that, because it's Christmas, he conducts questioning in what he regards as 'a very amiable manner' (*'n baie gemoedelike trant*).[157] Auret is studying down the corridor in Room 1015, the office of newly promoted Lieutenant Pitout, whom Gavin had accused of trying to seduce him. Shortly after midday, when Neil is taken back down to the cells, Auret is called to Room 1009, Major Cronwright's office, and offered a beer. Cronwright is throwing a small Christmas party for his men, with members of the top brass from the ninth floor, like Colonel Muller and Brigadier Theunis 'Rooi Rus' Swanepoel, dropping in. At one stage, Whitehead comes to sit next to Auret. 'Look, do you think that Neil might be SACTU?' he asks. Auret goes through all the reasons again with him why the unions – and Neil – keep away from SACTU: 'You people have got an absolutely inflated view of SACTU's role in the labour movement.'[158]

When Cronwright joins the conversation, he asserts to Whitehead that he should forget Neil's involvement in underground activity, because if this was the case Barbara would have placed him in that capacity on her list. Whitehead must know that the conversation will be relayed to Neil. If he regards his boss's intervention as an indiscretion, he doesn't let on. Perhaps it makes him even more determined to prove his own theory.

Later that evening in the cells, it's hard for the detainees to avoid low spirits. Then, from somewhere distant, they hear singing. It comes and goes: 'Good King Wenceslas looked out on the feast of Stephen ...' A party of carol singers is circling John Vorster Square in a truck. The gesture cheers them. On Christmas Day, in the afternoon, Whitehead appears at Neil's cell, bearing a plate of cold meat from his family's table. Neil thanks him. Whitehead is pleased. When Neil says that he has run out of matches, Whitehead arranges that he gets some. Perhaps Whitehead thinks that Neil will now owe him something. Or perhaps he is simply relishing his own sense of munificence in conferring favours – and the power to withdraw them.

The weekend follows. No interrogation and no running up and down the corridor for exercise. Inside his cell, Neil has plenty of time for reading and reflection. For the past two years, there has been precious little space for contemplating personal matters. Does he think about arguments with Liz over this? He knows that it has been a major bone of contention. Later, Liz will say that it must have preyed on his mind: 'What you're there with is yourself and your life. If you've got problems you sit with them and they tear you apart, especially regrets.'

Auret can tell that he is 'thinking a lot'. Neil discusses his personal life 'quite extensively' with Auret, telling him what has happened in his relationship with Liz: 'He was quite optimistic about that. It was clear to me ... that in the long run he viewed them as a couple.'[159] Neil has no idea whether Liz is still in detention or how she is faring. But, inevitably, much of Neil's thinking revolves around Gavin, thankfully, safely out of the country, and Sipho ... hopefully, not detained.

Neil's interrogation resumes on Monday 28 December, and continues on Tuesday and Wednesday while he writes his statement by hand. Up until

Christmas, Whitehead has played along as 'good cop', but before the year is out there are clues that he has begun to strain at the bit. When Magistrate PC van der Merwe visits the cells on Tuesday, nearly a fortnight after his last visit, Neil is 'unavailable'. On Wednesday evening, Neil cuts his hair and beard with a small pair of borrowed scissors. Without a mirror, it's quite a feat. He has heard that his family has been granted a Christmas visit. Perhaps his father is coming to see him. Later, he will tell Naude that he wanted to show his parents that he still respected them.

On Thursday, New Year's Eve, Warrant Officer Danvey Maphophe collects Neil before noon and takes him to an office on the ninth floor. There he finds his mother and sister. Aubrey has said that Joy should take Jill. Years later, when his parents talk to me, words and images from the visit replay relentlessly:

> JOY: The last time I saw him, he was in detention at John Vorster Square … New Year's Eve.
>
> AUBREY: He told you don't worry about him, but it would be some time before he got out.
>
> JOY: The security police was there all the time, a black man, and there was to be no talk of any 'case', just personal affairs. So Jill and I sat with him there and talked for about half an hour.
>
> AUBREY: We periodically sent him things, and he told you they would not give these things to them, as a sort of punishment.
>
> JOY: We sent him dried fruit and cigarettes and so on.
>
> AUBREY: The stuff that was supposed to be in his cell, he had biscuits, dried fruit – which was a lot of tommyrot.
>
> JOY: When we got there we came with a box of things. We had to hand it to the security policeman, but I don't believe he ever got it again.
>
> AUBREY: They manipulated them by retaining any goodies …
>
> JOY: Of course he didn't have a belt on, laces in his shoes. He was looking thin too.

Mother and sister huddle, with Neil sitting between them, heads and knees close. He holds a hand from each. Maphophe sits nearby, listening, having warned Neil, 'Now, Aggett, you must say nothing about the case.' They can chat about Christmas. Jill and her family have been down in Somerset

West. Neil tells them how the carol singers had lifted the depressed mood on Christmas Eve. It's better being in John Vorster Square than Pretoria, where his cell had been both narrow, dirty and completely cut off from most normal sounds. At least he can hear some life going on outside in Johannesburg. You're thinner, notes Joy, but still looking fit. He smiles to reassure them. It's true: he lost weight in Pretoria. There was less food there and a lot of time for doing exercises. They speak a little about Liz. Her mother and father have been up from the Cape to see her. Neil listens intently, gleaning whatever he can. The conversation confirms that Liz is still 'inside'. He adds that his interrogation hasn't been too trying, but, realistically, his own detention might last at least six months longer. 'Aggett!' warns Maphophe, 'Nothing about the case!' Mother and sister ask if he has received parcels that have been sent in. Yes, some things, but then they were taken away. In that way detainees are manipulated. The words are out before Maphophe can stop him. Besides, it's not exactly to do with 'the case'.

At half past twelve, a white policeman replaces Maphophe, and pulls up his chair very close. Ten more minutes only. Joy has brought in her copy of *Zorba the Greek* and a couple of books that she thinks will be light reading for her son. Neil asks if they will please get him the medical textbook *Emergency Surgery* by Bailey. It's the book he has also mentioned to Yvette. That's what he'd like to study, he says, when he comes out of detention. Neil remains relaxed throughout. At 12.40pm, they embrace goodbye. As he goes out of the door, he drags his feet a bit and they realise that he has no laces in his shoes. The two women have managed to keep brave faces, but the shuffling almost undoes them. They hold each other, unaware that this will be their final image of him alive.

At 12.51pm, Neil is signed back into the second-floor cells. There's another long weekend ahead, inside his cell, to see in 1982. On Christmas Eve, he thought he'd be out by February and able to go on holiday. By New Year's Eve, his estimate has been revised to six months.

CHAPTER 33

Whitehead takes charge

NAUDE IS BUSY ON HIS FIRST DAY BACK AT WORK, MONDAY 4 January, checking statements of other detainees against Neil's. In the afternoon he tells Neil to begin typing out everything that he has written by hand, putting all names in capitals … that is, according to the Captain's benign account of the day. Later in the afternoon, however, when the cell doors are opened for their evening meal, Auret sees Neil limping towards his grille. 'What's up?' asks Auret. It's a very different story.

That morning, when the black policeman Detective Constable Magezi Eddie Chauke has fetched Neil from the cells, he is taken to the general office, Room 1011. Whitehead is waiting there with 'Schalk', the railway policeman, and Captain Andries Struwig, the officer who beat up Barbara. There are three desks in the room, one of which is shunted across the door. Chauke remains inside with the white policemen. Surrounded, Neil must strip, totally naked, and then run on the spot. 'You're going nowhere, just keep running.' Then it's press-ups. Squats. Star-jumps. Non-stop. All the while, the white policemen fire questions and abuse at him. 'You've written a statement but it is bullshit – we know that. This is just to give you a taste of what will happen if you do not agree to start writing a more comprehensive statement.'[160] Their questions are unspecific, vague, no details. His interrogators are fishing. There's a pool of sweat on the floor and he's now exhausted.

But Whitehead and Struwig decide he needs more incentive. Given the nod, 'Schalk' wraps a piece of protective clothing around his forearm. We have Neil's own words, dictated exactly a month later, in an affidavit to Sergeant Blom, telling us what happens next:

> … I was interrogated by Lt. Whitehead and every time that he had asked
> me a question and I denied it, he accusing [sic] me of calling him a liar.
> Then this Schalk would assault me. He hit me with his open hand through
> my face and I fell against the table with my back and I could feel a scab on
> my back. He also assaulted me with his fists by hitting me on the side of
> my temple and my chest. He also kicked me with his knee on the side of
> my thigh. This Schalk wore a watch which cut my right forearm and it was
> bleeding. Later this Schalk went to wash off the blood that was on him.
> While I was assaulted by him he grabbed me by the scrotum and squeezed
> my testicles.[161]

The 'interrogation' lasts for about three hours. While Neil is on the tenth floor, the Inspector of Detainees, Mr Abraham Johannes Mouton, who reports directly to the Minister of Justice, visits the cells: 'The detainee was again not available for an interview. The security police told me that he was out on investigation.'[162] This is the second time that Neil is 'not available', the Inspector's first visit having been made on 23 December to Pretoria Central because the security police had failed to inform him of Neil's transfer. While the magistrate is required to visit fortnightly, the Inspector of Detainees is simply expected to visit as frequently as possible. Neither is legally bound to ensure that they actually see all the detainees, but they have the power to insist that a detainee be made available for interview. On Monday 4 January, Inspector Mouton doesn't request that Neil be made available, nor does he arrange to return later in the day. As far as he's concerned, he has fulfilled his obligation.

By mid-afternoon, Neil informs MacPherson that he wants to see a doctor. He wants his injuries recorded. However the policeman who has brought him down has handed MacPherson a letter. Neil tells Auret that he thinks it must be an instruction not to let him see a doctor, because MacPherson is blocking him. Instead, next to 'Any Complaints?' in the Cell Register, MacPherson writes: 'Pain in ribs & back used one tablet'. A single 200mg Brufen … This MacPherson repeats over the next four days, despite Neil's repeated requests for a doctor. While the register indicates three meals being taken each day, Neil unusually writes nothing in the register that comprises the daily inventory. The entry for Cell 209, in Neil's handwriting, jumps three days from 3 January – 4 Slices Bread. Tea. Mince. Rice Potato Carrots – to 7 January – Mince. Rice. Beetroot. 4 Slices Bread. Tea. It's not clear whether Neil eats anything for the missing period or whether this is his only way of registering a protest and recording that something is amiss.

A memory of Keith Coleman's seems also to relate to this first assault. Keith acknowledges the problem of always remembering the correct sequence of events because 'being inside, time just changes'. Nevertheless, the memories themselves remain sharp: 'I remember going into his cell and seeing Neil sitting there and he looked terrible. Don't know if the word "devastated" is right. He looked stunned, literally stunned, and he brought me a shirt, and he came and said, "There's blood on my shirt. I'm keeping this as evidence of what these guys have done to me."' The details fit Neil's later account of Whitehead's introductory onslaught.

On the morning of Tuesday 5 January, Neil is taken out soon after eight, earlier than usual. He has to type his statement. Naude and Van Schalkwyk say that they take turns with Whitehead sitting in the room with Neil. By chance, as Constable Chauke returns him to the cells in the afternoon, they pass Barbara, who is being taken to Heidelberg police station. She sees Neil's torn shirt and scratch marks on his arm:

> His face just lit up and he kind of went to the back of the room and put his hand up, while they were getting the keys, and saluted me – which was quite a defiant thing to do in prison at that time. But he was just very warm, and I had been very concerned that he would be feeling that I had placed him in a very difficult position – him more than anyone else because he was a union person – and, in a sense, it's always been like a comfort that he had that response.

A generous, comradely salute forms Barbara's final image.

From Wednesday to Friday, Neil types, six and a half hours every day, signing and dating each typewritten page. By now, he knows that Cronwright is moving Naude to another case and putting Whitehead in full charge. Later, rumours will circulate that strings were pulled. On Monday 11 January, Whitehead orders Neil to index all persons and organisations mentioned. Five hours later, the work completed, Constable Maqubela takes him back to his cell. Whitehead intends to scour the statement, compare it with others, poke its fabric, and find which threads to pull. Back in his cell, Neil is left to contemplate what he has written.

CHAPTER 34

The first statement

NEIL HUDSON AGGETT

Born on 6th October at Nanyuki, Kenya.
Youngest son of J.A.E. AGGETT residing at:
P.O. Box 136,
Somerset West.

I

My father was a farmer in Nanyuki, and I had one elder brother, Michael and one older sister, Jill. I went to school when I was six at the Nanyuki primary school, where I was a weekly boarder. After that I went to the Nyeri primary school, where I was a boarder until the age of ten. In January 1964, my family and I left Kenya by ship and arrived in Durban. My father sold his farm and invested his money in South Africa …[163]

TELL US YOUR BACKGROUND … HOW SIMPLY HE BEGINS: CHILD-hood encapsulated in a few sentences. When he comes to his student days and conjures up a vivid image of Liz and himself in their early days, there's even a fleeting touch of his former poetry:

> LIZ FLOYD came to stay with me in Constantia in 1974, and we spent the
> next two years together, studying and staying on the farm. We did not go
> out much, but spent our time on the beach or in the forest, or sitting around
> a fire at the cottage …[164]

Nevertheless, even in this account of youth, the occasional awkward sentence
points to a jabbing question. There's a telltale phrase like, 'My friends at this
time were …'; 'At this time I was friendly with …'; 'It was during this time that
I met …' Each detainee is expected to produce, in capitals, a who's who.

Gavin's name appears for the first time when Neil writes of coming to
Tembisa Hospital around September 1977 after not being able to find work in
Cape Town. 'It was during this time that I met JENNY CUNNINGHAM, ANNIE
SMYTHE [sic], TAFFY ADLER and GAVIN ANDERSON [sic].' He puts his best
friend at the end of an eclectic list.

As Neil explains the evolution of his political outlook, his sentences become dense, his tone more intense. He gives rational grounds for what seems
so irrational to his interrogators, why a medical doctor should be working in
a trade union: 'sometimes I would stitch up a patient, only to have him return
the following week due to alcoholism, unemployment, or extreme poverty,
with another assault wound'. Many medical problems were 'basically social
problems', including those of people injured at work. 'Even if they did get
their compensation, they often lost their jobs, which meant that they could
not get another job due to the disability, and them and their families were
without means of support.'[165]

There's nothing that's illegal here, just common human concern. So it's not
surprising that he takes an interest in workman's compensation and says 'yes'
to Taffy Adler when 'he asked me if I would be interested to work in the
Industrial Aid Society'.[166] Neil says nothing about the highly charged debate
between 'workerists' and 'populists' of two years earlier … and nothing of
how Gavin and Sipho were marginalised after their banning by those taking charge of IAS and MAWU. By reversing roles with Taffy in how he enters
IAS ('he asked me'), he hopes to seal up questions that might lead towards
the Group of 7, Woodworkers and the network of discussion groups. At least
Captain Naude from East London hasn't picked up on this. He has been more
interested in Neil's links with Sisa, Thozamile and SAAWU. But Whitehead?

Neil tries to be as brief with his introduction to Food and Canning. Jan comes up in 1978 with a delegation of AFCWU workers to start a branch in Johannesburg and they stay with Neil in his house in Bertrams. Then, early in 1979, Oscar Mpetha comes up to continue the work and stays with Neil. Prompted by a question, or perhaps knowing that this is already in their files, Neil tells how Lisa Williamson, sister of the spy Craig, took Oscar to a meeting:

> He [Oscar] told me she had an elaborate plan to get money from overseas from her brother to set up Unions in South Africa, presumably s.a.c.t.u. It sounded far fetched, and I told Oscar so. He was not interested in her plan, and never took up the offer.[167]

This was before Craig Williamson had finally been exposed, but Neil had been able to pass on Gavin's warning. Here, he keeps to the bare bones. However, he still needs to explain how he has come to work in the union. So, between minimal details, he inserts a long philosophical passage in which Oscar, while staying with him in Bertrams, asks if he would be prepared to work unpaid: 'I felt that if I worked in a trade union I could at least contribute …'[168]

Patiently, earnestly, Neil explains a set of fundamental values, relating 'rights' with 'respect', outlining the open nature of his contacts and work in factories, where 'even the management seems happy now because there is a relationship of mutual respect …' While his interrogators want a picture of him as a conspiratorial communist, trying to undermine society, Neil presents universal liberal values as the basis of his actions effecting gradual change. 'So when Mr. MPETHA asked me if I would be prepared to work for the a.f.c.w.u., I said that I would.'[169]

He keeps details about Liz to a bare minimum. She too will be questioned about him, and the less said the better: 'In about mid 1979, LIZ FLOYD came up to stay with me in Joburg. We had personal problems and I felt it would be good to get away for a while …'[170]

Describing his trip to Umtata and Mount Fletcher, he sticks to his medical duties as a locum. After his return to Johannesburg, Jan comes up with a delegation for the Fatti's & Moni's boycott and stays with Neil and Liz. They discuss Neil's appointment to the union. In the abbreviated telling, Neil says nothing about Jan's reservations about him, including the business of avoiding army call-up. Instead he focuses on his resignation from the IAS, outlining how he handed his work over to three women doctors, Liz Floyd, Liz

Thomson and Jenny Cunningham. Although he and Liz have now moved into 420A Fox Street, 'generally we agreed not to discuss our work too much with each other, as we each had our own problems and were very busy'.[171]

A brief paragraph follows, perhaps in response to a question about social life:

> We were also involved at this time in a vegetable garden … and we would share the vegetables. It was a good way of getting out in the sun and using our bodies after a week in the office. It was here that I had met Dave Dyson [sic]. We also played together in the soccer team that used to play occasionally on Sundays. I also visited GAVIN ANDERSON [sic] a few times while he was living with his wife in Bertrams, in Ascot road, and he was also involved in the vegetable garden and playing soccer.[172]

They were like any group of friends engaging in normal weekend activity.

Describing his work at the union, Neil expands on events, meetings, boycotts, how the workers are organised, issues under debate. Many paragraphs are lengthy. There's nothing to hold him back when talking about his work, including his union's cooperation with SAAWU. Every now and again, he gives a list of names. Here, for the first, and only, time in his first statement he mentions his comrade Sipho taking part in a meeting on Prime Minister PW Botha's 'total strategy'. His interrogators must already have information and are cross-checking. To deny who was there would now be pointless:

> We also had a discussion that I was invited to by GAVIN ANDERSON [sic], at which BARBARA HOGAN, CEDRIC DE BEER? [sic], SIPHO KHUBEKA, VALLEY [sic] MOOSA and AURET VAN HEERDEN were present.[173]

It was just a general political discussion on problems faced by the government, asserts Neil, attended by a wide range of people. Not illegal. As Neil elaborates some of the issues discussed, he must be hoping intensely that whoever has told the security police about this meeting has managed to be circumspect. In that case, the most that could be deduced by the police is that Sipho and Gavin had been breaking their now-expired banning orders.

The truth was that the 'total strategy' meeting had been called to plan a response to a predicted clampdown on increasingly militant unions. The question had been, as Sipho Kubeka recalls, 'how to effectively continue running a union underground in case, when the leadership is arrested, offices are closed and money is taken by the government'. A solution would be to form underground structures that linked to the trade union movement via key shop stewards. But how, in those circumstances, would you ensure democracy?: 'If they linked the legal organisation to an underground structure, who would call the shots? Because the underground structure might end up undermining the legal structure.' No decisions were taken except to continue the discussion, but this is dangerous territory for Neil. If his interrogators have already elicited something about this 'underground structure' discussion from others, he knows that they'll use it to accuse him of lying about his commitment to open democratic process. But, at the moment, they're not revealing their hand.

From here on, in dense paragraph after paragraph, Neil itemises meeting after meeting, all above ground. They reflected an explosion of union activity, some of it clearly merging with wider community issues:

> I attended a meeting in the Selbourne Hall around Republic Day at which Sisa Njikelana was invited to speak about the Wilson Rowntree Boycott. The speakers at the meeting were Curtis Nkondo, SAMSON NDOU, MR. MAVI and SISA NJIKELANA. MR NKONDO spoke about the fact that the Republic was only based on the votes of the whites, and was not a true Republic representing all the people ... MR. NJIKELANA spoke about the dispute at Wilson Rowntree and called for the support of everyone in boycotting the products of Wilson Rowntree. After the meeting, the people present sang 'We shall overcome'. During the meeting, a traffic policeman came in to say that there was a bomb in the hall, but the people present took no notice and the meeting continued.[174]

In recounting the failed bomb hoax, has Neil just rubbed salt into a wound? His catalogue of meetings and union activity reflect strong criticism of the apartheid state. But everything Neil cites is legal.

What about Barbara Hogan? Yes, he says, he knows her, but his contact has been open and strictly limited:

> I had seen Barbara HOGAN and at some parties and I knew that she had been involved in the Fattis and Monis Boycott. She was also active on

the White Left but not wanting to get involved in White Left politics, because I saw my feild [sic] as being in the union and my actions under the control of our union membership, I was not keen to get involved with her. I knew that LIZ FLOYD was friendly with her, and saw her occasionally …[175]

Barbara was at his and Liz's house for professional reasons on the night Whitehead came to detain Sisa. She had come to supper to continue discussions with Sisa, before he returned to East London, about setting up an unemployed workers' union in the Transvaal. That's what SAAWU and Sisa were developing in East London. Neil expands at some length on why he doesn't think the idea will work in Johannesburg where SAAWU is still 'very young and weak',[176] emphasising the professional issues.

So what about Thozamile Gqweta? Neil says that Thozamile has told him about his detention and torture and how the security police wanted to establish links between him and the ANC: '… but he [Thozamile] only said that he had gone either to Swaziland or Leshoto [sic] to meet someone from S.A.C.T.U. and ask for money for S.A.A.W.U. We did not discuss this matter further, as he was busy describing his detention.'[177] Here too is a minefield. The line between SACTU and ANC is a fine one. Neil remembers Gavin's debriefing, how Gavin's interrogator called Alan Fine a 'slim kêrel' (clever chap) for asserting that his contacts were SACTU not ANC. But to Cronwright's men, the legal distinction is an own goal by their government. It obstructs them from securing more convictions in court. Stoking an interrogator's frustration can lead to fury.

Whitehead returns to Neil's contact with Gavin, this time after his detention. What did Gavin say before escaping the country? Neil sidesteps. He just saw him briefly at a protest meeting outside Khotso House: '… and he seemed depressed because he had been released and the others had not. Later I heard that he was in Botswana. I then wrote him a letter to cheer him up, and assure him that he still had my friendship and support, as I had not seen much of him in the last year.'[178] Neil knows that the security police must be kicking themselves for releasing Gavin. Regardless, he affirms their friendship.

The final pages of Neil's first statement contain passages that read like a manifesto. Under 'WHY I AM WORKING IN A TRADE UNION', he writes:

When OSCAR MPETHA approached me to ask if I wanted to work in Food and Canning, I was already aware that this was a trade Union with a proud history, that it was democratically controlled, and respected by other unionists ... My feeling was that I saw that changes in South Africa were necessary, and it was important that I contribute to these changes. I felt that the most positive area where I could be effective was in the trade unions, because here you were actually changing concrete conditions of existence and not just talking rhetorical politics.

I felt that if different people in all walks of life organized themselves in various democratic organizations, such as the Women's Organizations, the Community Organizations and Trade Unions, then gradually the laws could be changed, and if all these organizations linked together then they would provide a strong call for democracy and universal suffrage.[179]

The strength of feeling behind his avowal of democratic organisation and universal suffrage is palpable. With the apartheid state the antithesis of 'democracy and universal suffrage', his declaration is like a gauntlet thrown at his interrogators' feet. These fundamental moral principles, the basis of his loyalty to the union, are not negotiable.

When Whitehead pushes him to make a full declaration of his views on the ANC, SACTU, South African Communist Party and the white left, Neil asserts his truths as a principled citizen and unionist, without revealing his deeper radicalism. In a quiet, confident tone, he states that he is not a member of the ANC yet he is unwavering on the values of 'a democratic non-racial society in South Africa, with one man, one vote'. To Whitehead, it's a red rag.

In discussing the ANC and SACTU, Neil skilfully manages a difficult balancing act. Their alliance was 'a valid one in the past'. Yes, he would have supported them when they were open and above-ground, but he cannot reconcile himself to organisations that cannot function democratically. It is essential that people are involved in the decisions that affect their own destiny. When it comes to the Communist Party, he prudently restricts his comments to the distant past.[180] Neil keeps quiet about his intense dislike for the Party's top-down approach and avoids engaging in current matters that would reveal the depth of his political life. He is genuinely committed to democratic process, but aware of its problematic tension with necessary underground organisation. He would have understood, for instance, Sipho's classic example concerning self-defence in the township:

> A meeting would be called asking for contributions, saying that some people will also be trained in how to use these things. But the community will never be told that so and so is being trained or went to buy arms. That is playing with fire. So where does democracy come in here?

This is a door to be kept firmly shut. Throughout his interrogation, Neil has striven to remain coherent and principled. When Whitehead requires him to provide a summary of his views at the end of his statement, he keenly hopes that this will be the final hurdle:

MY VIEWS ON THE A.N.C., S.A.C.T.U., S.A.C.P., AND THE WHITE LEFT.

73.

THE A.N.C.

I support the principles of the Freedom Charter as being a basis for a democratic non-racial society in South Africa, with one man, one vote. However I am not a member of the A.N.C.... They seem to be more active outside South Africa than within it, and not very active in the areas that affect peoples daily lives. I believe we must fight against Apartheid, but this can only be done by involving people in the day to day struggles on the factory floor and in the community. What are needed are democratic organizations that people are involved in and that are controlled by the people themselves. This will bring about gradual change in all spheres of life. Without these democratic, open, legal organizations, there is no gaurantee [sic] that the people will have any control over their destiny. Most people in this country, black and white, want to see change come about, but this will not be possible through the actions of just a few people, but only through open, mass organizations. Furthermore, if there is no democratic control over the leadership of the A.N.C.., their policies may not correspond to what is wanted by the South African people.

74.

However, it is no use if the forms of organization are dictated to the people by the State, such as community councils, and the present restrict[ive] clauses relating to registered unions. The membership must be free to choose their own constitution, and run their organization free from State interference.

75.

S.A.C.T.U.

I have read about S.A.C.T.U. and as a non-racial, independent federation of trade unions, I think its history is commendable. Our Union was itself a leading member of S.A.C.T.U. and I think it was the correct decision of the membership to affiliate at that time. Politics always cuts accross [sic] trade union matters, particularly in South Africa where influx control and contract labour directly affect the lives of the Union membership. For this reason, the alliance of S.A.C.T.U.. and the A.N.C. was a valid one in the past. It was also important that the workers had their own organization within the alliance, to make sure that their aspirations were catered for. However when S.A.C.T.U. dissolved and went underground, a basic contradiction arose. It is impossible to have an underground trade union, because there can be no possible democratic [control] over the policies of that union. A trade union must be open, legal, and run democratically. It is for this reason that I believe that S.A.C.T.U. is taking a wrong path, although it has a good history.

THE S.A.C.P.

I know nothing about this organization apart from what I have read. I know that in the 1920's they took a very incorrect position of supporting the white workers in their struggles for protection against the black workers. This mistake has seemed to make them a spent force historically. I have also heard that they are close to Moscow, and this does not stand in their favour. What the workers and the people need are open democratic organizations in which they can participate.

THE WHITE LEFT:

As a trade unionist, I had neither the time nor the inclination to become involved in the circles of the white left. However, during the Wilson Rowntree boycott, S.A.A.W.U. needed any support they could get, and that is why we contacted Joanne Yawitch. Some of the white left were present at the first

Wilson Rowntree meeting, and others did some printing in our offices, but I do not know their names. I used to be friendly with GAVIN ANDERSON [sic] and DAVE DYSON [sic], and met some other young people while we worked in the vegetable garden, but never discussed labour or politics with them.

*   *   *

Rereading Neil's first statement almost thirty years later, Gavin is impressed:

> ... overall I'd say that he is holding up pretty well at this stage of his inter-rogation. He is keeping within the boundaries of what's expected, and not being radical or giving anyone away ... He comes across as a principled unionist, with exactly the values you'd expect from someone in his position at that time. Very impressive; he is well in command of himself at this point.

But Neil is also tired. In his final sentence, writing about 'The White Left', he states that he has neither the time nor inclination to become involved in its circles. But he then returns to the Vegetable Garden and how he 'used to be friendly with GAVIN ANDERSON [sic] and DAVE DYSON [sic] ... and some other young people ... but never discussed labour or politics with them'. Neil has forgotten that more than halfway through his 27 typed A4 pages he has mentioned talking with Gavin about the bitter divisions in the labour movement. This is just the kind of 'blip' on which Whitehead will be ready to pounce and call him a 'liar'.

CHAPTER 35

Limbo

O N MONDAY 11 JANUARY, WHITEHEAD INSTRUCTS NEIL TO TYPE an index of all the names he has mentioned. The process obliges Neil to review his statement, highlighting key targets of the questions. Gavin and Liz come out on top. Eleven mentions each, followed by Jan with eight, Barbara and Sisa, seven, Oscar, six, Thozamile, five, Sipho, one. It's surely a relief that Sipho appears low on his interrogators' radar. So far, nothing suggests that Cronwright's men are aware of Woodworkers, the Group of 7 and their other discussion groups. In focusing on his 'life story', Neil hasn't been specifically questioned about these, his closest comrades.

What is Neil's state of mind when he is returned to Cell 209, clocked in at 1.50pm, and left by Whitehead to wait? The only thing of which he is sure is that his statement will be dissected. Having managed to keep 'revolutionary practice' out of sight behind his principled unionist stance, perhaps he feels that he hasn't done too badly, and that his statement coheres well. The impression he gives Auret is one of optimism: 'He was very confident about his ground. He felt that there was nothing that they could actually incriminate him on or implicate him in. Again ironically this is partly because of Whitehead having monitored him so closely.'[181] When Auret picks up a hint from Cronwright that he wants to use them as state witnesses, the pair even speculate whether they might be released in February with a subpoena.

But Neil has also sensed a highly unpredictable dynamic with Whitehead. Not only did Whitehead supervise Van Schalkwyk's assault, but he plays power games, granting 'privileges', then withdrawing them. Neil also talks to Auret about a 'war of attrition'. Books are given, then taken away. Neil is convinced that his surgery textbooks have arrived but have been blocked. The beady-eyed, pudgy-faced security policeman appears to have a personal obsession with him and Liz. Why aren't they living more grandly, as would befit successful white doctors? Why aren't they earning more money? How can they be throwing away all their material advantages? There's only one explanation. They must be communists and members of the ANC.

The Special Branch conception of the underground is of a hierarchy of control. The Soviet Union and the '*rooi gevaar*' (red threat) is at the pinnacle, working its way down through the South African Communist Party into the ANC and its lower echelons. Viewed through sharply racialised spectacles, white communists subvert black people on behalf of a foreign power and ideology. Whitehead's own background and working life in the police are militaristic. The state's infiltrators into the ANC in exile and MK confirm the existence of hierarchical lines of command. Barbara's use of a term like 'under discipline' will have reinforced the view that the internal political underground is similarly structured.

Although such a crude notion doesn't fit the more organic, deeply woven networking of activists building alliances across various constituencies, both above-ground and underground, an interrogator intent on proving a theory will stop at nothing. Moreover, Whitehead wants to extract information not only on Neil but on what he knows about others. Gavin slipped out of their net. However, now they have his best buddy. Whitehead is determined not to make the same mistake.

When I ask Gavin what might go through Neil's mind in that limbo period after writing his first statement, he is struck by how Whitehead leaves Neil for nine days before having him brought up to the tenth floor again:

> This is a LONG time to be left ... He will have gone through nightmares imagining what they know and don't know, whether his statement covered things adequately or has opened him up for more probing because they have some detail that will show his statement was devious. And the sheer

loneliness means that he will have been almost hungry to talk; this is perhaps the most powerful thing that happened [in interrogation] – to bring to the front of his mind his entire life and ideas and then his recent political thoughts and work, and get him to write down a version, and then leave him to stew. That was a terrifying time for him and apart from all the terror he will have been desperate for ANY human contact. Intense interrogation followed by nothing, day after day and night after night, nothing except the mind churning and relentlessly constructing scenarios of what they know and don't know and what I've given and not given and whether I will be able to hold my head up afterwards. It's a gruelling time they gave him by being absent (sounds crazy, I know ...).

There is little to do apart from reading or exercising in his cell. Occasionally, MacPherson lets Neil run up and down the corridor, and if he's lucky, and MacPherson isn't watching, he might snatch a bit of conversation on the way to the shower. Once in a while, Neil gets the chance to communicate with Thabo Lerumo, an 18-year-old student whom MacPherson makes sweep the passages and cells. Neil slips Thabo copies of *Anna Karenina*, *Youth* and *Heart of Darkness*, which MacPherson finds and confiscates.[182] When he gets the chance, Neil also lends books to Eric Mntonga, chairman of SAAWU's East London branch, and probably to others. But most of the time, he is alone, 'in solitary'.

Perhaps it is also during these long nine days that Auret recalls Neil talking about Liz. In the waiting hours, does he wonder how she's coping? Does he feel responsible, even partly, for her arrest? Why hadn't he warned her earlier about her name on Barbara's list? He knows that he has hurt her. Yet, in spite of tensions and breakdowns, their relationship has lasted nine years since they first came together in the cottage up in Eagle's Nest. Here, in this cell, there are no barriers to obstruct a resurgence of angry, frustrated, loving, painful words from the past. Since arriving in Johannesburg, Neil has had little time for this kind of personal self-exploration. But in this obligatory lull, it must be difficult to avoid regrets, doubts and unanswered questions about friendships, family and future.

*   *   *

The second-floor register for the following week shows three brief interruptions to Neil's solitary confinement. On Monday 18 January, he receives a visit from Magistrate AGJ Wessels. The report, marked 'GEHEIM' (secret), is sent to the Director General of Justice, the Commissioner of Police, and the Commander of Security Police at John Vorster Square.

COMPLAINTS:	No.
REQUESTS:	'I would like my relatives to send two books. One is "Emergency Surgery". It is a text book by Bailey. The other book is "Accident and Emergency Medicine". It is a text book by Rutherford. It is at the flat of Doug Hindson. The first book my parents know of its whereabouts.'
HEALTH:	Good.
INJURIES:	'I had injuries on 4.1.82. I injured my back and left ribs as a result of an assault. I also cut my right forearm. Assault was by a sergeant of Railway Security Police. His first name is Schalk. This was on 10th Floor of John Vorster Square.'[183]

While most detainees keep quiet, Neil officially records his assault without registering it as a direct complaint and accusation. He knows the risk but goes ahead, on principle. This is also his third time asking for Bailey's *Emergency Surgery*. Sergeant Michael Joubert takes down Neil's request that he ring and ask David Dison for the two books, a jacket, a pair of trousers and a portable radio. The phone call will only be made 11 days later. Neil also tells Auret that he has a bloodstain on his pants and is thinking how he can get them out to Yvette with a message not to wash them. The stain would provide evidence for charging his interrogators after he is released. Neil has obviously said nothing to the magistrate about this further evidence of the assault. His captors could destroy it in a trice.

The second interruption that week is an ominously brief session on Wednesday 20 January with Whitehead, on the tenth floor. Neil is taken out at 10.22am by Constable Maqubela, and returned at 11.38am. At the inquest, Whitehead will say that he simply tells Neil there are points in his statement 'to clarify'. Through Auret, we hear a different story:

Also about in the middle of January Whitehead started telling him that we know you are lying and you must expect me to come back to you. He actually said to him 'I am going to come and fetch you late one night and I am going to take you out and we are going to give you an incredibly rough time.'[184]

It's a bully's threat, designed to prey on a detainee's imagination.

On Friday 22 January, the Inspector of Detainees visits the cells and speaks to Neil for the first time after eight weeks in detention. Neil has not been 'available' on either of his two previous visits, nor did the Inspector ask for him to be made available. His report to 'The Honourable the Minister of Justice' resounds with omissions and silences:

Dear Minister
DETAINEE IN TERMS OF SECTION 6:   Neil AGGETT
       DATE OF DETENTION: *10.12.1981*
       NAME OF INTERPRETER: -

The above named was interviewed by me for the 3rd time at John Vorster Square police station on the 22nd January 1982. The 2nd visit was on 4.1.1982. My report dated 6.1.1982 refers.

   The detainee commented as follows in regard to:

His health: *I am allright and don't wish to see a doctor.*

The food: *Is good – I have no complaints.*

The treatment: *I have no complaints.*

Other complaints: *None.*

Requests: *I need a pair of shorts and a jersey. Home address is 420A Fox Street, Jeppe.*

Remarks and recommendations: *The request was conveyed to the security police at John Vorster Square.*

Yours faithfully

       INSPECTOR OF DETAINEES[185]

As the Inspector disappears from sight, Neil knows that he is about to enter an almighty storm. If he slips, he brings others tumbling down. That, I imagine, is his worst fear.

CHAPTER 36

Behind the frosted glass

THE OFFICIAL RECORD OF MONDAY 25 JANUARY STATES THE BARE facts that Neil is taken 'Out for Investigation' at 8.59am and returned at 2.50pm. By chance, Maurice Smithers finds himself in an office adjoining Neil's interrogation room. Although detained out at Randburg, Maurice has been brought to John Vorster Square before being taken to see an optician. He has broken the right-hand lens of his glasses and is being allowed to have it repaired. Maurice is one of Yvette's friends, and has come to know Neil a little prior to detention. They were together at the swimming pool party out at Fourways. Maurice now identifies Neil through a frosted glass partition. Neil is standing, with six or seven policemen in the room with him. Maurice can hear voices but can't hear what is being said. After a short while, a number of policemen leave the adjoining office. Three remain. He can only see their top halves but thinks that Neil is wearing a white shirt.

At ten o'clock, Maurice is taken away. When he returns an hour later, he sees that Neil is still standing with three officers near him. After about five minutes, one of them indicates that Neil should go down on the floor. Neil goes down and is lost from view, but a large policeman appears to stand over him, take off his belt and bend down. Maurice sees the movement of the man's arm and hears 'a distinct sound as if flesh was being hit.'[186] Neil remains on the floor for five to ten minutes. It sounds and looks as if he is hit twice.

When Neil stands up, his back is towards the glass. He begins to run on the spot with his arms outstretched. Whenever his arms begin to sag or he stops running, a policeman hits him with an object that could be a rolled-up newspaper. At least twice, Maurice hears a policeman shout words to the effect of 'Who told you to stop?' It seems as if Neil is being questioned continuously. Maurice deduces that Neil is replying because he gestures with his outstretched arms.

A black policeman guarding Maurice is aware that he is watching the scene next door but doesn't try to prevent him. Maurice even asks the policeman the time in order to establish how long Neil's treatment is lasting. Running on the spot, with outstretched arms, continues for almost an hour, sometimes with knees raised high. From time to time, Neil appears to be ordered down on the floor, probably for press-ups. Maurice makes out a loud voice barking, 'Come on, just ten more!' He can tell that Neil is tiring because he keeps wiping his face. At one stage, he appears to stumble and is hit again with the 'rolled-up newspaper' object.

At about ten minutes past midday, there is a sudden flurry of activity and Maurice sees Neil bending down. From his gestures, Maurice wonders if he is pulling on trousers. Then Neil repeats the gestures and Maurice deduces that it must have been first underpants, then trousers. Neil then pulls on his shirt over his head and is immediately taken out of the office. Maurice is now convinced that Neil had been naked:

> The whole experience left a deep impression on me and made me very angry. For approximately one hour on each of the following three days, I ran on the spot with my arms outstretched, did push-ups and lifted my knees to attempt to simulate and experience what Dr Aggett had gone through. On the third day I was already experiencing searing pain in my legs and shoulders and I was unable to carry on with the exercises thereafter.

The shock of what he has witnessed also provokes Maurice, back in his Randburg cell, to make a note in tiny handwriting, detailing Neil's treatment. He doesn't know how he will get this miniature note out, but at least he has made a record.

*   *   *

There are no reliable witnesses to Neil's interrogation in the ensuing days. We have only the Cells Occurrence Book, indicating the times that he is up on the tenth floor, including the Thursday to Sunday session, set up by Whitehead as a 'long weekend':

Tuesday 26	taken out 8h25 by Maqubela, returned 15h43
Wednesday 27	taken out 8h21 by Maqubela, returned 15h25
Thursday 28	taken out 8h25 by Maqubela, returned 14h41;
	taken out 16h18 by Whitehead
Sunday 31	returned 03h30[187]

Between Tuesday and Thursday in that last week of January, we have a handful of recollections from fellow detainees. On Tuesday afternoon, Thozamile Gqweta is in the shower room. While he is cleaning his teeth at the tap beside the iron gate, Neil comes to fetch water. Whitehead has torn up his statement and he has been told to write a new one. Whitehead has threatened to 'take him out for the whole night'. His cell has been emptied of all reading material. 'This was all that Dr Aggett said to me. He was stopped from talking further by one of the policemen.'[188]

Another memory comes from Keith Coleman, and, although he cannot pinpoint the date, it fits this stage in Neil's interrogation. In a brief conversation through the bars of Neil's cell, Neil tells Keith that 'they' are now telling him what to write and even that isn't satisfying Whitehead:

> I remember how desperate Neil was, and how I said to him – he knew I was taking a risk just going in there – but I remember saying to him, 'Listen Neil, just keep strong. Remember we're with you. Just keep strong.' Which I really meant but it wasn't what he needed at that point, I think. [Pause] I think Neil needed something much more. It was an appeal for real help and I don't know what I could have done. I didn't hear it sufficiently clearly. I didn't know how close to the edge he was but that's what he was saying: 'I don't know how much more I can take.'

A final glimpse of Neil before his long weekend comes through Samson Ndou, GAWU's president. Arrested on the same day as Neil, he has only been transferred to John Vorster Square on Wednesday 27 January. Samson briefly encounters Neil in the clothes room on Thursday morning, and it's obvious to him that Neil is 'in bad condition'. He has known Neil as 'a dynamic energetic man' but now he shows 'no enthusiasm'. To Samson's experienced eye, he seems 'dispirited and broken'.[189]

Thirteen years older than Neil, this is Samson's third period of detention without trial. On this occasion, he has already been through the wringer. He has been stripped and pliers applied to his penis. While blindfolded, handcuffed and suspended upside down, with a wet towel wrapped around his chest, he has had electric shocks applied to his knee, testicles, penis and forehead. His interrogators laughed when he urinated on himself, declaring him to be a 'real kaffir'. They have stifled his screams by forcing a piece of cloth into his mouth. Despite threats from Struwig, the Koevoet helicopter-torturer, Samson has made a statement to the police with the intention of laying charges. When he meets Neil in the clothes room on Thursday 28 January, MacPherson is present, so their communication is limited. But Samson's depiction of Neil indicates that something is already happening to him that would make lifting his spirits very difficult.

We can only speculate at the source of this sudden alteration in confidence. While Maurice's account of Neil with outstretched arms behind the frosted glass suggests a macabre puppet show, Gavin writes that this is something he has never understood:

> How do you force someone to exercise? It would have been a good opportunity for him [Neil] to say 'Fuck you – you do press-ups yourself, you bloody idiot, in fact why don't you just go ...' and so invite an attack or beating that might mercifully lead to unconsciousness. Somehow, they got him to try and prove something ...

This was Pindile's advice, passed on to Gavin and Sipho. Get yourself knocked unconscious rather than being slowly worn down and finding yourself 'playing mind games where you can be tricked into letting slip some seemingly innocuous piece of information (like the reading group)'. Although no one in their circles has received formal training in dealing with torture, they have all shared bits of information and advice. When an interrogator is beating you senseless, you don't forget that he's your enemy. He is most dangerous when he offers you a cup of coffee and a cigarette. 'But Neil would have heard all the same kinds of thing from me and Sipho, and also people like Sisa and Thozamile and Oscar as well,' says Gavin. They had no illusions: 'We all gird-ed ourselves for this terror-laden experience that might befall us sometime, that was the nature of political work in that epoch.'

Pindile's logic is clear, but taunting someone to beat you up strikes me as dangerous in the extreme and requiring a certain kind of personality. Neil has been aiming not to antagonise. He is uncompromising, but his disposi-tion is more inclined to engagement. Yet has this led him unwittingly into Whitehead's mind game?

I seek Gavin's views on the process by which Neil may have found himself trapped. I also mention a memory from my own detention of unconsciously 'throwing a blanket' over things that I didn't want to remember, literally blanking them out. I recall the shock when my interrogators finally showed me a statement that referred to me. The shock wasn't because of the degree of implication. Painting an ANC slogan on a bridge and leafleting were relatively minor in the scale of things, and the police who raided my flat hadn't found the typewriter hidden by my brother behind the kitchen cupboard. But my mind had assumed a persona of complete innocence from which I was now thoroughly jolted.[190] Might Neil also have resorted to blanking out and bury-ing his revolutionary self while writing his first statement in his genuine trade unionist voice? Yes, Gavin thinks that the blanking-out rings true. But the signs of Neil's deep dispiritedness, before the long weekend, indicate that he has already experienced *umcentrierung* (shift in the centre of gravity). Gavin explains that '[This is] where the "facilitator"/psychologist/interrogator dis-places the centre of gravity by placing new information or data before the participant/s or shifts the emphasis so existing data is viewed in a new way or has to be explained in a new way.'[191] The interrogator suddenly jolts the de-tainee out of their story and forces a turning point. What then might be Neil's moment of *umcentrierung*? Gavin's theory is that Whitehead has managed to get Neil into a conversation where a thread of his deeper revolutionary optimism has been revealed. Once this shift has occurred, Neil can no longer present himself solely as the trade unionist who believes in gradual change. He is now in the domain, says Gavin, where 'he is fully acknowledging his political personality and clandestine practice, and it's a slippery slope'. When the interrogator gets a detainee to this point, torture is used to extract more specific information.

Although Neil has been careful about confining and circumscribing his own political activities, he knows that he has information that Whitehead wants. It mightn't be much, but enough to give a scent. At least Gavin is relatively safe in Botswana. But his greatest fear must be about saying anything that might lead to Sipho, or to the existence of his comrades' other networks. By the time he enters Whitehead's long weekend, it looks as if Neil fears that Whitehead has already found a thread and he is not going to let go of it.

CHAPTER 37

The long weekend

AFTER ALLOWING NEIL LESS THAN TWO HOURS BACK IN HIS CELL that Thursday afternoon, at 4.18pm, Whitehead personally collects his quarry from the second floor. He has arranged for other interrogators to assist him over the forthcoming nights and days. Detective Warrant Officers Disré Carr from Newcastle and Karel de Bruin from Ladybrand have already been working with Whitehead on Neil since Monday, making up the threesome seen by Maurice behind the frosted glass. While both are tall, Carr is notably burly. They continue their 'assistance' until Saturday 30 January when they are replaced by Captains Johannes Visser and Daniël Swanepoel. This is the same Visser who strangled Auret, then later massaged him. The final duo comprises Lieutenant Joseph Woensdregt and Detective Warrant Officer Nicolaas Deetlefs, the interrogator who struck Barbara, threatening 'other methods'. The henchmen take turns, allowing Whitehead time to sleep while Neil is kept under 62 uninterrupted hours of interrogation, from Thursday afternoon until the early hours of Sunday morning. At the inquest, each interrogator will claim that Neil has a camp bed for his personal use.

A brief paragraph in the affidavit that Neil dictates to Sergeant Blom the following Thursday tells a very different story:

I was kept awake since the morning 82.01.28 to the 82.01.30. During the night of the 82.01.29 Lt. Whitehead and another security sergeant who's [sic] name I don't know and another black male also a policemen [sic] were present when Lt. Whitehead blindfolded me with a towel. They made me sit down and handcuffed me behind my back. I was shocked through the handcuffs. I don't know what they used to shock me. I was shocked a few times. I have a scratch on my left pulse (radial nerve) where I was injured whilst being handcuffed.[192]

In trying to reconstruct what happened during Whitehead's long weekend, we also have Neil's notes and an unfinished second statement, both in his handwriting. There is also a typewritten version of the second statement with a number of discrepancies that call into doubt who typed it. But Whitehead's line of attack is best revealed by comparing the first and second statements, relying on Neil's handwritten version, and especially his notes. The latter are scrawled, enforced jottings made between the firing of questions.

The ten pages of notes show how Whitehead begins by pouncing onto his relationship with Gavin:

1. How I met Gavin
2. Reasons why we read *Capital*
3. Before FOSATU started – dec. on General Union
4. Ideas were put to the group
5. Also asked B Kay about going into FCWU. Why – Good organiz
6. My support for it initially
7. (Gang of four Opinion)
8. Gavin – couple of discussions – the SACTU position taken
9. Discussions Oscar on FOSATU. Both agreed FOSATU was taking a wrong path.
10. Reasons why Oscar was satisfied with me …
11. Taking Oscar to see Gavin + Sipho[193]

The first 11 items reveal three major threads that Whitehead wants to extract and tie together as evidence of Neil's 'communistic ideology'. Gavin is the first thread. The second is SACTU, including the dissident 'Gang of five'. Sometimes referred to as the 'Gang of four' (because only four were ostensibly ANC supporters in London), these were South African exiles linked to a Trotskyite group in Britain who, for a while, had managed to take over SACTU's news-paper *Workers' Unity* in London.[194] Highly critical of the ANC for organising on a nationalist rather than a class basis, they argued that SACTU's 'historical task' was to take the lead in organising the mass of workers, develop revolutionary consciousness through concrete struggles, with the eventual forcible seizure of power by a workers' army.[195] The third thread is the banned ANC itself, and people like Oscar, Barbara, Auret and other activists like Liz, whose role Whitehead is intent on linking to a major treason plot.

Although Barbara has listed Neil and Liz under 'Advisory/Reference People', Neil's stated support for SACTU in his first statement, and its alliance with the ANC as 'a valid one in the past', is something Whitehead grasps. Gavin's in-experienced interrogator Engelbrecht might have thought Alan Fine a '*slim kêrel*' for asserting his links were with the never-banned SACTU rather than the ANC, but Whitehead is determined to demonstrate that Neil's stated cri-tique of SACTU going underground ('It is impossible to have an underground trade union') is a cosmetic lie. Whitehead is now out to prove that Neil has spun a whole pack of lies – and he is the young blood who will bring Neil spinning down.

From the beginning of these notes, it feels as if the hooks are in. Whitehead latches onto Gavin. How did Neil know him? Why were they reading *Capital* together? Two copies of Marx's tome had been seized from Neil's house, but how does Whitehead know about their reading group? Does he surprise Neil with information from another source? By item 4, Neil is being made to explain the 'Group of 7' although he is managing not to call it that. Whitehead now thrusts questions about SACTU and the potential schism, then jumps to Oscar, again pressing Neil to clarify a political line, this time on FOSATU. By item 11, Whitehead has got Neil to make a link between Oscar, Gavin and Sipho.

Reading these notes and Neil's subsequent statement is painful. It's not just the reek of physical torment but the humiliation and mental anguish of a deeply principled and gentle young man at the hands of a laddishly pomp-ous, pitiless interrogator with his fastidiously parted hair and slightly flabby schoolboy face.

Numbered items on the first page of Neil's notes rapidly give way to un-numbered clusters of scrawled phrases and words, revealing the web of Whitehead's targets. Liz's name crops up ten times on the next three pages as Whitehead pushes Neil on her views regarding SACTU, registration, the

largely white Trade Union Council of South Africa (TUCSA) and FOSATU.
Pugnacious questions draw Neil on:

> Sympathies in SACTU. Against Registration
>> Favours strong/democratic/militant/progressive
>> Militant – aren't toothless like TUCSA. get some body & strength:
> Discussed FOSATU = Criticisms of FOSATU – Undemocratic elements.
> Registration position not viable. – Liz not trying to break FOSATU – not
> getting orders.

Having been led to acknowledge Liz's 'strong/democratic/militant/progres-
sive' sympathies with SACTU, Neil attempts to draw a line. No, she is 'not trying to break FOSATU', and no, she is 'not getting orders' from anyone.

Whitehead switches to Sisa. Neil acknowledges that he has helped Sisa with
meetings and transport, but no, he has not written speeches for Sisa. It's a single sentence, followed by a single phrase, 'Been to Barbara's flat once', before
Whitehead swoops back to SACTU:

> I support the direction of SACTU + I'm working in the same direction as
> SACTU but I'm not in SACTU: I've got no links to SACTU: I was furthering
> the aims but I didn't have any instructions.

For charges to stick in court, Whitehead needs evidence of a line of command. He changes tack, digging into Neil's perceptions of close friends and
their personal lives: Dave Dison, Gavin, and back to Liz. He pressures Neil to
make personal judgments:

> Liz: Domineering, Moralistic, Strong, also quite soft. Socializes easily with
> people on superficial level, but does not have close friendship on a deep
> level. Liz doesn't fit into my setup. Tension between us.

By now, Whitehead knows very well that he will find nothing to incriminate
Liz. However, he's not only poking and probing to unhinge Neil. He is personally fixated with their relationship. For Neil, caught in the nightmare of
torture, discussing an intimate relationship with this bully must have been a
source of great distress.

But Whitehead drives on. Does he interweave electric shocks and verbal prods? As Neil is pushed harder one way, then another, sometimes revealing names, afterwards he tries to limit the damage. Thus when Whitehead brings him back to the *Capital* reading group, Neil adds: 'Dissolved as soon as we finished reading. No resolutions.' In other words, this wasn't a formal study group, nor one that reported to another organisation. It wasn't a Communist Party cell.

When Whitehead probes into SAAWU, Neil acknowledges that SAAWU is 'very progressive' but denies knowledge of links between SAAWU and SACTU. Suddenly, in a lone sentence, midway through the notes, Neil writes: 'I am sympathetic to the ANC. Not a member of the ANC.' What provokes this? We can only imagine. Whitehead must finally feel that he's getting somewhere. So far, the evidence has been nebulous, but with Neil now acknowledging ANC sympathies, Whitehead just needs to bring to light the activities that prove Neil's union occupation is simply a cover for revolutionary underground work. The interrogation switches sharply to a factory and union focus:

> Factory discussion part of group discussion.
>> Build up organization inside the factory.
>> Groups of 3 – Meeting – co-ord with other factories
>> – Underground trade union
>> Worker's Unity – put forward this app.

How it would suit Whitehead to align Neil with SACTU's dissidents! They had slipped into SACTU in London as volunteers helping to edit *Workers' Unity*, and attempting a takeover from within. Whitehead's theory, it seems, is that Neil is a front man for Gavin and others, and together they are developing an 'underground trade union' that ultimately aims at the forcible seizure of state power. Having been pushed to acknowledge his familiarity with the SACTU dissidents' approach, Neil can see where Whitehead is leading him, and valiantly attempts to disprove his theory. Yes, they have discussed the 'underground trade union' idea, but they haven't agreed on its viability:

> Gavin and I meeting – TU discussions – Gavin invited myself Dave and
> Sipho – discussions. Not formal thing:- informal – types of org possible.
> Not following one or another. Not structured.

I decided   1. Not viable
             2. Anti-democratic no elements of a trade union. Gavin still
             thought viable.

Years later, looking at these notes and Neil's subsequent statement, Gavin
wryly comments that it had been the other way round. In their discussions
around the underground union idea, he recalls having been very sceptical. It
had been Neil, in his earlier, less-seasoned days, who thought the idea worth
exploring. But with Whitehead hammering him, and Gavin hopefully out of
reach in Botswana, Neil reverses their positions. In any event, nothing had
come of their discussions and Neil indicates this to Whitehead.

> I continued working in Union – discussing now + then with Gavin. He did
> not give me instructions. Discuss what was happening in the factory. Not a
> formal group that I left …

But Whitehead isn't going to let up, returning later to extract from Neil who
else was in the group:

> An actual underground union was not started, but discussions were started
> between myself, Dave Dyson [sic], Gavin Andersson, Sipho Kubheka –
> about 4 discussions.
>   No minutes gatherings –
>   Roughly 3-4 months – discussions – dissolved. At that time discussed in
> group of 7 to get other people into the group (other workers). I pulled out of
> it, the others may have continued discussion. No such union exists.

Despite Neil's reiteration that the underground union does not exist, mentioning Sipho's name in particular, as well as naming the 'Group of 7' as such,
must have weighed very heavily on Neil. He's slipping fast, and knows it.
Whitehead has forced him to revise the stance of the gradualist trade unionist, while the stilted sentence construction intimates that he is now being
pumped with his Afrikaans-speaking interrogators' words and terminology:

> I try to organize workers strongly as a class to be militant + to fight for their
> rights.

> Gavin knows I have an idealistic ideology …

What is an 'idealistic ideology'? Exhausted, Neil is losing to Whitehead's thrust:

> I know that Gavin was in the movement (ANC) …
>   Gavin said that Barbara was going into Botswana – Met with G + S. About military training.
>   Auret van Heerden was in movement but had gone to army.

Is this ANC 'military training' or the South African army training that Neil has been avoiding? Although unclear, it's most likely the latter with the reference to Auret going into the army.

> I was aware that Gavin, Auret and Barbara working together – never specifically told that they were in the ANC but I suspected it. I often saw Auret at Gavin's house …

Neil knows that Gavin hasn't been working in an ANC cell with Barbara and Auret, as Whitehead wants to imply. Yet Whitehead still hasn't got what he needs on Neil himself, and returns to SACTU. After getting Neil to say that he has been 'pushing the SACTU line', he engineers a long-winded passage on 'SACTU's reasons for going underground'. Whitehead wants to tie the knots that will prove Neil is part of a secret plot to 'organize militant wc [working class] into militant organization that could challenge the existing structure of society'.

In what must have been a major effort for Neil towards the end of three days and nights of interrogation, he struggles to pull himself out of the morass:

> I – the last year I was building up the structures of the union – because I saw it important as working legally. I do see Workers Unity has communistic ideology. During this time I didn't want contact with any political organization – important to develop the union. Being involved in the ANC was dangerous. I wanted

Does Whitehead stop him here, realising what Neil is doing? Neil has just undermined the underground story while signalling his interrogator's hand in the unlikely, non-English phrase 'communistic ideology', reflecting the Afrikaans usage of '*kommunistiese*'. Whitehead hasn't secured his great coup. Frustrated, he demands to know why Neil has become more active in the last year. In reply, Neil lists boycotts, strikes, discussion with Barbara about the unemployed workers' union and discussion with Oscar about registration. All legal.

In a final stab, Whitehead accuses Neil of having been recruited to the ANC through Gavin and SACTU. He fixes on the 'military training' meeting as evidence. Despite his mental and physical fatigue, Neil finds his foothold:

> The meeting that we had on military training was the closest that I came to working in the ANC. I was not recruited. I never made reports to Gavin. I told him about what was going on in the Union. I never wrote anything down for him. I was not aware that Gavin made reports to ['Botswana' scratched out] SACTU. I see it as a possibility because he had been to Botswana before to meet with the SACTU people and he could have had regular contact with them.
>
> I've never been recruited, though I have communistic ideas. Never been a member of the ANC, SACP and SACTU. I associated myself with SACTU.

Once again, 'communistic' reveals dictation. Whitehead has kept Neil awake for some 70 hours since Thursday morning. Yet after all the hours of non-stop 'fishing', replete with torture, Whitehead has produced nothing to back his grand theory. At 3.30am on Sunday, he finally allows Neil to be returned in handcuffs to his cell.

CHAPTER 38

'Broken'

O N SUNDAY MORNING WHEN AURET GETS UP, HE REALISES THAT Neil is back but doesn't see him all day:

> *Why was that strange?* Normally at meal times he would have come to the door and sort of spoken to me. I noticed that at lunchtime when the guard brought the food he called to Neil. I could only see to the northeastern corner of Neil's cell so I could not actually see his bed. I could just see the guard calling to him and the guard was getting no response. He then put Neil's food down in the doorway. At supper his food from lunch was still there untouched. The guard called to him again, again no response, again left food there. So both lots were now there. He did not take away the lunchtime food. I then called the guard and asked him what was going on with Neil. He said the [sic] Neil was sleeping.[196]

Auret has known of Whitehead's threat to Neil and seen Cell 209 empty since Thursday. On Friday afternoon, while studying in Lieutenant Pitout's tenth-floor office, he had overheard a conversation that could only have been about Neil. Captain Daniël Swanepoel came to tell Pitout that he had been put on duty for Sunday 6am to 6pm. Pitout wasn't happy, having made other arrangements, leading Swanepoel to reply, '*Kyk, ek glo nie hy sal so lank hou nie*' (Look, I don't think he'll last so long). Indeed, Pitout has not been required to give up his Sunday, and when Neil continues to sleep through the whole day, Auret makes his own deductions. He is so convinced that Neil has been badly tortured that when he receives a visit from his friend Ruth on Monday, he manages to tell her, 'I think they've broken Neil this weekend.'

Although the Cell Register shows that Neil takes no meals on Sunday 31 January, MacPherson nevertheless records Neil's health as 'Good'. At 8.24am on Monday morning, Neil is taken out again. Whitehead orders him to begin, or possibly continue, writing a new statement based on the notes he has made under interrogation. Neil is checked back into the cells at 3.30pm, at the same time as Samson Ndou, who recalls Neil looking 'tired, depressed and worried'.[197] Neil recognises Samson but merely nods his head at him.

In the evening, when Auret's door is opened, he sees Neil approaching his own door, but when Auret greets him, Neil hesitates in the middle of his cell. Puzzled, Auret beckons him to come closer. Neil points a finger up to the tenth floor, meaning 'the people upstairs'. Using signs and whispers, he indicates that 'they' know that he and Auret have been talking. He doesn't want to speak any more. 'How do they know?' Auret whispers back. Neil points around the corner. It seems that a guard has split on them. When Auret perseveres, asking what happened during the interrogation, Neil makes a sign with his hand 'as if a stick was being broken':

> He actually whispered the word at the same time 'I've broken'. He was incredibly downcast, everything about him spoke about defeat and resignation.

Auret wants to keep Neil talking. He has come nearer the grille, but is not in his usual close-up position. Auret lifts his fist to his head: 'What did they do, did they beat you up?' Thrashing his hands, Neil signals electric shocks. He then holds up two fingers to say that he has been kept awake and standing. When Auret asks about the implications, Neil whispers, 'I have admitted having had SACTU links. They forced me to admit that I am a Communist.' He starts to cry. 'They just must not ask me any more questions.'[198]

Their conversation stops shortly after that, Neil indicating that he is really scared about being found out. The following morning, Colonel Daniel Gert

Oosthuizen visits the detainees in their cells before commenting in the Cell Register at 6.53am: 'geen klagtes' (no complaints). On Tuesday 2 February, Neil is taken out at 8.17am and returned at 3.41pm. Although Auret doesn't recall seeing him, Neil appears to be eating again, signing the Food Register: 4 Slices Bread. Mince. Rice. Tea.

When Keith Coleman sees Neil, he is concerned that he is 'completely unresponsive'. They pass in the corridor but Neil won't look directly at him, appearing scared to be caught talking. Another time, Keith sees Neil pass by the window of his cell and calls out to him. Normally Neil acknowledges him. Now there's no response.

On Wednesday, Jabu Ngwenya, who has known Neil outside, is exercising in the corridor soon after eight o'clock in the morning. Jabu sees Neil entering the changing room and notices that he is struggling to walk 'as though there was something wrong with his testicles'.[199] On the pretext of getting water, Jabu follows Neil. 'How are you?' he asks. Face to face, he is shocked at how Neil has deteriorated, looking 'very tired, worried, pale and very thin'. Neil manages to tell him that he has been beaten up and given electric shocks. He tries to show Jabu his wrists, pulling up the sleeves of his jersey. But before Jabu can look properly, MacPherson enters and he has to leave.

Shortly afterwards, Neil is taken out at 8.20am. This is around the usual time, but he is returned to the cells much earlier than usual, soon after half past eleven in the morning. Around midday Auret is also brought back from studying in Pitout's office, where he has heard that the entire interrogation staff is going to Arthur Bloch Park, the rugby club in Mayfair, for a braai. When the doors are opened at the usual supper time, around 4pm, Neil comes to the door so Auret can speak to him:

> He was very very nervous about the fact that he had been brought down early. He interpreted this as meaning that they had started to interrogate other people on the basis of the things that he had said, and that they were now putting him aside to work on others. The person he specifically feared was Liz.

Auret tells him about the braai, and says that he is overreacting. But Neil remains 'incredibly depressed, tearful, totally different' from his former self. Auret tries to lift his spirits. No matter how bleak the situation looks at this point, there will always be positive and negative aspects. Neil shouldn't give up now. He should try and 'emphasise the positive aspects and kind of de-emphasise the negative aspects'.[200]

However, Auret fears that he's not getting through. They can't speak for long, and at one stage they hear a sound from up the passage, as if someone might be listening in to their conversation. Using sign language, Auret asks whether Neil is writing a statement. Neil shows with his fingers that he is busy typing. Does he know what is going to be happening to him? Neil shakes his head and points downwards. It seems that he is going to be staying here for the foreseeable future. Has he said anything to his interrogators about Auret? Neil points to him and raises his thumbs. Auret is all right.[201]

Next morning, Thursday 4 February, Auret passes Neil in the corridor outside their cells, on his way to the showers. Neil seems to be on his way back. He is by himself. Auret greets him enthusiastically with a 'Howzit Neil?' Neil looks up with 'virtually no acknowledgement or recognition in his eyes'. Slumped over, he just moves his right arm slightly to open and close it. Perhaps it is an attempt at a greeting, 'a kind of wave'. Auret sees no limp, no obvious physical injury, but Neil appears completely listless, unable to exchange even a few words before they each move on.

At 8.37am, Neil is taken out to continue writing his statement. While the pages of his first typed statement are dated and signed, no dates are marked on this second, handwritten statement. We have no firm indication whether it was begun during the long weekend of torture or afterwards, on Monday, but whichever it was, Whitehead's presence looms heavily over this second statement. Neil's usual neatly slanting script appears messy and uneven, with intermittent crossings-out and diagonal lines scratched almost randomly across sections. Is this Whitehead venting his spleen? Here and there, Neil scrawls out and replaces numbers above paragraphs. Some numbers, including sequences, are confusingly repeated. Whitehead reveals himself most directly, however, through dictation.

A new, telltale opening sentence is allocated its own paragraph:

I

I support the Marxist ideology and therefore I am
a communist. I am **II** also an idealist.
My father was a farmer in Nanyuki ...[202]

The first sentence is crudely Whitehead's. Neil would not make the error of describing Marxism as an 'ideology'. Marx offers a set of materialist theories about society, economics and history, providing a mode of analysis, not an ideology. Nor is someone who finds Marxist analysis useful necessarily 'a communist', Whitehead's second giveaway being the word 'therefore'. But the sentence 'I am also an idealist' is surely Neil's. Squeezed in at the end of section 'I', surrounding the Roman numeral 'II', the words that he adds pose a contradiction. Someone who adheres strictly to Marx's materialist philosophy is not going to describe himself as an 'idealist'. Spinning on his tightrope, Neil manages to complicate things should this come before a court. For reasons we shall never know, this additional sentence, undercutting the first, does not appear in the typed version of his second statement. Whitehead will claim at the inquest that the typing is done by a detective from Ladybrand, Warrant Officer Karel de Bruin. As the two of them sit in Whitehead's office, Neil continues to work on his handwritten statement, obliged to hand it over page by page.

Paragraph by paragraph, more names and events are added. Wherever he can, Neil limits the implications. Naming those with whom he had studied *Capital*, he immediately qualifies that it was 'in order to get a good understanding of the economics of Marxism, but we took no resolutions, and when we had finished reading Volume 1, the group dissolved'.[203] In paragraph 12, Neil names the six others who made up Gavin's Group of 7, but calls them 'M.A.W.U people'. By paragraph 16, on a page with words and phrases messily crossed out, Neil writes about 'Workers Unity' and discussions on 'underground unions'. He writes that they 'used to meet informally'. Whitehead's assertion that they were reporting to a higher authority is undermined:

> These meetings were not structured to follow on from each other. Gavin felt that we should develop underground unions in line with the S.A.C.T.U. position. As he put the idea forward, there should be workers organized in groups of three in all of the factories, and they should co-ordinate with each other. It would be secret, and it would mean that the state could not ban or crush such an organization. The structure would be something like this: –

At this point Neil concocts a drawing: three large circles represent three factories, each containing smaller circles – for different departments – in which three dots represent core activists. A dot in one circle is linked by a line to a dot in another, each dot making a new link to a different department and one to a different factory. Underneath, he does his best to make his illustration irrelevant:

> We never actually wrote down this structure, but it was brought up at the meetings we had with the M.A.W.U. people, who were asked to bring other people to the meeting, although they never did bring anyone else.[204]

Perhaps the diagram has its roots in hearing how Gavin and Sipho used to organise in the early 1970s as they tried to re-establish links in factories where union organisation had been smashed for a decade and more. Finding one person, they would seek to build a group of three in each department, each new person being carefully tested to check they were not one of the management's network of informers. It had been slow, careful work, some years before Neil had come to Johannesburg, to establish a strong core of support within each factory before expanding more overtly. Exhausted and under threat of further torture, it seems that Neil produces this scrappy diagram for Whitehead as the latter demands to know more about 'underground unions'. Moreover, Neil writes that Gavin had approved of them.

It's a twist of positions that Gavin believes must have weighed heavily on Neil. He and Gavin had looked at the writings of Santiago Carrillo, General Secretary of the Spanish Communist Party, on underground unionism. But Gavin says he had never been in favour of the idea. It had been Neil:

> … you can imagine that from those early kind of romantic, revolutionary days, he had quite a fascination with clandestine organisation. Once he was in the union he realised that he must very rigorously not be part of it, but he was alert to its existence and its importance.

Reading groups and discussions had necessarily been clandestine but the 'underground union' idea had been a non-starter. They had decided 'it really wasn't on' and they should combat anything that might divide the union into factions. In writing his second statement, Neil acknowledges his initial support for underground unions, then he positions Gavin as continuing to support the idea, while distancing himself:

> Later, I argued with Gavin saying that an underground union was impossible because it would not be a proper trade union, that was democratically controlled by the membership, and open ... The discussions we had about an underground union never materialized, and the underground union was never formed.[205]

Whitehead has Neil on the back foot as he attempts to deflect attention to Gavin. A strange discrepancy creeps in here between the handwritten and typed statements. If we accept Whitehead's account that his colleague De Bruin has begun typing up Neil's statement while Neil writes up his notes by hand in the first week of February, then it is Karel de Bruin who twice mistypes 'I argued with Gavin' as 'I agreed with Gavin'. Desperate to pin Neil down to illegality, Whitehead hopes to override his declaration that the underground union idea had been clearly rejected.

Whitehead's dictation emerges once again in the word 'communistic' as Neil writes about joining Food and Canning. Although Neil is by now becoming muddled and repeating whole sequences of paragraph numbers, he is aware enough to dissociate himself swiftly from Whitehead's intent, even though he can no longer maintain his narrative of being a moderate. Yes, he is militant and keen to organise workers 'as a class so that they would themselves bring about changes in society', but this does not mean that he supports 'infiltration and undemocratic activities':

> When I began working in A.F.C.W.U. I had communistic ideas, but I did not want to have anything to do with the A.N.C. or S.A.C.T.U. partly because it was dangerous, and partly because it was not democratic, and I felt that I should work to organize workers in a militant, progressive, democratic way as a class so that they would themselves bring about changes in society. I was not in favour of infiltration and undemocratic activities. I was sympathetic and supported S.A.C.T.U.'s general political direction, but I disagreed with their methods of underground trade unions and I did not want any contact with them.[206]

Neil frustrates Whitehead's attempt to link his union activities with an underground strategy influenced by the ANC, SACTU and the SACP, but knows that he has exposed and misrepresented Gavin.

Where he can, he tries to limit the damage. He makes a point of saying that he knows that Jan Theron had been against his appointment 'because I had not done my military training'.[207] After he writes about taking Oscar to meet Gavin and Sipho, Neil adds,

> I never wrote reports for anyone about the Unions [sic] activities, and never received instructions from anyone to do this or that, apart from the reports that we sent half-yearly to the National Executive Council, and the advice that Jan gave me over the phone …[208]

Under pressure to write about Oscar, Neil describes how Oscar would tell him stories about the ANC in the 1950s and how he combined his trade union and political activities: 'He said that you could not separate the two.'[209] But Neil also makes clear that he did not take instructions from Oscar. Their work was union work.

By paragraph 25, Neil is pushed to write about Liz, personally and politically:

> Occasionally, Liz FLOYD would mention the problems they were having in the I.A.S., but generally we agreed not to discuss our work too much with each other, as we each had our own problems and we were busy. There was also tension between us about political things, because initially in Cape Town, I had drawn Liz away from political activity, but since I had come up to Johannesburg, I was more politically active, so she felt that I did not respect her politically. Only twowards [sic] the end of 1981 did we discuss some things together … I was aware that Liz FLOYD disliked the F.O.S.A.T.U. leadership intensely. Her sympathies are in a S.A.C.T.U. direction against registration. But she was not trying to break F.O.S.A.T.U. and she did not get any orders.[210]

However much Neil asserts that their political conversations were limited and that Liz had no 'orders', with Whitehead's fanatical probing, writing anything about Liz could feel like capitulation – perhaps even betrayal. Gavin is at least out of reach, but she is in enemy hands.

Neil writes just three more pages. Sections 26 to 29 are mostly copied word for word from his first statement, and cover his early work in the union, moving with Liz into 420A Fox Street, the Vegetable Garden and organising workers at Fatti's & Moni's. Does Whitehead declare that he's fed up with this padding and accuse Neil of inciting workers to strike? Because now Neil begins to expand, writing at length about the struggle of the workers to gain recognition for their union and higher wages, while stressing that their work was about organisation, not incitement:

> We used to stress to the workers that they must be militant and united if they wanted to get the recognition of the management, and higher wages, but we never told them to strike.[211]

This isn't what Whitehead wants. In Neil's next paragraph, he names a woman worker at Fatti's & Moni's to whom he had given a copy of *Workers' Unity*. The document comes to an abrupt end at the top of page 30:

> I had been given about three copies of Workers Unity who knew that I was involved in trade unions and had received them by post. The other two copies I either destroyed or gave to Brian Cutler or Gavin Anderson [sic].[212]

His account has barely reached 1980 and he is less than a third of a way through his first statement. Is there a definite moment when he decides that he will write no more? We can never know. What is certain is that at 10.45am on Thursday 4 February, Neil signs a sworn affidavit that he has dictated to Sergeant Aletta Gertruida Blom, detailing maltreatment and torture by his interrogators. It's a brave step to take while still in their hands, and Whitehead learns about it immediately.

It's a fateful twist that Sergeant Blom should present herself on the tenth floor that morning. She is a detective sergeant in the uniformed police, seconded to the Investigation Unit that deals with criminal proceedings against members of the force. Her visit traces back to Neil's complaint to Magistrate Wessels on 18 January about his earlier assault. On 19 January, the magistrate writes to the Divisional Commander of the security police (*Afdelingsbevelvoerder, Veiligheidstak*) in Johannesburg. It's a postbag address, from where the letter will be taken to an office in John Vorster Square. Six days later, on Monday 25 January, the Divisional Commander writes to the District Detective Commander (*Distrikskommandant*), John Vorster Square. A further three days later, on Thursday 28 January, the latter passes the matter on to the Branch Commander, Detective Branch (*Takbevelvoerder, Speurtak*), John Vorster Square. But the communication is only registered as received on Monday 1 February. All the while, during this sequence of 'pass the parcel', Neil is being assaulted and tortured on the tenth floor. On Tuesday, a dossier numbered M.R.84/2/82 is opened for the complaint. On Wednesday, the dossier is signed for by the Investigation Unit of the uniformed branch and transferred to the detective division. Sergeant Blom receives the dossier on Thursday 4 February and ascends to the tenth floor to make her inquiries.

The Occurrence Book shows Neil returned to his cell at '15h49', time enough for Whitehead to promise retribution. That evening, when Neil comes to his grille he looks so awful that Auret decides not to attempt talking: 'It was actually disintegration where he was actually becoming a zombie. I felt that now if I tried to reach out to him and connect with him it would just make the whole situation worse.'[213]

Auret retreats from his own grille so Neil won't see him, but after the guard closes his door he watches Neil through his peephole until Neil's door is eventually closed too. Sitting on his mat at half-past seven, listening on his radio to 'Deadline Thursday Night', Auret cannot stop his mind going back to their encounter in the corridor and Neil's slumped over, zombie-like state: 'For the first time I actually began to worry that he might commit suicide. It was actually the first time while I was in detention I was worried about someone committing suicide. I just did not know what to do about it.'[214] Auret decides he will speak to Cronwright the next day. He will express his fear that Neil could be a suicide risk, who should possibly be transferred to a psychiatric ward or at least put in one of the suicide-proof cells.

CHAPTER 39

Two scenarios

O N DUTY THAT NIGHT IN THE CHARGE OFFICE, SERGEANT JAMES
Agenbag is assisted by another white officer, Warrant Officer
Johannes Marais, as well as a black constable, Mosoeu Sehloko,
keeper of the keys, who guards the second floor. Agenbag, an ordinary uniformed policeman, is also responsible for about 250 prisoners on the floors
above and below. Having begun his tour on the crowded third floor, Agenbag
descends to the second. At about 10.20pm he appears at Auret's door and
waves. Auret recalls waving back 'without really waking up'. Across the corridor, Sehloko now opens up Neil's door. Agenbag finds Neil lying on his
mat. Neil props himself up on his right elbow, lifts his thumb and winks.
Agenbag takes this as an 'okay' and proceeds. At 10.30pm, the register is filled
in by Marais: all cells have been visited and there have been 'geen klagtes' (no
complaints).

Agenbag's orders are to visit the political detainees every hour, but
nothing is recorded in the register for 11.30pm, nor 12.30pm. He will state
at the inquest that he had been busy preparing complaint statements and
charge letters for the following day, as well as helping with booking in
ordinary prisoners brought in by detectives. The Occurrence Book shows
three black prisoners admitted to first-floor cells before 1am on Friday

5 February. All the while, Constable Sehloko remains alone in charge of the second floor.

There are at least two possible scenarios of what happens next.

One ...

When Whitehead assesses that the other detainees will be asleep, he collects Neil personally to take him to the tenth floor. With Agenbag and Marais conveniently occupied on the first and third floors, Whitehead insists to Sehloko that no record is to be made in the Occurrence Book. A black constable is not going to defy a white officer. Within a couple of hours, Whitehead returns, accompanied by at least one or two others, carrying a body. Neil is either dead or near death, unconscious. Passing the cells of sleeping detainees, they aim to minimise their shuffling footsteps. Inside Cell 209, a long multicoloured strip of material, perhaps strewn on the mattress, would seem ideal for a noose. Once looped over Neil's head, the body has to be lifted. This is the most difficult part. Someone has to secure the cloth's loose end to the topmost bars of the grille at right angles to the cell door, then test the knot with sharp tugs before nodding the 'okay'. The others drop the body. They feel its swing, hear it crash against the metal, witness it jerk and shudder to a halt. Their entrance and exit unrecorded, the constable on duty, the keeper of the keys, will have seen and heard nothing.

He fell from the ninth floor
He hanged himself
He slipped on a piece of soap while washing ...

It has happened so often before to black detainees that this version of events is one that many believe to be true. Here was a young white man who refused to take his allotted place in white society and has been made to share the fate of these black comrades.

A variation of Scenario One is that the Special Branch officers enter the second floor from below, using a flight of stairs that circumvent the usual entrance gate. Complicity would still be required from the uniformed policeman on duty should they be seen. In this version, the murder is carried out in Cell 209 itself and Neil's body then strung up. Harrowing though it is to imagine what might have happened either in Whitehead's office or in Cell 209 in the above scenario, I find the alternative even more painful.

Two ...

Neil waits for the cell door to slam shut. He is counting on the sergeant not returning for a while. His decision has been made. Watching the police-woman commit his affidavit to paper in her large childlike script, he knew well what Whitehead's reaction would be. Yet as the time to act closes in, we can only guess what might be going through his mind. He has a couple of blank sheets of paper in his cell, but anything he writes to those he loves will go straight to his interrogators. There is another way. Each book sent in by friends or family has carried a fleeting physical connection to 'outside'. Moreover, once opened and entered, each book has offered an imaginative lifeline to the world beyond the perverted confines of John Vorster Square.

He must choose. Camus's *Selected Essays and Notebooks*? *The Portable Nietzsche*? Will these authors, his intimates on the mountain above Cape Town, provide him with the words he needs? But tonight he leaves them stacked with Tolstoy, Orwell, Huxley, Zamyatin, Bashevis Singer and others. Instead he is drawn to William Faulkner's prose, dense as thickets, and the young man Isaac, whose companions each year seek to hunt and kill the leg-endary, near-indestructible Old Ben, 'The Bear', in *Go Down, Moses*. The story is full of resonance for Neil. He places the book face down beside his mat, on pages 196 and 197, in the middle of a long argument in which Isaac explains why he is renouncing the land bequeathed to him by his slave-owning grand-father. Isaac argues that the land was never anyone's to sell, bequeath or own. Men are only meant to be stewards of the earth:

> He made the earth first and peopled it with dumb creatures, and then He created man to be His overseer on the earth and to hold suzerainty over the earth and the animals on it in His name, not to hold for himself and his descendants inviolable title for ever, generation after generation, to the oblongs and squares of the earth, but to hold the earth mutual and intact in the communal anonymity of brotherhood ...[215]

While Neil has long ago rejected the biblical authority quoted by Isaac, he perfectly understands the boy's intense, non-materialist bond to the land and his fierce questioning of inheritance. 'To hold the earth mutual and intact in the communal anonymity of brotherhood' has indeed been one of Neil's transforming principles.

But there's something else he must say. As he pulls out the copy of Nikos Kazantzakis's *Zorba the Greek*, he thinks of his mother, who brought it for him. *J. Aggett* appears in pen, in her handwriting, on the first page. He looks for the scene immediately before the murder of the widow ... where the dark, handsome young shepherd, who has come down from the hills for Easter, is leading the dance. There is something disturbing, almost inhuman, in his presence as his feet beat against the earth 'like wings':

> Every minute death was dying and being reborn, just like life. For thousands of years young girls and boys have danced beneath the tender foliage of the trees in spring – beneath the poplars, firs, oaks, planes and slender palms – and they will go on dancing for thousands more years, their faces consumed with desire. Faces change, crumble, return to earth; but others rise to take their place. There is only one dancer, but he has a thousand masks. He is always twenty. He is immortal.[216]

His mother, and others who love him, should think of him just as part of the cycle of life and death. He will die, but others will replace him. Perhaps the thought that he is part of a continuous cycle helps him as he prepares his final act. His interrogators have brought him to the depths of despondency, but in making his affidavit he has defied them. They have broken him down, physically and mentally, but he will allow them no more satisfaction.

He has worked out how to hang himself. Yvette's kikoi is the right length. First he makes a small loop at one end and knots it with a reef. He tugs, tests it. It has to take his full weight. He has to do this dispassionately, as when he prepares to operate on someone, a living human being who must be treated just as a body. Is this kikoi, which once adorned Yvette, its colours glinting in the sun beside the pool, now drained of memory? Reminiscence might derail his purpose.

He threads the kikoi through its own hole until he has a noose. Using both hands, he pulls it over his scalp, around his neck. The other end hangs down below his thighs. The tricky part will be to secure this end to the topmost crossbar of the iron grille. Clambering up, at right angles to the gate, he secures both feet on the lowest bar. He leans against the metal so as not to lose his balance, and stretches up. Grasping the crossbar above him with one hand, he lifts the loose end of his kikoi with the other, estimating the length he'll need to ensure that his feet won't reach the floor. Then begins the winding. It's tricky with only one hand – a balancing feat – and a challenge to twist the final knot. But medical training has made him methodical.

Does Neil pause at all? Does he allow himself some final moments to think about his comrades, friends, family? Does he try to replace the stagnant green cell walls with the memory of walking under palm trees along a beach with his mother … tracking impala through the bush … Jill as little mother in the school 'san' … lying beside Liz on their mountain under the night sky … digging with Gav in the Vegetable Garden … chatting in Sipho's backyard … driving Israel and fellow workers home, singing, in the kombi …

Or perhaps not … As with the kikoi, all recollections may have to be put aside and every atom of energy harnessed to carry out this final act. Of course we, I, cannot know. But if Neil did decide to end his life, the open books tell us that, despite all the pain and anguish exacted by his interrogators, in his final hours he is wresting back dominion over himself and who he is. He can accept philosophically his own death, whereas he could never have reconciled himself with being Whitehead's pawn.

Whichever scenario is closest to the truth, the pathologists' determination of time of death is undisputed. Neil died within the first hour of Friday morning.

CHAPTER 40

‚What is done in the dark …’

S ERGEANT AGENBAG WAS MEANT TO CHECK THE CELLS EVERY HOUR, but, according to the Occurrence Book, after his cell round with Constable André Martin at 10.30pm, the next ‘*Selle besoek*’ (cells visited) took place at 12.56am. At the inquest, both men would admit that this had been a false entry. The sergeant had fallen behind with paperwork, preparing court lists in the first-floor office. Having missed two cell visits, he instructed the constable to record that they had visited the cells on all three floors. He intended to do his round soon.

Approaching 1.30am, Sergeant Agenbag returned to the second floor. As usual, Constable Sehloko opened each cell door for the sergeant to inspect inside. After the sergeant stepped back into the corridor, Sehloko would lock up again. They worked quickly. Entering Cell 209, however, as Agenbag looked in the direction of the mat, his eyes were drawn to the right. A body was hanging down against the grille, suspended from ‘*'n stuk materiaal*’ (a piece of material), around the neck. *Kom! Kyk!* Sehloko would have heard the alarm in the sergeant’s voice. Agenbag slipped his hand through the bars to feel for a pulse. Nothing. He shifted his hand onto the stomach. No movement there as well. The prisoner was already dead. In his affidavit, Agenbag would assert how he had no way of entering the cell. Only the security police held the keys to the padlocks that secured the inner cells and he didn't know there were duplicates in the complaints office. This was, he would add in his statement, the first time in his police career that he had come across a '*selfmoord*' (suicide).

Agenbag hurried back to the first-floor cells to tell duty constables Martin and Enslin that 'a security prisoner Neil Aggett had hung himself' and that he was going to fetch Warrant Officer Marais from the charge office.[217] Although instructed by Agenbag to continue their work, the two constables couldn't resist nipping up to the second floor, asking Sehloko to show them the dead prisoner. Sehloko would be kept busy with a stream of visitors requiring him to open Cell 209. Shortly after quarter to two, Agenbag returned with Marais, who had accompanied him on his rounds the previous evening. Checking for himself that there was no pulse, Marais found the body still warm.

Back in the charge office, around 2am, Marais rang Lieutenant Colonel Christiaan Scholtz of the security police at his home. Scholtz immediately called and woke Colonel Muller, Divisional Commander of the Johannesburg security police, also at home. By 2.20am, when Scholtz arrived at John Vorster Square, Muller was already there. Now that the security police had arrived, Marais handed Agenbag a duplicate key for the inner padlock of Cell 209. Neil was still their prisoner, even dead.

Across the corridor, Auret was woken in the early hours of the morning by the noise outside his cell: 'I carried on sleeping and woke up in the middle of the night. I could hear voices on the steps and a general commotion outside my cell. I just realised that Neil had committed suicide from what I heard.'[218] Auret had no doubts that Neil had hung himself. He may have been woken by the visit of the top brass, or possibly a little later, when the news had been communicated down through the ranks. Amongst those Muller had to ring were the district medical officer, Dr Neilson, and the senior state pathologist, Dr Nicolaas Schepers.

The flurry of spectators grew. Struwig and Whitehead arrived shortly after 3am. Around 3.40am, back in the charge office, Colonel Muller instructed Captain Carel Victor to supervise the immediate investigation. Having organised a photographer, Victor proceeded to Cell 209, where he found Agenbag with Struwig and Whitehead. Victor felt Neil's arm, by now cold. Under Victor's instructions, Warrant Officer Charl Lambrecht from the fingerprinting department began by taking Neil's fingerprints from the bars directly above the knot in the material from which he hung, before shooting a sequence of photos:

> PHOTO 1. Towards cell door into cell 209 and deceased who is hanging from the bars with his back to the door.
> PHOTO 2. Towards the front facing the deceased where he hangs from the bars.
> PHOTO 3. Towards nearby facing the deceased's face and material from which he hangs.
> PHOTO 4. Towards cement benches with various articles and sleeping place from the eastern corner of the cell.[219]

Photography was still under way at 3.45am, when Cronwright arrived with Brigadier Theunis Swanepoel, Divisional Inspector in the SAP's Witwatersrand Division. Trained by French police in torture methods used in the Algerian war, 'Rooi Rus' (Red Russian) Swanepoel was experienced in matters of death.[220] He fingered Neil's body. From its coldness, and with rigor mortis setting in, he estimated that Neil had been dead for between three and four hours, from some time between midnight and 1am. Swanepoel's subsequent statement on the state of Neil and his cell was meticulously calculated:

> The body of the whiteman 'Dr. Neil Aggett' hung from a piece of striped material. The material was knotted at one end around his neck and the other end was knotted around the uppermost cross-bar.
>
> The body was clothed in blue jeans, dark blue jersey-type shirt with long sleeves. He was wearing grey socks and blue slippers. The body's feet were about 5-6 inches from the ground.[221]

After the photographer had completed his work, Swanepoel ordered the body to be brought down. With two uniformed constables, he helped to lift it up while Andries Struwig cut the material with a pair of scissors. It was quarter past four when Neil's body was taken away to the state mortuary

More than likely it was Swanepoel who had instructed that a photograph should be taken of the cement benches. What was the relevance of this, beyond showing the 'comforts' he would maintain that Neil had enjoyed in his cell?

I then examined further the cell of the deceased. I noticed there was a good deal of clean clothes in the cell – there were trousers, shirts, jerseys, underwear and a pair of shoes without laces. There were also a lot of packets of sweets, packets of biscuits and other food. Cigarettes, jigsaw puzzles, dice and about 20 books concerning medicine as well as ordinary tales. I noticed two books that were opened face downwards. The one book was 'Go down Moses' and was open at pages 196–197. The other was 'Zorba the Greek' and was open at pages 246–247. I took the two books and handed them over to Colonel Muller. I drew his attention to the particular pages.

The two books were on the bench directly beside the bed where the deceased lay.

The bed of the deceased was made of 3 cellmats, 2 blankets and a cushion.

Following my observation of the comforts in the deceased's cell, I got the impression that he had received better treatment than what I normally expected for any detainees.

The light in the cell 209 is not very bright.

I saw no injuries on the hands or face of the deceased.

I did not examine the rest of the body.[222]

After commenting that 'the light in cell 209 is not very bright' – detainees often complained about the constant light – and that he had seen no injuries on Neil's hands or face, Swanepoel finished with his instruction to Captain Victor to make a full inventory of the contents of the cell. Although he has made no mention of suicide, his subtext is clear. *Look how good we were to him. This detainee had nothing to complain about.* Therefore he must have hung himself for other reasons. Indeed, Swanepoel's theory was that detainee suicides were 'a communist plot' to discredit the security forces.[223]

To make his inventory, Victor sought assistance. Starting on the left side of the cell with the bedding and books on cement bench 'A', Victor sorted and dictated items for Warrant Officer Pretorius to write down. In addition to titles and authors of some 18 books, he described each item in detail, including the messages in Neil's Christmas cards and brand names of clothes and food:

> 1 open packet Safari raisins lying underneath the cell mats …
> 1 open packet Springbok mixed fruit pieces …
> 8 loose toffies [sic] …

1 packet Simba Savoury Snack biscuits, containing 13 pieces ...

1 packet Chesterfield cigarettes (30) – containing 17 cigarettes

...[224]

Among the clothes, one item stands out poignantly: '1 multi-coloured man's shirt make "Yves Boutique"'. The whole inventory was to fill two-and-a-half typed A4 pages, although it is possible that the list may have been expanded to include items Whitehead had confiscated.

When it was time for detainees to rise, eat and go to the showers, the news began licking its way out like wild fire. Anonymous messages appeared in the Food Register directly beneath Neil's final entry:

MAY YOUR SOUL REST IN PEACE. ALWAYS REMEMBERED.

THE BLOOD OF THE MARTYRS WILL NURTURE THE TREE OF LIBERATION

ALUTA CONTINUA

   We love you

   What is done in the dark will be brought to light that day[225]

Strangely, there were only these four. Perhaps MacPherson discovered what was happening and removed the book. Or maybe the register was swiftly requisitioned in preparation for the inquest. The authorities were experienced in dealing with deaths in detention. There had been a spate of them during the mass detentions of 1976 and 1977, but, with the exception of Steve Biko, the majority had never caused more than a ripple of short-lived interest within the mainstream press and media. Dead detainees had always been black. Disappearances, coupled with denials, threw a grey cloak over the exact numbers of deaths in detention of those held under security legislation.[226] Steve Biko was generally regarded as the 46th and Neil was possibly the 51st. What is in no doubt, however, is that he was the first white political detainee to die in the hands of the security police.

PART FIVE

Lies, Truth and Recognition

CHAPTER 41

_____

'Purging of grief through activity'

EVERY DAY SINCE HIS ARREST IN NOVEMBER, JILL HAD BEEN thinking of her younger brother, deprived of seeing the same sky as she did. Although in recent years they had spent little time together, as the family emissary Jill had kept in regular contact with Neil by phone. It had often been necessary to leave a message for him with one of the union's secretaries, but he would always ring back. In the year before his arrest, they had seen each other perhaps only twice. Once, in July, he had come to stay for the weekend in Irene, to celebrate his niece Katy's fourth birthday. Joy was visiting from Somerset West. It had been a long time since both women had been able to enjoy a simple family occasion with Neil. His mother took special pleasure in him making a 'fry-up' for their breakfast. Jill would remember how Neil had brought gifts for Katy's birthday:

> ... a very pretty dress and jumper – the only trouble being that the jumper was for a child aged 8!! I was very touched that he had remembered the birthday and thought 'what a boy thing to do – to get the size wrong!'

A posed photograph from that weekend captures a moment of smiles. Joy, in her tailored dark dress offset by a string of pearls, is in the centre, with the excited birthday girl, mischievous face and bow in hair, in front of her. Neil, bushily bearded and moustached, in open jacket and shirt, stands on his mother's right. To her left, slightly to the rear and in the shadow of a doorway, is Jill's husband, Paul. He too has a beard and moustache, but they are trimmer than Neil's. His fatherly hands sit reassuringly on the shoulders of Katy's older brother. Young Miles grins from under his fringe at his mother, the photographer. Examined more closely, it is the two children whose smiles seem to be naturally bubbling. Neil's jacket suggests that he might be about to leave, which might account for the touch of stoicism in Joy's expression. It would be their last photograph of him.

*   *   *

Little more than four months later, Jill had been obliged to ring her parents with the news of Neil's arrest. After she and her mother had been allowed to see him briefly in John Vorster Square briefly on Christmas Eve, she had been left with the image of Neil shuffling out of a room with no shoelaces. Prey to recurring nightmares since his detention, Jill recalls an 'extraordinary bright moonlit night' on the evening of Thursday 4 February. Her daughter was a 'non-sleeper' and she had been up regularly up to see to her:

> I too wasn't sleeping and remember looking out onto the garden, thinking about Neil and feeling overwhelmed with anxiety about the predicament he was in and wondering if he too could see out of his cell and see the same moon I was looking at. It was an intense and unforgettable period in the night – probably half an hour or so as I stood at the window. As I looked back to this incident in the days that followed, I imagined perhaps that I had been touched by his spirit.

Having managed to fall asleep, Jill woke around 6am with the phone ringing. A neighbour at their previous house in Eldoraigne wanted to let her know that a policeman was on his way. He had gone to their old address and the neighbour had redirected him. Jill's first thought was, naively she admits, 'They're releasing Neil!' However, when the policeman arrived with the news that her brother was dead, she instinctively cried, 'What have you done with him?' 'Nothing to do with me, ma'am,' he replied. This would be the only official contact that the security police initiated with the family. Jill was left to ring her parents at their home in Somerset West. They were expecting a phone call on 5 February, but not this early. It was their wedding anniversary.

In remembering the day on which everything changed for them, Joy's recall was slightly different. She told me that Colonel Muller had rung Aubrey on the morning that Neil died. With the pain and the passage of time, it seems her memory may have blurred. I suspect what happened was that, on learning the news, Aubrey had immediately decided to go to the top. He would have demanded to speak to Colonel Muller, and what Joy remembered very clearly was Aubrey shouting down the phone: 'You killed him! You killed him!' It was the beginning of a seismic shift.

Jill's next call was to the Colemans, who were still asleep. It wasn't yet 7am. Unable to speak with them, Jill rang David Dison, whom she had come to know a little through the DPSC. David, recently qualified and already acting as Neil's attorney, was working for a firm of commercial attorneys, Bell, Dewar & Hall. He told her to come in straight away. With arrangements hastily made for the children, Paul drove Jill to Johannesburg.

A few memories stand out from the haze of that day, in which Jill felt reduced to 'a bag of jelly': David stating that he was only a junior and they must meet a senior partner, William Lane; Paul volunteering to identify the body; and, most poignantly, later that afternoon at the airport, seeing her father arrive from Cape Town with her mother: 'He came off the plane an old man. Weeping, weeping. It was a terrible sight.'

Even before leaving home in Somerset West, in his distressed state, Aubrey had been obliged to face a *Cape Times* reporter on the doorstep. During the brief interview, in which Joy remained inside, Aubrey handed the reporter a short typewritten statement. They were going to do their 'utmost to find out why this happened'.[227] Essentially private people, there was no time for any kind of preparation before being thrust into a very public matter. Arriving exhausted at the Burgers' home, they learned that the phone had rung solidly all afternoon.

In contrast, the authorities' well-oiled machinery had been set in motion from early morning. At 8.45am, inside the mortuary on Hillbrow's ridge, just west of The Fort prison, state pathologist Dr Vernon Kemp opened his post-mortem on Body No 270/82. He began with an external examination before incising the scalp, opening the skull and sectioning the brain. Between 9.15am and 9.30am, he received a message that a pathologist appointed for the Aggett family was on his way. Their lawyers had wasted no time. William Lane had rung Senior Counsel George Bizos, who immediately advised him to ask Dr Jonathan Gluckman to attend the postmortem.[228] Gluckman, with a reputation as a dispassionate scientist, was willing to undertake inquests into suspicious deaths in custody. He was not available, but fortunately his colleague, Dr Jan Botha, was. Having received the message, Dr Kemp ceased work on the corpse to await the family's pathologist.

Dr Botha arrived around 9.45am. After making his own examination of the head, scalp and brain, the two pathologists then proceeded in tandem, each making his own report. As a non-medical reader, I struggle to grasp sentences – even just phrases – that I can vaguely comprehend in Dr Botha's densely technical terminology. Here, in these seven typed pages, lies a detailed, physical, external and internal description of someone who ten hours earlier was a living human being ... was Neil:

> Examination of the neck revealed the presence of a broad but irregular area of discolouration on the anterior surface of the neck extending from ear to ear, this being more pronounced in the vicinity of the right angle of the mandible, while further discolouration of the skin was observed in the left occipital region. I was informed that the changes seen in the vicinity of the one angle of the mandible corresponded to the position of the knot in the garment found around the deceased's neck.[229]

The language is unemotional, detached. This is what the young, warm-hearted student Neil had to learn around the dissecting table in medical school so he could become the doctor who could calmly talk about taking axes out of people's heads; the doctor with the reputation for the smoothest of 'cut downs'; who could read an autopsy report with comprehension and dispassion. I try to imagine his mother and sister facing these words, page after page ...

Hillbrow police station, where Liz had been held in the cells since the last week in December, lay to the northeast of The Fort, barely half a kilometre away from the mortuary on Joubert Street. For a month Liz had been left in solitary without interrogation, before being taken the previous day, Thursday 4 February, for a session on John Vorster Square's tenth floor. Whitehead had entered intermittently, saying that Neil had implicated her. He warned her, as did her interrogators, Carr and Olivier, that she was heading for a five-year sentence. Whitehead also threatened to keep her standing until Saturday. They told her things she knew could not be true but which were deeply unsettling, such as Neil saying he regretted ever going to the University of Cape Town. She knew they were attempting to play her off against Neil, yet it was hard not to be affected. On Friday morning, Liz had been preparing herself for another day of intimidation when she was informed that Neil was dead. Shocked and distraught, she was taken under armed guard to the psychiatric ward of the Johannesburg General Hospital in Parktown.[230] Her captors were taking no chances.

Meanwhile, the DPSC launched into action, with a public statement and a telegram to the Minister of Justice:

APPALLED AT DEATH IN DETENTION OF DETAINEE DR. NEIL AGGUTT [sic]. THIS DEATH CONFIRMS THAT DETENTION AND INTERROGATION PLACE INTOLERABLE PRESSURES ON DETAINEES. DEMAND IMMEDIATE RELEASE OF ALL DETAINEES, TOTAL ABOLITION OF DETENTION LEGIS-LATION AND THE RETURN TO THE RULE OF LAW FORTHWITH. DETAINEE PARENTS SUPPORT COMMITTEE[231]

The DPSC's public statement began with a reminder that the Minister of Police had stated in Parliament, only the day before, that 'great care was taken by his Department that the detainees did not harm themselves':

Why – we ask of the Minister – should detainees want 'to harm themselves' if it were not because of lengthy detention in solitary confinement – intoler-able pressure of interrogation under bullying, threatening and even black-mail condition – without any recourse to outside help, without any friendly presence to give comfort and guidance? We ask of the Minister whether any alleged suicide under such conditions should not be seen as anything other than murder?[232]

The news had begun swirling through friends in the 'outside' world from early morning. At least a couple of close friends have memories of the previous night. Yvette had been travelling through the bushveld, the kind of terrain that Neil had loved from childhood. Like Jill, she had been strangely conscious of the moon:

> … there was an amazing full moon in a clear sky. I watched it from the car as we drove – a group of us were doing a night drive taking a four-day weekend trip to the Eastern Transvaal to get some relief from the stress. I was staying at a remote hospital where a friend worked when I got the news of Neil's death over a party line. I always hoped, afterwards, that Neil had had a chance to look at that moon from his cell window (if he had one) while he made his decision.

Joanne Yawitch had been indoors, in the Crown Mines house that she had shared with Gavin. She recalls feeling emotionally fragile even before hearing the news:

> This will sound bizarre. The night that Neil killed himself, I was alone at home and I was feeling incredibly miserable, and very depressed. I just burst into tears and couldn't stop crying; and Gavin was in London at that stage and I kept on thinking about him. I cried for hours and hours and hours, and I just had this terrible feeling about Gavin, and then the next morning I was woken up … by Clive Cope saying that Neil had hanged himself. I will never forget … It was just absolutely awful, terrible.

It must have been soon after seven o'clock, and Jill's phone call to David Dison, when the grim news began to spread. Gavin had to be told. He was no longer in Botswana. Following a tip-off to his family from the Botswana security police that the South Africans were after him, his brother Neil had paid for a ticket to London, where he was pursuing his medical career in epidemiology. But when the first phone call came through to Neil Andersson's London flat from Johannesburg, Gavin wasn't there. Nor was he immediately contactable. He had gone with Eddie Wes and Eddie's film school colleagues to Osea Island, off the Essex coast in the Blackwater estuary. For Gavin, the wintry, bleak island landscape 'somehow fitted with my pained and dismal internal condition'. Eddie was helping a fellow student with an assignment and Gavin, who wasn't part of the crew, spent a lot of time walking, sketching, thinking. The alien environment was also distracting:

It was fun in a way, to be with this group of quintessentially English, early-20s young, inexperienced and very artistic types, with the director (about 24 years old) absolutely the king of the roost, confident and opinionated and definitive about everything. They knew nothing about our world and struggle and in fact couldn't care less about it. Their own world of music and film and vaguely counter-cultural art was totally unfamiliar to me, so that it was like being backstage at rehearsals for an outlandish play.

Gavin was on the point of being drawn into a scene as a boatman who rows the heroine to some mysterious assignation. He was looking forward to getting some rowing practice when, on the evening before the filming, he rang his brother's flat from a telephone booth. It was part of their agreed twice-a-week schedule. His brother asked him to sit down because he had some very bad news to share. Sitting on the floor of the cramped booth, Gavin learned that Neil was dead, his body found hanging in his cell.

Gavin can't remember much except that he pulled Eddie out of the shoot to tell him the news. For a long time, the two just hugged each other and howled with grief. It was high tide, which meant that Osea Island was cut off from the mainland. They had no alternative but to wait for the tide to recede so that Gavin could go across and catch a bus back to London:

> While waiting there was a kind of wide circle of silence around me, and the normal bantering of the film crew stopped altogether; only Eddie flitted in and out of my awareness, with a cup of tea, or an offer of food. Eventually the tide went out and I got across to the bus station. I guess that was only the following morning.

Back in London, Gavin found a score of messages at the flat. His brother had already been pushing away journalists. He was puzzled by the focus on Gavin, as well as the depth of Gavin's reaction, doing his best to counsel his older brother by trying to help him see things in perspective. It was he who had been the original friend at medical school in Cape Town, but it was only now that he realised how much closer Gavin and Neil had become, 'closer even than brothers'. There was so much that Gavin couldn't say.

With styes gathering on the lower and upper lids of each eye, Gavin felt his body breaking down, and for a while found it difficult to see. Although exhausted, he couldn't sleep, plagued by the thought that he, the real target, had evaded the police, only for them to get Neil. When Pedro Espi, a Crown Mines friend who was visiting his family home in Spain, rang and said, 'Come to us', Gavin escaped from London:

> ... the whole Espi family took me to their bosom as I tried to cope with the loss of my friend, and my feeling of guilt that it was not me who had died ... But it was safe there; I felt fully safe for the first time in more than 5 years. The time on the farm in Spain with Pedro helped me cling to sanity and to life.

On Saturday 6 February, Jane Barrett, another close friend of Gavin's back in Johannesburg, began writing an extended letter to him, a diary of sorts that continued over several days, in which she vividly described how friends were commemorating Neil. Even without knowing the depths of Gavin's feelings of guilt, she and other friends at home sensed how bereft he would be at the loss of his buddy-cum-brother and how adrift he would be in exile:

> Saturday
>
> ... Jo and I and all others close to you have been holding you close to our hearts over the last 2 terrible days. None of us will ever know the depth of your pain, but know that we are cradling you – and loving you dearly ... I hope we were able to convey that to you earlier over those painful telephone miles. I want to describe in detail all that has happened here since the devastation of yesterday – but right now my heart is too heavy with grief, and your pain to do that coherently. May Neil's spirit live on in you – his fineness will never die. We must trust that his soul & his convictions will remain burning alive in his friends and in those he worked with. Courage, dear one. –
>
> It feels like an eternity since I first heard the news of Neil's terrible death on Friday morning – The horror of those first minutes of comprehension returns periodically in a frightening blackness – Mostly, we are all filled with a numbness which almost disallows grief & anger. And for us perhaps things are made much easier by the urgency of things to be said & done – a purging of grief through activity.

I have repeatedly left, & come back to, this half-page over the last day. Before that I tore up 3 new pages. It is hard. News of Neil's death spread fast on Friday morning. A group of about 100 stunned people gathered speechlessly at midday – when the parents committee made their strong & courageous statement & the rest planned a 'service' for that night. – It was beautiful & simple, befitting of your comrade. – About 350 people coming together unpublically [sic] & unpretentiously to share their grief spontane-ously & from the heart. It was held in the old canteen at Wits, with seats in a circle, & Tom Waspe chairing informally – No planned or announced speeches – Memories and tributes expressed from the soul. And beautiful singing. We started with a few minutes silence – the room darkened, with candles burning. The concentration on Neil was intense, uninterrupted, & said so much for him. After a song Sipho was the first to stand – beautiful man standing brave & strong, sharing the history of Neil as he knew him – his work in the townships as a doctor, determined never to withhold his medical insights from those he treated, ready to be called out at any time, & refusing payment; his time in IAS, with a reference to the difficulties of the time; his work in FOSATU – again, difficulties; his dogged determination in Food & Cans – together with his work at Bara. Sipho spoke long & elabo-rately – people attentive – ending in a powerful Amandla. Then Ma Lydia [Mam'Lydia Kompe] – equally moving, simple. She spoke of him as a son – with a deep deep love & respect. She described their relationship – Neil with theoretical insights & expertise & she with experience of the factory floor – How they learned to learn from each other – how they needed each other. Her voice went quiet at times. She referred to the growers co-op, and later introduced a song Neil had taught you all while gardening. Smile [Mam'Lydia's husband, one of Neil's patients] stood gravely on her one side, & Lisa [Jacobson] on her other. Jeremy Baskin described a weekend in the Eastern Transvaal with Neil just before his detention – how they walked long together, talking. – About a waterfall they found together. Dave told of his special contribution to the IAS – of how he introduced a particular com-plaints system still used effectively today. And of his interest in Industrial Health. Parts of the meeting are a haze – Jo spoke. I can't remember what she said. I was moved at a time to remember the other detainees likely to learn of his death, & alone in their cells – And then to remember you as a special friend of Neil's & comrade of us all. I fear that many hardly heard me, as it was hard to talk through the tears welling inside me. There were others who spoke – some who had never met him, but who felt moved to speak. The meeting ended with a powerful rendition of Nkosi which would have made him proud. – And then groups gathered to talk of further action. Despite the grief there has been a strong determination to act. –

On Saturday afternoon a motorcade of 90 or more cars – lights on, black flags on arials [sic], & posters announcing 'His Spirit Lives On', & 'Kill Apartheid, not detainees' on their sides. 3 convoys of cars converged on the [John Vorster] Square, where they were met by swarms of police with cameras & notebooks (taking numberplates); traffic cops watching for petty offences (one person fined for not wearing a seatbelt & one for going thro' a red robot.); & a row of riot vans waiting inside the parking lot – there was nothing they could do, so we circled the building again & again. A few people … were arrested for 'unnecessary use of a hooter'. Liz [McGregor, a journalist] had earlier been arrested at the Fort after taking pictures of the motorcade – the cops suspected her of photographing the police station & were very heavy. She stood her ground & was eventually charged with 'disturbing the peace' – for blowing her hooter, also. She felt okay about it all until today, when she was heavily reprimanded by the Assistant Editor at the *Mail* – shitting on her for her 'partiality'. Things snapped for her then, & I saw her shortly afterwards, very upset. She has to pay a R50 fine by tomorrow. – She's okay now – a lot calmer. We spent a few hours together.

Then tomorrow there is a torch stand along Jan Smuts Ave during evening rush-hour. – Posters & torches. There should be about a hundred people, at least. And on Thursday a brief nationwide workstoppage – supported by FOSATU. They came out clear & strong from the start; although I don't recall any public statements as yet.

Neil will never be forgotten.–

The visits to other detainees on Saturday were a total whitewash – Visitors prevented from asking questions of any import, & in most cases attempts were made to prevent any reference to Neil. Most visitors were defiant however, & told of his death. – Those who have radios (a few of the longer term detainees) knew, & a few others had heard it thro' the grapevine. Others had seen the billboards' (newspaper) reference to a death in detention but didn't know who it was. Cedric [de Beer] had had no idea & was totally stunned; Barbara's first question was 'Who?' – She sobbed at the end of the visit; A few of us stood at the gate watching detainees being brought in & out – we had close glimpses of many – including Barbara [Hogan], Fink [Haysom], Morris [Maurice Smithers], & Monty [Narsoo]. Some saw Cedric earlier, looking very grave. – It was so wonderful to catch glimpses, but the context so ghastly. Most were very distraught at the news …

Tues … The funeral plans are running ahead. – It's to be on Saturday – late morning, starting at St Mary's Cathedral & moving to the cemetery. The union is involved in organising it together with a large working group. – Virginia Engel [from FCWU] is up here & Jan [Theron] is due in Jhb on Friday. He will pay tribute to Neil during the Service, – most of the rest will take place later. – with Sipho as a likely speaker, amongst others.– The Woodworkers are making Neil's coffin – mostly pine, but with teak beading – Also, instead of handles to carry it, it'll have poles so that numbers of people can carry it at the same time. Liz has requested chrystanthemums in pots around the graveside – so that people can take them away to plant. She also asked that Mannenberg be played at some stage during the funeral. – We are all hoping that she will be allowed to attend. There probably won't be a hearse, but the union kombi may be used. There will be lots of singing – especially of his favourite songs; minimal amount of religious content has been necessary to satisfy the family. – Jill, Neil's sister, has been amazingly supportive of all suggestions – His parents are still so stunned that its hard to gauge them.

I hope this hasn't read dispassionately – Its hard to know how best to let you know of all thats been happening. – Also hard to know to what extent you need contact & detail. I've been keeping clippings for you for a while, so these are all added to those on Neil – I hope it isn't too overwhelmingly depressing …

… it is now Wednesday afternoon & I have precious little time before getting this to Jane [Eagle, a friend who was travelling to Europe]. – Neil would be so proud of the unity displayed in response to his death. No ifs & buts & qualifications. – So even in death, he continues to work. You would be moved by the humbleness of people right now – no power politiking [sic]. Straight hard work with a sense of purpose. Even the TMS [Transvaal Medical Society] has organised a meeting & made a strong statement …

I spoke to your mother on Friday – early morning. I broke the news to her. It was horrible. Muff [Gavin's sister] was apparently away in the swamps

– even now I don't know where she is. Your mother was amazing – angry
& grieved, but somehow she managed to find strengthening words. It was
very important that day.

All love & strength to you.

Jane.[233]

The letter was the closest that Gavin could come to his comrades in their
mourning and 'purging of grief through activity'. In a different kind of exile
from that of Gavin, under armed guard in a hospital psychiatric ward, Liz was
forced to deal with her anguish completely alone.

Meanwhile, Neil's family was experiencing a distinct kind of aloneness.
The Neil they knew as son and brother was not the political Neil who had
so unexpectedly become the focus of a sweeping tide of attention. With a
German TV crew arriving at the house in Irene, Jill found herself thrust into
the role of family representative, talking to reporters from across the country and abroad, including the special correspondent of *The New York Times*,
Joseph Lelyveld. The first white death in detention was news. A lengthy article
appeared across the Atlantic the following day, headlined 'WHITE AIDE OF
NONWHITE SOUTH AFRICAN UNION FOUND HANGED IN CELL'.[234]

While Neil's comrades had to struggle with his loss, they nevertheless understood the political context and drew strength from collective resistance.
Certainly for black South Africans, another death in detention was no surprise. The words of this song by SAAWU workers in the Ciskei reflected the
ominous possibility that death would be the price of their resistance. It was
part of the process:

Thozamile, Thozamile, we are going to die in jail,
We go in, we go out, we shall surely die in jail ...[235]

For the Aggetts, however, the tragedy of Neil's death was the beginning of a
deeply painful journey that would take them into the ugly heart of the state
to which Aubrey had entrusted his family 18 years earlier. The DPSC offered
practical support and sympathy, but this particular journey was one that they
had to make by themselves.

CHAPTER 42

Public protests

ANGRY STATEMENTS AND PROTESTS FROM A WIDE RANGE OF organisations followed news of Neil's death. In large headlines, the *Cape Times* reported 'Storm over detainee's death in cell'.[236] There were unprecedented expressions of concern from the two major employer bodies: the Federated Chamber of Industries and Assocom. It was not hard to see why. Five major unions, previously on opposite sides of the fierce debates over registration, issued a joint statement with stark implications for the government's carefully constructed labour strategy. Unequivocal in their dismay, the two Food and Canning Workers' unions, the General Workers' Union, the Cape Municipal Workers' Association and FOSATU announced that as far as they were concerned 'the remnants of the government's labour reforms have died with Neil Aggett'. As long as the security police were free to act against unionists, there was 'no possibility of any further and future relations between the unions and the state'.[237] They were planning, they said, a joint day of mourning.

The DPSC's public statement, reflecting widespread disbelief that Neil's death was anything other than murder, flew in the face of a statement issued by the Commissioner of Police. After declaring that 'everything indicates' it was suicide, General Mike Geldenhuys, General Johan Coetzee's superior, added an account of cell inspection that would later be revealed as fiction. The Commissioner stated that 'When he [the detainee] was visited in the cell 30 minutes before he was discovered dead, everything was in order'.[238] In Parliament, the Leader of the Opposition, Dr Frederik van Zyl Slabbert, announced that he felt 'shame' at the death of Dr Aggett, recalling how the Minister of Police, Louis le Grange, had so recently assured Parliament that detainees were being held 'under the most favourable conditions possible ... All reasonable precautions are being taken to prevent any of them from in-juring themselves or from being injured in some other way or from com-mitting suicide.'[239] Le Grange had given his assurances only two days before Neil's death on presenting the findings of the Rabie Commission into security legislation. He had been happy to report Justice Rabie's satisfaction that the Terrorism Act provided detainees with regular visits from magistrates and inspectors.[240]

Separately from the impromptu gathering in the Wits canteen on the evening of Neil's death, the Wits SRC called an emergency meeting that day, issuing a statement that made Neil's death a clarion call in the struggle for de-mocracy: 'The death in detention of Dr Neil Aggett epitomizes the lengths to which the undemocratic South African state needs to go to suppress the call for democracy and freedom ...'[241] Describing Neil as 'a true patriot of South Africa whose life was dedicated to the struggle for freedom and justice in our country', the SRC said that his death served 'only to strengthen the resolve of all democrats to continue building a truly democratic South Africa'. The SRC passed a unanimous motion resolving:

1. to extend our sympathy and solidarity to Neil's family and friends.
2. to make known our absolute abhorrence for a system that allows for the murder of patriots working for a democratic society.
3. to intensify our demand for the unconditional release of all detainees.
4. to recommit ourselves to hold sacred those ideals which Neil strove for in his life.[242]

Similar sentiments were echoed in meetings across the country. At the University of the Western Cape – designated for Coloured students un-der apartheid laws – more than 500 people gathered to protest and pass a more militantly worded resolution in which this death was seen as 'the lat-est in a calculated process on the part of the State to silence and wipe out all opposition to its totalitarianism'.[243] The United Women's Organization, based in Cape Town and whose members were predominantly poor black women, made a moving tribute to Neil, adding their concern for Oscar Mpetha. Their statement carried a special poignancy given Oscar's mentorship of Neil. Very likely some of them had come to know Neil through Oscar:

> Even though he is no longer with us in the flesh, Neil Aggett will live on to inspire us. We are shocked at the death in detention of one of our most dedicated leaders in the workers' struggle. We are concerned for the safety of other detainees and awaiting trial prisoners. Oscar Mpetha has been admitted to Groote Schuur. How safe is he?[244]

On hearing of Neil's death, relatives of detainees in Cape Town gathered to present a memorandum to the head of the security police in the Cape. Mainly parents of students, they asked to see their own children:

> We do not know where they are being held or why. We do not know how they are, whether they eat or drink, how they are being treated – we do not even know if they are still alive. We make this approach to you sir because we have no other avenue open to us. We cannot approach the courts nor are lawyers allowed access to detainees …[245]

Brigadier Hennie Kotze refused to see them, agreeing only to see their legal representative and then refusing their request. It was a similar story in Durban, where 11 out of 12 families were refused permission to see detained relatives. Not even allowed into the grounds of the CR Swart Square police station, they were all photographed.

While Saturday's motorcade around John Vorster Square (described by Jane Barrett in her letter to Gavin) and Monday evening's torch stand along Jan Smuts Avenue were attended by many of Neil's friends, Food and Canning's call on Monday for a half-hour nationwide work stoppage on Thursday 11 February dramatically raised the scale of protest. The call received immediate support from FOSATU. Ironically, through his death Neil was forcing a degree of unity that he had not been able to achieve in life, given the half-hearted responses that he had met in setting up a Transvaal solidarity committee.

Opposing unions were now faced with a massive practical challenge. There had been no national stoppage for nearly twenty years. With less than three full days to organise, it was an exceptional test for the spectrum of emerging unions. Figures vary, but it seems that almost all of Food and Canning's 15 000 Transvaal and Cape workers supported the action. They were joined by some 4 000 to 5 000 members of the Cape-based General Workers' Union, and an estimated 10 000 to 12 000 members of the Council of Unions of South Africa (CUSA). Add to these FOSATU's carefully itemised 59 161 workers in 90 factories spanning the eastern and western Cape, Natal and the Transvaal, and the total is around 90 000.[246] Most of the workers taking part belonged to the older unions, reflecting the importance of solid shop-steward structures, with patient organisation as opposed to spontaneous militancy. While newer unions wanted to respond, simply putting out the call was not enough.

Numbers in individual factories varied from 50 at a Natal fertiliser plant to 7 000 at Volkswagen's factory in Uitenhage. But beyond the numbers were small, telling details. White workers joined the mainly black workforce at the Uitenhage plant. At Cadbury's in Port Elizabeth, some white managers attended a commemorative service, as did white foremen at Plascon, with all the workers observing a three-minute silence followed by prayers and 'Nkosi Sikelel' iAfrika'.[247] Both the Federated Chamber of Industries and the Steel and Engineering Industries Federation advised employers not to obstruct the stoppage.[248] Although the latter apparently also advised that workers should not be paid for the half-hour missed, many employers were reported to have made no deductions of wages. Interviewed for Britain's *TV Eye* programme, Tony Bloom, Chairman of the Premier Group, declared that he supported the stoppage. Detention without trial and its use against trade unionists would leave 'a legacy of bitterness', making life 'very difficult' for industrialists.[249] Neil had organised at Premier Group factories and negotiated with its head of Human Resources, and was therefore known personally. The fact that he was white, and the first white detainee to die in security police hands, finally focused white attention on an issue that black South Africans had known for years.[250]

If Whitehead and Cronwright had hoped that interest in the case would peak quickly, then die, this backing for the stoppage from a white captain of industry like Tony Bloom was very unwelcome. Moreover, senior figures from the National Mining Commission were now voicing in public their concern that detention of trade unionists was affecting labour relations, undermining labour reform and impairing the work of the Department of Manpower.[251] Instead of earning praise for rooting out 'terrorists', Cronwright and his team effectively found themselves accused of destabilising the economy. They had passed on strong intimations, already printed in the Afrikaans press, about Neil having been a member of a banned organisation, but had seen these treated with scepticism by critics. During the inquest, they would want to ensure that Neil was portrayed as a member of the illegal underground for which his union work had been just a cover.

In the meantime, with all the national and international attention, the security police must have debated how to handle the funeral. As the week after his death wore on, there were indications that the event could grow into something very large. The last major political funeral had been that of Steve Biko, in September 1977. Held in King William's Town, it had attracted diplomats from 13 Western countries, with over 10 000 mourners accompanying the coffin to the gravesite. Buses carrying many more thousands of mourners had been prevented from entering the town by heavily armed police. However, Biko had been a significant political figure, while Neil was a previously unknown doctor-cum-trade unionist. Why would black workers risk coming onto the streets of Johannesburg for a young white man whom most of them would never have known? Thursday's national stoppage must have given the authorities pause for thought.

CHAPTER 43

Funeral preparations

WHILE PUBLIC PROTESTS GATHERED PACE IN THE WEEK AFTER Neil's death, focusing on the iniquity of a system that allowed the security police unbridled power over detainees, the shaken family tried to hold themselves together as best they could. They had contacted Michael, now working in Israel at the Edinburgh Medical Missionary Society's 'Mustashfa Inglizi' (English hospital) in Nazareth. He promised to come as soon as possible. The day following Neil's death was spent, between interviews and phone calls, with friends and family – about 20 people – calling at the Burgers' house to offer sympathy and support. My parents were among the company, hoping to have a quiet time to talk, given their own experience of having children whose divergent views had led to jail. There were no quiet moments, however, and my mother would wait until after the funeral to send her thoughts in a letter.

Although memories are no longer clear on precise details and timing, it was probably during that first weekend that the Aggetts reluctantly agreed to the union organising Neil's funeral. While really wanting a quiet, private ceremony in which to mourn their loss, everything had changed for them and they were now adrift in uncharted waters. In handing over control of the funeral to the union, they nevertheless hoped that the ceremony would be dignified and not become a political rally. Shocked and angered by Neil's sudden death, Jan Theron spoke on the telephone, probably to Jill, offering the union's assurances that the funeral would be an occasion for workers to pay tribute to Neil and the union ideals to which he had dedicated himself.

Yet Food and Canning was walking a fine line. As Jan subsequently explained to me, there had been a number of events in the Cape, including a funeral in Worcester, that had been turned into political occasions, with workers turning up in ANC colours, and where the union 'had to carry the flak with Security Branch raids'. For a union working with the community this was inevitable, especially in the wake of the Fatti's & Moni's strike. However, the union was also contending with some major internal struggles with a right-wing faction, or 'old guard from the days of being a straight registered Coloured union':

> We weren't saying no to political involvement – we never did – but on our terms … I thought it was also mistaken politically to almost say, 'Yes, he [Neil] was involved in the underground' … I mean he wasn't involved in the underground at the point when he died. If he had been involved in the underground, maybe he would have been prepared to deal with detention in the way that a person in the underground might, with the knowledge and the mental preparation that maybe comes with doing that.

These were clearly concerns for the union itself, and not appropriate to share with the distressed family. As preparations for the funeral took place, the issue of how Neil should be represented, including what symbols to use, came into sharp focus and would be strongly contested.

With union staff busy organising Thursday's work stoppage, a funeral committee was set up to include union representation alongside a group of Neil's friends and fellow activists. Doug Hindson, the editor of the *South African Labour Bulletin*, whose flat Neil had used in the months before his arrest, was surprised when approached to take the role of chair. His FOSATU sympathies meant that he had been on the opposite side of the earlier 'workerist' versus 'populist' division, but the request reflected Neil's own work towards rapprochement:

The reason I did it, I felt bloody upset that this person had been brutalised. It was more a personal thing, I just saw in Neil an integrity. There was all the political rhetoric and manoeuvring but here was a guy who could be carving out a career but he devoted his life to helping people who were vulnerable …

Furthermore, Doug agreed for the committee meetings to be held in his flat in Diamond Court. Although his consent arose out of a personal commitment to Neil, it set in motion a chain of events that were to change his life. Special Branch intimidation, of the kind meted out to 'populists', began soon afterwards, including phone-tapping and heavy-breathing calls in the middle of the night. Years later, talking to me over the phone from France, I could still hear the emotional toll in his voice. The harassment, which went on for years, had affected his family life and left him with some profound regrets. Nevertheless, Doug felt that he had done the right thing, honouring the spirit of Neil's own dedication.

Also playing a major role in the funeral committee was David Webster, a senior lecturer in Social Anthropology at Wits, who had become involved in the DPSC following the detention of a number of his students, including Barbara Hogan. For David Webster too, involvement in the funeral committee may have been a significant marker on the road that would lead to his assassination seven years later by a covert government hit squad.[252]

Woodworkers immediately offered to make Neil's coffin, with Sipho in charge of the process. It was a communal act of love and respect for someone very close:

> To the Woodworkers' Cooperative, Neil's death was a terrible blow because we were very close with him … [He] would sit down with us, talk with us and to my family it was a terrible blow. In fact the pain that I had when Neil died is more than the pains which I felt for my own family members that died – that is as close as I was with him.

For Sipho, there was an additionally intimate personal-political identification:

> As a unionist, I was also like Neil: I had very little time for my family. Thandi had given birth to our third child and it was Neil who fetched Thandi at the

hospital and brought her home. I was not there, so that is as much as how we were close.

This was a coffin not just for a comrade, but a brother.

The first requirement was a visit to the mortuary to take measurements. When Sipho and a comrade arrived, they didn't enter but asked the mortuary attendants to measure the body. Neil's solid pine coffin would be something simple and utilitarian, except for the teak beading. It was like no other task they had undertaken. In Yvette's eyes, 'It was a real act of love for him and the respect and care with which his loving comrades handled it was incredibly important for me and I'm sure everyone. From getting the measurements through to sending him on his way on the day.'

The committee also had to decide whether the coffin should be left open at the funeral for mourners to file past and pay their respects. While discussion initially focused on different cultural practices and which to prioritise, the question was resolved after someone explained what would have happened to Neil's face in the autopsy. The coffin would remain closed.

One of the major discussions in the funeral committee was whether members of the crowd might try to place an ANC flag on the coffin, thereby turning the funeral into an ANC rally. Jan, who was being kept closely informed back at Food and Canning headquarters in Cape Town, was made aware that there was a certain amount of support for the ANC flag idea. Jan strongly disagreed, believing that if this were to happen, Neil would simply be represented as the latest person who had died 'in the long miserable annals of the repressive apartheid regime ... and not really having much regard to who had died, why they had died, why they had been detained in the first place, what they were doing and what the significance of their work was ...'

Neil was a unionist, accountable to the workers whom he represented. Moreover, to have the ANC flag laid over the coffin would politically compromise the union's task of trying to create a strong workers' organisation at a delicate and critical stage of building unity between different factions, as was happening through the national work stoppage. The gesture would also play completely into police hands.

However, the AFCWU also contained many ANC supporters who felt the time was right to push for the flag and that it would be welcomed as an expression of worker and political militancy. After heated discussion, the committee's decision was to drape Neil's coffin with the AFCWU/FCWU red flag, with its white lettering and central icon of interlocking black hands. Yvette recalls how those who had argued for it hoped that the crowd would give it respect and not try to replace it. The decision was 'in no ways meant as a slight to the ANC, nor as any denial of where Neil's sympathies lay. But it was a very careful and political decision' that was intended to emphasise his trade unionist role and what Neil stood for in the struggle for 'workers' rights, moral rights'.

The pallbearers – the subject of another thorough discussion – were chosen to include his family, the union and those close to Neil. One group would carry the coffin a short distance, then pass it over to the next, in a kind of symbolic order. The family were to be included in the heart of the church, progressing to the final group that would emerge outside to convey the coffin to the hearse. The concluding group would have to be the strongest, able to withstand the buffeting of what was expected to be a large crowd.

Jill recalls Doug Hindson and David Webster coming to their house to talk with the family about the funeral and the committee's decisions. Doug was quiet and intense, while David came across as gently genial, trying to accommodate the family's feelings. Jill recalled her parents' incomprehension and sense of being marginalised:

> [They] felt they were being mown down, not having a say in anything and they kept on saying 'He's our son, he's our son!' … It was just very difficult for all of us to understand anything, to be honest. Paul and I were perhaps a little more aware of the danger Neil was in when he was detained, but I don't think my parents really got that. They just thought he'd come in for questioning. They'd known about you and your brother Paul, and you both survived.

Although there was no intent to offend the family, decisions were being made without reference to them. They had been allotted their set place in a funeral that would largely reflect Neil's world and his beliefs. Realising that there was not much room for them in this world, they stepped back. In Yvette's assessment, the family 'really handed a lot over and honoured Neil in a huge way by not standing in the way of the funeral proceedings'. Her speculation was that Jill probably played a large role in this.

There were many other matters, however, to occupy the family. The question of legal representation remained firmly in the family's hands, with Aubrey insisting on having the very best legal team for the inquest, which he would fund from his savings. Bell, Dewar & Hall, where David Dison worked, was one of Johannesburg's oldest firms and highly prestigious. Aubrey would have been unaware that it was also the most liberal and political of the commercial chambers, its clients including the Anglican Diocese of Johannesburg and Bishop Desmond Tutu. An active Anglican, William Lane had also been Bram Fischer's personal attorney, looking after his estate after his death.

To the Aggetts, William Lane came across as a solid, knowledgeable, unassuming attorney. However, when he proposed George Bizos as Senior Counsel, Aubrey faced the challenge of dealing with his prejudices. The high-profile advocate, who had represented Nelson Mandela and Bram Fischer, and the families of Ahmed Timol and Steve Biko at their respective inquests, had probably been involved in more political trials than anyone else, taking on cases that the vast majority of the legal fraternity avoided. In his autobiography, *Odyssey to Freedom*, George Bizos describes being one of a small group of lawyers who made use of a 'few procedural safeguards' to defend many black, and some white, men and women who the regime wanted either to imprison or execute as 'terrorists':

> The dice were loaded against our clients. Many were wrongly accused of serious, even heinous crimes. Confessions were often extracted from them under torture, although torture was routinely denied and often coupled with an allegation that we, their lawyers, were engaged in a campaign to besmirch the good name of the South African Police.[253]

For Joy and Aubrey, as for other white South Africans who simply trusted the police, the name 'George Bizos' was itself loaded. But now, with the collapse of his previously solid frame of reference, Aubrey in particular was forced to make an unprecedented intellectual and emotional leap, as he acknowledged in an interview some time later:

> You take the Biko affair. I heard about Biko. I thought he was probably a bad fellow who got what he deserved. Since our troubles I have read a lot about Biko, and to my mind, there's no argument: Biko was murdered. But I've only come to feel this way about things since this tragedy happened to us …[254]

Initially, everything was happening so rapidly that there was little time for Neil's parents to make sense of conflicting thoughts and emotions. On Sunday 7 February, Paul drove the family to Johannesburg for an 11am meeting arranged by David Dison with George Bizos. Perhaps it was here, in the hushed calm of a lawyer's office, that they first began to get a measure of the grim reality ahead. How do you reach the truth in a corrupt sea of lies? Aubrey, who had always been formidably strong-minded, was, for the first time in his life, completely adrift. He underwent a painful process of re-perception, and as time wore on both he and Joy would be deeply impressed by the rationality and integrity of the legal team who undertook the inquest. Indeed the legal team provided their only raft.

Although the family had reluctantly consented to a public funeral under the aegis of the union, they still desperately wanted something of themselves in the funeral service. On Monday, Paul once again drove them into Johannesburg to speak to the Dean of St Mary's Cathedral. With its brown stone exterior and red-tiled roof, the Anglican cathedral remained one of the few non-racial churches in central Johannesburg under apartheid. Dean Simeon Nkoane, like his predecessor Desmond Tutu, was carrying on the tradition of speaking out against government policies. What Dean Nkoane could tell the family about the funeral programme, however, was limited, as the committee was still busy working out the details. But at least the family, who felt they might have some say in the flowers and the music, arranged to meet the organist later in the week.

On Tuesday, the family stayed at home, receiving Liz Floyd's parents, who had come up from Cape Town to visit their daughter, still under guard in hospital. Paul's diary records that Yvette called as well. Although she was active in the funeral committee, she came in her personal capacity, bringing condolences as a friend of Neil's, making a bridge to the family. Apart from David Dison, who had been Neil's friend and on whom they would rely professionally, she was the only member of Neil's former world who they would recall reaching out personally. It was a kindness that they appreciated.

Back in Johannesburg, the toxicological examination of Neil's internal organs was under way. On Monday, barely a kilometre away from the cathedral, where the Aggetts were speaking to the Dean, a bottle containing specimens of Neil's brain, heart and lung, and skin from his neck and back, was sent by the Commander of the South African Police mortuary to the police's own Medico-Legal Laboratories in Braamfontein.²⁵⁵ On Tuesday, a 'Viscera box' marked 'S.A.P. Jhbg. No.12' and sealed with police seal No. 582, was received from the Medico-Legal Laboratories at the government's Chemical Laboratory in Johannesburg.²⁵⁶ Inside was 'An earthenware jar marked "J.V. Square P.M. 270/82" containing liver and kidneys'. The clinical reports would indicate that no narcotic drugs were detected in the organs, along with no trace of the metals arsenic, mercury and antimony. The blood sample contained no carbon monoxide or alcohol.²⁵⁷ The security police had secured a clean bill of health.

On Wednesday, Michael returned from Israel, entering in his diary, 'Met by Mom, Dad, Paul and Jill. There was rain and lightning. Many visitors.' Neighbours and relatives were continuing to rally round, bringing meals and flowers. To Jill, Irene was 'always a little enclave on the outskirts of Pretoria of white liberalism'. A couple of her former tennis group were Black Sash members, white women who carried out silent protests against apartheid's unjust laws. They were more aware than most white South Africans of what went on inside the country's prisons. But Jill found support coming from an even wider spectrum of shocked 'non-political' friends.

Without any awareness of union history, the significance of Thursday's national work stoppage was difficult for Neil's family to grasp beyond that it was both a protest and a tribute. The news of a memorial service at Baragwanath Hospital was more comprehensible. Organised by the Transvaal Medical Society, recently renamed the Health Workers' Association, the service was attended by some 500 people, including nurses, doctors and others, many of whom had known and worked with Neil.

Thursday's protests and commemoration were removed from their more immediate concern that afternoon, with Michael joining the family for a meeting at the lawyer's office. William Lane had something to tell them that had come from a fellow detainee – and was, in Jill's words, 'very shocking and upsetting'. It was an account of Neil being beaten and forced to exercise, as witnessed by Maurice Smithers through frosted glass on Monday 25 January. On learning that Neil had died, Maurice had immediately rewritten his earlier note, again in miniature, on a piece of paper only 3 x 10cm. This time, he mentioned that he knew of Neil's death. During his special family visit the following day, he had managed to smuggle the note to his sister, tightly folded inside a matchbox with a false bottom. To protect his identity, on no account should his name, or the date of the attack on Neil, be revealed. There were also plans afoot to make the note public that the Aggetts could not yet be told. Their knowledge of this world of secrets and horrors was just beginning.

Jill recalls how her mother remained stoic that afternoon until they reached the cathedral, where they were meeting the dean and the organist. Beneath the soaring Romanesque arches and the massive pipe organ, Joy suddenly yielded to her grief: '[She] just broke down and wept uncontrollably for the first time – she didn't actually collapse but it was the first time I had seen her sob and just express her devastation.'

On Friday morning, Joy and Aubrey had to face a TV crew in the house. Jan Theron, having just flown in from Cape Town, also came to give his condolences. It was the first time that they had met him, and Joy and Aubrey may well have felt wary of the General Secretary of the union to which Neil had given his allegiance above medicine. Unaware of Jan's initial reluctance to employ Neil, perhaps Aubrey had even felt that Jan may have somehow lured Neil in, remembering his words to his son: 'I said, "What pay are you getting for this?" and he said, "I'm not getting any pay but they'll pay me later when they've got some funds." He worked for nothing for the union. Never got a penny.'

Another visitor that Friday was Hugh Stevenson, Suffragan Bishop of Pretoria, who was the Burgers' local parish priest in Irene, and who had agreed to conduct the service and final burial rites by the graveside. His familiar presence offered a small measure of reassurance.

Apart from the family having some say in the music, the committee had been happy for Jill to take on the flowers. No one knew whether Liz Floyd would be allowed to attend the funeral, but Liz Thomson had conveyed her wish that there be yellow chrysanthemums in pots for mourners to take away and plant. Jill organised for a florist friend to bring the potted chrysanthemums, along with other flowers, to the cathedral, and on Friday Michael travelled with a small group of Jill's supportive friends from Irene to help with the arrangement.

Michael's diary gives no inkling of his feelings about the loss of the brother who had once followed in his footsteps, before losing faith. Serious and reserved, Michael must have felt deeply upset, especially for his parents' pain. His last close memories of Neil were of the young student rebelling against conformity. In 1995, he took me to see Eagle's Nest, where Neil and Liz had lived in their labourer's cottage, with no hot water or electricity. One of the few memories that Michael shared with me, reflecting his perception of a younger brother prepared to throw caution to the wind, involved a journey made by Neil during his end-of-year hitchhiking vacation in 1974. This was Neil, student and romantic idealist:

> When Mozambique became independent, remember there was a lot of upset then, FRELIMO taking over, and Neil set off for that country and went down almost to Lourenço Marques but didn't quite get that far and then was arrested on his way out and was held there for a day or so. By the FRELIMO soldiers. It was a little bit of excitement, I think. I don't know too much about it, but when he got back, my parents were really very upset that he'd done that. They felt it was a very foolish move because it was obviously very dangerous to be there, and fortunately he had been able to talk his way out of it, but he had been held there for a time … When he got back he told us the story … It may have been just the excitement of seeing what was going on there perhaps, I've no idea, Beverley.

Without him explicitly saying so, my sense was that he always felt that Neil should have listened to their father, and had been wrong to ignore Aubrey's paternal warnings. Michael was left with his incomprehension. With Neil's death, there could now be no chance for the brothers to come together, perhaps in time negotiating a new, more equal relationship in which Michael could meet an older, more seasoned Neil. Denied that possibility, Michael was left helping with the flowers.

Just after six o'clock on Friday, on the eve of the funeral, a uniformed officer from Hillbrow police station, Captain Daniel Brand, was driving past Wits University, down Bertha Street, when he heard a blast and saw pieces of paper flying around near the corner with Stiemens Street. At the scene he found pieces of red plastic from an exploded bucket, the remains of a Zobo pocketwatch, bits of metal and wood and 150 pamphlets referring to Neil:

PEOPLE'S HERO – DR. NEIL AGGETT …

MASS RALLY – ST. MARY'S CATHEDRAL SATURDAY – 13 FEBRUARY 1982 –

11AM. BE THERE! – WEAR THE MOVEMENT'S COLOURS!

Printed to an unusually high quality, the leaflets purported to be issued by 'the underground of the African National Congress, the South African Communist Party, Umkhonto We [sic] Sizwe and the South African Congress of Trade Unions.' Not only was it unusual to see SACTU allied in this way, but it was an odd place and time to leave a leaflet bomb, given that most students would have gone home by the evening. When the leaflet was subsequently presented by the security police at the inquest as evidence of Neil's associations, its authenticity would be contested by the family's legal team.

A note in Michael's diary suggests they were informed that evening: 'Heard of letter bomb accusing Neil of ANC membership.' Previously, they might have accepted without question a police statement about an explosion, but they were rapidly learning not to take for granted what they had always believed. Whatever its provenance, the leaflet bomb on the eve of Neil's funeral added to their confusion and fears as this very private family prepared to face in public what for any family would be traumatic … to bury a younger member.

CHAPTER 44

'A man of the people'

THE AGGETTS SET OFF EARLY. THEY HAD RECEIVED PERMISSION TO visit Liz in Johannesburg General Hospital's psychiatric wing before the funeral. The security police had no intention of letting her photograph be displayed across the world and had turned down her request to attend. An armed guard stood outside the door to her room, while a policewoman remained inside throughout the visit. Jill recalls her shock at seeing Liz:

> [She] was very pale and spaced out, completely shattered. She said at the time, 'I can barely remember my name.' She was mentally drained, emptied. 'I can't add or do anything. My mind has gone.'

The last time they had met, about six months earlier, Jill and Paul had come to Johannesburg with the children, meeting Liz and Neil in Kensington's Rhodes Park so the children could play while they talked. Afterwards, invited to 420A Fox Street for a meal, they had bathed the children there, preparing them for bed. It was a simple family get-together, almost normal, except that it was a rare event. Joy and Aubrey, however, knew Liz even less, and on the few occasions when they had met, they had always been wary. They associated her with Neil's diversion from the conventional career path that they'd imagined for him. Nevertheless, seeing her present state was disturbing. To Aubrey, she was 'in a helluva mess', while Joy recalled Michael saying 'a little prayer'.

The church service at St Mary's was due to begin at 11.30am. When the family arrived, roads around the cathedral had been blocked off and were being monitored by the security police. Paul drove the Burgers' bright yellow Cortina station wagon, with Aubrey in the front beside him. Jill, Joy and her sister, Madge, were squeezed in the back. Michael crouched in the boot. Since they were due to follow the hearse, the car was allowed through the cordon and permitted to park. Already it was a hot highveld day as they struggled to make their way through the singing, chanting crowd waiting around the building.

Inside the cathedral, in strong contrast to the usual sombre quiet of an English church prior to a funeral service, lilting emotional voices in mass harmony were paying tribute to Neil. They were singing the union songs he had loved, interspersed with pained, angry cries of '*Amandla! Ngawethu!*' Seats had been reserved for the family in the front row of the nave. Designed to seat 1 400, the cathedral was overflowing. Pews were packed and mourners stood in aisles or wherever they could squeeze in. From the organ loft, organist Richard Cock could see people sitting on top of the covered doorways of the porch, inside the side door of the cathedral.

In the congregation were the families of other detainees who knew that the Aggetts' loss could so easily be their own. While Jill knew people from DPSC meetings, for her parents only a handful of relatives and the white uniforms of 200 or so nurses could provide any note of familiarity in this vast assembly. The nurses had arrived in procession from Baragwanath, ululating and singing as they had made their way into the central area of the nave and the upstairs gallery, alongside hundreds of workers, many in union T-shirts. In among the mourners, foreign and local camera crews and reporters had positioned themselves around the cathedral.

The simple pine coffin lay in the apse, carried in by union pallbearers some 15 minutes before the service was due to begin. Sprays of red and white carnations partially covered the large white letters of 'FCWU' and 'AFCWU' on the union's red flag, on either side of its central circle of clasped black hands. Dozens of yellow chrysanthemum plants and burning candles surrounded the coffin, auguring a service that would be infused with the social and political world that Neil had embraced. This was to be a funeral not simply to mourn but to raise spirits for the ongoing struggle.

The union had printed a funeral programme, a single sheet folded into four pages, with a black and white picture of Neil on the front, his beard and moustache a little trimmer than in his final family photograph. The portrait was ensconced between two captions: 'DIED IN DETENTION 5.2.1982' above, and the union's motto, 'AN INJURY TO ONE IS AN INJURY TO ALL', below. On the back page were the words of 'Nkosi Sikelel' iAfrika', unknown to most white South Africans at that time. Inside, a Tribute was followed by an out-line of proceedings, divided into stages: Church Service, Funeral Procession, Burial Service and Tributes and Messages. There was also a note about trans-port arrangements between the cathedral and West Park Cemetery, about nine kilometres away through northwestern 'white' suburbs. Black mourners would also require help getting back to Park Station, from where they had to travel to their townships to be out of the city by night. Whatever Neil had done to challenge apartheid during his life, he could not avoid being buried in a whites-only cemetery.

A second handout, a service sheet from 'The Cathedral Church of Saint Mary the Virgin, Johannesburg', with the words of the hymns, songs and prayers, reflected an interweaving of Anglican and African traditions: 'Umzima lomthwalo/Ufuna sihlangane' (The load is heavy/It needs us to come together) coming between 'The Lord's My Shepherd' and 'Guide Me, O Thou Great Redeemer'; and the measured tones of 'O God, Our Help in Ages Past' giving way to the farewell and promise to meet again in 'Hamba kahle sihlobo sethu' (Go well, our brother), to be sung while the coffin was carried from the cathedral. But the neatly printed sheets give little clue to the overwhelming emotion inside the building. Tasked with bringing the vigorous impromptu singing to a close, Richard Cock played a piece by the nineteenth-century composer Thomas Walmisley, which opened very loudly and ended softly. The mourners responded, allowing the service to begin with Psalm 23.

Jan Theron's tribute to Neil, given on behalf of the union, preceded both the Scripture reading and the Dean's sermon. Sipho stood beside him, translat-ing. Gaunt and tall in front of his comrade's coffin, Jan expressed sympathy with the family before speaking passionately, at times tearfully, of Neil's work towards the unity of all workers and thereby his contribution to the country: 'When they speak of suicide, we say he was killed. We put the blame where it lies, with the government of the country and with the security police who do its dirty work for it.'[258] Joseph Lelyveld, reporting for *The New York Times*, noted that '[T]he union leader ... sounded tense and angry. But when his words were translated into Zulu for the mainly black congregation of about 2 000 that filled the cathedral, they came across as warm and expressive.'[259]

While Jan spoke as someone who had lost a younger comrade, Sipho spoke as one who had also lost a brother. Countering the hints in pro-government newspapers that Neil was an ANC operative and that he was to have been a state witness in a major political trial, Jan lambasted the regime's claims that it was ready to accept free trade unions. Instead, in its attempts to discredit militant unions as being manipulated by the underground, the government was preparing for a show trial against trade unions, a trial in which comrades would be pushed to give evidence against one another. Jan's tribute lasted almost half an hour, ending with a raised-fist cry of '*Amandla!*' The response from mourners rose to the vaults. Dean Nkoane's subsequent sermon lauded Neil's commitment to the principle of a just society. The Dean reminded the congregation about 'all our brothers in detention. It is my hope that many South Africans will today make the decision that will change the kind of life we live in this country.'[260]

For those who knew Neil well, the music that reminded them most vividly of the life extinguished was Abdullah Ibrahim's 'Mannenberg', Liz's special request. Quintessential South African jazz, it was Neil's favourite. Friends remembered how Neil would keep 'Mannenberg' playing at parties by sneaking the needle back to the beginning. Unrecorded on the cathedral's programme, it was inserted before the final isiZulu hymn, '*Hamba kahle sihlobo sethu*'.

In the carefully planned relay of carrying out the coffin, with Aubrey barely able to stand, Paul and Michael represented the family. Yvette recalls being overwhelmed when it came to her turn:

> The atmosphere was so powerful, filled with beautiful, loud, strong African singing. The singing just filled the space and went through one. The coffin was so heavy, Neil was so heavy. I really had to use all my strength to carry my bit. When I had handed over I kept walking after it for a few paces in a daze.

A friendly hand helped to steady her.

As the coffin emerged from the door of the cathedral, the crowd outside surged forward, singing '*Aggett wethu/Somlandela noma siyabosha*' (Our Aggett/We shall follow even if we are being imprisoned). A hand-held camera captured glimpses of the coffin's progress as church officials and pallbearers made their way slowly towards the hearse. Within seconds of the coffin's appearance, two striking ANC flags were unfurled above the crush of bodies, the black, green and gold in full view of the security police perched on the fourth and fifth floors of the block of flats across the road.

This was what Jan and those who had prevailed in the fierce debate on the committee had hoped wouldn't happen. Steven Friedman would later write about workers who chose not to challenge the ANC activists for fear of prompting an incident and detracting from the focus of the day. He added that the 'hijacking' would become a source of tension, as some unionists charged that the ANC had claimed as their own someone who, while sympathetic, had carefully avoided them:

> 'The flag was only part of the problem: workers wanted to know whose leader Neil was anyway: who had he died for?' said a unionist. 'I guess this is the only kind of meeting these people are allowed, so they feel they ought to make the most of it,' mused another. As tensions between unions and black political groups grew, unionists cited the funeral incident repeatedly.[261]

However, many workers were clearly jubilant at this display of defiance by the banned ANC. What wasn't in doubt was workers' anger and militancy. For his American readers, Joseph Lelyveld described the procession as 'a startling sight' and 'the largest display of black political feeling' that had been seen in white areas since the Congress movement had been forced to go underground.[262]

A printed sheet also appeared outside the cathedral, with the words of seven songs honouring Neil as one in a line of heroes fighting for freedom, including,

> *Kubi kubi Siyaya, siyaya, siyaya*
> *Noma kubi*
> *Kwashu Sisulu Siyaya Siyaya*
> *Kwashu Neil Aggett Siyaya Siyaya*

Kwashu Mandela Siyaya Siyaya
Noma kubi

[In trials and tribulations we are marching on, we are marching on
Despite trials and tribulations
Sisulu said we are marching on
Neil Aggett said we are marching on
Mandela said we are marching on
Despite trials and tribulations]

Often sung and adapted, especially by ANC-aligned workers at meetings, these were songs that Neil had loved. Although unattributed, the source of the songsheet was almost certainly the same ANC activists behind the unfurling of the flag. Its version of '*Unzima lomthwalo*' reflected a far deeper militancy than that on the cathedral programme, including the lines:

Ayangena ayaphuma ayadidizela
Ayasaba amagwala (amaBhunu)
Wenagw' ebaleka
Ayasaba amagwala (amaBhunu)

[They are joining, they are pulling out, they are confused
The cowards (Boers) are scared
They are running away
The cowards (Boers) are scared]

While not understanding the meaning of the words being sung openly and jubilantly on the streets of Johannesburg, the family could feel the revolutionary tone. Sitting inside the yellow Cortina, behind the hearse, in the midst of a 'huge sea of people' on this 'baking, baking hot day', they waited for at least half an hour before the procession began to move, on foot, in buses and in cars. From inside their stiflingly hot car, the journey felt painfully slow, moving at the pace of the jogging, marching crowd around them. All the way to the cemetery, Jill was aware of police 'sharpshooters' on top of office blocks and along the road. At one point, police tried to stop the funeral procession, 'squatting down in the road, pointing guns at us and everyone there.

Eventually they got out of the way and let the cortege move on.' Inside the family car, everything felt unreal.

The atmosphere outside was very different. The same hand-held camera that captured the raising of the ANC flag was now embedded in the surge of mourners, recording the journey to the graveside. Directed by Mark Newman, the remarkable film sweeps the viewer forward to the rhythm of stamping feet, singing and chanting as the procession makes its way through downtown Johannesburg and into the white suburbs.[263] Workers hang out of buses, wave posters, fling out pamphlets, wave hats, raise branches and clench fists, while feet race forward. In the midst of the marchers, a wheelchair spins in full flow with the determined energy of the vast mass.

Newman was recording history in the making. He chose to do so from the viewpoint of the workers, who, in coming to honour Neil, were voicing their commitment to continue the struggle for which he had died. We see bemusement and shock on the faces of white residents. A group of children, torsos dripping from their swimming pool, scurry over a wall to see what is happening. Bafflement and uncertainty vie with their excitement. Two black policemen glance at each other as if they too cannot believe what they are seeing. Their astonished open mouths seem to hover on the brink of smiles.

West Park Cemetery had never seen a funeral like this. Newman catches a swathe of mourners entering the high stone gateway on foot. Beyond the entrance, they spread out through the extensive, sprawling cemetery reserved for Johannesburg's white deceased. They seem anxious to cover the remaining kilometre or two as quickly as possible. Something that was not caught on Newman's film occurred earlier, when those in the front of the procession reached the entrance and stopped the hearse. From inside the car, the family saw the coffin lifted out and raised aloft. From here, volunteer pallbearers carried their comrade under the banner of his union for this final journey. The open grave was waiting beneath a jacaranda tree, with the Melville Koppies in view. The Koppies had been a favourite place for Gavin to come with Neil to sit and talk:

> In the winter you can find spots where the wind does not reach, the sun holds sway. And you can watch back down to the bottom of the path and see that nobody is following you. It's a lovely place to talk. You can curl up in the sun for hours.

A bench had been placed alongside the grave for the family. A photograph catches them sitting in front of a throng of people and union banners. Their shoes on the red earth are almost within touching distance of Neil's coffin, poised on struts above the dark hole beneath. Aubrey's head is bowed, and all their eyes are averted to the right, as if unable to bear the sight in front of them. Another image, taken by a photographer perched in the tree above, reveals that they are also turning aside from a multitude of cameras on the other side of the coffin.[264] Bishop Stevenson stands surrounded by mourners to the family's right, prayer book in one hand and funeral programme in the other. The tilt of the family's heads suggests that they are waiting for him to speak, for this private, public agony to be over. This could be the moment before the committal. Three young men, crouched on the ground, also wait. One stretches out his hand to touch the teak beading. Another clasps his knees, eyes fixed on the coffin, as if in silent conversation. White and black, they are a reflection of the wider crowd.

Among the quieter, poignant moments in Newman's film is the reciting of the Lord's Prayer as the coffin is lowered. The camera focuses briefly on the family and closes in on Joy's anguished face. The family left soon after the service, not waiting for the reading of tributes and messages. Exhausted and anxious to get away from the crowds after a gruelling day, they didn't manage to escape the press. Jill recalls being asked 'stupid questions despite [us] all being clearly in distress – and then everything appears in the papers the next day'.

Underneath the jacaranda tree, a group of comrades filled the grave, red dust rising as their spades hit the earth, while others rapidly erected a small stage with microphone and speakers. Photographs of the vast assembly show a few umbrellas, hats and even posters used to cover heads, but most mourners stood or sat on the grass, brows furrowed and intense, unprotected from the sun. Yvette found herself so far away that she was unable to get anywhere near the grave to witness the lowering of Neil's coffin. She was even too far off to hear the words spoken.

Speeches made on behalf of FOSATU, the General and Allied Workers' Union and the General Workers' Union, and later published, pointedly called for solidarity and unity. Dave Lewis, General Secretary of the General Workers' Union, exhorted workers to end the factionalism dividing them. That had been Neil's work, he said, and should be his legacy:

Neil's vision wasn't just with the Food and Canning Workers' Union, with the workers that he organised. Neil saw all workers … I think Neil's death is a great price to pay for the unity of the union movement, but I think that the trade unions must see now clearly who the common enemy is. We must take the example that the workers showed on Thursday. And we must take the example of this funeral and I think we must start to think about uniting the trade union movement. And that must be the monument that we must build to Neil Aggett. We don't want a big building on a hill. The Monument that we must build to Neil must be the unity of the trade union movement.[265]

Lewis included a more personal note, although never diverting from his political focus. Workers would mourn Neil, he said, by taking forward his work, but they would also remember his personal qualities:

… we will also remember Neil as a kind, gentle person – that is what we will remember. Neil as a democrat who never wanted personal glory … and I think we should remember Neil in the words that a great comrade of Neil's used to describe him as. Comrade Oscar Mpetha, who is one of the great leaders of the South African people … said of Neil, he said a very short and simple thing about Neil, he said that Neil was a 'man of the people' and there's no greater thing that can be said about anybody …[266]

Oscar Mpetha had managed to send two messages from his prison cell:

To the family of Neil Aggett:
I received with great horror the news of what happened to Comrade Neil and we all grieved at this. Neil was a man of the people and not only the Whites but the African people grieve with you.
To the meeting:
It is a pity that I am under these government controls and I cannot be at the meeting. I assure you I am with you in spirit.
Forward with the struggle.[267]

The emotion Oscar permits himself in addressing the family is harnessed to explain Neil's significance. In contrast, his message to his union comrades is understated and businesslike. Yet the death of the young man he had mentored must have surely hit the old man hard.

Most of the tributes to Neil came from organisations representing workers, students and women across the country, too many for all to be read out, especially as speeches were also being translated into isiZulu. A telegram from the International Confederation of Free Trade Unions stated that it had called for an inquiry and the release of all trade union detainees. A telegram from Archbishop Denis Hurley, President of the Southern African Bishops' Conference, deplored 'cruel inhuman conditions' and called for the end of detention without trial:

> PRAYING GOD NEIL WOULD NOT HAVE DIED IN VAIN THAT TRADE
> UNIONS MOVEMENT WILL GO FROM STRENGTH TO STRENGTH.[268]

There was a message, too, from Neil's old school. Eschewing political content, it spoke more personally:

> The Head, Staff and pupils of Kingswood College, Grahamstown, remember with pride and affection the life of one of its promising old boys.
>
> Our prayers are with you today, and our sympathy extends to all those near and dear to Dr Aggett.[269]

Perhaps the hardest task on the podium that day fell to Sipho, in reading the tribute sent by Gavin. Intimate emotion throbbed beneath the words that were yoked into their shared struggle. It was up to them to realise 'the ideals and the cause' for which their fallen brother had worked so hard:

> Our brother, Neil Aggett, has been killed in detention. Though he is not the first brave person to die at the hands of the security police, this fact does not make his death any the more acceptable.
>
> All of us who knew and loved Neil will forever grieve for this gentle and considerate man. We will remember his warmth and keen sense of humour, his calm strength and fairness, his deep commitment to people and to building democratic organization. It is difficult to accept that we have been robbed of his presence for always.
>
> But in the middle of this terrible moment, when we stop to mourn the

loss of such a wonderful person, let us also rejoice that in the end he has been victorious over his persecutors, over his killers. Because the ideals and the cause for which Neil Aggett worked so hard, these didn't die on the 5th February. They live more strongly than ever in all of us, run deep through millions of hearts, and will find expression one day in a song that will break down the walls of the prisons, a song that will be heard all around the world and through all the centuries.

Neil's death serves us notice that it is now time. It is now time for all democrats, all lovers of freedom and of peace, to unite, to work together, to surge forward in a determined and unstoppable wave, sweeping away forever all traces of this opressive regime, and to build a new South Africa, a South Africa which is worthy of sacrifices by such brave martyrs.

May Neil's death bring focus to our resolve.

His life will be a shining example through the hard years that lie ahead.

Go well dear brother, sweet friend, true comrade.[270]

In mourning their brother, friend and comrade, Gavin and Sipho dealt with their own grief by turning a terrible loss into a victory. Neil's persecutors and the oppressive state would be defeated by Neil's death spurring on 'all democrats, all lovers of freedom and of peace, to unite … and to build a new South Africa.' Neil was now a martyr to the cause and his death a sacrifice that should not be in vain. Its political meaning had to take precedence over the personal. Years later, when I asked Sipho about the funeral, he responded that I was 'going into an area which is not pleasant for me' and only hinted at a personal sense of loss by mentioning that he and his wife had named their youngest son Sicelo Neil. It was more important to Sipho to outline its wider political meaning:

The funeral was the first of its kind in Jo'burg because it was held in the city centre … It unified many organisations. It brought people from the townships who were ordinary workers, members of unions; and I must say that as we were going towards the cemetery, Jo'burg was completely liberated that day. So the massiveness of the people there transformed Jo'burg that day – and Jo'burg as Jo'burg came to a standstill.

For Neil's comrades, his funeral would be remembered as a transforming moment. In contrast, his family struggled to find any meaning in his death.

CHAPTER 45

'We have been deeply touched'

REPORTS ON THE FUNERAL RANGED WIDELY. THE ENGLISH-language newspaper *The Citizen* ran a full-page report, highlighting the defiant singing in its headline, '"Freedom" songs at funeral of Dr Aggett', and pointedly enclosing 'freedom' in quotation marks. The reporter, Marilyn Cohen, wrote of the 'solemn dignity' of St Mary's Cathedral being 'rocked with "freedom" songs, chants of "amandla" and clenched-fist salutes' before the service began:

> Many turned the sombre proceedings into a political rally. Dr Aggett's parents, Aubrey (69) and Joyce (64), his brother Michael and sister, Mrs Jill Berger [sic], were all but forgotten by the 'mourners'.[271]

Quotation marks around the word 'mourners' implicitly questioned how so many black people, who couldn't have known Neil personally, could possibly be genuine. Using the family as her focus, the reporter's critique surfaced: Neil's funeral had been taken over.

In sharp contrast, under the headline 'Farewell to Dr Aggett', Sam Mabe of the *Sowetan* wrote unreservedly of a hero's funeral:

> In what could have been one of the biggest and the most spectacular funerals

of a white person in South Africa, mourners chanted freedom songs and marched through the streets of central Johannesburg on a seven-kilometre trip to the cemetery.[272]

Mabe didn't mention the family, but concentrated on the widespread public anger at the government whose hands, according to one funeral speaker, 'were full of the blood of "our leaders"'. Estimating the crowd at over 15 000 (treble that estimated by white media), he described mourners who had come from all over South Africa as being 'led by the black, green and gold national flags of the ANC'.

Each narrative spoke to, and reflected, its respective audience, white and black. It would take Desmond Tutu to point out to white readers in *The Star* that black mourners had come to the funeral to pay respect to this young white man. He wrote of an 'incredible demonstration of affection and regard for a young white man by thousands of blacks'. Neil had been given the kind of salute reserved for those considered heroes, 'really special people'. Bishop Tutu went on to say,

> I am sad that Neil's parents did not understand what happened because they ought to be proud of their son who evoked so much admiration and gratitude. Our young blacks and all blacks hate racism with every fibre of their being. There is hope still for South Africa even at this late hour. Will someone please awake?[273]

It appears that the bishop had seen an article suggesting that Neil's parents had been unhappy with the political nature of the funeral but hadn't seen the family's letter the following week to the *Sunday Times* and other newspapers:

P.O. Box 136
Somerset West, 7130
Cape.

20th February, 1982
The Editor,

Dear Sir,
We should be grateful if, through your correspondence columns, we, the

family of Neil Aggett, could thank most sincerely all the devoted friends who supported him during his detention, and who then organized and supervised his funeral; also those who travelled long distances to be present at the ceremony.

We have been deeply touched by the many messages of sympathy and expressions of kindness and help we have received, and our sadness has been lightened by the wonderful tributes that have been paid to him. We shall try to acknowledge personally as many as possible.

Yours faithfully,

Joy and Aubrey Aggett

Michael and Jill.[274]

For the grieving family it had been a day of suppressed private emotion, under the glare of cameras and caught in the midst of much that they couldn't comprehend. At least one cousin had expressed her fears of a 'political funeral' and potential violence, recommending that the family only attend the service in the cathedral. Many years later, she acknowledged how much she had been brainwashed, but at the time those fears felt palpable and she had expressed them to Joy. Nevertheless, they had followed Neil's coffin to the grave. If some of the media, encouraged by the security police, were looking for a story about dissension between the family and the union, the Aggetts' letter to the press sent out a clear marker that they did not wish to be used in this way.

Among the many letters of condolence were some from people who had also suffered tragedies at the hands of the state. The mother of Ahmed Timol, whom the security police alleged had 'jumped' out of a tenth-floor window in John Vorster Square in 1971, sent a handwritten note:

Roodepoort

Dear Mr & Mrs Agget & Family,

My deepest sympathies on the loss of your son Neil. I can imagine how you must be feeling because I felt the same when I lost my son also while in detention and also the same age.

Please be brave. God is great and may He rest his soul in peace.

Yours truly

Mrs Hawa Timol[275]

Another letter came from Victoria Mxenge, whose husband Griffiths, having survived banning and imprisonment on Robben Island, had been found savagely murdered barely a week before Neil's arrest. Her typewritten letter, dictated on headed notepaper from the attorneys' office that she had shared with her late husband, simply mentions not being well prepared to offer comfort, before going on to offer a moving tribute to Neil:

Durban, 11 – 2 – 82

Dear Friends,
The news of Neil's death in detention was shocking to say the least.

I am singularly ill-equiped [sic] to comfort you but rest assured that I share your grief and sorrow.

Neil was a man of deep compassion and a firm believer in justice for all people. Small wonder that he took up the cause for the underdog with such passion and tenacity.

We all admired and revered your late son. He was a gentle and humane person, the epitome of a patriot. He was the kind of man whose death makes the rest of us feel that in some way we have lost part of ourselves.

The knowledge that others care should comfort you.

Yours faithfully

V.N. MXENGE[276]

Whether or not Joy and Aubrey realised who the writer was, they would surely have been touched by its deep humanity. Three years later, Victoria Mxenge would be assassinated herself, shortly before she was due to represent defendants in a treason trial. The Timols and Mxenges inhabited a very different world from Joy and Aubrey, and their letters of genuine sympathy offered a fundamental challenge to lifelong perceptions fostered within the mainstream white community, perceptions reinforced by much of its media. Writing from exile in Lesotho, Phyllis Naidoo, a banned lawyer active in the underground, picked up on how Neil's parents had been represented in the *Sunday Times* and how their letter of thanks had made a difference:

Maseru, 14th March 1982

Dear Family,

The *Sunday Times* published your 'Thanks' in a not much read page …

Had I not read your letter I would have gone on thinking & having the impression that was left by the same paper of the 14th. No I was not angry at the article I was saddened that Neils parents did not know their own son. Your letter cleared that up & I thank all of you. The first article complained that Neil's body was borne to his grave on a tide of emotion. For crying out aloud what did they expect? Why should not there be unbridled anger when a son of the soil dies in the hands of those who are paid by our taxes to protect us?

I do hope Liz Floyd is much improved & that you will give her the support she sorely needs right now.

I have wished you all strength, courage lots of it. I have cried with you for you & with you [sic]. I know it will be impossible to share the pain of his death with you, his family. I trust you will have the strength to cope. I am proud of your son, that White SA could produce a son such as he, another Bram Fisher/Dennis Goldberg. People who would lay down their lives for a free SA from its racial shackles.

The country came to a halt to honour your son for half an hour.

Very few statesmen in the world can boast of such honour. I salute you his family.

I am an exile. Don't bother to reply now. Someday in the future when we can boast of our freedom we shall meet.

Sincerely

Phyllis Naidoo[277]

How much could Neil's parents identify with what is expressed by 'an exile' whom a couple of months earlier they might easily have dismissed as a 'terrorist'? A couple of years earlier, they were unlikely to have paid much attention to an item of news about a parcel bomb, sent from South Africa to Maseru, that had blown off the hand of a priest, Father John Osmers, who was known to help young South African refugees. The bomb had seriously injured others, including one Phyllis Naidoo. Yet her letter offered a bridge across the gulf.

A letter from Rob Adam's mother, written in a sympathetic, personal tone,

offered a more gentle challenge to the Aggetts to feel proud of Neil. After saying that she and her husband had attended the 'magnificent service' in the
cathedral, Barbara Adam then explains that their son Robert had also been
detained and was now a prisoner awaiting trial. During a visit, he had spoken
of how he and Neil had become friends in prison without being able to see
each other:

> [They] used to 'talk' by knocking on the wall dividing them. I believe they
> even evolved a game of chess together at that time.
>
> Robert wrote us such a lovely letter last month, and perhaps it will help
> you a little if I quote a couple of sentences to you, and we can all four under-
> stand a little of what motivated our very fine young people to-day.
>
> 'I don't know whether it is a curse or a blessing to fight for one [sic] prin-
> ciples. But it is true to say that history would remain static if people were
> not prepared to do so. Things are much easier to bear if I look at myself as
> an agent in history rather than as an individual. I think that much emo-
> tional suffering is a product of over emphasis on one's own importance in
> the scale of things ... and that individual tragedy is a necessary debit in the
> fight for a common happiness.'[278]

Young white activists had fought on a matter of principle, placing 'common
happiness' above 'individual tragedy'. In quoting from her son's letter, Barbara
Adam offered the Aggetts a way of understanding the motivation of 'our very
fine young people' who shared a different paradigm for living. Whatever the
unhappy consequences, the idealistic motivation deserved respect. For Rob
Adam and his parents, it made the prospect of a long prison sentence more
bearable. Barbara Adam ended her letter with encouragement to Neil's parents to recall the happy memories of Neil as a little boy and to 'remember that
he is at peace now, and will be happy for eternity. I firmly believe that.'[279]

My mother's letter to Joy and Aubrey presented a different view, although
she too wrote from the shared perspective of white parents whose children
had bucked the system:

> I must tell you again with what real grief we share your sorrow. We under-
> stand it perhaps more than most, because inevitably there is a feeling of
> 'There but for the grace of God ...'

We know the sorrow will be with you always, but we are sure you will be given the strength to bear it – maybe, in time, even to come to terms with it. We have learned to accept the fact that however deep the bond of family love, our children's thoughts and feelings are their own, and we cannot always share them. But there is the comfort of that unalterable, lasting bond.[280]

My parents' adjustment was to separate the personal and the political, yet affirming parental love and the personal bond between parent and child. For some parents, that would be too difficult, but my mother's letter reminds me of how we operated, despite the politics in the air we all breathed. Maintaining our connection meant, as far as possible, avoiding any political comment. Reading my mother's letter, at this distance, also helps to remind me why my own letter to the Aggetts, written in England, sounds so guarded and emotionally stunted:

Oxhey, Herts
24th February 1982

Dear Jill, Joy, Aubrey, Michael and family,
　I don't know whether this will find you still all together. I have been wanting to write, but finding the words is difficult. 'Condolences' are so totally inadequate. Perhaps all I can say is that I have been thinking a lot about Neil. I should have liked to have known more of him – he must have been enormously courageous and brave. He must be a great loss. From what I have read he seems to have been so very well liked and respected.
　The publicity must be a big strain on you all. Yet we must believe that ultimately the truth will prevail, despite all the odds.
　I imagine Neil would have believed that too – to take on the odds he did. May he be well remembered.
　With love to you all in this very difficult time for you,
　Beverley.[281]

It's not unusual to feel inadequate in expressing condolences, a feeling exacerbated when you do not really know the people to whom you are writing. But I wonder if my inadequacy here lies beyond that? The worlds in which we existed were so sharply different, and I was inhibited by deep habits of caution and silence. Perhaps, if I had read my cousins' letter to the *Sunday Times*, saying how they had been deeply touched by the many tributes to Neil, I would have been less restrained. The walls of their former world had been fractured, and in the coming months they would experience first-hand some of the apartheid state's dirty tricks, discovering the lengths to which it would go to distort the truth.

The process of negotiating joint decisions, involving the family, union and Liz (after her release), would not always be easy. One such matter was the wording of Neil's headstone. After the very public and political funeral, his parents hoped that the gravestone could at least be privately decided by the family alone. However, although paid for by Aubrey, the grave below Melville Koppies could never be regarded as purely personal. In the end, the agreed wording was moving and simple:

DEARLY LOVED

NEIL HUDSON AGGETT

6.10.1953

5.2.1982

PHYSICIAN AND TRADE UNIONIST

Below this was engraved Food and Canning's symbol of four black clasped hands against a white circle, underscored by the words 'DIED IN DETENTION'.

Despite Joy and Aubrey's sense of hurt, and indeed bemusement, they conducted themselves with dignity. They implicitly understood that, given any whiff of dissension, the security police and their pet reporters would be quick to churn up a sensationalist story.

CHAPTER 46

In pursuit of a wider justice: 'Do it!'

O N THE TUESDAY FOLLOWING THE FUNERAL, HELEN SUZMAN, MP
for the Progressive Party, caused a furore in Parliament by reading out Maurice Smithers's smuggled note. His sister had driven
to Cape Town to hand it to her personally. They met at night in the centre
of Cape Town, in what Suzman later described as a 'cloak-and-dagger business'.[282] She needed a magnifying glass to read it, and then waited for the par-
liamentary debate on the Rabie Commission report. Justice Rabie had not
spoken with any detainees or ex-detainees before pronouncing his satisfaction that they were adequately protected through visits from magistrates and
inspectors. Suzman asked the Minister of Police Louis le Grange whether he
could give categorical assurance that 'inhuman and degrading methods of
interrogation' were not being used by the security police. 'Yes, I can give that
assurance,' Le Grange replied. Having got the Minister to repeat his assurance,
she then asked if he could verify an allegation that had come to her notice.
Withholding the name of the note's author, simply saying that it came from
a detainee, she read Maurice's account of Neil being held naked and beaten
'with a belt or with a rolled-up newspaper'. Only at the end of the account
did she reveal that the man 'who was allegedly subjected to this inhuman
and degrading treatment was Dr Neil Aggett at John Vorster Square. I ask the

Minister to investigate the truth of this allegation.'[283] Had she mentioned Neil's name at the beginning, the Speaker would undoubtedly have stopped her on the grounds that the matter was *sub judice* even though an inquest had not yet been announced.

Maurice's letter was a bombshell. Le Grange repeated at least twice, 'that can definitely not be true'. Fully expecting that her speech would be struck out of the Hansard record, she had already handed a copy of it to a reporter from the Argus group. By evening, it was in the newspapers and in the public domain. Both the ministers of Police (Louis le Grange) and of Justice (Kobie Coetsee) were furious, launching accusations that the letter she had read was fabricated. With calls to name her source, Suzman declared she would first require proper assurances that the note's author would not be victimised. However, the response that she found most 'extraordinary' was that of Adriaan Vlok, a National Party MP who would become Minister of Law and Order in 1986. Why should Suzman be concerned about solitary confinement and the loneliness of detainees? 'In the same breath she says they are interrogated for hours. I want to ask her – in that case when are they lonely?'[284]

In her terrier fashion, Helen Suzman went on to raise questions in Parliament about the postmortem. Had the Aggett family been informed about the postmortem? What time had it commenced, and had the Aggetts' private pathologist been present at commencement? Declaring that he was treating the matter as *sub judice*, the Minister of Justice, Kobie Coetsee, wouldn't comment. Nevertheless, the pressure was on, and on the same day the Chief Magistrate of Johannesburg announced that an inquest would be held as soon as possible. In a 'Darling All' letter the following week to her family abroad, Suzman wrote of being in the government's 'dog-box'. She had been obliged 'to work a very cunning trick' in order to 'use this information in Parliament because otherwise it could never have been published owing to the Police Act and the Prisons Act'.[285]

The Detainee Parents' Support Committee continued to express concern over the medical supervision of detainees. In a telegram to the Minister of Justice, it pressed that all detainees be examined by, and have access to, an independent panel of doctors. The Minister refused. On Monday 1 March, the DPSC sent the Minister a further telegram:

How many detainees have been hospitalised? For what complaints are they being treated? Have their families been informed? Has the Minister taken any steps to alleviate the conditions leading to their hospitalisation? Has the Minister taken any steps to modify interrogation techniques?

The Minister replied tersely, also by telegram: 'I am not prepared to take part in a organised question and answer campaign by telegram.'[286]

The inquest date was set for Tuesday 2 March at the Johannesburg Magistrate's Court. With a foundation stone laid in 1936, the court building covered the equivalent of four city blocks. Each of the entrances on the north, west and east side was dwarfed by columns soaring up to a three-storey-high lintel. The more ordinary southern entrance, however, was reserved for black people. Despite being constructed before the Afrikaner Nationalists took power, the design consciously reflected everyday apartheid, as in this 1941 comment:

> The native and Asiatic witness-rooms are so placed that these people have no need to use the public concourse or the European section.[287]

Hundreds of thousands of people had passed through these courts for falling foul of the pass laws and other draconian legislation. In the 1950s, the attorney offices of Nelson Mandela and Oliver Tambo had been situated in Chancellor House, directly opposite the northern entrance of the courts in Fox Street. After his arrest in 1962, Mandela was due to be tried here until a last-minute switch of venue to the Old Synagogue Court in Pretoria where he had stated from the dock that he had been made a criminal by the law, not because of what he had done 'but because of what I thought, because of my conscience'.[288]

Conscience was what had brought thousands to be sentenced here during the Defiance Campaign and for many subsequent acts of resistance.[289] Conscience lay at the heart of Neil's political choices, which had placed him on a collision course with the apartheid state. Whitehead had dreamt of nailing Neil in the dock, a 'criminal'. While those plans had gone awry and there was an inquest rather than a trial, the contest was far from over. In Advocate Bizos, the Aggett family could not have asked for anyone who understood more clearly the nature of the battle ahead to lead the team representing the family of a young man of conscience against a brutal, corrupt, depraved security force. The full team was now assembled, with Denis Kuny as junior counsel and Mohamed Navsa as his pupil, while William Lane as senior attorney had David Dison as his junior and a young articled clerk, James Sutherland.

Jill attended the opening of the inquest on behalf of the family. Her parents had returned to Somerset West, having been advised by their lawyers that it would only be a short hearing. The small courtroom was filled to the brim. Local and international reporters crammed into the press benches, while DPSC supporters, who had earlier mounted a placard protest outside the courts, packed the gallery, leaving standing room only in the aisle and doorway. George Bizos opened with an application for a postponement, stating that Neil's fellow detainees would have 'vital information' relating to the inquest, and without access to them and their testimony it would not be possible 'to make a meaningful contribution to the proceedings'.[290] He also wanted the legal team to make an immediate inspection of the cell in which Neil had died, as well as the adjacent cells and the interrogation rooms. The magistrate, Lourens de Kock, baulked at the latter, insisting that the authorities would have to be given time to make alternative arrangements for detainees before any inspection. Bizos made no headway with arguing that the purpose of the inspection was precisely to see things as they were, not rearranged.

It was, as the lawyers predicted, a short hearing. After 35 minutes, the magistrate reluctantly agreed to postpone proceedings until 13 April. At this stage, the family and its legal team had not yet seen the affidavits from both the security and ordinary policemen charged with looking after Neil. The magistrate assured them that these would be made available straight away, while Piet Schabort, Senior Counsel for the Minister of Police, with Schalk Burger as his junior, said that he would need to seek instructions regarding interviews with detainees and an inspection in loco.

Advocate Bizos had begun with a bold move. Even if they managed to get affidavits from Neil's fellow detainees, they would still have to argue their relevance to the inquest. It was a strategy that came with a high price for the Aggetts. They would have to accept the police version of suicide, something that Aubrey had instinctively rejected. But the legal team had their reasons.

Eleven years earlier, George Bizos SC and Isie Maisels QC had jointly represented the Timol family, arguing that the young teacher had been directly killed by his interrogators. The police version was that he had jumped out of the tenth floor window to escape betraying his comrades. To support this, the security police had concocted a fake document, supposedly issued by the South African Communist Party, exhorting its members to commit suicide when necessary:

> Rather commit suicide than betray the organization … Vorster and his murderers will not halt our people when we have comrades like Archbishop Hurley, Rowley Arenstein, Vernon Berrangé, Isie Maisels, M.D. Naidoo, George Bizos and others who have been fighting with us since the days of Rivonia.[291]

The collection of names was a giveaway and, quite correctly, the police counsel regarded it as defamatory to link a Roman Catholic bishop and lawyers prominent in defending political activists to the banned Communist Party. Hence, instead of presenting the document as state evidence, the police counsel had shown it to Bizos and Maisels, saying that he would not be using it. Nevertheless, on behalf of his police clients, he continued to put forward the argument that Ahmed Timol, as a good communist, was prepared to die rather than betray his comrades. Unsurprisingly, the magistrate had accepted the police version of Timol's death and concluded that no one was to blame.

In planning their approach, the Aggetts' legal team had taken the Timol experience into account. If they tried to prove the police had physically killed Neil, without any witnesses who could offer direct evidence, they would end up losing. However, if they accepted that Neil's death could have been suicide and that his death had been induced by the circumstances under which he had been held and interrogated, they could open up a wider inquiry. The magistrate would be under greater obligation to admit the evidence of fellow detainees. Although suicide was not an offence under South African law, those responsible for inducing a person to commit suicide might be held criminally liable.

The lawyers knew from experience how hard it could be for the family to accept that their loved one might have committed suicide. The findings of their pathologist, Dr Botha, were compatible with possible suicide and didn't offer any concrete evidence to prove otherwise. It was, however, the copy of *Zorba the Greek*, lying open at the passage about the unending cycle of life and death, that made George Bizos inclined to believe Neil might have taken his own life. Writing about the Aggett inquest, he records how they put the problem to Aubrey. They explained that if they adopted the view that it was suicide, a number of possibilities would follow. The police might be held legally responsible. The evidence of other fellow detainees, interrogated by Cronwright's same team, might become admissible. The inquest would thus become more of an indictment against detention without trial. Joy had been in tears, 'hardly in a state to take part in the decision'. Bizos recalled Aubrey's reaction: 'He looked at me sternly. I was not sure what was going through his mind. He looked at his daughter Jill, who nodded. With a deliberate and almost a commanding voice, he said, "Do it."'[292]

Recollecting the same scene, in an interview in Oxford in 2011, George Bizos spoke of how Aubrey had required them to explain 'over and over again the legal niceties':

> I said, 'Mr Aggett, I know how difficult it is, but in order to prove this, for the benefit of others, we have to, in the alternative, assume that he committed suicide and enquire as to *why* he was pushed and to the extent he was pushed … and when he understood, he said, 'I trust you. Do it.' He was very angry. He called them bastards. 'Do it to these bastards!' Changed his view.[293]

From this early encounter, George Bizos quickly gauged Aubrey's strength of character and that this was no easy client. As he got to learn more about Neil, he would have sensed that, however different their outlooks, there were also essential character connections between the young man with his uncompromising principles and this deeply conservative, no-nonsense father. Bizos was keenly aware of the tragedy for this particular family: 'I felt that he [Aubrey] had feelings of guilt about their relationship but he took a very brave decision.' Whatever its divisions, this was a family that retained deep bonds. Jill had 'this sort of brotherly, filial, love for her brother'. Their advocate had been moved by their plight.

At the very end of our interview in Oxford, almost as we were going through the door, not hiding his emotion, George Bizos repeated Joy's words: 'They could not understand my sensitive son.' The depth of his sentiment, in remembering events of some 30 years ago, was a strong reminder of how the lawyers who undertook political cases were directly exposed to the personal stories. They too had to find ways of coping with the emotional toll.

In the coming months of the inquest, the lawyers would inevitably learn more about Neil himself. Through David Dison, they would come to know something of Neil's complexity, of someone who was 'very, very idealistic, tense' … who 'read Marx but he was a humanist', not 'a hard-line Marxist' … a dedicated grassroots trade unionist … 'not these hard corporatist trade unionists' … who 'wasn't sealed off' … who was 'a complete and utter stoic' … and who was 'a difficult guy in the sense that it was difficult to maintain a constant relationship with him, because his standards were so different to ours'. Yet this inflexible stoicism was combined with an inner sensitivity, clearly appreciated by George Bizos, who, in writing about the case years later, included both Joy's memory of her 'sensitive son' and Liz Floyd's memory of 'a very gentle person, a very intelligent person … very warm to people, although he wouldn't be the kind of person who would go around being very friendly to everybody. If he got close to somebody, he would be very warm to them, and considerate. He thought about things a lot. He was very concerned about what was going on around him.'[294]

Neil was ultimately 'a thinker' and, as David Dison knew, he didn't fit his interrogators' pigeon-holed minds. They had pursued and seized a beautifully complicated, deeply humane and healthy young man, and had destroyed him while he was in their custody. This individual narrative would rest at the core of the inquest. However, Aubrey's go-ahead to the legal team was hugely significant. In aiming to establish induced suicide, through offering evidence from Neil's fellow detainees, the inquest would provide a rare public means of truth-seeking, and form an indictment against detention without trial. Aubrey, who was prepared to commit his life's savings to pay for the best lawyers, had agreed a strategy in pursuit of a wider justice. The political implications were diametrically at odds with everything that he had previously believed.

Neil would have approved.

CHAPTER 47

'Snooping around people's houses'

I N THE MIDDLE OF MARCH, NEIL'S PARENTS CAME UP FROM SOMERSET West for a briefing with the lawyers, leaving their house in the care of their domestic worker, Sarah Isaacs, and her husband, Isak. A neighbour was on call if they needed any help. Aubrey also informed the Somerset West police station that they would be away for a few days. Around 9pm on Monday 15 March, the phone rang at the Burgers' house in Irene. A 'Paul Edwards' asked to speak to Jill's father. He was asleep, said Jill. What did it concern? The speaker claimed to be a private investigator, tasked with finding material on Neil for an overseas client who wished to write a book, like Donald Woods had written about Steve Biko. He had already visited Neil's old school, Kingswood, and spoken with the teachers. They would vouch for him. But now, having travelled all the way to Somerset West, he was distressed to find that the Aggetts were away. He had asked the maid to let him look around the house for any photos of Neil, but an 'aggressive' neighbour had suddenly arrived and called the police. He claimed that he was now in a state of shock. Jill coolly suggested that he was 'in the wrong line of work and shouldn't go snooping around people's houses'.[295]

The family was immediately suspicious. On their return home, a fuller story of the break-in emerged. The man who called himself 'Paul Edwards', later revealed to be security policeman Paul Erasmus, had inveigled his way into the house. He had ignored Sarah's requests to come back when her employers had returned. Once inside the house, Erasmus declared that the police had given him their address, and told Sarah's husband that he wanted to speak to her alone. Given an order by a white man, Isak obeyed. Nevertheless, he made a note of the registration number of the yellow car parked outside.

Spinning his 'private detective' story, Erasmus demanded that Sarah show him where to find photos of Neil and letters written to his mother. Ignoring her pleas to wait for her employers, he began scratching through drawers for papers to read. Suddenly, said Sarah, he pulled out a gun, threatening to shoot her if she lied to him. If she got him the letters and photos, however, he would give her R200.

Sarah, who would later sign her affidavit with an 'x', said nothing about not being able to read. Using the excuse of needing the toilet, she managed to leave the lounge and tell her husband to alert the neighbour. William Anderson found Erasmus still rifling through the front room. Unable to impress Anderson with his story, Erasmus left without arguing.

Anderson immediately rang the police station to report the incident, adding that he had noted the intruder's vehicle registration number. To his surprise, he was asked, was the number FVP782T? It was. Oh, said the warrant officer, someone had come to the police station earlier, seeking directions to the Aggetts' house. Later that night, three police officers arrived at Anderson's house. Two were uniformed; the third was in plain clothes, fairly tall but rather slight of build. Declaring himself the duty officer for the night, he produced his identity document. His name: Lieutenant Whitehead.

Sarah, too, would report in her statement how two uniformed policemen had come to the Aggett house later that night, returning shortly afterwards with a third man in plain clothes. He had shown her his ID and told her his name, but she had forgotten it. She had asked this plain-clothes officer, should she ring her employers? No, he replied. Don't worry them. He would come to talk with them when they returned.

The following morning, the intruder who had aimed his gun at her returned in his yellow car. This time, backed up by police instructions, she would only speak to him through the window. Once again, he had asked for photos of Neil. As soon as he left, she rang the police station, and within ten minutes some policemen arrived to take fingerprints. They were different from the previous night's group.

Alarmed by the details, Aubrey demanded that the local police come to his house and explain what they knew. Silence descended. No police officer would admit to having known a Lieutenant Whitehead. In his affidavit of 30 March, Aubrey stated:

> Captain Holting, after taking my statement, asked me if I suspected any-
> body, whereupon I answered in the negative. He then asked me if I sus-
> pected 'the Security'. My reply thereto was that 'that is a thought'.[296]

Later, Aubrey would say that the break-in at their home gave them such direct experience of the lengths to which the security police would go that it finalised his view about the corruption of the entire system. This was not a matter of a few 'bad apples'. It was obvious that the local police had been made complicit, instructed not to provide further information. Authorisation must have come from higher up. When Aubrey proceeded to lay a criminal charge of illegal entry, the Cape Attorney General initially refused to prosecute. He claimed that the police had a taped conversation in which Sarah Isaacs had contradicted her statement. After obtaining a copy of the tape, Aubrey's lawyers discovered that it revealed Erasmus maligning the Aggetts to Sarah, offering her a bribe, and threatening her with jail if she were to talk. The tape provided more reason than ever to prosecute.

When confronted with the break-in at the inquest, Whitehead would claim that the security police had information that Gavin Andersson was hiding in the Aggett's home. It was a poor cover story, given that the Aggetts had never known Gavin. Changing tack, Whitehead then tried to shift responsibility to the state's legal team. Their counsel needed documents to help their psychologist in his report on the detainee's state of mind. That too wasn't a bright suggestion. Senior Counsel for the police, Piet Schabort, was obliged to approach George Bizos to offer assurances that he and his junior, Schalk Burger, had nothing to do with this, which Bizos believed. Moreover, the Minister of Police, Louis le Grange, asked Schabort to apologise to Aubrey on his behalf for the invasion of his privacy, and was prepared to grant Aubrey an audience to apologise in person. Bizos relayed a blunt response from his client: Advocate Schabort should inform the Minister that he was not interested in any apology from the Minister who was in charge of the people who had caused his son's death. Schabort replied that 'he understood how the old man felt'.[297] Whatever Piet Schabort's personal views, however, there would be no justice when the Somerset West case eventually came to court, six months after the end of the inquest. Charges against Whitehead were withdrawn and Paul Erasmus fined a mere R200, with no questions asked about who had authorised their illegal activity.

It would be many years before a fuller story emerged. Paul Erasmus came before the Truth and Reconciliation Commission (TRC) in October 2000 applying for amnesty for some 87 'incidents'. I say 'fuller' rather than 'full' because, while a condition of amnesty was a willingness to tell the whole truth, there were a few aspects of Erasmus's account that differed significantly from the statements sworn for the inquest by Sarah Isaacs and the neighbour, William Anderson. In Erasmus's TRC submission, there was no gun and the domestic worker had 'allowed' him 'to literally search the house'. It was not a break-in. It was just that he had 'bluffed her a little bit'. When it came to the neighbour, Erasmus's version was that he had been caught leaving 'on the veranda', rather than in the act of poking through drawers in the front room.[298]

Nevertheless, despite his omissions, what Erasmus had to say about his colleagues and superiors, and the impunity with which they operated, seemed thoroughly credible. There had been little contact between him and Whitehead as colleagues prior to Neil's death. But Erasmus recalled how Whitehead had approached him for the enterprise:

> He came into my office one day and said that I had been chosen for a very specialised covert mission. He then took me to – I wasn't very happy about this because I didn't like him, I doubted his ability as a field operative, I'd heard stories about him, but … I was then taken by him to see – I've got to think about this, Brig Muller. Brig Muller told me that I was to accompany Lieut Whitehead on a mission. We were given laissez-faire and our brief was quite simply to prove or gather evidence as to the psychological makeup of Dr Neil Aggett … our job was to find, which Whitehead referred to in Afrikaans, as a 'naald in 'n hooimied' [a needle in a haystack], was to find evidence that Neil Aggett had suicidal tendencies from the time that he was a child. We were given money from the Secret Account. My expertise

which had been steadily growing, due to various covert activities that I'd been involved in over the previous three years, was called on.

I was told to set up a cover story for these investigations. I was told that Whitehead – Whitehead in fact told me that he couldn't be too exposed himself, because he would have to feature at the inquest, I would have to do the work, as in I had to become somebody else. Which I did, I became Paul Edwards, private investigator.[299]

No expense was spared. Muller knew that they could not afford 'another Biko thing'. Using a government vehicle (the yellow car), and with the assurance that SB commanders in various divisions had been briefed to help them – with whatever they needed – they had driven first to Grahamstown and Neil's old school, Kingswood College. According to Erasmus, the headmaster had fallen for the story that he was Paul Edwards, a private investigator working for an overseas writer client. He claimed that he and Whitehead had been shown photos and school records. Having found nothing of interest, they had then made their way to Somerset West, where, after filling up with petrol at the local police station, Whitehead had stayed in a restaurant while Erasmus had driven to the Aggetts' house.

In Erasmus's version, he believed that he would have got away without being identified had Whitehead not 'made a mistake' in going first to the Somerset West police station, allowing the warrant officer on duty to make the connection when the neighbour had rung the local police to report the intrusion:

So now we had a problem. As I understood it, a couple of things then happened. Mr Anderson, the neighbour, tried to save face by not having been able to physically stop me, by saying that I pointed a firearm at him. Sarah, the domestic, feared she would lose her job and she said that she'd caught me inside the house. So the next thing I looked I was charged with, I believe at one stage even attempted murder. I was charged with housebreaking, illegal search, pointing a firearm and a whole variety of things. This terrified me. The following morning at 6 o'clock when all of this had happened, we were summoned to the office of the Divisional Commander for the Western Province, Brig Kotze, who tore strips off Whitehead and I, and he told us in no uncertain terms to get the hell out of his division and to get back to Johannesburg. We'd wrecked this whole thing, compromised possibly the forthcoming Aggett Inquest, we'd placed the Minister in a situation, I mean we just literally destroyed the security situation in the country. So Whitehead and I got in the car, we drove back to Johannesburg.

Hauled in front of the recently promoted Brigadier Muller, Erasmus denied carrying out a break-in or that he'd pulled out a gun. Nevertheless, Muller was not pleased. The affair had been reported upward to the highest levels. General Coetzee, Head of the Security Police, the Minister of Police and the Minister of Justice had all been informed, including, Erasmus believed, all the way to the top: 'I think the State President had been informed, because damage control now had to be instituted. We'd compromised the inquest.'

Erasmus was instructed to make a statement, and on 14 May Brigadier Muller drove with Whitehead and Erasmus to Pretoria. Having been summoned to meet Coetzee and the police top brass, presumably in the General's heavily panelled office, they were all very nervous. While still drinking coffee, they were asked to list how many people knew what had really happened. First on the list was the uniformed warrant officer at Somerset West police station, marked down as a 'gattoesteker' (backstabber) because he had wrecked their operation. How could they 'close him down'? There was also the furious Divisional Commander for the Western Province, as well as the neighbour and the domestic worker:

> There was no ways [sic] that through the existing situation, that all of these people could be somehow intimidated, persuaded or otherwise told to forget about this thing. They had to find some way to dance along these issues. The big thing being the forthcoming Aggett Inquest, or the looming Aggett Inquest.

Having ruled out a 'shut down' operation, they proceeded onto a 'brainstorming session' on a strategy to deal with the issue. Erasmus, whose original statement had been typed, was instructed every now and again to leave the office. The General's position was that they had to have a cover story in which Whitehead could be excluded. Erasmus would therefore have to change his statement:

> ... it would be convenient to say that we had gone down to Somerset West,
> for the love of God, not to look for evidence relating to the inquest, but to
> do a bona fide Security Branch investigation whereby we were looking for
> Gavin Anderson [sic]. What made this more convenient was that the neigh-
> bour's name was Anderson, which also helped to sort of muddy the water
> and give a little bit of credibility to this. I believe it was Gen Coetzee – the
> statements are here, available, he actually took my statement and told me
> what to write in it, he changed my words and added in things and I think
> deleted some.

In his new statement, Erasmus had to say that he 'was never instructed by
Brigadier Muller or any other superior officer ... to conduct the investigation into the past history of the late Dr Aggett, and the methods used were
planned solely by Lieut Whitehead and myself'. It seems that Whitehead, because of his undeniable presence in Somerset West – having claimed to be the
duty officer at the local police station – could not be so simply written out of
the story after all.

In his submission to the TRC, Erasmus now extended the net of those
drawn into the General's plan to include the Cape Attorney General. Erasmus
was told that he would be charged, and must plead guilty. It would look as if
he were likely to be jailed, but instead he would be given a fine. This he would
pay out of the money given to him from a secret fund. The charges against
Whitehead, however, would, in due course, be dropped so as to diminish the
link to the inquest, thus leaving Erasmus to take the flak on his own. Erasmus
understood General Coetzee – 'a man that I regarded as God himself, the top
intelligence man in this country' – to promise that he would benefit from this
'sacrifice' and that his career prospects, as a young detective sergeant, would
not be affected by this criminal record.

Erasmus was duly found guilty, paying his R200 fine from the Pretoria,
rather than the Johannesburg, Secret Fund. However, when General Coetzee's
promise regarding his career was not kept, he began to feel that there were
other forces at work. Whitehead's father was a brigadier in the police, and, subsequently, his wife's father became the Deputy Head of National Intelligence,
so he was well connected. In 1982, it seems that Whitehead had been studying law by correspondence through UNISA, intending to change career. To be
convicted of illegal search or housebreaking would put paid to becoming a

lawyer. This, said Erasmus, he had learned from several senior officers, and furthermore,

> Whitehead had secretly said … he had told me to go to the house, but he told me not to go into the house. Pretending to be my friend and looking after my interests and everything like that, he had actually double-dealed me and sold me down the river to protect himself. I found that out in 1988 and yes, I did get a conduct sheet and criminal record and I lost my promotions.

Erasmus went on to offer the TRC panel at least two other pertinent pieces of information regarding the Aggett inquest. A state psychiatrist had been employed to advise on what evidence Whitehead and Erasmus should look for, in order to show that Neil had been mentally unstable and a natural candidate for suicide. According to Erasmus, during their 'joy-ride' around the country, Whitehead had reported to the psychiatrist daily. Although Erasmus didn't name him, this was Jan Adriaan Plomp, a Professor of Psychiatry from the University of Pretoria, who would sit through most of the inquest, on call to analyse evidence for police counsel, and would be the state's final witness.

The other piece of information concerned 'mock trials', held 'flat out' during the inquest, in which Whitehead and other officers rehearsed being cross-examined by 'George the Greek'. These were based on private deliberations among the Aggett lawyers, which had been detected by the use of 'tomatoes' – concealed electronic bugs that could pick up conversations across a room. By the time Erasmus was applying for amnesty, in 2000, this information was not new to George Bizos. In the mid-1990s, a special investigation under Transvaal Attorney General Jan D'Oliviera into security-force hit squads had established the bugging of his chambers during the Aggett inquest.

Aubrey did not live to hear the full extent of security police perfidy. Any political detainee could have told him that breaking into his house under a false identity was par for the course. When Neil had criticised the apartheid state, Aubrey's attitude had been that his son was 'playing with fire'. Like most white South Africans, he had dismissed talk about abuse of power as designed to undermine the state and police. The break-in at their home, on top of their personal tragedy, was unnerving and unsettling. But, in a strange, painful way, it may also have brought Aubrey a little closer to understanding his son.

CHAPTER 48

Whose voices shall be heard?

TEN DAYS AFTER THE BUNGLED ILLEGAL ENTRY INTO THE AGGETT home, Barbara Hogan was charged under the Terrorism Act. Only one person from her 'Close Comrades' list – trade unionist Alan Fine – was included in the charge, along with a former Methodist minister, Cedric Mayson. This was hardly the mass treason trial about which the police had boasted. On the same day, Friday 26 March, seven white detainees were released without charge, most having been held between five and six months in solitary confinement. Liz Floyd and Maurice Smithers were among them. Issuing a joint statement through the DPSC, the group declared that any jubilation at their release 'was soured by the fact of the continued detention of our friends and in particular Neil Aggett's tragic death'.[300] Looking at their photograph in the *Sunday Times*, it's hard not to imagine Neil standing alongside the others. Instead, his presence hovers in Liz's traumatised gaze and Maurice's frenzied stare.

The inquest was to resume after the Easter weekend, on Tuesday 13 April. Police documents passed on to the family's lawyers already formed a docket an inch thick. Every officer who had had dealings with Neil had made an affidavit. There were also relevant pages from the Cell Register, Occurrence Book and Meal Register, plus inventories of items seized on his arrest, items found in his cell on the day of death, receipts signed by Neil, reports by magistrates and the Inspector of Detainees and all the other official documentation. The initial six-week postponement had provided vital time for the legal team to begin reconstructing what might have happened inside John Vorster Square. One of the most critical documents secured from the police was Neil's affidavit of complaint made to Detective Sergeant Aletta Gertruida Blom on the day before he died. It was with this that the Aggett lawyers intended to begin.

An important development was that Maurice Smithers, despite his fears of further retribution, had met the lawyers and made a full affidavit on Monday 12 April, confirming and elaborating the contents of his smuggled note. The next day, during the morning tea break at the inquest, two security policemen handed Maurice a two-year banning order. As George Bizos had just informed the court that he was to be a witness – an announcement that identified him as the author of the smuggled note – many assumed that this was an attempt to silence him. Under pressure, the Minister of Police, Le Grange, was obliged to offer public assurances that the ban would not prevent the former detainee giving testimony.

The presiding magistrate had also been changed. It was well known that the security police would ask the control prosecutor to set down cases in a particular court presided over by a sympathetic magistrate. Petrus (Piet) AJ Kotzé had begun his career in the eastern Cape in the 1960s, prosecuting in political trials where hundreds of defendants were sent to Robben Island. By the time he came to the Magistrate's Court in Johannesburg in the 1970s, his prestige was reflected in the position of his office, on the ground floor of the northeastern corner, ironically opposite the former offices of Mandela and Tambo.[301] As senior public prosecutor, he led the evidence in the Timol inquest. By 1982, Kotzé was a very senior magistrate, experienced in political cases and trusted to oversee juniors. He was to be assisted in the Aggett inquest by an assessor, Professor Lionel Shelsey (LS) Smith, a Chief Government Pathologist and Professor of Forensic Medicine and Toxicology at the University of Cape Town. It is very likely that the professor had taught Neil.

*   *   *

Medical evidence came first, with District Surgeon Dr Vernon Kemp presenting postmortem findings for the state. Before cross-examining the witness,

George Bizos announced that he would read the affidavit that Neil had made to Sergeant Blom, 14 hours before his death, about how he had been assaulted and tortured. Advocate Schabort jumped in: the statement was inadmissible. The magistrate shouldn't allow it to be read in this inquest as it could be used in a criminal prosecution. Besides, Schabort argued, the police had made numerous statements rebutting the 'allegations'. Advocate Bizos retorted that they would indeed cross-examine every police witness on the 'happy relationships' which each officer claimed to have existed:[302]

> We do not concede that it will be established … that Dr Aggett committed suicide. Our alternative argument is going to be that, if it was suicide, it was an induced suicide … induced suicide is a crime.[303]

It was to be the first of many sharp exchanges at the opening of a long, gladiatorial contest inside the drab confines of Courtroom 18.

To the Aggetts' relief, the magistrate ruled in favour of George Bizos reading Neil's affidavit out in court so that the details could be put to Dr Kemp. This small advance was immediately challenged, the security police instructing Schabort to apply to the Supreme Court to have the magistrate's decision overruled. At the end of the afternoon, during which the court was shown the strip of cloth found around Neil's neck, a grim sight for family and friends, the inquest was postponed. Neil's parents returned to Somerset West to wait a further six weeks.

The lawyers' work continued. After two applications, they received permission for an 'informal visit' to John Vorster Square. Maurice Smithers could accompany them. He recalls how they were all 'a little nervous' about what they would find there. Police counsel wanted to show that he couldn't have seen what he claimed to have seen. Maurice, who was re-entering the lion's den, recalls 'being very happy I was in the company of so many friendly lawyers'. Apart from the family's legal team, however, the police lawyers and the magistrate also entered the room where Maurice had been held on 25 January. He went into the interrogation room on the other side of the frosted glass:

> Proof was instant and unanimous – I was easily recognisable and my movements were clearly defined. So it was obvious to all that it would have been possible for me to recognise Neil and to have seen what was going on in the

room where he was. This didn't mean I was telling the truth, of course. It just meant the state could not dismiss my evidence on the grounds that I could not have seen through the glass.

The visit received some minor attention in the press. Then all was quiet until Thursday 3 June with a splash of coverage on the Supreme Court decision not to intervene in the magistrate's ruling on the admissibility of Neil's affidavit. A front-page photograph in the *Rand Daily Mail* showed Jill, eyes down but smiling with relief, along with Paul, who cut a sombre figure next to Audrey Coleman of the DPSC, as the three descended the courthouse steps. The large headline proclaimed 'Dr Aggett's SP torture statement'. Printed in full alongside, and headed 'Last statement before he died', was the affidavit that Neil had dictated to Sergeant Blom.[304]

Inside the Supreme Court, Piet Schabort had argued before Justice CF Eloff and Justice Richard Goldstone that Neil's affidavit shouldn't be made public in 'the interests of national security'.[305] The working methods of the security police would be disclosed while the person who had made the statement could not be cross-examined. In giving judgment, Justice Eloff approached the matter from another angle, asking, were the statement not used, would the public not suspect that something was not right about the circumstances surrounding Dr Aggett's death?[306] Furthermore, it had already been published in the court records. Magistrate Kotzé's ruling was upheld. The Minister of Police was ordered to contribute towards the family's legal costs.

Back in the Magistrate's Court, Bizos pressed Dr Vernon Kemp on what he had found at the postmortem. Johannesburg's Chief District Surgeon said that he had only found a small scar about 5cm above Neil's right wrist. It was consistent with the account of assault. Dr Kemp was prepared to say that he regarded an interrogation session of 62 hours to be 'abnormal' but added that he was not aware of interrogation methods, as the security police had never sought his advice.[307] Bizos pursued the role of the district surgeon, a matter that had featured strongly in the Biko inquest. Dr Kemp seemed surprised to learn that Section 6 of the Terrorism Act allowed for him, as an officer employed in the service of the state, to make unannounced visits and expect to see a detainee at any time.[308] In his experience, it was customary to fit in with the security police. 'You can't just go barging into someone else's department,' said Dr Kemp.[309] Asked what his response would have been had he known that Neil had been interrogated for over 61 hours, the Chief District Surgeon said that he would have told them that they were 'overdoing things'. As a state employee, he was careful to be circumspect.

Under cross-examination, Dr Kemp and a second state medical witness, Johannesburg's Senior Government Pathologist, Dr Nicolaas Schepers, nevertheless agreed that it was impossible to conclude medically that the death was definitely suicide. Dr Schepers had examined a sample of Neil's brain, which had been bloodless, indicating suicide. Dr Schepers pointed out that there was no sign of a struggle that would have caused Neil's face to turn blue, and the rush of blood would have ruptured capillaries in the eyes. However, pressed by Bizos, he conceded that Neil's pale face did not rule out the possibility of him being hanged while unconscious.[310]

Dr Jan Botha, who had conducted the postmortem for the Aggetts, was also unable to say whether Neil had 'voluntarily elevated himself with a cloth around his neck or whether he was elevated in an unconscious or semiconscious [state]'.[311] A final medical witness, the Chief State Pathologist from Pretoria, Professor Johan Loubser, had read the reports. While agreeing that death had been caused by hanging, he agreed under cross-examination that it was possible for a layperson to confuse death with unconsciousness. It was also possible for about five people to lift up and suspend a limp body into a hanging position without damaging the skin. The family's lawyers wanted to show that, while they had no direct evidence, it was not out of the question that Neil had been strung up while unconscious.

Next to give evidence were the ordinary police officers responsible for the care of detainees in their cells. Little love was lost between them and security police. A junior 'security' could punch above his weight with an 'ordinary'. Nevertheless, they had their own patches to protect. Constable André Martin, the officer on duty the night Neil died, had already admitted in his affidavit to making a false entry in the Occurrence Book. Neil had not been visited, as written in the book, at '00h56'. There had been a three-hour gap between the 10.30pm visit and 1.30am, when he was found dead. Advocate Kuny probed the constable, getting him to explain how, by entering from ground level and coming up the internal stairs, it was possible to gain entry to the second-floor cells without being seen by the night duty officer. Occasionally, a security policeman would go directly to the cell to fetch a detainee, before checking the detainee out in the Occurrence Book. In other words, the security police had their own set of keys to both the outer wooden cell door and the padlocks for the inner grille gates.[312]

Next, Denis Kuny tackled Warrant Officer MacPherson, in charge of the second-floor cells. Why hadn't he ensured that Neil had seen the Inspector of Detainees on 4 January, and why, on 6 January, when Neil was still complaining of pain, was he not seen by the visiting magistrate? MacPherson rapidly claimed the limits of his domain: Neil hadn't been in his cell … A telephone hadn't been available … Nor could he leave the inspector or magistrate alone with another detainee on the second floor while he went to the tenth floor. The detainee might flee! Moreover, MacPherson insisted, the Inspector stated that he was in a hurry and couldn't wait.[313]

There was also the matter of the pain in Neil's back, marked in MacPherson's book over three days, from 4 January. Why had he not called a doctor to see Neil? It wasn't necessary, MacPherson replied. Neil was a doctor and happy to prescribe a painkiller for himself. However, he could not say why the dose of 200mg Brufen was six times lower than the dosage that should have been prescribed.[314] Neil's affidavit to Sergeant Blom gave a different picture, pointedly stating 'I was not seen by a doctor'.[315] But MacPherson's priorities were clear. He was not going to rock the boat.

The high point of the inquest's first full week came at the end on Friday 11 June. A visibly nervous Sergeant Aletta Gertruida Blom, the uniformed policewoman who had taken down Neil's final statement of complaint in a childish script, gave her testimony in front of a court packed with male SB officers. George Bizos was not impressed. Nor did he think Neil would have felt reassured that she could offer him any protection. Whoever had appointed her to the Investigation Unit, responsible for dealing with complaints against the police, had not been looking for the qualities of a confident, independent mind.

In court, Sergeant Blom appeared as anxious about her audience as she was over Advocate Bizos's questions. Having caught Warrant Officer Lawrence Prince shaking his head in a signal to the witness, Bizos angrily objected. Although Magistrate Kotzé issued a warning, the incident reflected the unhealthy relationship. It was clear that the timorous Blom would make known to the overbearing security police any allegations against them 'on a systematic basis', said Bizos. 'Dr Aggett is not able to say what happened to him … Evidence will depend on what happened to others who made statements to this witness (Sergeant Blom), and the court may draw the inference that it was part of the system.'[316] At this stage, Magistrate Kotzé had still to give his decision about the admissibility of similar fact sworn statements from other detainees.

Maurice Smithers followed Sergeant Blom on the witness stand. The *in situ* visit had at least established that, from the room where he had been waiting on Monday 25 January, he was able to see through the frosted glass into Room 1012. Although Maurice felt that he gave his evidence 'competently and comprehensively', it was not easy. Still recovering from solitary confinement and acclimatising to being banned, he had 'to relive the Neil situation all over again', with the police denying everything:

> The cops carrying out the torture denied even being there on the day. They also denied that Neil was there. The black cop who was guarding me and from whom I was asking the time periodically ... denied that he owned a watch and said therefore that he could not have told me the time. Of course, he also said that he saw nothing going on in the next room.

'I do not remember' and 'I do not know' formed a constant refrain in the replies of black officers to the family's counsel. For instance, asked if he would call for help if he had seen Dr Aggett being maltreated, Maurice's guard, Constable Makhetha, replied, 'what other people do, I do not notice'.[317]

The prevalence of assaults on detainees, however, was confirmed by the Inspector of Detainees, Abraham Johannes Mouton. But that was all. There were times when detainees told him they had been assaulted 'but refused to give details', telling him they 'were scared the information would filter back to the security police'. If they did not say anything, he could not draw the complaints out of them. Mouton insisted that, if a detainee needed a doctor, he informed the station commander: 'When I have done that, my duty is completed.'[318] Beyond that, he could not go. Nevertheless, he rejected the suggestion by Bizos that he was 'helpless'. He conveyed complaints to the Minister of Justice. But he could not himself give instructions to the security police.[319]

Probed by Bizos, the Inspector gave details of his visits to a number of detainees and former detainees, including five whose affidavits were being submitted for inclusion at the inquest. He denied being in a hurry on Monday 4 January, as claimed by Warrant Officer MacPherson, when he called to see

Dr Aggett. When he called again, on Friday 22 January, he gained the impression that Dr Aggett was completely normal, with no complaints. Liz Floyd would later say that the Inspector appeared to listen with concern but 'he had no power to intervene'. His 'apologetic manner' was hardly reassuring.[320]

The challenge for the family's legal team was now to have testimony included from other detainees who were interrogated by members of Major Cronwright's team around the same time as Neil. Over the past week they had been collecting affidavits from released detainees, but the security police were making access to those still in their custody very difficult. The magistrate was becoming impatient but granted a short adjournment until Monday 21 June, when he would hear each side's arguments before ruling on the admissibility of similar fact evidence.

On Monday, the two senior counsels, Bizos and Schabort, embarked on a classic courtroom duel. Arguing for Magistrate Kotzé to accept 13 detainee affidavits, Advocate Bizos outlined a pattern of ill treatment. There were physical assaults of varying intensity and frequency, coupled with the humiliation of being made to undress, having genitals attacked, and being laughed and sneered at. Some detainees spoke of sleep deprivation, long periods of standing, being forced to perform strenuous physical exercise, being hooded, subjected to electrical shocks, hit with various objects and threatened with further assaults, even death.

Bizos argued that the allegations showed great similarity to the complaints mentioned by Neil in his sworn statement, as well as with what Maurice Smithers saw meted out. The affidavits contradicted the denials by Neil's interrogators that he was not ill-treated; their refrain that he was always in a genial mood (*gemoedelike stemming*); their assertions that he was in good physical and mental shape in his last week. He had been subjected to unlawful treatment, and the police had failed to ensure that his complaints were properly investigated. Moreover, the affidavits suggested the strong possibility that Neil was threatened after making his complaint to Sergeant Blom. A number of detainees spoke of being confronted by their interrogators after making complaints – and of giving in to pressure to withdraw them.[321] The affidavits revealed the futility of the complaints system. Dr Aggett, said Bizos, may have come to believe that death was preferable to continued mental and physical abuse.

Advocate Schabort, on behalf of the police, could muster nothing to compare with the logic of Advocate Bizos, let alone his moral indignation. He stated that the affidavits were irrelevant to the medical findings of death by hanging, and if other detainees had been reluctant to lodge complaints, there was no evidence that this had been the case with Dr Aggett. There were 57 detainees in John Vorster Square at the time of Dr Aggett's death, but the lawyers had only obtained affidavits from about a quarter of them. It was not a comprehensive study and he appealed to the magistrate to 'draw the line'.[322]

Once again, as with the admission of Neil's complaint to Sergeant Blom, Magistrate Kotzé cannot have been unaware of the eyes of the media at home and abroad. Ruling that eight affidavits could be admitted, he refused the other five.[323] However, the cat was out of the bag, with the abuses listed by George Bizos widely quoted in the press. As Joseph Lelyveld noted in *The New York Times*, it was 'a legal breakthrough that seems likely to turn the inquest into an inquiry into police interrogation methods'.[324]

The expansion of the inquest had financial implications. By 16 June, Aubrey's initial R50 000 was already used up, with a R27 000 shortfall in the budget rising rapidly. Although Aubrey had given an undertaking to pay more if called upon, between June and November William Lane was to send a series of confidential memos to 'Supporters of the Aggett family', each with a detailed summary of developments, financial statement and budget. He explained that while the first purpose of the inquest was to ascertain the cause of Neil's death, 'other surrounding issues are of such magnitude as to justify us in concluding that there are others who would wish to help relieve Mr Aggett of the financial burden'.[325] Aubrey's brother-in-law, George Allison, a well-known Johannesburg accountant and company director, who was married to Joy's sister Madge, assisted in seeking donations.

William Lane's style in describing the inquest made compelling reading. The July statement of accounts showed that, inside South Africa, donations ranged from R500 from the Cape Town Municipal Workers, collected from individual workers, to R10 000 from the South African Council of Churches. From abroad, the American Lawyers' Committee for Civil Rights had donated R14 297, while 'A firm of solicitors in England acting for a client' had sent R29 602. The Aggetts would not have known that the highly respected firm of Carruthers & Co, in London's West End, was actually a conduit for money from the banned International Defence and Aid Fund (IDAF), the brainchild of Canon John Collins of St Paul's Cathedral. Apartheid intelligence agents, including Craig Williamson, had done their best to unmask Defence and Aid's system of 'illegally' providing funds for political defendants, but the irrepressible Canon and his colleagues managed to outsmart them all.[326] It was the kind of international 'interference' that made security police blood boil.

CHAPTER 49

'Mr Bizos is changing the scope of this inquest …'

BRIGADIER HENDRIK CHRISTOFFEL MULLER, HEAD OF JOHANNES-burg's security police, was next on the stand, agreeing to answer questions in English. 'I am indebted to the brigadier for his courtesy,' said Bizos.[327] Short and sinewy, with weathered skin, Muller could be mistaken for a 'farmer in church', as Lelyveld observed.[328] At the same time, he remained very much the smooth bureaucrat, apart from the odd occasion when the affable mask was seen to slip. One such moment was when Bizos pressed him to explain why a visiting magistrate had twice been unable to see Neil. 'These persons are detained for interrogation. They are not detained to be kept in detention for visits by magistrates,' he suddenly snapped.[329]

Muller affirmed complete faith in his officers regardless of any questionable activities. Asked about Captain Struwig, who previously had been found by the Appellate Division – then the country's highest court – to have compelled false confessions from witnesses, Muller replied that he could not remember the matter. However, if the allegations were true, he was 'still satisfied that Captain Struwig is acceptable to me as a member of my staff'.[330]

When Muller said that he instructed the treatment of detainees to be 'as humane as possible',[331] his definition of 'humane' was sufficiently broad to include Neil's 62-hour interrogation session. Questioned on 'intensive interrogation', he stated that it happened 'from time to time ... for purposes of continuity or following a request from a detainee to finalise his interrogation. There is nothing sinister in it.'[332] However, after Bizos indicated that intensive interrogation had been ruled unlawful in the Supreme Court following a successful action against the police in 1978, Muller attempted to backtrack.[333] Pressed to give details of who was responsible for Neil's investigation, he emphatically denied being 'actively engaged' himself.[334] Although Muller appeared largely unruffled while giving evidence over three days, Advocate Schabort protested to the magistrate that Bizos was changing the scope of this inquest into 'a commission of inquiry into detention in general'.[335] The culture of impunity in which the security police operated was being laid bare.

Major Arthur Benoni Cronwright followed his boss onto the witness stand. Although the major had authorised the 'long weekend', he claimed not to have read Neil's affidavit to Sergeant Blom, on the grounds of not wanting to interfere with the investigation into his death. He had called Lieutenant Whitehead and Sergeant van Schalkwyk into his office following Neil's earlier complaint to Magistrate Wessels and they denied any ill treatment. That was sufficient. Why, asked Bizos, should detainees make false complaints? There have never been any prosecutions, replied Cronwright. As far as he was concerned, any complaints were properly investigated. To Cronwright, who divided the world into the saved and the damned, all his officers were in the first category while Neil and his ilk were beyond redemption. Dr Aggett and his girlfriend were named, he said, in another detainee's statement as members of an 'ANC cell'. He was referring to Barbara Hogan's 'Close Comrades' list.[336] Challenged on this, he refused to concede that they had actually been listed as labour experts. When Bizos queried why the police had not recorded Dr Aggett's 'negative answers' regarding his alleged links to the banned ANC, Cronwright gave the chilling reply that 'The Commissioner of Police is not interested in negative answers.'[337]

Cronwright also claimed that 'vertroulike inligting' (secret information) obtained from Neil was so important and vital to ongoing investigations that he was withholding it from the Transvaal Attorney General, the court and the Aggett family's lawyers.[338] This claim contained a barely veiled threat directed at Bizos himself; these 'confidential' contents would damage 'a very respected person present in this court today and who is named and who would be warned about the investigation'.[339] To Cronwright, Bizos was clearly a member of the banned South African Communist Party, and it was only a matter of time before they would nail him. As Bizos told the magistrate, the fairness of the inquiry was in question when 'one of our hands [is] tied to our backs, because information has not been made available'.[340]

On behalf of his clients, Piet Schabort insisted that as the investigation was not yet complete, there were 'dozens of pages' of handwritten notes that could not be submitted to the inquest.[341] Muller too had alluded to Neil having made 'new revelations', yet was not prepared to reveal anything more, maintaining that a number of 'new names',[342] given by Neil, were sent to Pretoria in a telex with an application to proceed with arrests. A new story began to emerge, according to which Neil was alleged to have overhead some officers preparing the telex. In this scenario, apparently overcome by guilt at having betrayed his comrades, Neil then took his life. According to Muller, the application for arrests had been rejected; hence the investigation was ongoing.

Cross-examined about Neil's appearance on the day before his death, Cronwright asserted that he was neat, calm and normal, with no signs of depression. Had Dr Aggett been coherent? 'Oh, yes, he was far more intelligent than any of us,' the major replied.[343] Asked by his counsel to read out the opening of Neil's second statement, Cronwright must have enjoyed reciting what he proclaimed was the detainee's key admission: 'I support the Marxist ideology and therefore I am a communist.' Bizos immediately pointed out that the major was reading from a typed and unsigned copy of a statement that could not be regarded legally as a statement.[344] This typed copy differed from the statement in Neil's handwriting, where it appeared that this opening sentence could have been inserted afterwards, under duress, to precede the paragraph about his family background. Moreover, the major omitted to read the subsequent sentence, squeezed into the handwritten statement, 'I am also an idealist.' Suspiciously absent from the typed statement, these five words would become a later focus for argument. Marxists subscribing to a materialist philosophy would surely not describe themselves as 'idealists', thus undercutting the veracity of the supposed admission. Nevertheless, four newspaper crime correspondents reported receiving phone calls from the security police, urging them to use the declaration: 'I support the Marxist ideology and therefore I am a communist.' The government-controlled South African Broadcasting Corporation, which had ignored much of the inquest, took a sudden interest and broadcast the statement.[345]

After three days of evidence from Cronwright, the inquest was postponed from 29 June until 20 September to allow the lawyers to meet other commitments. These included George Bizos representing Barbara Hogan on her charge of high treason in the Johannesburg Supreme Court in July. Pleading guilty to membership of the ANC, Barbara attempted damage limitation for some of those she had named in 'Close Comrades'. As an awaiting-trial prisoner with access to newspapers, and aware of developments in the inquest, she made a point of referring to Neil and her involvement with him during the Fatti's & Moni's boycott. She spoke of 'a tension problem' between them, saying that Neil 'resented' her presence at meetings: 'I can definitely say he was not an ANC member. He himself told me that and the ANC assured me of the same fact.'[346] While Barbara's testimony would have no bearing on the inquest, her comments were at least in the public domain, with 'Aggett "definitely not" an ANC man' making the *Rand Daily Mail*'s headline.

Unlike the other lawyers, David Dison had another kind of commitment, not of his choosing. After his initial army training in 1972, he had managed to avoid further military service for ten years. But finally he had been arrested, charged, tried and convicted of failure to go on an army camp. From army barracks in Pretoria, he was taken as a 'non-effective troop' to Oshakati, close to the border with southern Angola. The town was a base for the South African Defence Force in its brutal war to suppress Namibian independence while bloodily involved in Angola's civil war. For ten weeks, David found himself working in the kitchen of a 'scary camp', with mortars screaming through the night. The experience was 'like being transported into Francis Ford Coppola's *Apocalypse Now*'.

Back in Johannesburg, more detainees were being released. Some had witnessed Neil's deterioration in his last days, including Auret van Heerden, who had been in detention for almost ten months. Auret's information confirmed the lawyers' view of induced suicide and that the security police were guilty of culpable homicide. But Cronwright had also threatened Auret about giving evidence, and he wanted a little time to decide about an affidavit.

On Sunday 8 August, Ernest Moabi Dipale was found hanging from a strip of cloth tied to his cell window on the second floor of the cells at John Vorster Square. Six months earlier, in January, the 21-year-old had occupied Cell 208, next to Neil. He had been released at the end of the month, while Neil was up on the tenth floor, only to be rearrested six months later in Soweto. Within three days, he was dead. Three days later, in St Anthony's Church in Durban, Jill addressed a DPSC meeting of over 400 people. Max Coleman had asked her to talk about the personal impact of Neil's death and her response to this latest tragedy. Jill, who had never spoken in public before, had no qualms. Neil's death and the revelations at the inquest had left her 'so emotionally numb' that she had no hesitation in 'accepting the opportunity to reiterate my horror that Neil's death had not brought an end to callous and inhumane treatment and murder in police cells'. Looking back, Jill felt that she had been so traumatised by events that she 'felt very little emotion about anything'.

*   *   *

When the inquest resumed on 20 September, the family steeled themselves to hear testimony from detainees who had witnessed Neil's last days. Preceding them on the witness stand, Yvette Breytenbach spoke warmly of Neil's character. He was a man of purpose, she testified, committed to change through trade union activism. He was 'a particularly sincere and honest friend who was against racial discrimination and wanted to work for a democratic society'.[347] A week before he had been detained, Neil had told her not to worry as he wasn't a member of the ANC and felt that he had nothing to fear. When she saw Neil in John Vorster Square on a special pre-Christmas visit, he appeared physically well, in a good state of mind and not at all despondent. He was optimistic, telling her not to cancel a booking she had made for a group holiday in February. He was hoping to be free by then. Quizzed about Neil's relationship with Liz, Yvette denied Schabort's suggestion that it had been floundering and that her relationship with Neil was a 'love affair'.[348]

Keith Coleman followed Yvette. Banned but permitted to give evidence, he told the court of four occasions when he had seen Neil inside John Vorster Square. He acknowledged that his five months in solitary confinement had distorted his view of time and he couldn't give dates. Nevertheless, he recalled that Neil had initially been 'alert' and 'responsive'.[349] On one occasion, Neil asked him for food and cigarettes, as his privileges had been taken away, but he was 'handling' it.[350] He also told Keith that he was keeping a shirt torn by a policeman as evidence of assault and planned to lay a charge when released. However, in what would be the last week of Neil's life, Keith noticed a distinct change. Seeing Neil walk by his cell, Keith banged from inside on his window, but Neil had ignored him. Another time, he greeted Neil as they passed each other in the corridor. Although Neil turned towards him, he didn't look at Keith. He was 'unresponsive', as if in another world, completely introspective: 'That is what frightened me.'[351]

The following day, a packed court heard Liz Floyd quietly and steadily describe the terrors of the tenth floor. Although held first in a police cell in Bronkhorstspruit, with very little interrogation, she was transferred to Hillbrow police station but interrogated at John Vorster Square. During the first week of January, she heard what sounded like a man screaming in pain, and on another occasion saw a black woman taken into the office opposite, and then heard the sound of crying and screaming. One of her interrogators, Disré Carr, spent nearly an hour telling her about detainees who jumped to their death through a window, including someone who, he claimed, had been caught by a leg and a foot. Liz stressed the intimidating and disorienting nature of detention: 'I think that anybody in this Court would find it very difficult to sit in solitary, without reading material, apart from a Bible, for even one week.'[352]

Warrant Officer Prince was one of those who shouted and screamed at her, while her interrogators reiterated that her statement was useless compared to information given, so they claimed, by Neil. She was 'insolent' and could be sentenced to five years for 'withholding information'.[353] On 4 February, she was handcuffed on Lieutenant Whitehead's orders and made to stand until she complained of her arthritis and was given a chair. Whitehead, frequently aggressive, told her things about Neil that she knew couldn't be true, including that Neil regretted going to the University of Cape Town to study medicine. He also repeatedly accused her of writing a document she had never seen. Finally she flipped, swearing at him, 'I'm tired of you and your fucking document.' Whitehead's response was that he would hit her, to which she replied that she would hit him back:

> He treated me like a liar … I am a fairly senior doctor, I am a person who is not used to being treated as a liar. Even if I am on the 10th floor of John Vorster Square, I expect to be treated with respect and I expect to treat other people with respect.[354]

Liz knew that her interrogators were trying to play her and Neil off against each other. When they told her that Neil had had affairs with other women, she had replied that she knew what they were trying to do and did not believe them, so they had backed off. In normal circumstances, she told the court, Neil was not the sort of person who would have committed suicide. Liz revealed nothing of her sense that, under the extreme pressure of solitary confinement, aggression and torture, Neil may have reverted to his earlier more introverted self and chosen suicide as a means of taking back control.

Over the next four days, the testimony of six more witnesses revealed a grim picture of Neil's final days, while some offered their own evidence of ill treatment and torture. The student Thabo Lerumo, awaiting trial under the Terrorism Act, testified to the change in Neil's demeanour, from being 'happy' to becoming 'not at ease'.[355] He recorded how, as he had swept the corridor on 4 February, Neil had been escorted past him by two policemen. He had seen tears in Neil's eyes and a spot of blood on his left forehead. He had tried to greet him but had been stopped. To demonstrate Neil's difficulty in walking, the student stooped over, with his hands crossing in front of him, shuffling slowly.

Ismail Momoniat, a senior Mathematics lecturer at the University of the Witwatersrand, who had been released in June, told how he had seen Neil for the last time on Wednesday 3 February. They were both on the first floor to sign out before being taken to the tenth floor. Referring to the date, Bizos pointed out that there had been 11 minutes between their signing-out times that Wednesday, but only two minutes on Thursday. As a mathematician, could he put a percentage on the likelihood of which it had been? It was probably Thursday 4 February, Momoniat corrected himself, adding, 'Perhaps maths is a better discipline than human memory.'[356]

His substantive evidence was that Neil hadn't responded to his greeting, which he found 'extremely strange because when you are in detention one looks forward to these occasions'. Instead, Neil had seemed oblivious to everything around him: 'He was in a daze ... just staring blankly at the wall.' Momoniat also noted that, towards the right side of his forehead, there appeared to be a large mark, half to three-quarters of an inch in diameter. 'It looked to me to be either to be a scar or a bruise. But it was a mark that stood out.'[357] This difference in recollecting the precise location of the blood mark on Neil's forehead – whether towards the right side (Momoniat) or on the left (Lerumo) was just the kind of variation the state would pounce on. No allowance was to be given for the disorienting effects of detention, to which Liz had testified.

Premanathan Naidoo, then serving a year's imprisonment for harbouring an escaped prisoner, followed with horrifying details of a sustained period of torture in November when he had been kept awake for almost a week, with only a few hours of sleep. He had been made to exercise intensively; given electric shocks; beaten, punched and kicked; forced to stand for long periods and to kneel until the skin on his knee broke; kept naked; and threatened with death. At one point he had become so tired that he had fallen asleep while standing. He had woken up to find himself confessing to something about which he had not even been questioned. Schabort accused him of telling a 'train of lies and half-truths ... aimed at disparaging the police', but the litany of abuse sounded all too credible.[358]

Sisa Njikelana, Neil's comrade from SAAWU now awaiting trial, became the fourth witness to note the marked change in Neil. His own experience offered an explanation of what might have happened. Major Cronwright had personally assaulted Sisa, pushing him against a wall and slapping and punching him. In the first week of January, he had been put into leg-irons that ran through handcuffs, forcing him to squat. With a canvas bag pulled over his head, he was subjected to electric shocks, which made his whole body vibrate. Asked by Schabort why he had not reported the maltreatment to the Inspector of Detainees, he replied that he had feared 'repercussions'.[359] Sisa had seen Neil on various occasions, and in January Neil had shown him a large triangular red mark on his arm. But when he saw Neil a week before his death, he could tell that something was deeply wrong: 'He appeared very much depressed and morose as if he was somebody that was bereaved.'[360] This was not the Neil Aggett he knew.

Taking the stand on Monday 27 September, Shirish Nanabhai, serving a three-year sentence for helping an escaped prisoner, offered further evidence of being manacled wrist to ankle and forced to crouch, with a canvas bag over his head, while being given electric shocks. He named 'Schalkie', Carr and Venter as the officers involved, the first two both having dealt with Neil.[361]

Trade unionist Jabu Ngwenya's subsequent evidence concerned a quick exchange with Neil on 3 February, although he acknowledged that 'when one is in detention, one is very forgetful, you forget many things. I had no calendar ...'.[362] Nevertheless, certain details were sharp. On meeting Neil in the corridor, where Jabu had been running for exercise, Jabu had followed him into the changing room on the pretext of wanting some water. As well as looking depressed, pale and unusually lean-faced, with his cheekbones showing, Neil 'was not walking normally. It appeared to me as though there was something wrong with his private parts, because he was walking wide-legged.'[363] Neil began to tell him how he had been assaulted and given electric shocks. He was pulling up his jersey sleeve to show something, when MacPherson walked in and Jabu was obliged to leave. He had been assaulted and tortured himself, as well as having Cronwright threaten him with death. After 312 days in detention, he had finally been released, without charges, just a few days earlier. Bravely, he intended bringing charges against the police.

Listening to this catalogue of cruelty unleashed on defenceless detainees, the family drew strength from the energy and passion of their legal team who, as well as being first-rate lawyers, were activists in the cause of justice. The inquest was, in David Dison's words, 'such an important channel', as well as a massive forensic case, requiring a considerable level of skill, work and commitment. Every day, William Lane's wife Elizabeth would bring a basket with sandwiches, buns and a Thermos flask of coffee for them all. The Aggetts appreciated the kindness. It helped them feel, said Jill, as if family and lawyers had become 'a little team', and they 'got fond of each other'. To the lawyers, Jill was the mediator who held things together. Aubrey always remained, as George Bizos would put it, 'a little bit more difficult to deal with'. Nevertheless, when William Lane told Aubrey, 'You had a very fine son', Jill knew that it meant a great deal to her father. In her words, their lawyers 'were very supportive in a very human way', and the family came to trust them implicitly.

CHAPTER 50

The Controller

I T WAS TIME NOW FOR THE FAMILY TO BRACE THEMSELVES TO LISTEN to Neil's interrogators. As the inquest stretched from September into October, the police officers who followed each other on the witness stand were practised in denial, some more adept than others. Captain Naude, Neil's first chief interrogator, brought in from East London for his trade union knowledge, commented on Neil's complaint of assault on 4 January: 'It was possible Dr Aggett was assaulted – but it was very improbable ... I would not have turned a blind eye to an assault.'[364] Naude maintained that his relationship with Neil was good. After all, they were both from the Cape. But it seems that the captain, whom Neil believed had been ready to recommend his release, had now shifted his position. Testifying in front of his fellow officers, Naude said that he had concluded from what Barbara Hogan had written that Neil was an 'ANC sympathizer'. He had come into line, adding, 'There is no difference between a sympathizer and a member. Being a sympathizer means you give your support to the ANC.'[365]

After Naude came a string of Cronwright's officers who had played second fiddle to Whitehead, including some whom the family's lawyers regarded as the 'night nurses' tasked with keeping Neil awake over the long weekend. First came the two Detective Warrant Officers brought in to work together on Neil's interrogation from Monday 25 January, Karel de Bruin and Disré Carr. Cross-examined by Denis Kuny, the older, softly-spoken De Bruin maintained that Neil had not been made to do strenuous exercises in the office behind the frosted glass, as observed by Maurice Smithers. Nor had he, De Bruin, been present during any assault. He found Neil 'very co-operative and I had no problem with him'.[366] Over the long weekend, Dr Aggett was given a camp bed, De Bruin asserted. Dr Aggett chose to stay on the tenth floor because he wanted 'sy hart wou skoonmaak' (to clear his heart) and be 'finished with' his statement.[367] On 4 February, De Bruin observed him to be 'dood normaal' (dead normal) as usual.[368] As the officer who had typed his second statement, he denied that the detainee's handwriting showed any signs of increasing shakiness.

Carr was not so smooth, and there were heated exchanges with Bizos. When Magistrate Kotzé intervened, it was to admonish Advocate Bizos to keep the examination on 'a high level'. He was 'not going to allow emotions to run away like this!'[369] Carr was obliged, however, to agree with Bizos that he had spent 25 to 30 hours with Neil yet was unable to name the law under which trade unions were registered. It was clear that he had not been brought in from Newcastle for his knowledge of labour matters.

On Thursday 30 September, the same day De Bruin and Carr gave their evidence, the DPSC presented the Minister of Police with 70 statements from ex-detainees, rebutting his denials of torture in April. They included multiple cases of sleep deprivation, enforced standing, enforced physical exercise (including holding objects aloft), electric shocks, suspension in mid-air, suffocation, assaults such as dragging by the hair and crushing of toes with chairs or bricks, attacks on genitals, and being kept naked for long periods. In addition, there was psychological torture and intimidation by hooding, death threats with a cocked firearm in the mouth, and threats to children, parents and spouses. Arguing that evidence of torture was an integral feature of the detention system, the DPSC stated that at least 20 commissioned officers up to the rank of major had been named.[370]

The Minister's response was swift and dismissive, accusing the DPSC of seeking sensational publicity. There was no question of him setting up any investigation. While editorials in the English-speaking press ranged from moral condemnation to restrained concern, a letter published in *The Star* from the 'Chairman, Security Forces Support Committee' may have reflected more accurately a significant sector of white opinion. Under the headline 'SP DETAINS LITTLE WOLVES', the letter denounced the DPSC as parents of ANC members who were not entitled to any sympathy.[371] The writer went on to attack the Anglican Church for allying itself with 'communist-inspired terrorism', suggesting that the church should 'throw in its lot with the SACP/ANC alliance and relocate in Tanzania'. With the Minister of Police giving his officers carte blanche, Magistrate Kotzé may have asked himself whether he had already gone too far in allowing any similar fact evidence at all.

On the witness stand, one police witness after another painted a picture of Neil as a contented, healthy detainee in his final days. According to Captain Johannes Visser, Neil 'looked fresh' at 6am during interrogation on the morning of Saturday 30 January in Room 1020, showing himself ready 'to open up his heart and write a statement of the whole truth'. Asked by Denis Kuny why Neil had changed his mind and become more relaxed, Visser claimed it was 'probably the way we had talked to him'.[372]

The next witness, Captain Daniël Swanepoel, spoke of confronting Neil with classified information that he couldn't reveal to the court. He flatly denied Bizos's suggestion that his role had been to pressurise. No, he and the detainee had enjoyed reminiscing about childhood.

By the evening of Saturday 30 January, when Lieutenant Whitehead took over with Detective Warrant Officer Deetlefs and Lieutenant Woensdregt, according to the latter pair, Neil was confiding that he was a communist who wanted to mobilise workers in a general strike. Both reported him to be normal, relaxed and rested. Deetlefs said that Neil had written four pages but the court was not permitted to see them.[373] According to Woensdregt, Neil offered them a list of names connected with the ANC and SACTU but was too scared to write them down in his own handwriting. Hence Deetlefs had done the writing. Asked by Bizos why Neil would have volunteered names but not written them down, Woensdregt replied, 'It could be that he liked us, that he preferred our approach'.[374] In due course, the story about Deetlefs writing names dictated by Neil would be elaborated by Whitehead.

When it came to the two black officers, Warrant Officer Danvey Maphophe and Constable Magezi Eddie Chauke, each emphasised the limited nature of their roles and that neither had seen anything untoward. The penultimate witness before Whitehead, like all the others, had seen nothing amiss. This was the hefty railway policeman, Detective Sergeant 'Schalkie' van Schalkwyk, implicated in three formal assault complaints – by Neil, Prema Naidoo and Shirish Nanabhai. He said that he hadn't asked many questions during Neil's December interrogation, and only briefly on 4 January, because his knowledge of trade unions was very limited. In fact, he had been there to learn security police techniques. Dr Aggett, he said, never complained but had always been friendly, drank tea, ate and smoked with his interrogators. When Lieutenant Stephan (Steven) Peter Whitehead followed 'Schalkie' onto the stand on Wednesday 6 October, he must have felt satisfied that the stage had been well set.

Reporters remarked on the tall, clean-shaven 25-year-old's chubby boyish looks, except that this image didn't fit the picture of the ambitious, determined policeman that would emerge over the next three days. The smart black suit, 'fashionable teardrop glasses' and 'what look like Gucci shoes' provided some clues.[375] Throughout cross-examination, Whitehead kept his back turned to Bizos. Facing and addressing only the magistrate, the lieutenant appeared to stare through his thin metal-rimmed glasses at the national coat of arms above Magistrate Kotzé. While Whitehead referred to Bizos only as 'the Advocate', Bizos aptly named him 'the Controller'. It was a legal duel for which Neil's chief interrogator appeared surprisingly well prepared. Whatever suspicions George Bizos had about the occasional bugging of his chambers by the security police, it would be more than ten years before he learned about the extent of Whitehead's advantage. The security police would study transcripts of the lawyers' discussions and rehearse the forthcoming cross-examination. The family's lawyers were deprived of the element of surprise, in Bizos's words, 'the cross-examiner's strongest weapon':

> Of course the magistrate could not have known then, and I am absolutely certain that neither Piet Schabort nor Schalk Burger even suspected it, otherwise they would have thrown their brief back to the State Attorney.[376]

Whitehead's role in the bungled break-in at the Aggetts' home in Somerset West had shown his limitations. Liz Floyd had also assessed him as a 'dumb interrogator', which for her meant that he was more to be feared, especially since he was, as she would tell me, 'obsessively immature'. Out of his comfort zone on the witness stand, but aided by tape recordings and 'mock trials', Whitehead was determined not to be caught off-guard. Perhaps staring at the coat of arms helped him to concentrate. His superiors were counting on him.

Whitehead projected his relationship' with Neil as friendly 'under the circumstances':[377] he had bought Neil cigarettes, offered him sandwiches and, on 20 January, shared his birthday cake. He had wanted to be friendly with Liz too, but said that she had been aggressive to him. In his narrative, he became the victim, the interrogator who was only doing his job. After learning of Neil's affidavit to Sergeant Blom, he tackled him: 'I stood in front of the table, looked him in the eye and said, "Is this how you treat people who have been good to you until now?" I turned around and walked out of the office.'[378]

Once again, the court heard that the camp bed over the long weekend was set up at Neil's own bidding. On Thursday 28 January, Whitehead claimed to have visited Neil in his cell to tell him 'the game was now up', confronting him with 'certain facts'. In Whitehead's version, Neil had agreed to undergo 'more intensive questioning' because he 'realised we knew more than he had thought and was then prepared to tell the truth and give us his full co-operation'.[379]

Whitehead lost no time in propounding the 'betrayed comrade' suicide theory, in which Neil overheard him sending a telex, on Thursday 4 February, requesting the arrest of people he had named. The relevant information was in four pages of notes that had to remain confidential because of ongoing investigations. Whitehead added that Neil also feared prosecution. Questioned by Bizos why he had made no mention in his affidavit following Neil's death of these particular factors, which he now claimed had led Neil to suicide, Whitehead replied that he hadn't included these 'facts' because they were 'privileged' information.[380]

Bizos focused at length on Neil's alleged confession that he was a communist, submitting written evidence from Tom Lodge, a Politics lecturer at the University of the Witwatersrand. After close textual analysis of Neil's handwritten statement and the two typed statements, Lodge made a number of points. It was evident to him that 'Dr Aggett's libertarian ideal of open democratic organizations controlled from below has little in common with the tight, autocratic and hierarchical structure of "Democratic Centralism" which is characteristic of most Communist parties including the SACP'. Moreover, the language in which Neil had made his confession 'invites disbelief'. 'Communists would not describe Marxism as an "Ideology"', wrote Lodge, but as a set of theories and a way of analysing society, history and economics. 'Only someone with a very naïve conception of Marxism would state "I support the Marxist Ideology and therefore I am a Communist" and this did not sound at all like Neil.'[381]

Bizos put it to Whitehead that the opening sentence of Neil's second statement was his own work. Did he know that the words 'I am an idealist' contradicted the previous sentence? No, said Whitehead, he didn't. Indeed, Tom Lodge believed that this sentence was not a casual inclusion by Neil, but 'intended to make nonsense of what has preceded it'. Nor did Whitehead appear to know that the word 'communistic' was not a common adjective in English, suggesting translation from the derogatory Afrikaans 'kommunistiese'.[382] Not knowing became a frequent refrain for Whitehead.

Whitehead operated solely within his own mental loop. The reality of Neil being at his mercy became painfully clear. Did the lieutenant agree that Dr Aggett was in an impossible situation? 'Unless he agreed with the information which you had,' declared Bizos, 'he could not make a satisfactory statement. Would you have ever been satisfied that your information was incorrect and that Dr Aggett was telling the truth?'[383] No, it was not so, dissented Whitehead.

Truth meant Whitehead's truth. To him, there were three kinds of ANC members: full card-carrying members, active supporters and sympathisers. He acknowledged that Neil had repeatedly denied being a full member, yet he was somewhere between the latter two. Questioned by Bizos whether sympathy is 'prima facie evidence of the commission of some offence', he replied that was correct, but claimed that further information had led to Neil's detention. Asked where the law stated that a sympathiser was guilty of an offence, Whitehead replied that it wasn't contained in the Act but should be seen in 'a wider context'.[384] He dismissed Bizos's references to Neil's democratic ideas and his 'strong objections to infiltration from outside'.[385] More important was that Neil had attended a meeting about military training and the South African Defence Force, chaired by Gavin Andersson, whom he said Dr Aggett knew to be an ANC member. This showed where Dr Aggett's sympathies lay. Added to this, he had avoided his military service. 'Your Worship,' said Whitehead, 'in the total context, with Dr Aggett's sympathies and collaboration, and the fact he was a Marxist, it's obvious that he was guilty.'[386] He had watched Dr Aggett for three years, said Whitehead, and had 'other' information.

There were veiled references to Gavin, whose name re-emerged during cross-examination on the bungled break-in at the Aggetts' home, with

Whitehead flimsily claiming that he had sent Paul Erasmus to look for Gavin Andersson in Somerset West. Pressed under cross-examination, Whitehead then tried to shift the blame, stating that his advocate had asked if he could find something to help build up a psychiatric picture.[387] With Schabort immediately standing up in court to contradict this, Magistrate Kotzé was offered firm evidence from within the police side itself of Whitehead's unreliability as a witness. Challenged by Bizos about having told the Aggetts' neighbour that he was the duty officer of the local security police, Whitehead reluctantly conceded that it had not been the 'full truth'.[388]

Inquiring why Whitehead had made no reference to Neil's complaints of torture, Bizos suggested there was a 'conspiracy of silence' between him and his colleagues.[389] Yet again, the court heard that Neil's appearance on the day before his death was 'quite normal', with no signs of being a 'suicide risk':[390]

> MR BIZOS: Did anybody tell you that it was important … for a detainee, with all the anxieties that detention induces, to be away from his interrogator in order that he may sleep in peace … so that the anxiety created in the interrogation situation may be wiped out?
> LT WHITEHEAD: Your Worship, no one told me that, but I can affirm that no anxiety is created during detention.[391]

Whitehead was on the witness stand for just under nine hours, spread over three days, frequently prefacing his answers with 'As I have already told the court'. Like someone who had learned his lines, he was not going to be shifted. At one point, Whitehead complained that he knew what it was like to be asked the same question over and over again, to which Bizos retorted that he had been in the witness box for only three and a half hours, compared with Neil's 62 hours of interrogation. 'You've still got a long way to go before you start complaining,' Bizos added.[392] An immediate reprimand followed from the magistrate, during which Whitehead was seen to smile. Magistrate Kotzé's repeated warnings to Bizos about his manner of questioning must have reassured the lieutenant that he was projecting the right image of an officer only doing his job.

The correspondent for the *Sowetan* remarked on Whitehead's voice, noting that he spoke in a 'barely audible tone in Afrikaans, as all security policemen have chosen to do, despite the fact that Mr and Mrs Aggett, immigrant parents of the trade unionist, understand little of the language.'[393] The Aggetts sat in the well of the court near their lawyers, within metres of the throng of SB officers who came regularly to support their colleagues. With little Afrikaans, Joy and Aubrey probably focused on the body language of the men they held responsible for Neil's death. It must have been impossible not to imagine Neil in the same room as the slick-suited Whitehead.

A rare interview with Aubrey, by Joe Openshaw from *The Star*, provided a glimpse of what he was going through at the inquest. Openshaw reported that Aubrey had already spent R55 000[394] – and was prepared to spend double that – to make public the evidence relating to his son's death and to 'ensure that Neil did not die in vain':

> 'I have only to think of what that kid went through and I break down,' he says, his eyes filling with tears. During a recent operation he was found to be diabetic. 'Doctors say the diabetes has been caused by shock and strain,' he says. 'I can accept diabetes. But whatever the outcome of the inquest, my family and I will be the losers ... big losers. We have lost Neil. This loss and the expense will be warranted if the laws relating to detention are changed. We hope that in future people in the position my son was in will be judged and sentenced by those duly appointed for this task – magistrates and judges.'[395]

How could Aubrey forget Neil's letter offering reconciliation? 'Despite all that has happened between us I do not feel any enmity as long as we realize that we have differences and we cannot impose our view of things on the other person ... We are living in troubled times and I think we must realize that human friendship must stand above any petty differences we have with people.' How could Aubrey ever forgive himself for not visiting his son in John Vorster Square? Few readers of *The Star*, who might appreciate a father's grief, would have known the full personal tragedy. While Aubrey's intense feelings of guilt were probably sensed only by those very close to him, they were picked up by George Bizos, who, with his sensitive antennae, witnessed 'a transformative process' in the father who made no secret of his background and former views.[396] Aubrey's new understanding owed much to his lawyers, and also to the Colemans and the 'sub-culture', as George Bizos called it, within the DPSC that not only supported detainees' families but mobilised their concerted challenge to detention without trial. *The Star*'s interview, however, revealed that Aubrey was still counting on the independence of the judiciary. The family was holding on to whatever straws of hope they could.

The following week, on 13 October, after Whitehead's testimony was completed, the Aggetts' lawyers made another application to Magistrate Kotzé to admit further detainee affidavits. Most of the day was spent on argument over whether evidence could be heard from Auret van Heerden, Barbara Hogan, Eric Mntonga and the Reverend Frank Chikane. New affidavits had also been made by three others whose earlier statements had been refused on the grounds that they were too vague. If the magistrate excluded this evidence, argued Bizos, there would always be a question mark over the correctness of the finding. Van Heerden's evidence was possibly more important than any of the evidence already given by other detainees. Piet Schabort resisted, declaring that the proceedings were becoming prohibitively long. If there were to be evidence from these detainees, at least 20 policemen would be implicated and would have to be called. Kotzé adjourned the inquest once again. He would rule on the admissibility of the new affidavits on Monday 25 October.

In the intervening week, George Bizos attended the Supreme Court to hear judgment in Barbara Hogan's trial. She had pleaded not guilty to the charge of high treason, but admitted that she had joined the ANC while visiting Swaziland in 1977. Dressed in ANC colours and carrying yellow daffodils, like members of the packed public gallery, Barbara stood calmly in the dock to hear her sentence. Ten years. It was worse than anyone had expected. Bravely smiling, she turned to supporters, holding up a clenched fist and chanting '*Amandla!*' before being led down to the cells.

Barbara was not only the first woman to be convicted of treason; she was the first political detainee to be charged with treason, rather than with furthering the objects of a banned organisation. Indeed, she had done nothing more than 'furthering the objects', without being involved in any violence. However, the judge, Mr Justice AP van Dyk, quoted extensively from Craig Williamson's evidence, 'testified as an expert' on the inner workings of the ANC, and saw fit to add that, in wartime, the death sentence was often imposed for treason.[397] He refused leave to appeal. Cronwright and his men hadn't managed to get their mass treason trial but must have celebrated.

George Bizos would later comment that Barbara was one of the most cruelly punished of the many political prisoners he had defended.[398] In addition to the state's punitive sentence, Barbara had to live with her own sense of guilt over the fate of some of her comrades, including Neil.

CHAPTER 51

A shameful collaboration

MAGISTRATE KOTZÉ CHOSE NOT TO HEAR ANY FURTHER SIMILAR fact evidence. There were to be no more graphic accounts of torture. However, this did not stop Bizos from producing a piece of equipment with a button electrode that could deliver electric shocks. The pathologist Dr Jonathan Gluckman had discovered, by chance, in a physiotherapist's consulting rooms, an electrotherapy machine that would deliver an identical pattern to that described by senior district surgeon Dr Norman Jacobson to Sergeant Blom concerning Shirish Nanabhai.[399] At the request of the Aggett lawyers, the police had been required to pass on Dr Jacobson's affidavit. Called to the witness stand and shown the button electrode, the doctor acknowledged there was 'a distinct possibility' that this was the kind of instrument that had caused the circular scars found on the arms of Shirish Nanabhai, each the size of a 10-cent piece, with multiple pinpoint puncture marks. To Bizos and the legal team, here was the corroboration they needed.

Although Kotzé ruled against any further evidence of torture, he was obliged to allow one final detainee to give evidence. Auret van Heerden had been released without charges in July, after ten months in detention. Towards the end of September, he made an affidavit, covering what he knew about Neil as well as his own experiences at the hands of his interrogators. In permitting

386

Auret to be called as a witness, Kotzé ruled that he should speak only about Neil. He must have read Auret's preamble, stating how it had taken much soul-searching and anxiety to give details of his own horrific torture because of his fears of victimisation. But with Kotzé drawing the line, the personal torture section of the affidavit was, in any event, inadmissible. Perhaps the magistrate was also conscious of the presence in the gallery of an observer from Amnesty International, who had come to hear the 27-year-old former NUSAS president. Bushy-haired and heavily bearded, Auret cut a sombre figure on the witness stand in his dark-grey business suit. His sad, deep-set eyes hinted at the unspoken testimony. Those who knew Auret expected that, under cross-examination, he should at least be a sharp match for Schabort.

From his cell opposite number 209, Auret had been in a better position than any other detainee to comment on Neil's worsening condition. Previously, he and Neil had managed to speak daily. Auret testified that after three days and nights of interrogation Neil couldn't be woken to eat, leaving his breakfast and lunch untouched. Auret had watched the guard call into the cell, but, getting no response, he told Auret that Neil was sleeping. Later, when he saw Neil for himself, Neil 'looked frightened': 'He indicated that he didn't want to talk, and with a combination of sign language and whispers, pointed at the people upstairs, which was the way we always referred to the security police ... he made a motion with his hands as if he was breaking a twig ... and said, "I've broken".' Neil also indicated that he had been forced to stand, and had been given electric shocks until he had said that he had links with SACTU and was a communist. After telling Auret, 'they must just not ask me more questions', he had burst into tears.[400]

Auret spoke of Neil's deterioration to a zombie-like state in the ensuing days. When walking, Neil shuffled with a stoop, 'dragging his feet as if he had no strength left ... and his response to things going on around him, to me in particular, was very removed. I found difficulty in getting through to him'.[401] By Thursday night, Auret began to think of reporting Neil as a suicide risk. On hearing a commotion outside his cell in the early hours of Friday 5 February, he knew 'the worst had happened'.[402]

A month earlier, Neil had told Auret about his assault on Monday 4 January, when, on the tenth floor, he had been stripped, beaten and made to exercise for a few hours until 'a pool of sweat lay under his body'. On that occasion, Sergeant van Schalkwyk had wrapped a piece of cloth around his arm and

388   DEATH OF AN IDEALIST

clubbed him, saying that it was 'just a taste of what would happen … if he did not give the Security Police the answers which they were looking for.'[403] Auret had seen the scar where the policeman's watch had cut Neil and how Neil said he hoped that his friends wouldn't wash a pair of trousers sent out of prison with blood on them. Neil had also spoken of his belief that Whitehead was withdrawing his privileges as part of his 'war of attrition.'[404]

Although warned not to refer to his own interrogation, Auret validated Neil's report of torture by adding that he had been shocked on his testicles, which had also been crushed, and that he had been throttled to the point where he thought he would die. He was still being victimised by the police; Cronwright had threatened him with jail, banning and house arrest if he gave evidence at the inquest. Despite these threats Auret had come forward, going further, briefly and bravely, to defy Kotzé's restriction.

Time and again in cross-examination, Auret's responses highlighted the callousness of the state's defence of detention. It was strange, said Schabort, that Dr Aggett didn't complain that he had been shocked through the testicles. Auret replied pointedly, 'I don't find anything that a detainee does after a couple of months in solitary confinement strange.'[405] The Minister of Police's counsel remained impervious:

> MR SCHABORT: You told his Worship yesterday that the deceased had told you that he had been shocked on his testicles. That, I suppose, was that the most shocking aspect of his report to you?
>
> MR VAN HEERDEN: Shocking is an unfortunate choice of words, Mr Schabort.[406]

Why, queried Schabort, should Auret and Neil have discussed tactics when interrogation was 'perfectly simple' if the detainee had nothing to hide? Auret was cutting. When one is being strangled to the point of death, 'tactics become a very real issue of survival.'[407] No amount of truthfulness could satisfy an interrogator who had an unshakeable set of assumptions about a detainee. Challenged on his use of the term 'solitary confinement', Auret was similarly concise: 'Mr Schabort, when you are locked in your cell alone for 289 days, I do not know what else you would call it.'[408]

Auret's cross-examination continued into a second day, which also saw

Major Cronwright recalled. Cronwright denied assaulting Sisa Njikelana and, shortly after Neil's death, threatening Auret with dire consequences if he were to speak out. That evening, looking exhausted and tense, Auret gave a press conference at Khotso House, attended mainly by foreign correspondents. Steering clear of his treatment during interrogation, he nevertheless spoke of strange occurrences at his home and some intimidating incidents since his release.

*   *   *

During Auret's testimony, for the first time, no family members were in court. On 22 October, Jill and Aubrey had flown to Washington to receive a George Meany Award, given posthumously to Neil, from the giant American Federation of Labor and Congress of Industrial Organization (AFL-CIO). The other recipient was Chief Mangosuthu Buthelezi, head of the Kwazulu 'home-land' and the Zulu nationalist movement, Inkatha. Also sitting at Table One at the Capital Hilton Hotel, with top officials from the largest federation of un-ions in the USA, were Frederick O'Neal, the first African-American president of the Actors' Equity Association and US statesman Lawrence Eagleburger, then Ronald Reagan's Undersecretary of State for Political Affairs. The cousin whom I have come to imagine would surely have eschewed this acknow-ledgement. Nevertheless, I suspect he would have been touched that his fa-ther chose to accept it. Speaking at the ceremony, 'with what sounded like a catch in his voice', Aubrey stated that it was a great honour to accept the award on behalf of his late son. Here was an opportunity to acknowledge his son the unionist.[409]

It was Jill who made the acceptance speech. Declaring that she had no wish to prejudice the inquest and would therefore not comment on the culpability or otherwise of the security police, Jill was forthright in criticising the apartheid government for its attack on independent trade unions that expressed militant opposition to the government dictating how they should organise themselves:

> One can only condemn in the strongest terms the legislation introduced by the South African Government which allows a handful of security police-men to detain without trial in solitary confinement, and treat in any way they see fit, people whose ideologies conflict with their own.[410]

She included some personal comments about the nightmare for a family, knowing that a loved one was at the mercy of policemen who were accountable to no one: 'There wasn't an hour when I didn't think of him – sitting alone in his grim cell when I enjoyed the freedom of going where and when I wanted in the glorious sunshine.' Neil's death had realised their nightmares, bringing home to them the 'appalling truth of what detention actually means'. In conclusion, she quoted from the Wisdom of Solomon about the fate of 'the poor and honest man ... the just man' whom the powerful tread underfoot and destroy.[411] Jill drew on her biblical understanding to make sense of what had happened to Neil. Had she been addressing Food and Canning union members, these words from Solomon would have resonated with their direct experience of being trampled underfoot and need for spiritual hope. Most likely, they would have followed her address with a song to share the pain: '*Unzima lomthwalo ufuna simanyane ...*' (This burden is heavy, it needs our unity). Instead, Jill's American audience, making their own connections to Neil's story, rose to their feet to give their ovation.

*   *   *

The inquest had begun with medical evidence, in which the experts on each side had agreed that suicide was physically indicated, although this was not entirely conclusive. Presenting similar fact evidence, the family's counsel had argued that if Neil had indeed taken his life, he had been induced to do so. Police testimony about Neil's 'happy relationship' with his interrogators had been strongly contested by former detainees, who offered personal accounts of torture as well as observations of Neil's deterioration in his final week. With all the first-hand testimony completed, the inquest was drawing to a close. However, there remained two final expert witnesses who would be asked to comment on Neil's state of mind: a psychologist for the family and a psychiatrist for the police. With Aubrey and Jill still abroad, Paul had managed to release himself from work so he could accompany Joy for the last few days.

Professor Charles Vorster of the Rand Afrikaans University, a practising clinical psychologist, had been appointed by the family's legal team to compile a psychological report on Neil. He had spoken with family and friends, examined Neil's teenage journal and various letters, as well as his statements made under interrogation. Professor Vorster painted a picture of a well-integrated, independent and idealistic young man, strongly dedicated to improving workers' conditions. Although Neil had become distanced from his parents, especially his father, and was trying to avoid military service, he was free of any serious psychological pathology. Actively involved in pursuing his ideals, his alleged suicide was a contradiction. Cross-examining Vorster, Schabort asserted that Neil had been a 'loner' at university.[412] Didn't this suggest suicidal tendencies? No, said the professor. Could Neil have presented himself as depressed to other detainees while appearing normal to the police? Unlikely, said Professor Vorster.[413]

The final witness was spruce little Professor Jan Adriaan Plomp, who had been sitting among his police clients through much of the proceedings. Plomp was head psychiatrist at Weskoppies Institute, one of South Africa's oldest psychiatric hospitals (originally Pretoria Lunatic Asylum), which was linked to the University of Pretoria. As a psychiatrist, he was a member of the medical profession. Two weeks earlier, Joy had added to her file of news cuttings a report about a small group of doctors who were threatening legal action against the South African Medical and Dental Council. The outspoken doctors attacked the Council over its long-standing failure to investigate properly the conduct of four doctors who had seen Steve Biko before his death. One of the complainants, Professor Frances Ames, warned that 'unless the Biko issue is publicly dealt with, the medical profession in South Africa is doomed to a loss of ethics and morality'.[414] In Neil's case, no doctor had seen him in detention. Medical involvement only came afterwards, and there had been no significant professional disagreement between the medical experts for the family and the police over postmortem findings. The police's Professor Plomp, however, was to present a picture of Neil sharply different from that indicated by Professor Vorster.

Although Plomp had read some of Neil's teenage writing, he had made no attempt to speak to any family or friends, relying instead on information supplied by his clients. Plomp was not afraid to pontificate on Marxism, about which he clearly knew nothing, and drew a link to suicide:

> His [Dr Aggett's] journal shows that he was disillusioned with religion and, in his declaration to the security police, he mentions that he adheres to Marxism, an ideology which excludes religion. It must be mentioned here that loss of religious conviction and religious participation is one of the

aspects of social isolation which is regarded by experts as one of the most significant in suicide.[415]

Neil's social isolation was reinforced for Plomp by 'his connection with the trade union movement which is regarded by many in the Republic of South Africa with political distrust'.[416]

Developing a picture of Neil as someone with a tendency to 'social isolation', the professor cited the rift between Neil and his father. Cross-examining Plomp, Bizos asked why he had not dealt with any of Neil's allegations of being assaulted, deprived of sleep, isolated in solitary confinement and compelled to implicate friends under interrogation. Instead he had focused on Neil's arguments with his father over the length of his beard. Challenged to acknowledge that death may have seemed preferable to Neil than any repetition of what he had already experienced, including electric shocks, the professor had to admit that he couldn't rule this out. If Neil had indeed been kept awake for 62 hours, Plomp found himself obliged to agree with Bizos that a form of psychosis would result.

Plomp and his clients must have felt that the ground had begun to slip. The next day in the witness stand, asserting that it would be wrong to say that assault was the only factor triggering suicide, the professor expounded on theories that shifted culpability away from the police. The court was offered a messianic suicide, in which Neil wanted to be a martyr for a cause, knowing that his death would have wide repercussions. Furthermore, Plomp concurred with Schabort that Neil's handwriting supported police testimony that he was not in a zombie-like state in the week before his death. According to the professor, the detainee was relatively, if not completely, normal.

Plomp also pushed the guilt theory. If Neil had overheard the police sending a telex asking for the arrest of people he had named, as had been testified, this alone would have been sufficient to drive him to suicide. He would have been overcome with guilt and worried how his friends would react to him afterwards. According to Plomp, Neil may have decided to give fellow detainees the impression that he had been badly assaulted and was depressed, while in front of the police he could have continued to act normally.[417] To those who knew Neil, Plomp's characterisation of him as someone capable of acting and deceiving fellow detainees revealed how little the dapper psychiatrist understood him. The security police must have been delighted with their final trump card: a member of the medical profession who was happy to impugn the integrity of Dr Aggett and validate their theories. It was a shameful collaboration.

Although Joy could observe Plomp's body language, she needed Paul to translate his Afrikaans. She had always respected medical people and had taken a quiet pride in both of her sons joining the profession. When she had seen Neil for the last time on New Year's Eve and he had asked for a copy of Bailey's *Emergency Surgery*, she had held out hope that he would return to full-time medicine in due course, after he was free. When Neil had chosen to dedicate himself to union work, Aubrey had railed against his son for throwing away his medical training. Yet here was this psychiatrist, with all his years in the profession, squandering something much more precious as he viewed Neil through the eyes of his captors, incapable of independent judgment. Throughout the angry years of his rift with Neil, Aubrey may have thought his son defiant, foolhardy and naive. But the son who had written, 'I think we must realize that human friendship must stand above any petty differences we have with people', at least remained worthy of respect. Professor Ames's warning on the state of South Africa's medical profession was resonant in Plomp's performance. For Joy, to hear her son diminished to a liar, by someone who had taken the same Hippocratic oath, must have been deeply depressing.

CHAPTER 52

Summing up

T HE MARATHON INQUEST WAS NEARING ITS END, WITH FINAL submissions starting on its 42nd day. It was being reported as the longest and most expensive inquest in South African history. Stretched out over more than nine months, at times the waiting for the family must have seemed interminable. With Jill and Aubrey due to return from the United States at the end of the week, only Joy and Paul were in court on 2 November to hear George Bizos present a meticulously detailed argument that would continue into the following day. His combination of formidable intellect, moral authority, compassion and passion offered a bulwark against the undermining words of the police.

Bizos began by reminding the court of the obligations of police. Whatever their powers under the Terrorism Act, they had a duty to release Dr Aggett in good health, both in body and in mind. They were not entitled to subject him to any form of assault or use 'third degree methods' while attempting to obtain a statement from him.[418] Yet instead of observing their duty of care, they had subjected Dr Aggett to the most extreme and severe physical and mental pressure. Bizos also reminded the court that any person who puts another in a position to commit suicide is guilty of an offence. In this respect, he would argue that both Major Cronwright and Lieutenant Whitehead were guilty of culpable homicide.[419]

His portrait of Neil's character and background was markedly different from that insinuated by the police and the chief psychiatrist of Weskoppies. George Bizos spoke of Neil as a highly intelligent, dedicated person who had foregone the material advantages that he might have enjoyed from a medical career for the sake of working for a trade union. He lived an austere, non-materialistic life, working very hard for the union, with extra work at Baragwanath Hospital and very little time for relaxation. Purposeful and directed, there was no indication that he 'was likely to contemplate taking his own life'.[420]

When it came to Lieutenant Whitehead, Bizos assessed him as 'immature, ambitious, aggressive' and an obsessive interrogator who refused 'to accept answers which didn't conform to his view of the facts'.[421] He had been an uncomfortable, sometimes evasive, witness who 'did not have the stature and composure one would have expected of a lieutenant charged with such an important investigation and interrogation'.[422] Having kept Neil under surveillance for about three years, he 'firmly believed in his own mind that Dr Aggett was involved in illegal activity'.[423] Bizos asked for this to be contrasted with Neil being 'an intelligent, headstrong, determined, principled, idealistic person who was obviously not prepared to be driven to make concessions readily or easily'. Thus the stage was set 'for a classic conflict situation'.[424]

Bizos pointed to the significant omission from Whitehead's detailed affidavit, made soon after Neil's death, of any reference to 'Dr Aggett's alleged momentous disclosures' on the last night of his 62-hour interrogation, for which the police had subsequently claimed privilege and the reason for his suicide.[425] Why would Neil have given this information to Warrant Officer Deetlefs, who had no background in the investigation, and why would he not have written it himself, if he was giving it voluntarily? The alleged disclosures were completely uncorroborated. Neil was alleged to have overheard a telex being composed on the basis of his disclosures, yet the Commissioner of Police had declined to order the arrests of the people he had supposedly named. The police claim of privilege was spurious and should be dismissed, declared Bizos.

A further discrepancy existed between Whitehead's earlier affidavit, in which he had spoken of the decision to interrogate Neil in a 'more intensive manner',[426] and his evidence on the witness stand, in which he and other officers tried to suggest that the 62-hour interrogation had been at

Neil's own request so he could 'clear' or 'open up his heart'. During that period he had been interrogated by no less than eight security policemen, and a ninth black officer had been present for some of the time. Even on the police's own version that Neil could sleep on a camp bed – which was not consistent with Neil's affidavit and not conceded – he had been subjected to exhausting periods of interrogation. Whitehead's affidavit had failed to mention Neil's complaint to the magistrate about being assaulted on 4 January and his own response to the allegation, as well as Neil's later affidavit to Sergeant Blom.

Bizos also reminded Magistrate Kotzé about Whitehead's admission that he was partially responsible for the planned illegal entry to the Aggetts' home, and the attempt to bribe their employee. Whitehead's explanation that he was looking for Gavin Andersson was 'so flimsy that it can be rejected out of hand'.[427] The substantial point was that the lieutenant had been prepared to misuse his position as a police officer, flout the law and commit perjury to conceal the true purpose of the incident.[428]

It was, however, Major Cronwright who had been in overall charge and who had given his approval for the 62-hour interrogation. During the first period of interrogation, he had been regularly advised by Captain Naude, until the investigation had been handed over to the newly promoted lieutenant in early January. Although the major said Dr Aggett's first statement did not contain the truth, he subsequently conceded that he had never read it, merely relying on Whitehead's word. The major had also relied heavily on the 'Close Comrades' document as proof that Dr Aggett formed part of an ANC cell. This was just one of the documents, along with Neil's statements, that the police had tried to withhold from the court. Yet, when it had been made available in September, it showed precisely the contrary. Bizos reminded the court of Major Cronwright's reason why Dr Aggett had not been given the chance to refute this misreading of Barbara Hogan's list: that the police had 'no interest in negative answers'.[429]

The court should also recall the manner in which the major had dealt with Dr Aggett's complaint to the magistrate on 18 January. When the letter had reached him, after taking seven days to travel half a kilometre from the magistrate's office to the major's desk, Cronwright had called in Lieutenant Whitehead and Detective Sergeant van Schalkwyk, who both denied the charge, whereupon the lieutenant was allowed to continue interrogation. Dr

Aggett would be alive if detainees' complaints of ill treatment had not been handled in such a 'flat-footed, lackadaisical manner'.[430]

Bizos went on to comment that the security police under Major Cronwright were, with the possible exception of Captain Naude, a closely-knit group whose loyalty to one another is greater than their respect for the truth. Apart from a frequently 'parrot-like fashion' of delivery,[431] there were a number of vital questions still to be answered on the probabilities. If Dr Aggett was well treated, as they all claimed, why did he complain of being assaulted? If he wasn't assaulted on 25 January, how did Maurice Smithers, Jabu Ngwenya and Auret van Heerden offer corroborating information when they had no opportunity to communicate with each other? Why was Dr Aggett's 'request' to remain on the tenth floor for 62 hours not mentioned in the earlier police affidavits? Why was Dr Aggett not allowed to return to his cell to shower, brush his teeth and change his clothing? Why was he not seen by the magistrate on 1 February? Why was he kept away from the magistrate, the Inspector of Detainees and a doctor for over two weeks after he was injured on 4 January? Why had Major Cronwright appointed an inept young policewoman to investigate Dr Aggett's complaint against officers who were senior to her? Sergeant Blom could not have inspired confidence in the complainant. Why had she immediately made known the contents of Dr Aggett's affidavit of 4 February to Major Cronwright and Lieutenant Whitehead? Even if Dr Aggett had not been threatened with another 'long weekend', he might well have feared such a repeat experience.

Over the course of the day, counsel for the family raised a string of queries, inconsistencies and contradictions that the legal team expected Magistrate Kotzé to address. If the police version of events was conceded, that they had seen no particular cause for alarm and that Dr Aggett was not likely to commit suicide, why did he then take his life? If their belated 'betrayal' explanation was correct, would he have betrayed his friends had he not been deprived of sleep, had he not been assaulted, had he not been shocked? The only explanation could be that he had been pressured unlawfully, until he broke. Why else would he have written in his second statement that he was a communist because he supported 'the Marxist ideology'? It was a most unlikely phrase and not one that he would have used. Why should he have chosen to squeeze in the sentence 'I am also an idealist' other than to negate the preceding sentence? Why was the sentence about being a communist placed as a banner headline in the typed statement? Why did Dr Aggett use the un-English word 'communistic'? There was no shortage of discrepancies and unanswered questions.

Denis Kuny addressed the evidence from detainees, pointing out that many were still in custody and could therefore not communicate with each other and conspire to furnish false evidence. The fact that they each spoke independently testified to their credibility. The apparent contradictions were minor and did not mean that the whole of their evidence on Dr Aggett's deteriorating condition should be rejected. Nor had counsel for the police dealt with the evidence of Prema Naidoo and Shirish Nanabhai,[432] both currently serving sentences. If their evidence of torture and ill treatment was accepted, it meant that the police had lied in their earlier denials, and were therefore probably also lying about Dr Aggett. Nor had the police given an explanation as to why he had committed suicide if he had been as healthy and composed as their witnesses suggested.

Calling for Major Cronwright and Lieutenant Whitehead to be found guilty of culpable homicide, Bizos returned to his premise of the responsibility of the police to maintain their detainees in good health, physical and mental. Yes, the security police had been granted enormous powers but 'we are all subject to the law of the land and its processes which protect the dignity and sanctity of human life'.[433]

Piet Schabort's submission for the police was considerably shorter than that of his opponents. With his main thrust that there was not enough evidence for anyone to be held responsible, he returned to the betrayal theory as the 'trigger' for suicide. Taking the uncorroborated and privileged 'disclosures' as fact, he argued that guilt could have driven Dr Aggett to take his life. Even if allegations of assault were to be proved, said Schabort, there was no proven connection between the alleged assaults and the suicide. Maurice Smithers, he asserted, had fabricated his evidence after Dr Aggett's death in order to cause a sensation. There were contradictions in the evidence of former detainees, which Schabort declared 'is totally irreconcilable with the objective evidence of Professor Jan Plomp'.[434] Thus the useful professor, who had relied heavily on the security police to assess Neil's character, was the provider of 'objective evidence'.

Neil's complaint to Sergeant Blom was discredited by Schabort because his account of torture did not tally in all details with the statement from Auret van Heerden. Either there was no assault, or Dr Aggett was lying in his statement of complaint, or he lied to Van Heerden, or Van Heerden lied to the court.[435] Here was the rub: 'lying ... lied ... lied'. With no reference to the disorienting effects of solitary confinement, the only explanation was that one or other detainee was lying. Neil had written the words 'I am a communist', which the police had ensured were circulated widely. To most white South Africans, communists would do anything to promote their cause, including lying. Schabort ended by calling on the magistrate to reject the 'fabricated and partisan' evidence of the detainees.[436]

So the police case was simple. Having been found out and having given names, the detainee had taken his life rather than face his friends. So, he was a liar ... and a coward. Moreover, according to Professor Plomp, his death could be seen as a final act calculated to damage the police by prompting an investigation into detention. In other words, Dr Aggett was also a betrayer of the state.

This kind of misrepresentation by counsel for the police came as no surprise to Neil's comrades and friends. Telling a reporter why she had sat through all 42 days of the inquest, Liz Floyd explained how it felt like an extension of the process of interrogation: 'It was as if Neil was virtually on trial and I had to play a role in that ... In a sense the inquest was a prolongation of detention; going into the witness box I could not get it out of my head that it was like interrogation.'[437]

Liz knew what to expect in the inquest and had steeled herself – a considerable feat. After two months in a psychiatric ward, she had been released with a diagnosis of 'post-traumatic stress syndrome'. Whenever the inquest was in session, she told the reporter, her symptoms manifested themselves again and got worse. Her memory would go. She couldn't remember places or people's names. She couldn't sleep. She would become tense and withdrawn. It was like being back inside John Vorster Square. Each detainee who had given evidence, submitting to being interrogated under cross-examination, had to grapple with demons. Liz spoke of her life coming under the microscope of four different groups of investigators: security police, psychologists, lawyers and the press. In the end, she said, you even start questioning yourself.

Joy, like Jill, probably managed to hold herself together during the inquest through a form of emotional cautery. But to hear her son's character maligned must have sorely chafed at the wound. Jill, who had returned with Aubrey from the United States on the final day of the inquest, had read the summings-up in a newspaper in New York. From the start, their lawyers had tried to prepare them not to have unrealistic expectations of 'openness and fairness'. Jill recalled their initial puzzlement when William Lane had told them to put any documents that they received from him under lock and key. The break-in at her parents' home had brought home 'how low' the police would go.

Nevertheless, the family was still heartened by what their lawyers had so skilfully managed to put into the public domain. Nearly thirty years later, Jill still recalls the thrust of fear and hope in their expectations: 'I think we knew in our heart of hearts what the outcome would be, but always had the hope that the magistrate would in some way criticise the police if not actually accuse them of murder.' They could not give up on receiving a modicum of justice.

CHAPTER 53

'No one to blame'

O N 20 DECEMBER, A CROWD BEGAN FILLING THE CORRIDOR
outside Courtroom 18, two hours before Magistrate Kotzé was due
to begin his summary of the evidence. Press and TV reporters, local
and overseas, formed about a third of the hundred or more people. Rivalling
the media, the security police arrived in force with their lawyers and a con-
tingent of uniformed officers. No doubt Cronwright, in his shiny Kelly-green
suit, and his men had come to see the former eastern Cape prosecutor do his
duty and prove that he remained on side. Uniformed police lined the pas-
sageway, with a couple at the doors, screening entrants with a metal detector.
Arriving just before 11am, the start of proceedings, Joy and Aubrey found
themselves mobbed by reporters, as did Liz. It was the middle of the summer school holidays, and the Burgers had taken their children away for a
complete break. Helen Suzman, who had read out Maurice Smithers' note in
Parliament, came to offer support and hear the verdict, while Jan Theron had
travelled from Cape Town to represent the union. Not everyone could fit into
the crammed gallery, and there were reports of altercations as people were
turned away.

The three-minute verdict in the Biko inquest had provoked international
outrage, and Magistrate Kotzé was not going to fall into the same hole. His

summary and evaluation of the evidence, taking almost five hours on the first day, required a late sitting and an extension into the next day. He and his assessor, Professor LS Smith, had concurred that there was no dispute over the medical evidence relating to death by suicidal hanging. However, the finding on the cause of death was a matter of law and his sole decision. There were two conflicting versions, one containing assault and extreme ill treatment and the other of ordinary, normal interrogation of a detainee, with unforeseen consequences. It was soon obvious which narrative Kotzé favoured as he read all 187 pages of his judgment.

He began with evidence from the police, clearly impressed by the degree of corroboration. (What Kotzé so readily regarded as a sign of reliability would be revealed for what it was a decade later when the truth emerged about the bugging of George Bizos's chambers.) While announcing that he intended to treat the evidence of Major Cronwright and Lieutenant Whitehead 'with caution', he felt that the two of them had withstood a 'long, thorough and merciless' cross-examination by counsel for the family.[438] In this telling phrase, Kotzé revealed that he was not without the ability to empathise. But it was the security police, subjected to Bizos's 'merciless' grilling, who needed his protection, rather than any political detainee. Instead of scrutinising a 'pattern of behaviour' by the police, as well as the uncanny similarity in so many of their statements, Kotzé instinctively felt that the detainees were ganging up on the police.

Almost every detainee called by the Aggett lawyers was marked down as unreliable. According to Kotzé, their observations of Dr Aggett were 'so contradictory in detail and so contradicted by reliable evidence that they could not be accepted as the truth on a balance of probabilities'.[439] Similar fact evidence of torture from Prema Naidoo and Shirish Nanabhai was dismissed as coming from two aggrieved political prisoners who had been convicted of helping another political prisoner escape. Nor had they complained to the Inspector of Detainees at the time. Kotzé's imagination did not, or would not, extend to accepting that a detainee who had been tortured might not complain while still in their interrogator's clutches. He rejected outright the idea that the marks on Nanabhai's arm could have been made by a small electrode, similar to that produced in court by George Bizos, despite the district surgeon's confirmation that this was possible. The district surgeon had noted four marks, while Nanabhai mentioned two. Kotzé even mused that Nanabhai may have made the marks himself to discredit a possible confession.

Nor did the magistrate's imagination extend to the effects of solitary confinement on memory. Rejecting the evidence of one detainee after another who had seen Neil after the long weekend, Kotzé revealed his narrowness of vision, as well as some bizarre prejudices. Thabo Lerumo had 'frequently rubbed his chin, mouth slightly opened when he listened to questions. He looked hither and thither for no reason.' He was adamant he saw Dr Aggett in the cells during November, which was obviously wrong.[440] Sisa Njikelana's account of assault was dismissed because he had not complained to the Inspector of Detainees. Keith Coleman had 'something to say about a torn shirt' belonging to Dr Aggett, but he was uncertain about details: 'More than once Mr Coleman blamed the effects of solitary confinement for his inability to explain certain situations. Yet certain things he does remember clearly, somewhat selective indeed.'[441] Jabu Ngwenya was 'deliberately vague when questioned about details', answering 'with a degree of arrogance'.[442] Here was a black man who didn't know his place.

One by one, Kotzé scraped away at the detainees' testimonies. Liz Floyd was dismissed as unreliable because of a variation of 15 minutes in the amount of time she had been made to stand, according to her affidavit and her oral testimony. With Maurice Smithers, Kotzé picked on the fact that he had sworn his written affidavit with the prescribed oath, 'So help me God', but, in court, had said that he was only prepared to affirm the truth because he was not a believer. This discredited him in Kotzé's book. In addition, Maurice had signed himself as 'Morice' in the note smuggled out of prison. Moreover, he had written that he had seen Neil hit with what could have been a rolled-up newspaper, but, in giving evidence, he said that it had appeared to be a newspaper but he could not be absolutely sure. Kotzé turned Maurice's honesty on its head. He was incapable of imagining a situation in which a detainee felt so impelled to smuggle out an urgent note that he would risk being caught and seriously punished.

One detainee would fare even worse than the others in Kotzé's judgment. At first, it seemed that Auret van Heerden would be just one more untrustworthy detainee. Kotzé compared Neil's complaint to Magistrate Wessels of the assault on 4 January with Auret's recollection of what Neil had told him during snatched conversations across the prison corridor. The 'discrepancies', which he regarded as 'conspicuous', appeared to be differing amounts of detail and a slight variation in the naming of the policeman who had beaten up Neil in Whitehead's presence. Neil had reported 'a Sergeant of the Railway Police. His first name is Schalk', whereas Auret remembered Neil speaking of 'a Railway policeman who had been seconded to this investigation by the name of Van Schalkwyk'.[443] Auret had added that he was not sure of the policeman's rank. Under cross-examination, Van Schalkwyk had acknowledged that Neil used to address him as 'Schalk', but Kotzé chose to ignore this corroboration. When it came to detainees, his mindset was one of disbelief, and he intended to return to Auret.

Kotzé did accept that it was problematic for Magistrate Wessels' letter to have taken a week to travel barely a kilometre to Cronwright's desk. However, he immediately muted any criticism so that it was not even a tap on the wrist. More than once, he resorted to saying, 'It is a fact of life that we find degrees of experience and zeal in every profession.'[444] Thus Warrant Officer MacPherson's behaviour in keeping the Inspector of Detainees away from Neil was nothing more than carelessness, yet another fact of life. He pulled out the same homily in relation to the string of policemen who assisted Whitehead over the final long weekend, and who were regarded by the Aggett lawyers as the 'night nurses'. With little or no knowledge of trade unions, they were in no position to interrogate Neil. Kotzé dismissed the family's concerns that their function was to intimidate and keep him awake, intoning, 'We have no reliable facts to substantiate this allegation.'[445]

Nor did Kotzé pay attention to the significant discrepancy between Whitehead's affidavit, in which he had stated that 'intensive interrogation' was needed to fill in gaps in Neil's statement, and his testimony in court, where he claimed that the long weekend had been at Neil's own request. Kotzé was happy to accept the police at their word that Neil had made 'revelations' to the uninformed Deetlefs. He raised no questions about the convenient claim of 'privilege'.

Dismissing the evidence of every witness who testified to Neil's pitiable physical and mental state after the long weekend, Kotzé accepted every police assertion that he was in good health. When it came to the contents of Neil's affidavit to Sergeant Blom, with its references to assault and torture, Kotzé was happy to accept that the police did not know Neil was suicidal, while rejecting all the evidence from detainees, with the exception of some segments of Auret van Heerden's testimony. If Auret had known that Neil was suicidal, why had he not informed the authorities and raised the alarm? Kotzé's answer to this was murky speculation about Auret and Neil being in the underground ANC, implying that Auret, as Neil's senior, might have wanted him out of the way so that he could not give any more information.[446]

To explain the suicide, Kotzé adopted the 'betrayed comrades' theory of Professor Plomp, never questioning why the psychiatrist had not even bothered to speak to the family and friends of a subject he had never met. The magistrate, who had shown himself incapable of imagining even the most basic conditions of life for a detainee, offered a potted psychological theory of what had gone on inside Neil's head as a man 'devoted to a cause' who had disclosed 'particulars of his activities' with names:

> These disclosures must have brought about a feeling of uncertainty about his future and the realization that steps could be taken against his associates. The possibility of a sense of guilt towards his associates, a sense of betrayal of his friends and associates, is large. He had to face some of his associates and to admit the disclosures, an anticipation or feeling of rejection by them cannot be excluded. Unfortunately, it was during this crucial period that he had to be informed *inter alia* that a friend could not afford to provide him with a portable radio in the cell.[447]

Returning his verdict of suicidal hanging, Magistrate Kotzé ruled that death was not brought about by any act or omission on the part of the police.

For the Aggett lawyers, it was a classic judgment based on 'revelations' cloaked under a never-to-be-revealed 'certificate of privilege'. The magistrate had addressed none of the vital questions on the probabilities that they had posed, and the suggestion that Neil's fellow detainee, Auret van Heerden, could be held morally responsible was outrageous. In George Bizos's words, 'It was an unbelievable judgement.'[448]

CHAPTER 54

The unanswered question

OR NEIL'S PARENTS, SITTING IN SILENCE, THIS WAS A CONCLUSION they had not wanted to contemplate. Within minutes, confronted by the press and holding back tears, Aubrey rejected the magistrate's findings: 'They are beyond my understanding. I am only a farmer but I cannot accept the verdict.' Joy limited herself to saying that while she had held out little hope, she hadn't expected it to be this bad.[449] To another reporter, Aubrey railed at the unfettered power of a state that could declare key documents secret. The magistrate had criticised their witnesses for being inconsistent and not knowing exact hours and dates. Yet people in detention didn't have diaries, calendars or even pencils to make notes. In fact, if the reporter were to ask him the date right now, he would not be able to give it.[450]

Photographs capture their stoic, inward-drawn faces. The prolonged inquest had absorbed much of their life savings, but any hope that it might lay some ghosts to rest had collapsed.

Years later, I can still hear the frustrated resignation in Aubrey's voice:

> Beverley, you must realise I am prejudiced although I try to be as objective as possible. The chap who really annoys me is the magistrate … Whatever the evidence, the verdict would have been the same.

With his son's death, he had travelled an arduous, anguished road that had taken him to a very different place from his starting point. What would it take to jolt open the eyes and ears of a man like Magistrate Kotzé? What if a son or daughter had made choices like Neil's, with similar tragic consequences? Would this magistrate have had the courage to remove his blinkers and make the kind of journey that Aubrey had undertaken?

Neil's dominant, difficult father, once actively involved in suppressing an anti-colonial rebellion in Kenya, had made a personal journey that had challenged him to his core. He had also assisted in enabling a light to be shone on the savage abuse of political detainees who challenged apartheid. Despite Aubrey's instinct that his son had been tortured to death, by agreeing that his lawyers make the argument for 'induced suicide' he had funded a unique confrontation between Neil's fellow detainees and the security police, inside a court of law. The information given under oath by the detainees had now entered the public domain, circumventing the Police Act's prohibition on publishing anything about the hidden world inside prisons and police stations. Neil would surely have admired both his parents for their courage in looking beyond their own loss to pursue the cause of justice with the slenderest of hope.

While Joy and Aubrey began their lonely return home to Somerset West, Liz made her way with Jan Theron and others to the Food and Canning office for a joint union and DPSC press conference. Foreign and local reporters crowded into the cramped, sparsely furnished room that Neil had helped turn into an effective office for its worker members. A photograph catches Liz in mid-speech, strands of long blonde hair falling across gaunt cheeks, unspoken pain reflected in both her face and that of Israel Mogoatlhe, chairman of the branch, as he leans forward intently to listen. The mood of the meeting was angry, determined. Whatever the verdict, Liz asserted, not everyone would believe it: 'I believe Neil was tortured. He saw no relief from those conditions and expected the pressure to increase. He got to the stage where he was totally desperate and suicide was the only way out.'[451] Liz proceeded to ask the critical question that remained unanswered because the magistrate in South Africa's longest, costliest inquest had not put his mind to its simple logic. If the security police had dealt with Neil in the way they say they did, then why was he dead? Moreover, Liz added, why have over 50 other people died in detention?

Jan Theron expressed 'total outrage' on behalf of the union. The findings opened the way for the security police to continue acting against trade unionists with impunity. What happened to Neil would happen to others. His view would be echoed by others as the day wore on. Leaders of other unions, including FOSATU, civic organisations, politicians and churches joined in condemnation not just of the verdict but of detention without trial that left detainees at the mercy of their interrogators. Bishop Tutu commented that this was even a worse shock than the Biko verdict because of the attempts to justify the death. It was, he said, 'unbelievable'.[452] Dr Nthato Motlana, chairman of the Soweto Committee of Ten, responded in similar vein:

> It painfully reminds one of the infamous Biko case where something similar has been said. It is inconceivable that nobody is being held responsible. I will join others all over the world who will reject the finding completely.[453]

At home and abroad, parallels were drawn with the Biko inquest. While the US State Department would only gingerly comment that 'all detainees be treated humanely wherever they are held', Thomas Downey, Democratic Representative for New York and chairman of the ad hoc Congressional Monitoring Group on South Africa let rip against a decision that cleared the security police and placed 'moral blame' on Auret van Heerden. It was 'nothing short of obscene': 'After the travesty of the Biko case, I thought the South African Government would take this matter more seriously … Apparently I was wrong.'[454] In London, the head of Amnesty International's medical group, Elizabeth Gordon, commented that the verdict was not a surprise. Whether or not Neil Aggett committed suicide was irrelevant. What mattered was that he was a man 'broken by the treatment a political detainee receives in South Africa'.[455]

Both during and after the inquest, Liz Floyd's press interviews revealed her dignity in handling her own trauma. As she would suggest in testimony more than 15 years later to the Truth and Reconciliation Commission, this required the silencing of emotion. Despite the personal difficulties she and Neil had experienced, and that Whitehead had tried to exploit, she had allowed none of this to emerge. That she recovered from psychological free fall following Neil's death showed tremendous inner strength. She continued to work with the DPSC, placing her personal experience of disintegration into the context of detention, and using her medical expertise to focus on the mental health of detainees.

Nevertheless, in conversation in 1995, I felt an underlying anger in Liz that went beyond the regime and its henchmen who had driven Neil to take his life. There was also frustration with the liberation movement's idealisation of the 'martyr figure' who completely sublimates their own personal needs to the dictates of the cause. This tendency caused activists to disregard what might otherwise be picked up as signs of stress. She saw herself as now 'much better educated':

> It fits in with the hero approach. One of the things that Neil is recognised for, as a hero, is someone who put his work infinitely ahead of his own needs and that is heroised. That's also dangerous, but he was also a candidate for that kind of extreme … it's almost sort of martyrdom and people don't consciously do it. It's out of control. So that's why I'm saying there was quite a self-destructive component in it. Obviously there are a lot of political people who do it. While other people see this martyr figure as this tremendous value, for me it was destroying somebody, and having somebody destroyed like that to me is no credit to a movement … with people like Barbara Hogan becoming this hero because she was sent to jail for so many years, I just think it's an incredible waste, and I think that people who say this is heroism, it's just a lot of nonsense, and to have Botswana people putting people in that vulnerable position, it's just – it's nonsense.

Liz's critique was of a political culture that rapidly turned people into heroes while avoiding self-examination. Barbara Hogan's breaches of security, with their tragic consequences, were part of a larger problem in underground communications linking internal activists to the ANC in Botswana. The fact that such links had been known, or suspected, by a much wider circle of activists than ANC operatives was itself indicative of lack of rigour. With her brutal ten-year jail sentence, Barbara became a hero for the movement, but to Liz it was all part of 'an incredible waste'.

In an environment with a heady mix of political activists – unionists, students, lecturers, community workers and others – where discussion raged about strategies and tactics, it could never be easy maintaining clear boundaries between above-ground and underground work. But the laxity of which

Liz and others spoke, in general terms and from an above-ground perspective, was echoed in Gavin's detailed account of the Woodworkers' security concerns about Craig Williamson. Despite the misgivings of these internal political activists being communicated through ANC channels, they had been overruled by Williamson's powerful supporters in the external leadership, until he was finally outed at the end of 1979. Despite their errors, the reports of the spy Karl Edwards reveal just how porous ANC underground communication was already at the time when Barbara undertook her role.

With the burden of guilt that Barbara carried for 'Close Comrades', she was probably too honourable to accept the 'hero' accolade.[456] But a friend like Liz was entitled to be furious about the waste of human life and to raise probing questions about the movement's use of people who were extremely well-intentioned yet naive; who 'felt the pressure to produce, show the relevance of the white left' but who were so poorly trained. While training people inside the country presented particular challenges, what explained the lack of training and the negligent security in a designated ANC forward area outside the country?

Liz expressed none of this to reporters who quizzed her after the inquest verdict. She spoke of a 'terrible year' and, no, the inquest had not helped erase any of the pain. It had made it worse. 'It will take a very long time to get over Neil', she told a reporter from *The Star* after the press conference, before returning the interview's focus from the personal to the political: 'They will not get rid of the problem just because they have done away with Neil.'[457] As well as the obvious desire for privacy, talking about the political was more controllable than opening the lid on her emotions. Throughout my own interviews with Liz, I recognised how much more at ease she was with analysis and critical comment than personal narrative. The contradiction was that much of her insightful analysis related to the suppression of the personal through commitment to a collective struggle.

While Liz committed herself to working with the DPSC, Gavin experienced a different kind of loneliness in exile in Botswana. He found a job as production manager at Camphill Community Rankoromane in the furniture workshop. At the time of the inquest, he was still finding his feet in the factory and in the village, and, as he put it in April 2011, in a deeply reflective email, 'learning to work within the exile structures of the ANC'. At least half of his attention had been back in South Africa. David Dison visited a few times, bringing updates or because the lawyers felt he could help them understand something. David would come with stories of minor harassment at the border, on one occasion having been taken to the security police in Zeerust. They wanted him to convey a message: tell Gavin that he needn't worry. He can come back and there'll be no problem ...

Angered by Whitehead's testimony in October, Gavin had immediately written a letter to the *Rand Daily Mail* that would only be published after the verdict, for legal fears of contempt. In his letter, he rejected Whitehead's peddling of the absurd tale that the raid on the Aggett family home was because the security police believed he was hiding there. Whitehead and his superiors knew very well that he had left South Africa 'perfectly legally, legitimately and openly'. Gavin ended his letter by exhorting readers to look to the future:

> Please allow me to make two final observations.
>
> Firstly, the 'reality' manufactured in the interrogation chambers (turned from true stock on a lathe that is twisted) can in no way impede the struggle for a new, democratic South Africa.
>
> Secondly, whatever it was that inspired Lieut Whitehead's vision as he stared at the coat of arms in the inquest court, this had nothing at all to do with the qualities of honesty and integrity, much less the service of humanity.[458]

Both in spirit and in his use of metaphor, here was a Woodworker speaking.

Yet while Gavin was outwardly functioning, and establishing himself in Botswana, the following description, in his April 2011 email, vividly reveals his inner torment:

> It was a horrible time, the time of my greatest pain and guilt at having drawn Neil closer to the struggle and to the Movement than he might otherwise have gone. Guilt that he was dead instead of me i suppose. A time when each day we heard another little part of the story that enabled us to piece together the picture of the torment of his last days. A time of extreme loneliness for me, with all whom i had come to love and all my real comrades back in SA. A time of puzzlement at the poor security amongst the ANC exile structures, and the out-of-touchness of some of the cadres. A time of great tension as i worked through the rumours that Auret was a spy, and

heard the various theories about what would happen to Barbara and others, and was sent letters with snippets that people had gleaned from visits to the detainees. A time of vigilance as i waited to see if any of our movement organization within the unions had been compromised (and it turned out that it had not, and was to remain intact right through until 1990!)

It wasn't a time where there was much sleep. Jumpiness and paranoia constant companions, night times devoted to going over the events of the last years and the detention again and again.

Time and again, Gavin must have replayed his conversation with Neil and Sipho about whether he should accept going 'under discipline' and direct underground linkage with the ANC. He would have recalled Neil's concerns about direct accountability to the workers of his union and Neil's reservations about a struggle directed from outside. He and Sipho had talked Neil round to their view that the time was right to bring internal and external organisation together. Only he, Gavin, would formally link ... But the bond of brothers who shared their commitment to the struggle remained strong. So did their manner of working through collaborative, critical discussion. Whatever care had been taken, Neil knew too much.

CHAPTER 55

Truth and Reconciliation?

F OR GEORGE BIZOS, A SENSE OF OUTRAGE AT THE INJUSTICE WAS
not something that could be turned off when the case was over. Indeed,
for all the Aggett lawyers the verdict must have affected them more
than if they had simply lost a well-reasoned argument. Attorneys and counsel
prepared to take on cases involving the security police had to be passionate
about justice and have the courage to become potential targets themselves.
They were rare.

Interviewing George Bizos almost thirty years later in Oxford, where he
came to give the 2011 Bram Fischer Memorial Lecture, I was touched by the
intensity of his emotion as well as the clarity of his recollection. Holding back
tears, he referred me to the dedication in his 1998 book *No One To Blame?*,
about some of the political inquests in which he had been involved as counsel,
including Neil's:

> You know my dedication is 'for all those for whom justice was not only
> blind but was deaf and dumb'. That's really what it was. That's really what
> it was.

Although the Aggett legal team could regard Neil's inquest as 'a victory of sorts' for what it exposed, it may well have hastened the rise of the state's death squads.[459] To Liz Floyd, the 1981 arrests and the subsequent events were 'ideologically ... a complete watershed'. The state had been out to create a mass treason trial, but, apart from sending Barbara Hogan to prison for ten years, the project 'blew up in their faces'. The security police had been used to intimidating black detainee families away from the glare of publicity. But these arrests stirred up white middle-class parents who, because of their children, became actively involved with a growing labour movement and a human rights movement with access to media inside and outside the country, as well as an international anti-apartheid movement. To Liz, the detainee support movement took them 'right through to '91 and ... internationally it is an absolutely remarkable experience. It compares with Chile and the Philippines.'

However, never again would the security forces find themselves faced with another Aggett-style inquest. As resistance to apartheid intensified, increasing numbers of activists were simply 'eliminated'. Without formal arrest, there was no documentation. Political assassinations in which bodies were disposed of – burnt or hacked beyond recognition, buried in the remote veld or dumped in the sea – replaced expensive inquests and the façade of accountability to a court of justice.

Neil's death was one of many, each with its own horrific story, reflecting the gross violations of human rights that were common currency under apartheid. The release of Nelson Mandela in February 1990, eight years after Neil's death, set in motion the turbulent negotiations for an interim constitution for a democratic country. It was impossible to move forward without tackling the question of past human rights violations and the fractious question of amnesty. Without the possibility of amnesty for agents of the apartheid state, the ANC would not have obtained a political settlement with the old regime. Avoiding civil war demanded a compromise on justice. Under the heading 'National Unity and Reconciliation', the 1993 Interim Constitution concluded with an exhortation:

> ... there is a need for understanding but not for vengeance, a need for reparation but not for retaliation, a need for ubuntu but not for victimization.
>
> In order to advance such reconciliation and reconstruction, amnesty shall be granted in respect of acts, and committed in the course of the conflicts of the past ...

> With this Constitution and these commitments we, the people of South
> Africa, open a new chapter in the history of our country.[460]

Yet gaining support within the ANC for an even-handed truth commission
was no easy matter. At a heated meeting of the National Executive Committee
in 1993, not everyone supported the principle of impartiality.[461] It was hard
to swallow that the brutal aggressor state should now be the beneficiary of
such an equitable approach. There was also a further concern. Abuses in ANC
training camps in Angola had been revealed by the ANC's own internal commissions.[462] Some of those present appeared to justify these, arguing that the
liberation struggle had been conducted against a ruthless, powerful enemy
that would stop at nothing to infiltrate and destroy the ANC from within.

Pallo Jordan summed up the dilemma. 'Comrades,' he said, 'I've learned
something very interesting today. There is such a thing as regime torture, and
there is ANC torture, and regime torture is bad and ANC torture is good; thank
you for enlightening me!'[463] It was left to Kader Asmal, the lawyer who had
led the Irish Anti-Apartheid Movement, to articulate the politically awkward,
but morally sound, principle that human rights were human rights, belonging to all human beings. Any torture or violation, committed by whichever
party, had to be investigated even-handedly, on a national basis. The moral
argument won the day, giving impetus to the establishment of the Truth and
Reconciliation Commission (TRC).

Soon after the ANC's 1994 accession to power in the Government of National
Unity, the new Minister of Justice, Dullah Omar, once a security police victim himself, called on the Legal Resources Centre's Senior Counsel, George
Bizos, and Counsel Mohamed Navsa (who had been Denis Kuny's pupil at
the Aggett inquest), to assist in drafting amnesty legislation that would take
account of the feelings and rights of victims. There were many fears and questions to address from members of Parliament's cross-party Justice Committee.
Reassurance was needed about the stated impartiality. Applicants for amnesty
would be required to tell the complete truth about their own roles and the
roles of others, especially about those who had given orders for a crime to be
committed. Applicants had to show that they had acted in good faith, on the
bidding of a known political organisation, not for monetary gain, and that
they had not used excessive means for their ends. The aim was to expose the
truth and have perpetrators at least acknowledge their crimes. Archbishop

Desmond Tutu, the TRC's chairperson, summed up the fine line in a letter to the *Sunday Times*: 'The commission remains a risky and delicate business, but it is still the only alternative to Nuremberg on the one hand and amnesia on the other.'[464]

Some families, including Steve Biko's, could not bring themselves to accept the possibility of amnesty for the murderers of their loved ones. However, they were unsuccessful in their application to the Constitutional Court for the TRC amnesty hearings to be declared unconstitutional. Justice Ismail Mahomed spoke of a complicated, painful balance between the need for national reconciliation affecting future generations and the right to justice for victims of past abuse. The future had to take precedence.

The Aggetts were among the thousands who applied to the Commission to seek out the truth. In a fax from England, where the Burgers emigrated after the inquest, Jill wrote to the TRC's Cape Town office on 16 April 1996 on behalf of her parents. The previous day, the first two hours of the opening hearing in East London had been televised and broadcast live. Now in their eighties and in poor health, Joy and Aubrey immediately wanted to see what could be done in relation to Neil. Referring in her fax to her brother having been 'murdered by the South African Security Police', Jill explained that, for her parents, 'who never cease to mourn him', there was a need 'to get to the real truth'. They had heard Paul Erasmus on the radio referring to Cronwright as 'a monster' who demanded that the interrogators 'break Aggett by tomorrow night':

> During the inquest into Neil's death we heard some very distressing evidence given by fellow detainees of Neil's treatment and condition while he was in John Vorster Square. We feel that at last we might be able to get a full and true account of the days and hours that preceded his death and who was responsible for taking such a valuable life. We have full details of the people involved in Neil's interrogation – Stephen Whitehead was his chief interrogator – and we are hopeful that all these people are called to give a 'true' account of what happened. Am I correct in assuming that if they are not prepared to appear before the Truth Commission and if there is sufficient evidence from other parties, that they may be prosecuted? [465]

Jill added that they 'would also like to know what has happened to the chief

TRUTH AND RECONCILIATION?   417

perpetrators of his tortuous death' and that despite her parents' ill health, they were willing to help with information.

The letter expressed the unresolved nightmare for families of security police victims. With a loved one destroyed, the perpetrators of the crime continued to dominate constantly reimagined scenes. The perpetrators remained powerful, and beyond reach. Beneath Jill's carefully restrained phrasing, there is the desperate desire to see 'all these people ... called to give a "true" account' in the hope that the truth might bring some relief. But it is her question about potential prosecution of those perpetrators not willing to appear before the TRC that indicates how families of victims hoped that the new state would take action to bring non-compliant perpetrators to book.

Within two days of Jill's fax, Joy and Aubrey received a reply from TRC Commissioner Dr Wendy Orr, Regional Convenor for the Western Cape, inviting either one or both of them to make a formal statement to the Commission.[466] They could either go to the TRC office in Cape Town or a 'statement taker' would come to see them. Dr Orr also answered Jill's question about potential criminal prosecution:

> Perpetrators have until 15/12/96 to apply for amnesty, a condition of which is full disclosure. If they do not do so by this date and our investigations produce evidence of involvement in a gross human rights violation, they will be subject to criminal prosecution.[467]

The Promotion of National Unity and Reconciliation Act, the legislative basis for the TRC, provided both a carrot and a stick to encourage perpetrators to come clean.

The Aggetts lost no time. Michael, who had settled in Somerset West with his wife Mavis and five boys, took his parents to make a statement at the Cape Town office. The Commission's two-year time frame was exceptionally tight. With many thousands of statements, it was possible to listen to less than a fifth in person. Over a period of 14 months, commissioners travelled the length and breadth of the country, from large urban centres to remote rural towns, to conduct hearings into human rights violations. Everywhere they went, the blue-and-white banner of the Commission was hung behind a table for the chairperson and his small band. With 21 commissioners, they were at least able to take turns in listening to the accumulation of harrowing evidence. Not so for chairperson Archbishop Tutu and his deputy, Dr Alex Boraine, who week after week were present at most hearings.

In front of the Commission table, set at the same level, was a table for witnesses, some of whom were accompanied by professional comforters. On one side were three or four cubicles for translators, so witnesses could speak in their language of choice. A continuous live radio broadcast was funded by the Norwegian government, and a weekly Sunday television round-up of the hearings and findings was presented by Max du Preez, the founding editor of the anti-apartheid, Afrikaans-language newspaper, *Vrye Weekblad*. Joy and Aubrey may well have been startled to catch a glimpse of Neil's body hanging from the bars of his cell in the collage of images introducing the early programmes of the weekly round-up.

After its dramatic opening hearings in East London, the Commission moved on to Cape Town, and by its third week was listening to testimony in the cavernous, five-storey Central Methodist Church in downtown Johannesburg. In the week beginning Monday 29 April 1996, there were accounts of assassinations; the young wife and elderly mother told of the death of the recently qualified young lawyer Bheki Mlangeni, … 'pieces of him and brains of Bheki were scattered all around', blown up by a bomb in a tape recorder. There was testimony about David Webster, once active on Neil's funeral committee, who was gunned down outside his home as he and his partner returned with their dogs from a run. There was the father of eight-year-old Cornio Smit, an Afrikaner boy killed by an ANC bomb at a shopping centre in Amanzimtoti, talking about how he had identified his child in the mortuary by looking for a little cut under his chin, and telling the Commissioners that many white people, including his family and friends, could not understand why he had told a journalist that his son was 'a hero' because 'he died in the cause of the oppressed people'. The death of his child had transformed his way of seeing. To reconcile himself with the horror, he had placed himself in 'the other person's shoes' without any rights, 'so I realised how it must have felt for them'.[468]

That week, the commissioners on the Human Rights Violations Committee in Gauteng and the audience listened to three tales of deaths in detention, across three decades, in Johannesburg's police headquarters. When Babla Saloojee had hurtled to his death in 1964, it had been from a seventh-floor window of The Grays, the precursor to John Vorster Square. His chief interrogator had been the same 'Rooi Rus' Swanepoel who ordered Neil's body to be cut down. Babla's widow Rokaya told of an inquest lasting five minutes: 'When I said I would like to say something, I'd like to know why was there blood on my husband's clothing, the magistrate said "That will be all".'[469] To the frail mother of Ahmed Timol, her son's death in 1971 had never left her: 'I want to know who assaulted him … It took me quite a bit of difficulty to raise my children. It is twenty-five years now and I will not forget what happened …'[470]

The third case was that of Neil. On Thursday 2 May, with George Bizos and the Premier of Gauteng Province, Tokyo Sexwale, in the audience, as well as embassy officials from Norway, Sweden and the Netherlands, Liz Floyd used her half hour on the witness stand to speak not only about what happened to Neil in 1982, but to castigate the whole system of detention without trial. Her focus was on the serious personal damage and psychological disintegration caused by the combination of solitary confinement and torture such as electric shock: 'We know that sleep deprivation completely disorganizes people.' She spoke of 'a culture of silence'. There was secrecy about activity and there were issues about which people found it hard to talk. Many detainees would simply say that it was 'part of the struggle':

> The legislation didn't allow it, the press weren't allowed to publish things, but in addition to that, I think a lot of us took these things as part of the struggle and felt we must take it upon our shoulders … Part of the struggle was to destroy you – and admitting that the struggle had damaged you or admitting that the security police had got the better of you – so one tends not to talk about those problems.[471]

Asked to comment on Neil himself, Liz spoke of the particular pressures he had been under in the months before his arrest, the intensity of his union work, as well as the fact that he was avoiding his army call-up. Although there was scepticism about police claims of suicides in detention, in Neil's case she didn't rule it out, but it was 'a technicality'. If he hadn't been detained, he wouldn't have died: 'I think that the experience with Neil really taught the public that the psychological effects of torture are very, very significant.'

Turning her focus to the interrogators, Liz thought it possible that some might even come forward to the TRC. Others, however, were unreachable and beyond rehabilitation. These were 'people who in general society would be regarded as psychopaths, who are professional interrogators ... and I think society needs protection from them'. They haven't disappeared, she said. Some had gone into other jobs, while there were 'some other dirty units in the police that collect them'. Liz proceeded to name Whitehead as head of the interrogation team and Cronwright as his superior. It was clear that she placed both of them in the category from which society needed protection. Neither had applied for amnesty.

A further concern for Liz was the need to educate South Africans about what had happened through the 1980s, when 'thousands upon thousands' of people had been detained. There were 'quite a lot of white people in this country who have taken on into the new political period as if there was no problem'. Liz clearly hoped that the TRC would ensure that 'they can't pretend that it didn't happen'. The fact of Neil being white had also had a particular effect at the time:

> ... what was a little bit unusual about Neil was that he was the first white person to die in detention. For the black people involved in our struggle, that was particularly significant, that there was a white person who had not held back when things got really tough and has paid the ultimate price. And the response from people was quite dramatic specifically on that issue. And I think, for me, it demonstrates how deep racism in our country goes, that when a white person demonstrates that level of commitment, how much it means to people.

Before thanking Liz for testifying, with his almost eternal optimism, Archbishop Tutu offered a different perspective:

> ... what struck me as giving such great hope for this country was that the overwhelming majority of those who attended the funeral which was at St Mary's Cathedral were what were called actually young blacks from the townships, that the cockles of your heart were warmed, even at that time, to see that there was a commitment, it seemed, which went beyond sloganeering to non-racialism, because here was a white doctor and you referred to the depth of racism. But maybe, taking it more positively, I mean here were many of these young people, who had often had unfortunate experiences with their compatriots who were not black, coming out in quite huge

numbers and doing the salute for him, which was the toyitoyi. Even in those dark days, you felt there was this tremendous light that it was going to be alright, that people really didn't want to look at skin colour. They would say, were you for or against the struggle? And that determined whether you were accepted or not accepted.[472]

In Somerset West, the Aggetts had gathered to listen to Liz over the radio. They attached a microphone to an audio-tape machine on loan to Joy from the Society for the Blind in order to make a recording to send to Jill in England. The sound was a little scratchy, and the last couple of minutes of Liz's testimony were cut off. But that fragile half-hour cassette tape, which Jill would pass on to me, seemed oddly emblematic of the TRC itself. Its mission was huge, its means terribly limited.

CHAPTER 56

Truth and recognition

THE HEARINGS ON HUMAN RIGHTS VIOLATIONS WERE ONLY THE first stage of the TRC process, and were followed by special hearings on specific topics, community-based workshops on reparations and reconciliation, and amnesty hearings, leading to over 7 000 decisions that would take until 2001 to be processed. The Commission was also tasked with devising a policy on reparations, which it was up to government to implement.

Aubrey did not live to hear the Commission's findings. Early in December 1996, seven months after Liz gave her testimony, he was diagnosed with lung cancer and decided not to have treatment. Jill flew back from England, in time to see her father before he died a few days before Christmas, having been cared for at home by his family and a visiting nurse from the hospice. He was 84. The previous year, when I had asked him whether, despite their differences, he felt there were qualities Neil had inherited from him, he had replied that he was sure there were. 'I think he was a very stubborn boy ...' Aubrey's own stubbornness made his painful journey after Neil's death all the more striking.

The Truth and Reconciliation Commission Report, handed to President Mandela on 28 October 1998, unequivocally reversed Magistrate Kotzé's 'no one to blame' verdict:

THE COMMISSION FINDS THAT THE INTENSIVE INTERROGATION OF DR
AGGETT BY MAJOR A CRONWRIGHT AND LIEUTENANT WHITEHEAD,
AND THE TREATMENT HE RECEIVED WHILE IN DETENTION FOR MORE
THAN SEVENTY DAYS WERE DIRECTLY RESPONSIBLE FOR THE MENTAL
AND PHYSICAL CONDITION OF DR AGGETT WHICH LED HIM TO TAKE
HIS OWN LIFE. THE COMMISSION FINDS THE FORMER STATE, THE MINIS-
TER OF POLICE, THE COMMISSIONER OF POLICE AND THE HEAD OF THE
SECURITY BRANCH RESPONSIBLE FOR THE DETENTION, TORTURE AND
DEATH OF DR NEIL AGGETT, CONSTITUTING GROSS VIOLATIONS OF HU-
MAN RIGHTS. THE COMMISSION FINDS FURTHER THAT A STATEMENT BY
DR AGGETT TO A MAGISTRATE ABOUT HIS ASSAULT AND TORTURE WAS
ONLY INVESTIGATED THREE WEEKS LATER. THE COMMISSION FINDS
THAT THE FAILURE OF THE MAGISTRATE TO TAKE THE COMPLAINT SE-
RIOUSLY IS AN OMISSION THAT LED TO HIS DEATH. THE COMMISSION
FINDS THAT THE FAILURE OF MAGISTRATES TO TAKE THE COMPLAINTS
OF DETAINEES SERIOUSLY AND THEIR RELIANCE ON THE EVIDENCE OF
THE POLICE CONTRIBUTED TO A CULTURE OF IMPUNITY THAT LED TO
FURTHER GROSS VIOLATIONS OF HUMAN RIGHTS. THE COMMISSION
FINDS THE MINISTER OF JUSTICE RESPONSIBLE FOR THESE GROSS VIO-
LATIONS OF HUMAN RIGHTS.[473]

The Commission's indictment of the chain of command above Cronwright –
from the Head of the Security Police (General Johan Coetzee), the
Commissioner of Police (General Mike Geldenhuys), up to the Minister of
Police (Louis le Grange) and indeed the former state – struck chords of truth,
although there were hardly going to be judicial consequences for these office bearers. Similarly, criticism of the magistrates who failed to act seriously on complaints of detainees, and of the former Minister of Justice (Kobie
Coetsee), who was ultimately 'responsible for these gross violations of human
rights', was about laying down a moral marker. On the other hand, naming
Whitehead and Cronwright as perpetrators who had been 'directly responsible' for inducing Neil to take his own life raised immediate questions of
what would happen next. Neither had applied for amnesty. For the Aggetts,
as for other families where the truth had at least been acknowledged by the
Commission, the question was whether those named as perpetrators would
now be charged, as Dr Orr had indicated was in the legislation.

Any hopes, however, that the new state would carry out criminal prosecutions began to fade with time. George Bizos, who drafted the provisions of Section 20 of the Promotion of National Unity and Reconciliation Act with Mohamed Navsa, told me, in 2011, of his disappointment that the state had not taken action, even in cases with first-hand evidence of the murder of political activists:

> There's a confused policy in the prosecuting authority as to how they should deal with it. The Goniwe [case] is much clearer – murder. They took them and killed them, burnt their bodies. They admitted it in the application for amnesty.[474] The judge, Zietsman, who held the second inquest found that they were culpable. But they didn't charge them. They say, you know, it was difficult to get witnesses, people – and they haven't got the means, they've got other problems. So there hasn't been one case where people committed serious crimes, which could be proved – but they were not prosecuted. So from that point of view, I think the provisions, the amnesty provisions, were frustrated really.

The 'resources' argument – that it would be far too expensive to prosecute every perpetrator who had not received amnesty, so it was better to prosecute none – has been challenged. In a discussion paper exploring a feasible prosecutions strategy, Howard Varney, a Johannesburg attorney and member of the International Center for Transitional Justice, has proposed guidelines that would focus on the more flagrant offences and middle- to higher-ranking officers.[475] While acknowledging that the field was 'a veritable minefield', he indicated that a way forward was possible. However, a prosecutorial strategy would have to be even-handed, in the spirit of the TRC. This means that members of the ruling party who had been refused amnesty could also find themselves facing charges. Might this account for the lack of political will to pursue the perpetrators without amnesty?

While the Commission's term was limited, its momentous vision and purpose made it integral to the future. The apartheid regime's desire to 'let bygones be bygones' had been rightly rejected. Introducing the Commission's Final Report, Archbishop Tutu wrote of how wounds from the past that remained unhealed would fester. Denial of the horrendous experiences of victims victimised them even further. However, there was also a pragmatic aspect: '... the past refuses to lie down quietly. It has an uncanny habit of returning to haunt one.'[476] Dealing with the past was not a matter of being obsessed with looking backwards, but of serving the present and the future.

It has fallen to civil society to scrutinise the Commission's progress and its aftermath. Some who played a role in opposition to the old regime find themselves monitoring the new ruling party that they helped bring to power. One example has been the Khulumani Support Group. Arising out of small discussion groups in Soweto, initiated by Mam'Sylvia Dhlomo-Jele, a former member of the DPSC, Khulumani's original aim was to encourage victims to engage with the TRC.[477] By providing a forum for its members to articulate their pain and concerns, Khulumani ('speaking out' in isiZulu) rapidly became a critical advocacy organisation for victims. With many of its members unemployed and poverty-stricken, Khulumani has continued to pursue the call for reparations and practical measures to redress apartheid's legacy of injustice.

In giving testimony to the Commission, Liz Floyd's broader focus on the legacy of damage reflected a strongly pragmatic and more socially-based approach than if she had concentrated solely on the individual perpetrators responsible for Neil's death. She also held the view that the TRC would have been better named the 'Truth and Recognition Commission'. One could not ensure reconciliation, but at least there was now a record, hence recognition, of the terrible abuses of the past.

*   *   *

However, not even that TRC legacy of recognition and acknowledgement of past abuses can be taken for granted. This would emerge in an unexpected legal challenge to a victim's 'right to truth', a salutary reminder of how easily fundamental principles and freedoms can be washed away in South Africa's still-fragile democracy.

The case goes back to 1986 and the bombing of Magoo's Bar and the 'Why Not' Restaurant in Durban, in which three people were killed and nearly 70 injured. MK cell leader Robert McBride was convicted for the bombing, sentenced to death, later reprieved, and released in 1992 on the grounds that he had been politically motivated. While the TRC found the bombing to be a gross violation of human rights, McBride was nevertheless granted amnesty. He went on to become an MP and to serve in the new ANC government before being appointed, in 2003, to the role of Police Chief of the large East Rand municipality of Ekurhuleni, including Tembisa, where Neil used to work. When *The Citizen* newspaper published a series of highly critical articles, questioning the candidacy of a 'murderer', McBride sued for defamation. He argued that his TRC amnesty had expunged his conviction 'for all purposes'. No one should be allowed to say that he had committed 'murder'. Both the High Court and the Supreme Court of Appeal ruled in his favour, supporting this literal interpretation, and imposing a heavy fine on the newspaper.

As none of those held responsible for Neil's death had applied for, nor received, amnesty, the Supreme Court ruling did not directly apply to my writing about Neil. But it didn't require much imagination to see the implications. What if Cronwright and Whitehead had applied for, and received, amnesty from the TRC? Would the McBride ruling mean that no one could write about what had happened to Neil inside John Vorster Square? Could Jill be sued for talking about her brother's 'murder'?

At the eleventh hour, the implications of McBride's successful defamation action were spelt out for others. In making a final appeal to the Constitutional Court, the highest court in constitutional matters, *The Citizen* was joined by two relatives of apartheid victims in an 'amicus brief'. Joyce Mbizana's brother, Justice, had been tortured and bludgeoned to death by security forces, and Mbasa Mxenge's parents, the lawyers Griffiths and Victoria Mxenge, had each been brutally assassinated. Supported by the South African Coalition for Transitional Justice, including the Khulumani Support Group, the relatives submitted that the ruling in favour of McBride denied them the right to speak freely about the crimes committed against their family members. Amnesty could not alter the historical facts, they said. To be prevented from speaking the truth, for fear of being sued for defamation, stripped them of their dignity.

Seven years after McBride began his initial defamation action, in April 2011, the Constitutional Court finally reaffirmed the priority of truth, ruling against the lower courts' interpretation of the TRC statute. Justice Edwin Cameron, on behalf of the majority of the Constitutional Court, described the family members as asserting 'a subjective and expressive entitlement' that sprang from their 'dignity as siblings and children':

> They seek to vindicate their right to describe with truth and accuracy the
> perpetrators of the gross wrongs inflicted on their loved ones. They claim

the entitlement, despite amnesty, to continue to call the unlawful inten-
tional killing of their loved ones 'murder', and those who perpetrated the
killings 'murderers'. The literal reading urged by Mr McBride would render
these descriptions false, and impose legally enforced inhibition on those
expressing them.[478]

That cannot be correct, stated Justice Cameron. The aim of the TRC statute
was national reconciliation, premised on full disclosure of the truth. It was
not conceivable that its provisions 'could muzzle truth and render true statements about our history false ...':

> The interpretation urged on us by Mr McBride would be antithetical to the
> adequate compilation of that collective memory. It is in conflict with the
> statute's context and historical setting, and is at odds with one of the moral
> impulses of the reconciliation process itself.[479]

The literal meaning urged by McBride also denied the 'expressive rights' of
others who, like the family members before the court, wished to speak the
truth about the perpetrators who had killed their relatives. The Bill of Rights,
included in the Constitution, protected their right to freedom of expression
and valued 'the dignity of their bereavement and the integrity of their memory'. It followed that a sound interpretation of Section 20 of the Promotion
of National Unity and Reconciliation Act 'must afford weight to these rights'.
While finding that *The Citizen*'s repeated use of the epithets 'murderer' and
'criminal' were both 'vengeful, and distasteful', Justice Cameron stated that
this opinion on the tone of the articles was not the issue:

> And the Reconciliation Act does not afford those who were granted am-
> nesty moral absolution, or freedom from opprobrious condemnation. Nor
> does it muzzle those who choose to discuss their deeds in abrasive, chal-
> lenging and confrontational terms.[480]

Here we have it. The TRC had offered amnesty from prosecution, not ab-
solution. Those who had killed, on whichever side, had still killed. While
the Constitutional Court upheld *The Citizen*'s main appeal and dismissed
McBride's cross-appeal, it nevertheless found that *The Citizen* had defamed

him by claiming falsely that he was not contrite.[481] The significance of the judgment went well beyond Robert McBride. I felt a personal sense of relief at its multi-layered wisdom. The Constitutional Court, which owed its existence to the ANC in the founding of the new democracy, had sensitively examined the whole picture, going back to the underlying principles of the Truth and Reconciliation Commission. All those people who lost relatives, or indeed anyone, on whichever side, who wishes to speak about actions for which amnesty has been granted, are entitled to do so freely. The gathering of this collective memory, however painful or politically uncomfortable, remains essential in the interests of truth, without which there is no chance of healing.

Epilogue

THREE IMAGES, PINNED ABOVE MY DESK DURING MY YEARS OF writing, capture moments from Neil's journey. The earliest was his mother's favourite: her three-year-old son posing for the camera next to one of his father's workers beside the flooded Ewaso Ng'iro river. The second is Eddie Wes's celebratory image of the Vegetable Gardeners with their Woodworker wheelbarrow, stacked with cabbages. The third, taken shortly before Neil's burial, is of his parents surrounded by workers and banners, their feet on the red earth barely a metre away from the coffin. These three photographs have acted as stopping places for reflection. They have been signposts on my own journey to understand the stories behind each image and the connections between the child in the first, the man in the second and the invisible yet powerful presence in the third.

Had Neil survived his ordeal inside John Vorster Square, he would now be middle-aged, approaching 60, and I can't help wondering what he might be doing in today's South Africa. At his funeral, the ANC claimed him as one of their own: this young white man who had bucked an autocratic father and a repressive state to review his world according to first moral principles. He died an uncompromising idealist. In David Dison's words, 'Honesty killed him.' He shared the Freedom Charter vision and, as journalist Percy Qoboza wrote at the time, 'whatever Dr Neil Aggett may or may not have done, it is obvious he represented an ideal for many, many people in this country.'[482]

With the liberation movement's leadership either in jail or exile, Neil was part of a new generation inside the country that began thinking afresh on how to meet the challenges of their time. They used words and ideas to transform and mobilise from the grassroots up. Promoting concepts of representation and accountability, they helped create a bedrock of civil society that fed into the United Democratic Front, the non-racial, broad coalition of hundreds of union, student, church, civic and other organisations. Had Neil been alive, whether at its launch in Mitchell's Plain on 20 August 1983 or elsewhere, he would have been among those singing with high hopes for a future without oppression of one by another. *Siyaya, noma kubi.* We are going forward, no matter what.[483]

In my imaginings, however, the cousin whom I have come to know through the words of others would, today, still be active in the ongoing struggle to empower poor people who feel deeply disconnected from the decision makers. I have no doubt that he would understand the frustration and marginalisation expressed by the Khulumani Support Group when it says that there has been an 'elite transition' and that 'victims were used to facilitate an elite transition'.[484] Had he become a decision-maker himself, in a government role, he would be one of those who remain sensitive to the people they are designated to serve.

For Neil and his close comrades, the liberation struggle was not about changing whose turn it was to eat. It was about creating a different kind of society, different kinds of relationships and responsibilities. Neil, the unpaid trade union organiser, who spoke out against those who were 'eating the workers' money' would have been appalled at the desire to leap into luxury lifestyles, the opulence, greed and self-interest leading to corruption. As his union comrade Israel Mogoatlhe remembered him saying, '… we must follow the constitution … even if I, Neil, eat the workers' money, I must be disciplined'.

If I were to add one more picture to those above my desk, it is one that has to be imagined. Taken inside John Vorster Square, it shows Neil slipping the student Thabo Lerumo two books: Tolstoy's *Anna Karenina* and a Conrad collection with *Youth* and *Heart of Darkness*. Food for the stomach is not enough. Feeding the mind is equally essential. Neil's final communication to us, defying prison walls, came through two works of literature, left open beside his mat. Kazantzakis's young girls and boys perform their eternal dance each spring: 'Faces change, crumble, return to earth; but others rise to take their place.' Faulkner's young man Isaac argues that men were only ever meant to be stewards 'to hold the earth mutual and intact in the communal anonymity of brotherhood …' Having owed so much to literature for mind food, Neil would surely be concerned that, in today's South Africa, books often appear scorned.

In May 2011, I asked Gavin to speculate on what Neil might be doing:

> I think it is different today from how it was in our time. For us it was rather a radical activity to build the union movement and a genuinely important site of engagement in the struggle for democracy (and socialism!).
>
> My guess is that Neil would have gone more towards the kind of contribution that informed him at the start of his time here in Jozi, when he tried to work at the IAS. At that stage his dream was to get a decent medical scheme for workers, and even to organise around the need for health care. I can imagine that in our present society, where there is such poor access for those precariously in work or completely unemployed, that he'd be interested to work with that kind of massive societal problem … he was very proud of being a doctor and very determined to contribute in ways that helped those who tend to be excluded from the system.

All Gavin's projections of the paths that Neil might have chosen contain a common thread of being 'in harmony with his dream of the society we need to create'. Gavin's own varied career, in a wide range of development projects, has reflected a similar integrity.

This strong sense of 'the society we need to create' was likewise present when Liz Floyd delivered the fifth Neil Aggett Memorial Lecture at Neil's old school, Kingswood College, in March 2010. She spoke in the school's chapel, to which the Old Kingswoodian Club and the family had 20 years earlier donated a stained-glass window, inscribed 'In memory of Neil Hudson Aggett', and 'Did my heart not grieve for the poor?', the latter from the Book of Job. Whatever Neil might have thought, the image of a Christ figure ministering to a poor man was one that enabled his family to make sense of their loss. Liz Floyd's audience comprised mainly current pupils, teachers and a gathering of

Neil's old school friends, 'The Class of 1970'. As Director of the Multi-sectoral AIDS Unit in the Gauteng Department of Health, Liz was engaged with the kind of 'massive societal problem' mentioned by Gavin.

She spoke vividly of Neil and the 'generation who decided to stay and fight' despite intimidation, detention, prison. But the thrust of her talk was South Africa today, and the future role of these young people of Kingswood College, no longer all white as in Neil's day. Whatever had been achieved since the first democratic elections, they lived in a society and world of 'haves' and 'have nots'. She was direct:

> Your presence at this school means you are part of the top five percent of youth in the country in terms of income, education and future employment.[485]

The Methodist traditions of the school offered them 'a set of human values including the value of community service'.

> You need to learn about and understand the country we live in: the effects of the past on people, how the different cultural backgrounds affect the way people live their lives today and the daily realities of unemployment and poverty, with the loss of hope that goes with it.

They were not expected to become 'another Neil Aggett'. Nor was Liz setting up Neil as an icon. Instead, she exhorted today's 'top five percent of youth' to reach out beyond the confines of their privilege, and recognise that the issues of concern to Neil were still very much around them.[486] Her realism was striking and her message straightforward: 'You have a lot to offer and your contribution counts.' Unspoken, but powerfully present in Liz's words to this younger generation, was the dream of the equal, just society urgently awaiting creation.

Sources and Notes

The main South African libraries holding documentary material on Neil Aggett are the University of Cape Town (UCT) Manuscripts and Archives: Neil Aggett Papers, BC1110 (donated by his parents) and Food and Canning Workers' Union (FCWU) Archive, BC721; and the University of the Witwatersrand (UWL) Historical Papers: Record of Inquest Enquiry and associated legal papers including the dockets prepared by the Aggett legal team, AK2216. The University of the Western Cape (UWC) – Robben Island Mayibuye Archive holds some audio-visual items. When quoting from the Record of the Inquest, in which the inquest transcript extends to nearly 4 000 pages, I have given detailed references. With archive material such as the schoolboy diaries, student journal and letters, I have cited the source on its first appearance only.

Primary material for this biography comes from interviews, which will be archived in due course at the University of the Witwatersrand Historical Papers. A list of interviewees follows the references. I have cited interviews only where the source is not otherwise apparent.

Prologue

1 *The Guardian*, 6.2.82.
2 *The New York Times*, 6.2.82.
3 'My View by Bishop Desmond Tutu', *The Star*, 25.2.82.
4 Bram Fischer SC, from a prominent Afrikaner family, led the defence team in the Rivonia Trial while secretly leading the banned South African Communist Party. Granted bail during his own subsequent trial, so he might act in an ongoing patent case in the Privy Council in London, he returned to South Africa but jumped

433

bail and went underground. He was caught nine months later and sentenced to life imprisonment.

5 'We will try to find out why', *Cape Times*, 6.2.82.

6 Kubeka was previously spelt with an 'h', hence variations in spelling.

PART ONE
Beginnings and Transformation

CHAPTER 1 From Cape to Kenya

7 Neil Aggett, First Statement, 6-8.1.82, section 1, Record of Inquest Enquiry on Dr Aggett, University of Witwatersrand Libraries Historical Papers, AK2216, B1, Docket 1.73.

8 Two and a half thousand indentured Indian labourers died while working on the railway to Kisumu, four for each mile of track laid, some of them eaten by lions according to Dr Sultan H Somjee, curator of 'The Asian African Heritage: Identity and History', National Museums of Kenya/Asian African Heritage Trust, Nairobi, 2000.

9 David Anderson, *Histories of the Hanged*, London: Weidenfeld & Nicolson, 2005, p16.

CHAPTER 2 Settlers and resistance

10 The *kipande* (from the Swahili word for 'piece') was an identification and employment card that every African male, from the age of 16, was obliged to carry or face imprisonment.

11 Jomo Kenyatta, *Facing Mount Kenya*, with an introduction by B Malinowski, London: Secker & Warburg, 1938.

12 Henry Muoria, *Ngoro ya Ugikuyu Ni ya Gutoria* (The Gikuyu Spirit is for Winning), Ngoro: 5, 1947, in C Pugliese, in ES Atieno Odhiambo & J Lonsdale, Mau Mau & Nationhood, Oxford: James Currey, 2003, p101.

13 Quoted in Donald L Barnett & Karari Njama, *Mau Mau From Within*, New York and London: Modern Reader Paperbacks, 1966, p76.

14 Anderson, *Histories of the Hanged*, p66.

15 *Ibid*, p67.

16 *Daily Mirror*, 12.12.52.

17 Michael Blundell, *So Rough a Wind*, London: Weidenfeld & Nicolson, 1964, pp126–27.

CHAPTER 3 From Kenya to the Cape: 'We'll march on'

18 Ol Pejeta was then owned by Marcus Wickham Boynton, a school friend of Lord Delamere, who had been anxious to buy the farm for years. Ol Pejeta was subsequently sold to the multi-millionaire Adnan Khashoggi and later to Tiny Rowland. The huge estate now operates as a non-profit wildlife conservancy working with the Kenyan government.

CHAPTER 4 Kingswood College: 'avoiding evil of every kind'

19 Only one person ignored the ban and went out of his way to talk to Andrew Rein. He was a teacher who didn't quite fit the mould and didn't use the cane; Clive Ulyate was a former Springbok rugby player and an outstanding all-round sportsman, including a cricketer. He taught their class English in the middle years.

20 South Africa refused to hand back South West Africa to the United Nations in 1966 after its mandate to administer the territory was withdrawn. Guerrilla attacks on the South African Defence Force in the north of the country launched the Namibian War of Independence, which would last over 20 years. The UN General Assembly changed the territory's name to Namibia in 1968.

21 The other two were Grant Dewar and David Pitman.

22 John & Charles Wesley, *Selected Writings and Hymns*, edited by Frank Whaling, 'The Nature, Design, and General Rules of the United Societies … 1743', Mahwah, NJ: Paulist Press, 1981.

23 Diary, 1 January 1970, Neil Aggett Papers, University of Cape Town (UCT) Libraries, Manuscripts and Archives, BC1110.

24 Josiah Mwangi Kariuki, *'Mau Mau' Detainee: The Account by a Kenya African of his Experiences in Detention Camps 1953-1960*, London: Oxford University Press, 1963.

CHAPTER 5 University: 'the long-haired coterie'

25 'The mills indiscriminately spewed blue dust clouds over the countryside, and whenever the wind rose, a blue haze hovered over the dumps.' Sleggs et al, 1961, quoted in Jock McCulloch, 'Asbestos Mining in Southern Africa, 1893-2002', in *International Journal of Occupational and Environmental Health*, Vol 9, 2003, pp230-235.

26 Trefor Jenkins, 'In Memoriam', George Trevor Nurse (1928–2010), *South African Medical Journal*, March 2011, Vol 101, No 3.

27 Journal, Neil Aggett Papers.

28 Jenkins, 'In Memoriam'.

29 The Driekoppen residence has been renamed Kopano.

30 Oswald Joseph Mtshali, *Sounds of a Cowhide Drum*, Johannesburg: Renoster Books, 1971.

31 *Ibid*.

32 *Sunday Times*, 1.1.1972.

33 Hugh Montefiore, 'The World at Stake in 1972', *Cape Times*, 31 December 1971. The emphasis is Neil's.

34 Professor ZK Matthews spoke on 'African awakening and the universities' in 1961, in the wake of the Extension of Universities Act designed to segregate students in higher education.

35 Alpheus Hamilton Zulu, 'The Dilemma of the Black South African', TB Davie Memorial Lecture, University of Cape Town, 17 May 1972. Neil Aggett Papers.

36 Steve Biko's unswerving message had been that white liberals should stop telling black people 'how best to respond to the kick'. [Steve Biko, 'White Racism and Black Consciousness' in *I Write What I Like*, edited by Aelred Stubbs, London: Penguin, 1978, p80.] If they were 'true liberals' they should recognise that they themselves were

oppressed and fight for their own freedom of mind 'not that of the nebulous "they" [black people] with whom they can hardly claim identification'.

37 Along with Biko, Abram Onkgopotse Tiro was one of the founders of the South African Students' Organization (SASO), which had broken away in 1969 from the non-racial but predominantly white, and white-led, National Union of Students (NUSAS). Less than two years after Tiro's speech and expulsion, he was blown up by a parcel bomb, having fled into exile in Botswana.

38 Juhan Kuus, *South Africa in Black and White*, London: Harrap, 1987.

39 'At that time I had a disagreement with my father over my refusal to shave my beard, and from that time received no further assistance from him.' Aggett, First Statement, 6-8.1.82, section 4, Record of Inquest.

CHAPTER 6 Searching

40 Neil Aggett Papers.

41 It's strange to think that at the time of writing this letter, Neil was just a few miles away from where I was living in north London with my husband Nandha. I was pregnant and soon to give birth to our second child. We welcomed visitors from 'home' bringing news of the country to which we could not return. However, my solitary cousin was making his own journey.

42 This is a reference to the famously eccentric bookshop on the Left Bank, Shakespeare & Co, created and run by George Whitman, with his motto, 'Be not inhospitable to strangers lest they be angels in disguise'.

CHAPTER 7 'We should throw stones'

43 Food and Canning Workers' founder Ray Alexander came to South Africa from Latvia as a teenage communist. She immediately became active in her new country, involving herself in campaigns against the pass laws and in the Anti-Fascist League. By 1934, she was Secretary of the Communist Party of South Africa (CPSA), going on to set up FCWU; 14 years later, in 1955, she helped establish the non-racial South African Congress of Trade Unions (SACTU), closely allied to the ANC. The banning of anyone designated 'communist' and the repression of the 1960s effectively crushed SACTU and its ANC-aligned member unions.

PART TWO
Comrades

CHAPTER 8 Jozi: Comrades

44 Aggett, First Statement, 6-8.1.82, section 8, Record of Inquest.

45 At the time, Robert Manci led by example, making his own tea, helping labourers un-
load goods in the yard, and eschewing the privileges of a suit-wearing clerk. In Sipho
Kubeka's view, this began a profound change in relationships as trust developed across
the worker hierarchy.

46 There was a strong emphasis on the ideas of Rick Turner, the banned University of
Natal lecturer, about developing worker control by using and expanding legal space.

47 Pindile Mfeti's detention followed the surprise arrest of the exiled Afrikaner writer
Breyten Breytenbach, who had set up an organisation for white radicals in Paris called
Okhela (isiZulu for 'ignite the flames'). It was a dramatic affair, with Breytenbach
returning to South Africa in disguise and with a forged French passport, to make
contact with trade unionists. However, Okhela had been infiltrated in Paris and the
security police tailed the writer-cum-revolutionary before pouncing. Following the
round-up of Breytenbach's contacts, Pindile's name was given by a detainee.

48 Another strategy was to have an 'alternate' for every shop steward on a factory's shop-
steward committee, ready to step into the shoes of anyone who was removed.

49 Heinemann was co-owned by the American firm and prominent South African
company Barlow Rand.

50 Steven Friedman, *Building Tomorrow Today: African Workers in Trade Unions
1970–1984*, Johannesburg: Ravan Press, 1987, p115.

51 *The Star*, 30 3.76.

52 *Rand Daily Mail*, 31.3.76

53 The security police claimed that Luke 'Storey' Mazwembe had hung himself with
strips of blanket tied with twine. They could not explain how a razor blade and twine
were in the cell. Nor could they explain the wounds across his body, denying torture.
The magistrate cleared them, saying that he assumed the twine and razor blade had
been accidentally left in the cell by an unknown person.

54 Jeanette Curtis was caught in the same round-up as Pindile Mfeti.

55 *Rand Daily Mail*, 16.9.77, quoted by Hilda Bernstein, No. 46 – Steve Biko, London:
International Defence and Aid Fund, 1978, p20.

CHAPTER 10 Breaking the rules, making the rules

56 Paul Erasmus would seek amnesty for this from the Truth and Reconciliation
Commission, as well as for an incident related to Neil's parents' house.

57 Mam'Lydia Kompe became an ANC Member of Parliament in 1994.

58 See Terry Bell, with Dumisa Ntsebeza, *Unfinished Business*, London: Verso, 2003,
pp98–99.

CHAPTER 11 Arguments, debates and stepping stones

59 Friedman, *Building Tomorrow*, p92.

60 Friedman, *Building Tomorrow*, p152.

61 Santiago Carillo was General Secretary of the Communist Party of Spain, 1960–1982.

62 Friedman, *Building Tomorrow*, p184.

CHAPTER 12 Into the union

63 Barbara Hogan, interview 20.7.95.

64 Oscar Mpetha, General Organizer's Report, circa June 1979, Food & Canning Workers' Union (FCWU) Archive, University of Cape Town Libraries, Manuscripts and Archives, BC721.

65 Jan Theron, 'A Chronology of the Fattis & Monis Dispute' 10.8.79. Subsequent details are drawn from this report by the General Secretary, FCWU Archive.

66 Catholic Students' Society, University of the Witwatersrand, circa July 1979, FCWU Archive.

CHAPTER 13 Learning the ropes

67 Aggett, First Statement, 6-8.1.82, section 15, Record of Inquest.

68 Marius Schoon was an Afrikaner who broke with apartheid. He served 12 years for an unsuccessful attempt at blowing up a radio transmitter at Hillbrow police station in 1964, organised by an agent provocateur.

69 Karl Edwards, KZR/rs, 'An Operational Analysis of the SCHOON NETWORK'., August 1980, National Intelligence Service file sent to The Commissioner SAP for Capt. Williamson by AJ Kruger, Divisional Head, NIS September 1980, UWC – Robben Island Mayibuye Archive, MCH 121-1, Mac Maharaj.

70 For a detailed account of NIS infiltration of the ANC through Williamson, see Bell, with Ntsebeza, *Unfinished Business*.

71 Friedman, *Building Tomorrow*, p188.

72 Jan Theron, interview 12.4.95.

73 Athalie Crawford, interview 22.7.95.

74 Minutes of AFCWU Transvaal Branch Executive Committee, 16.11.79, FCWU Archive.

75 Secretary C Bogatsu's Report, *Ibid*.

76 Letter from Neil Aggett to Oscar Mpetha, 4.12.79, *Ibid*.

CHAPTER 15 'Point by point by point'

77 Branch Executive Committee Minutes, 27.4.80, FCWU.

78 Minutes of Branch Executive meeting, Lekton House, Johannesburg, 28 June 1980, FCWU Archive.

79 AFCWU Johannesburg Branch Newsletter, 5 November 1980, FCWU Archive.

CHAPTER 16 Eating the workers' money

80 Minutes of Branch Executive meeting, Lekton House, 24.9.80, FCWU Archive.

81 *Ibid*.

82 Minutes of Branch Executive meeting, Lekton House, 10.2.81, FCWU Archive.

83 Minutes of the General Meeting, Endulwini Church, 15.2.81, FCWU Archive.

CHAPTER 17 Gavin and an ANC link?

84 Pindile Mfeti mysteriously disappeared from Butterworth in 1987 and the truth has never emerged.

85 'On the whole I think that it can be said that my relationship to outside was based upon a formal commitment to the A.N.C. but that in actual practice I worked fairly independently of outside, relying for the bulk of my political guidance and activity on comrades loyal to the A.N.C. inside South Africa, some of whom were formally linked to the movement and others not.' Barbara Hogan, 'Problems Arising in Internal Work', 1981, *The State* vs *Barbara Hogan*, Supreme Court of SA (Witwatersrand), Case No 163/82, Exhibit B2.

86 The letter to ANC National Executive Committee member Henry Makgoti reveals the breadth of what was discussed. See Karl Edwards, Schoon Network. 'The Schoons and Internal Reconstruction', p8.

PART THREE
The Rising Tide

CHAPTER 18 The rising tide

87 More commonly spelt today as Tozamile Botha.

88 Friedman, *Building Tomorrow*, p216.

89 Friedman, *Building Tomorrow*, p220.

90 Friedman, *Building Tomorrow*, p225.

91 Despite international protests, the case went ahead, with Oscar Mpetha finally sentenced to five years after losing an appeal. His diabetes led to one of his legs being amputated and he spent much of his sentence in hospital.

92 Minutes of Branch Executive meeting, Lekton House, 10.2.81, FCWU Archive.

CHAPTER 19 Publicly and privately

93 Neil Aggett Papers.

94 Friedman, *Building Tomorrow*, p258.

95 AFCWU Branch Report to National Executive Council, 22.3.81, FCWU Archive.

96 Letter to Jan Theron, 20.5.81, FCWU Archive.

97 Friedman, *Building Tomorrow*, p243.

98 Howard Barrell, 'Conscripts to their Age: African National Congress Operational Strategy, 1976-1986', DPhil thesis in Politics, Faculty of Social Studies, University of Oxford, 1993, Ch 6.

99 Mac Maharaj, in Padraig O'Malley, *Shades of Difference: Mac Maharaj and the Struggle for South Africa*, New York: Viking, 2007, pp224–25.

CHAPTER 20 The Anti-Republic Day Campaign, and two heady weeks

100 *Africa Report*, interview by Anthony Hughes with Oliver Tambo, New York,
    September-October 1981. Available from http://www.anc.org.za/show.php?id=4389
101 Promotion of Access to Information Act 2 of 2000 (PAIA).
102 Bell, with Ntsebeza, *Unfinished Business*, p9.
103 Julie Frederickse, *South Africa: A Different Kind of War*, London: James Currey with
    Ravan Press (Johannesburg) and Mambo Press (Gweru), 1986, p40.

CHAPTER 21 Daily reality, 'discipline' and a relationship cracks

104 See also Maharaj, in O'Malley, *Shades of Difference*, p224.

CHAPTER 22 Unions on the move

105 Letter to the General Secretary, 23.6.81, FCWU Archive. Emphasis in the original.
106 Friedman, *Building Tomorrow*, p245.
107 Sydney Mufamadi had recently been fired as a messenger from a firm of attorneys,
    after being identified in a newspaper photograph addressing workers. In 1994, he
    was appointed Minister of Safety and Security.
108 AFCWU Branch Executive Minutes, 27.8.81, FCWU Archive.
109 41st FCWU/AFCWU Annual Conference Report, 19-20 September 1981, FCWU
    Archive.
110 AFCWU Transvaal Newsletter, August 1981, FCWU Archive.

CHAPTER 23 Conscription?

111 *Passing the Message*, Film by Cliff Bestall and Michael Gavshon, 1981, UWC-Robben
    Island Museum Mayibuye Archives, University of Western Cape.
112 FCWU/AFCWU Annual Report, 1981, FCWU Archive.

CHAPTER 24 Close Comrades

113 Barbara Hogan, 'Problems Arising in Internal Work'.
114 Half a page has been blanked out, by whom I don't know. The document, passed on
    to me by Barbara, went through unknown hands before ending up as a state exhibit
    in her trial.
115 Barbara Hogan, 'Close Comrades', *The State* vs *Barbara Hogan*, Supreme Court of SA
    (Witwatersrand), Case No 163/82, Exhibit B3.
116 Newsletter, 'Missions & Movements', *Episcopal Churchmen for South Africa* (ECSA),
    August 1982.
117 In the 1970s, Cronwright had led the harassment of students at Wits. It was said that
    he hated them with added passion after he fell down a flight of stairs, injuring his
    back, in a physical fight at the university. In 1975, Cronwright instigated charges

of conspiracy and furthering the aims of communism against five NUSAS leaders. When their year-long trial, in which George Bizos led the defence team, ended in a 'not guilty' verdict, Cronwright was said to be furious.

118 'A born-again Christian as interrogated', *Christian Science Monitor*, January 1979.

119 George Bizos, *No One to Blame?*, Cape Town: David Philip Publishers and Mayibuye Books, 1998, p115.

CHAPTER 25 John Vorster Square

120 Chris van Wyk, *It is Time to Go Home*, Johannesburg: Ad Donker, 1979.

121 Engelbrecht's first name and rank are not known.

CHAPTER 26 Gavin's getaway

122 Pravin Gordhan, then a pharmacist at King Edward VII Hospital, was dismissed after being detained in 1981. He continued with underground work, and was arrested in 1990. An ANC MP from 1994 to 1998, he served as Commissioner of the South African Revenue Service from 1999 and was appointed Minister of Finance in May 2009.

123 '*Nnya Rra*' means 'No, sir' in Setswana.

CHAPTER 27 'Stay well, bro, & keep strong'

124 Gavin Andersson, personal papers

CHAPTER 28 'We can use other methods'

125 Barbara Hogan, Affidavit, 22.9.82, Docket 4, 2.I, Record of Inquest.

126 Hogan, unsigned statement, Docket 3, 1.4, Record of Inquest.

127 Keith Coleman, interview, 21.3.10.

128 Later in her detention, Barbara Hogan was to lay charges against Warrant Officers Prince and Deetlefs in Case No 8/931/82. The two were subsequently charged in the Johannesburg Magistrate's Court but found not guilty despite the District Surgeon testifying that, in his opinion, she had been assaulted. 'But that outcome was normal in those days' [Hogan, email, 13.7.11].

129 Judgment, *The State* vs *Barbara Hogan*, Supreme Court of SA (Witwatersrand), Case No 163/82.

130 Auret van Heerden, Affidavit, 20.9.82, Docket 4, 1A, Record of Inquest.

131 *Ibid.*

132 Van Heerden, Supplementary points arising out of Affidavit, 24.9.82, Docket 4, 1D, Record of Inquest.

133 *Ibid.*

134 *Ibid*

135 Van Heerden, Affidavit, 20.9.82, Docket 4, 1A, Record of Inquest.
136 Ariel Dorfman, 'Are there times when we have to accept torture? – Every regime that commits this crime does so in the name of salvation', *The Guardian*, 8.5.2004.

PART FOUR
Seventy Days

CHAPTER 29 Arrest

137 Bridget King, email, 15.2.11.
138 Michael Stephen Joubert, Vol 1, p231, Record of Inquest.
139 Lelyveld, *The New York Times*, 5.1.83.
140 Exhibit, Docket 3, 4.4, Record of Inquest.

CHAPTER 30 Pretoria Central Prison

141 *The Star*, 27.11.81.
142 Khotso House, the headquarters of the South African Council of Churches, offered premises to various anti-apartheid organisations. It was bombed by the security forces in 1988.
143 Emma Mashinini, *Strikes Have Followed Me All My Life*, London: The Women's Press, 1989, p54.
144 Josephus Johannes Hendrik Delport, Affidavit, 10.3.82, Docket 1.70, Record of Inquest.

CHAPTER 31 John Vorster Square: 'Try not to threaten them'

145 Report by Magistrate AH Louw, Docket 1.60, Record of Inquest.
146 James Andrew van Schalkwyk, Affidavit, 19.2.82, Docket 1.48, Record of Inquest.
147 Walter MacPherson, Affidavit, 15.2.82, Docket 1.24, Record of Inquest.
148 Van Heerden, Statement, 16.9.82, Docket 4.1B, Record of Inquest.
149 John Edward Lloyd, Affidavit with page from 'parcel register', Docket 1.2, Record of Inquest.
150 Coleman, interview, 21.3.10.
151 Report of Chief Magistrate regarding visit of Magistrate PC van der Merwe, 18.1.81, Docket 1.61, Record of Inquest.

CHAPTER 32 Christmas Visits: 'Don't worry'

152 Stephan Peter Whitehead, Affidavit, 19.2.82, Docket 1.47, Record of Inquest.
153 Yvette Breytenbach, Affidavit, 18.6.82, Docket 2.1021, Record of Inquest.

154 Six Christmas cards – six in and six out – were negotiated two weeks earlier by the DPSC with Colonel Muller, along with weekly (Friday morning) acceptance of food parcels and clothing, plus books, games and puzzles approved by the commanding officer. Dirty washing could also be returned. See Minutes meeting, DPSC & Col Muller, 10.12.81, in Mashinini, *Strikes*, 1989, p139.

155 Whitehead, Affidavit, 19.2.82, Docket 1.47, Record of Inquest.

156 The DPSC delegation to Colonel Muller on 10 December 1981 that secured a raft of agreements, including the Christmas arrangements, reflected non-racial unity: Mrs K Naidoo, Mrs P Hogan, Mr T Mashinini, Dr HJ Koornhoff, Dr IM Cachalia and Dr M Coleman. The meeting began with the delegation emphasising that their purpose was to secure equal treatment for all detainees, parents and spouses of detainees. No one was making requests specifically for their own relatives. See Mashinini, *Strikes*, 1989.

157 Whitehead, Affidavit.

158 Van Heerden, Statement, 16.9.82.

159 *Ibid.*

CHAPTER 33 Whitehead takes charge

160 Van Heerden, *Ibid.*

161 Aggett, Affidavit to Sgt G Blom, 4.2.82, Docket 3, 4.1, Record of Inquest.

162 Inspector of Detainees to Minister of Justice, 6.1.82, Docket 1.63, Record of Inquest.

CHAPTER 34 The first statement

163 Aggett, First Statement, 6-8.1.82.

164 *Ibid*, section 5.

165 *Ibid*, section 8.

166 *Ibid*, section 10.

167 *Ibid*, section 14.

168 *Ibid*, section 15.

169 *Ibid*, section 16.

170 *Ibid*, section 17.

171 *Ibid*, section 18.

172 *Ibid*, section 20.

173 *Ibid*, section 32.

174 *Ibid*, section 36.

175 *Ibid*, section 59.

176 *Ibid*, section 59.

177 *Ibid*, section 63.

178 *Ibid*, section 66.

179 *Ibid*, sections 67 & 68.

180 Gavin Andersson recalls that, only a few months earlier, Neil had led a discussion in their reading group about a paper by Joe Slovo and expressed very definite opinions.

CHAPTER 35 Limbo

181 Van Heerden, Statement, 16.9.82.
182 Thabo Lerumo, Affidavit, Docket 2.1015, Record of Inquest.
183 Report of Chief Magistrate, 19.1.82, Docket 1.67, Record of Inquest.
184 Van Heerden, Statement, 16.09.82.
185 Report by Inspector of Detainees, 26.1.82, Docket 1.66, Record of Inquest.

CHAPTER 36 Behind the frosted glass

186 Maurice Peter Smithers, Affidavit, 12.4.82, Docket 2.1001, Record of Inquest.
187 Cells Occurrence Book, Docket 1.41, Record of Inquest.
188 Thozamile Gqweta, Affidavit, 15.6.82, Docket 2.1012, Record of Inquest.
189 Samson Ndou, Affidavit, 14.6.82, Docket 2.1011, Record of Inquest.
190 My shock was twofold. The statement was my brother's, and I immediately knew that he must have been tortured. My image was of a rock cracking. He had been made to stand without sleep for almost three full days and nights, and after a couple of days, made to stand again for a further 40 hours before he agreed to make a statement.
191 The principle of *umcentrierung* was proposed by one of the founders of Gestalt psychology, Max Wertheimer.

CHAPTER 37 The long weekend

192 Aggett, Affidavit to Sgt Blom, 4.2.82, Docket 3.4.1, Record of Inquest.
193 Aggett, Notes under interrogation, 25-28.1.82, Docket 5, 4.2, Record of Inquest.
194 The office was in the flat of John Gaetsewe, whom Pindile Mfeti had taken Gavin Andersson to meet in Botswana, and who was now based in London.
195 'Petersen Memorandum address to the National Executive Committee of SACTU', 8 April 1979.

CHAPTER 38 'Broken'

196 Van Heerden, Statement, 16.09.82. Emphasis in the original.
197 Ndou, Affidavit, Docket 2.1011, Record of Inquest.
198 Van Heerden, Statement, 16.09.82,
199 Jabu Gabriel Ngwenya, Affidavit, Docket 2.1016, Record of Inquest.
200 Van Heerden, Statement 16.9.82.
201 *Ibid.*
202 Aggett, handwritten (unsigned and undated) second statement, Docket 1.74, Record of Inquest.
203 *Ibid*, section 11.
204 *Ibid*, section 19.
205 *Ibid*, section 18.

206 *Ibid*, second section numbered 21.
207 *Ibid*, second section numbered 18.
208 *Ibid*, second section numbered 19.
209 *Ibid*, second section numbered 24.
210 *Ibid*, section 25.
211 *Ibid*, section 28.
212 *Ibid*, section 28.
213 Van Heerden, Statement, 16.9.82.
214 *Ibid*.

CHAPTER 39 Two scenarios

215 William Faulkner, 'The Bear', *Go Down, Moses*, Harmondsworth: Penguin, 1960, p196.
216 Nikos Kazantzakis, *Zorba the Greek*, London: Faber & Faber, 1961, pp246–47.

CHAPTER 40 'What is done in the dark …'

217 André Martin, Affidavit, Docket 1, p76, Record of Inquest.
218 Van Heerden, Statement, 16.9.82.
219 Charl Wynand Lambrecht, Docket 1.27, 1.28, Record of Inquest.
220 In 1964, as a leading member of the Special Branch 'sabotage squad', Swanepoel claimed that the detainee Babla Salojee had deliberately jumped to his death out of a seventh-storey window in The Grays, Johannesburg's former police headquarters. According to (then) Captain Swanepoel, the slightly-built Salojee had 'escaped' by slipping past three burly policemen [Bell, with Ntsebeza, *Unfinished Business*, p45]. Those who survived Swanepoel's 'standing torture' included my husband Nandha, whom he had threatened with having his body dumped down a mine. One of their people would investigate, he added, and that would be 'end of story'. By 1966, Major Swanepoel commanded the new security police camp in South West Africa's far north and the counterinsurgency unit that became the notorious Koevoet [TRC Report, Vol 3, Ch 6, p164]. Death was integral to Swanepoel's repertoire. He is said to have commanded the policemen who, in 1976, open fire on black schoolchildren in Soweto and Alexandra [TRC Report, Vol 3, Ch 6, p110].
221 Theunis Jacobus Swanepoel, Affidavit, Docket 1.29, Record of Inquest.
222 *Ibid*.
223 TRC Final Report, Vol 2, Ch 3, p168.
224 Inventory of Cell 209, Docket 1.25, Record of Inquest.
225 Meal Register extract, Docket 1.59, Record of Inquest.
226 Numbers for deaths in general police custody were even higher. Bernstein, 1978, p150.

PART FIVE
Lies, Truth and Recognition

CHAPTER 41 'Purging of grief through activity'

227 'We will try to find out why', *Cape Times*, 6.2.82

228 Bizos, *No One to Blame?*, p435.

229 Family pathologist JBC Botha, Autopsy Report, 25.3.82, Docket 1.76, Record of Inquest.

230 Now Charlotte Maxeke Johannesburg Academic Hospital.

231 DPSC telegram, 5.2.82, Neil Aggett Papers.

232 *Ibid.*

233 Jane Barrett to Gavin Andersson, 6-9.2.82, Andersson personal papers.

234 *The New York Times*, 6.2.82.

235 Frederickse, *South Africa*, p112.

CHAPTER 42 Public protests

236 *Cape Times*, 6.2.82.

237 *Ibid.*

238 *Ibid.*

239 Quoted in Bizos, 1998, p103.

240 Pieter Jacobus Rabie served as Chief Justice of South Africa from 1982 to 1989.

241 University of the Witwatersrand Students' Representative Council, 5.2.82, Neil Aggett Papers.

242 *Ibid.*

243 'Storm over detainee's death in cell', *Cape Times*, 6.2.82.

244 *Ibid.*

245 'City parents ask to see detainees', *Cape Argus*, 8.2.82.

246 'Thousands mourn for Neil Aggett – first national stoppage for twenty years', *FOSATU Worker News*, March 1982.

247 *Ibid.*

248 'A new spirit is abroad on factory floors', *Rand Daily Mail*, 19.2.82.

249 *TV Eye*, Producer/writer Linda McDougall, Thames Television, March 1982.

250 By early January 1982, the number of detainees had risen to 159 [IDAF, *Focus* 39, March-April 1982] and at least two deaths in detention had passed with little comment. In the Transkei, 60-year-old Manana Mgqweto, staunchly opposed to Bantustan government, died on 17 September. In the northern Bantustan of Venda, 28-year-old Tshifhiwa Muofhe, a Lutheran lay preacher, insurance salesman and formerly a leading member of the banned Black People's Convention, died on 12 November, two days after being seized by Venda's security police. A Lutheran bishop was refused entry to Venda to officiate at his funeral and Bishop Desmond Tutu, attempting to visit detained churchmen, was expelled from the territory. [*Episcopal Churchmen for South Africa*, ECSA Newsletter, 8.2.82, Room 1005, 853 Broadway,

New York, August 1982. African Activist Archive, http://www.africanactivist.msu.edu].

251 Friedman, *Building Tomorrow*, p302.

CHAPTER 43 Funeral preparations

252 On May Day 1989, David Webster was gunned down outside his home, a few blocks away from where Neil and Liz had lived at 420A Fox Street. He had been writing about repression and violence in South Africa and how, having failed to control government opposition through detention and intimidation, the state had switched to assassination.

253 George Bizos, *Odyssey to Freedom*, Johannesburg and Cape Town: Random House in association with Umuzi, 2007, p166.

254 Interview, Pretoria, 30 June 1982, UWC – Robben Island Mayibuye Archive, MCA-496-P1, quoted in Frederickse, *South Africa*, p116.

255 Nicolaas Jacobus Schepers, Senior Government Pathologist, Docket 1.5, Record of Inquest.

256 Maurice Freiman, Asst Chief of Chemical Laboratories, Docket 1.5, Record of Inquest.

257 *Ibid*, and Docket 1.12.

CHAPTER 44 'A man of the people'

258 Lelyveld, 'Thousands Mourn a "Martyr" in South Africa', *The New York Times*, 14.2.82.

259 *Ibid.*

260 '"Freedom" songs at funeral of Dr Aggett', *The Citizen*, 15.2.82.

261 Friedman, *Building Tomorrow*, p284.

262 Lelyveld, *The New York Times*, 14.2.82.

263 Mark Newman (dir), *A Film on the Funeral of Neil Aggett*, InterChurch Media Programme, 1982.

264 The photo appeared in *The Citizen*, 15.2.82.

265 Dave Lewis, *South African Labour Bulletin*, Vol 7, No 6/7, April 1982, pp167–70.

266 *Ibid.*

267 Oscar Mpetha, Neil Aggett Papers.

268 Archbishop Denis Hurley, *Ibid.*

269 Headmaster, Kingswood College, *Ibid.*

270 Andersson, *Ibid.*

CHAPTER 45 'We have been deeply touched'

271 '"Freedom" songs at funeral of Dr Aggett', *The Citizen*, 15.2.82.

272 'Farewell to Dr Aggett', *Sowetan*, 15.2.82.

273 '"Mourners" tribute to a white man was a mark of respect', *The Star*, 25.2.82.

274 Aggetts to *Sunday Times*, 20.2.82, Neil Aggett Papers.

275 Hawa Timol to Aggetts, undated, *Ibid.*

276 Victoria Mxenge to Aggetts, 11.2.82, *Ibid.*

277 Phyllis Naidoo to Aggetts, 14.3.82, *Ibid.*

278 Barbara Adam to Aggetts, 11.2.82, *Ibid.*

279 *Ibid.*

280 Evelyn Trewhela to Aggetts, 14.2.82, *Ibid.*

281 Author to Aggetts, 24.2.82. *Ibid.*

CHAPTER 46 In pursuit of a wider justice: 'Do it!'

282 Helen Suzman, *In No Uncertain Terms,* Johannesburg: Jonathan Ball Publishers, 1993, p232.

283 *Ibid*, p234.

284 Quoted by Suzman, *Ibid*, p236.

285 Helen Suzman, letter to family, 23.2.82, by permission of Frances Suzman Jowell.

286 *Critical Health*, No 7, April 1982.

287 *The South African Building*, August 1941, in Magistrates' Courts: blasts, apartheid, art, www.joburg.org.za.

288 Nelson Mandela, *In His Own Words*, London: Abacus, 2004, p24.

289 It was inside this building, in April 1965, that my brother had declared, before being sentenced, 'I would like to make this a better country for all its people, and not just for the privileged minority to which I was born' [Author's personal papers].

290 Inquest Enquiry Opening, Johannesburg Magistrate's Court, 2.3.82, Record of Inquest. Miscellaneous additions.

291 Quoted in Bizos, *No One to Blame?*, 1998, p27.

292 Bizos, *Ibid*, p105.

293 George Bizos, aged 82, came to England in February 2011 to deliver a lecture in honour of his friend and fellow advocate Bram Fischer QC, at Rhodes House, Oxford. The setting for our interview the following morning, in a comfortable sitting room overlooking a serene, walled English garden, was in sharp contrast with his subject matter.

294 Elizabeth Floyd, in Bizos, 1998, p106, taken from Record of Inquest, Vol 4, p1268.

CHAPTER 47 'Snooping around people's houses'

295 Jill Burger, Statement, 15.3.82, Docket 3.13, Record of Inquest.

296 Aubrey Aggett, Affidavit, 30.3.82, Docket 3.13, Record of Inquest.

297 Bizos, *No One to Blame?*, p114.

298 Erasmus, TRC Amnesty Hearing, AM3690/96, 16.10.2000. Available from http://www.justice.gov.za/trc/amntrans/2000/201016jh.htm.

299 *Ibid.* Colonel Hendrik Muller was promoted to Brigadier in 1982. This and subsequent quotations are from Erasmus's testimony to the TRC.

CHAPTER 48 Whose voices shall be heard?

300 'Released detainees are "jubilant but soured"', *Sunday Times*, 28.3.82.
301 Bizos, *No One to Blame?*, p124.
302 Vol 1, p57, Record of Inquest.
303 *Ibid*, p59.
304 'Last statement before he died', *Rand Daily Mail*, 3.6.82.
305 Judgment, Supreme Court of South Africa, Transvaal Provincial Division, Case 6533/1982, p9.
306 'Dr Aggett's SP torture statement', *Rand Daily Mail*, 3.6.82.
307 Vol 1, p84, Record of Inquest. Sixty-two hours was the time determined by the family's legal team for the 'long weekend' interrogation.
308 For Section 6(6) of the Terrorism Act, on which George Bizos based his interpretation, see David Dyzenhaus, *Judging the Judges, Judging Ourselves: Truth, Reconciliation and the Apartheid Legal Order*, Oxford: Hart, 1998, p63.
309 *Ibid*, p91.
310 *Ibid*, p150.
311 *Ibid*, Vol 1, pp189-90.
312 Vol 1, p292, Record of Inquest.
313 This would not be Inspector Mouton's version when he took the witness stand a few days later. Not only was he not in a hurry but had he been told that Dr Aggett was on the tenth floor, he claimed that he would have gone up there himself.
314 Vol 1, p315, Record of Inquest.
315 Aggett, Affidavit to Sgt Gertruida Blom, 4.2.82, Docket 3, 4.1, Record of Inquest.
316 Vol 2, p485, Record of Inquest.
317 *Ibid*, p598.
318 *Ibid*, pp695-97.
319 *Ibid*, Vol 3, p771.
320 *Ibid*, Vol 4, pp1337-38.
321 'Dispute over affidavits at inquest', *Rand Daily Mail*, 22.6.82.
322 *Ibid*.
323 Affidavits were refused from Firoz Cachalia, Thozamile Gqweta, Oscar Mpetha, Monty Narsoo and Samson Ndou.
324 'South African Police Acts Revealed', *The New York Times*, 24.6.82.
325 William Lane, 14.7.82, Miscellaneous attorney correspondence, Record of Inquest.
326 Over a quarter of a century, almost £100 000 000 was smuggled into South Africa to help those accused of political offences, and their families. See Denis Herbstein, *White Lies: Canon Collins and the Secret War Against Apartheid*, Oxford: James Currey, 2004, p328.

CHAPTER 49 'Mr Bizos is changing the scope of this inquest ...'

327 Vol 3, p841, Record of Inquest.
328 Lelyveld, *The New York Times*, 24.6.82.

329 Vol 3, p872, Record of Inquest.
330 *Ibid*, p947.
331 *Ibid*, p910.
332 *Ibid*, p898.
333 *Ibid*, p901. Bizos was referring to *Cynthia Mongwene vs Minister of Police*, No 12531/78.
334 *Ibid*, p918.
335 *Ibid*, p915
336 *Ibid*, p1086.
337 *Ibid*, p1090.
338 *Ibid*, p1154.
339 *Ibid*, p1156.
340 *Ibid*, p1155.
341 *Ibid*, p1152.
342 *Ibid*.
343 *Sunday Times*, 4.7.82.
344 Docket 1.74, Record of Inquest.
345 'The amazing Aggett Dossier', *Sunday Express*, 4.7.82.
346 'Aggett "definitely not" an ANC man', *Rand Daily Mail*, 26.8.82.
347 Vol 4, p1196, Record of Inquest.
348 *Ibid*, p1205.
349 *Ibid*, p1225.
350 *Ibid*, p1220.
351 *Ibid*, pp1226-27.
352 *Ibid*, p1298.
353 *Ibid*, pp1278-79.
354 *Ibid*, pp1304-305.
355 *Ibid*, p1372.
356 *Ibid*, p1438.
357 *Ibid*, pp1411-12.
358 *Ibid*, Vol 4, p1501.
359 *Ibid*, p1552.
360 *Ibid*, p1537.
361 *Ibid*, Vol 5, p1592.
362 *Ibid*, p1641.
363 *Ibid*, p1642.

CHAPTER 50   The Controller

364 Vol 5, p1729, Record of Inquest.
365 *Ibid*, p1767.
366 *Ibid*, p1804.
367 *Ibid*, p1831.
368 *Ibid*, p1804.

369 *Ibid*, pp1865-68

370 'Minister to reply today to detainee torture claims', *Rand Dail Mail*, 1.10.82.

371 *The Star*, 2.10.82.

372 Vol 6, pp1996-98, Record of Inquest.

373 *Ibid*, p2067.

374 *Ibid*, p2110.

375 'The Controller', *Sunday Times*, 10.10.82.

376 Bizos, *No One to Blame?*, p121.

377 Vol 6, p2241, Record of Inquest.

378 *Ibid*, p2241

379 *Ibid*, p2232.

380 *Ibid*, p2249.

381 Tom Lodge, Affidavit, 12.4.82, Docket 2.1002, Record of Inquest.

382 Vol 6, pp2301-6, Record of Inquest.

383 *Ibid*, pp2292-93.

384 *Ibid*, pp2327-29.

385 *Ibid*, p2296.

386 *Ibid*, p2294.

387 *Ibid*, p2371.

388 *Ibid*, p2377.

389 *Ibid*, p2257.

390 *Ibid*, p2259.

391 *Ibid*, Vol 7, p2436.

392 *Ibid*, Vol 6, p2332.

393 'Aggett's Jailer', *Sowetan*, 11.10.82.

394 The equivalent sum in today's money would be many times higher. Helen Suzman records that by the end of the inquest the Aggetts had spent R87 000. 'The rest of the enormous costs were met by church bodies, private donors and sympathetic trade unions.' *In No Uncertain Terms*, p237.

395 'Stricken father's ordeal seen as bequest', *The Star*, 7.10.82.

396 Bizos, interview, 25.2.11.

397 Judgment, *The State* vs *Barbara Hogan*.

398 Interview with Thomas Karis and Gail Gerhart, New York, 1989, http://www.disa.ukzn.ac.za.

CHAPTER 51 A shameful collaboration

399 Norman Jacobson, Affidavit, 24.2.82, Docket 3.3, Record of Inquest.

400 Vol 7, pp2667-69, Record of Inquest.

401 *Ibid*, p2671.

402 *Ibid*, p2672.

403 *Ibid*, pp2661-62.

404 *Ibid*, p2663.

405 *Ibid*, p2740.

406 *Ibid*, p2737.

407 *Ibid*, p2688.

408 *Ibid*, p2756.

409 'Standing ovation for the Aggetts', *The Star*, 27.10.82.

410 Jill Burger, George Meany Human Rights Award acceptance speech, Washington, DC, 26.10.82, Neil Aggett Papers.

411 'But the souls of the just are in God's hand and torment shall not touch them. In the eyes of foolish men they seemed to be dead, their departure was reckoned as defeat and their going from us as disaster. But they are at peace …', Wisdom of Solomon, 3:1.

412 Vol 8, pp2986–87, Record of Inquest.

413 *Ibid*, p3029.

414 'Deadline on action over "Biko doctors' conduct"', *Rand Daily Mail*, 18.10.82.

415 Report by Jan Adriaan Plomp, Exhibits B6.6, p11, Record of Inquest.

416 *Ibid*, p13.

417 Vol 8, p3139, Record of Inquest.

CHAPTER 52 Summing up

418 Heads of Argument, 10.1, Box C, Record of Inquest.

419 *Ibid*, 12.11.

420 *Ibid*, 5.2.

421 *Ibid*, 31.3

422 *Ibid*.

423 *Ibid*, 21.8.

424 *Ibid*, 31.4

425 *Ibid*, 23.2.

426 Whitehead, Affidavit, 19.2.82, Docket 1.47, Record of Inquest.

427 *Ibid*, 33.1.

428 *Ibid*, 34.

429 *Ibid*, 38.2.

430 *Ibid*, 14.1.4.

431 *Ibid*, 19.5.

432 *Ibid*, 25.5.

433 *Ibid*, 62.

434 'Detainees "made up evidence"', *Cape Times*, 5.11.82.

435 'A diary of alleged police torture and assaults and the nightmare his parents have to live with', *Sunday Tribune*, 7.11.82.

436 'Reject fabrications, Aggett inquest told', *Rand Daily Mail*, 4.11.82.

437 'The suffering of the young woman doctor who lives on', *Sunday Tribune*, 7.11.82.

CHAPTER 53 'No one to blame'

438 Vol 9, p3678, Record of Inquest.

439 *Ibid*, p3686.

440 *Ibid*, p3669.
441 *Ibid*, p3665.
442 *Ibid*, p3670.
443 *Ibid*, pp3682-83.
444 *Ibid*, p3690.
445 *Ibid*.
446 *Ibid*, pp3695-96.
447 *Ibid*, Vol 9, p3705-6.
448 Bizos, *No One to Blame?*, p124.

CHAPTER 54 The unanswered question

449 'Aggett finding upsets family', *The Citizen*, 22.12.82.
450 'Mrs Aggett says she's disappointed by the verdict', *The Star*, 22.12.82.
451 'Outrage at Neil Aggett finding', *Rand Daily Mail*, 22.12.82.
452 *Ibid*.
453 *Ibid*.
454 'Detainees: US puts case', *The Star*, 23.12.82.
455 'Aggett "broken", says Amnesty', *The Star*, 23.12.82.
456 After her release in 1990, Barbara Hogan went on to play an important role in the ANC's transition to government, serving as a dedicated, respected MP and an honest Minister of Health prepared to tackle the HIV/AIDS crisis. After being shifted by President Jacob Zuma to Minister of Public Enterprises, she was dropped from his Cabinet in October 2010.
457 'Evidence withheld, says Floyd', *The Star*, 22.12.82.
458 Andersson, letter to *Rand Daily Mail*, 22.12.82.

CHAPTER 55 Truth and Reconciliation?

459 Bizos, *No One to Blame?*, p5.
460 Constitution of the Republic of South Africa, Act 200 of 1993 (Interim Constitution).
461 Albie Sachs, 'Post-Apartheid South Africa: Truth, Reconciliation and Justice', The Fourth DT Lakdawala Memorial Lecture, New Delhi, 18 December 1998, quoted in Alex Boraine, *A Country Unmasked: Inside South Africa's Truth and Reconciliation Commission*, Oxford: Oxford University Press, 2000, pp258-60.
462 The ANC appointed various internal commissions to investigate abuses in its camps, of which only the Motsuenyane Commission publicly named some individuals believed to be responsible. While the reports of the Skweyiya Commission and the earlier Stuart Commission are available on the ANC's website, the more searching Motsuenyane report is not.
463 As a leading member of the ANC's information department, Pallo Jordan was detained for six weeks by the ANC's internal police in 1983 for jokingly referring to them as 'AmaPoyisa' – the regime's police.

464 Desmond Tutu, letter to *Sunday Times*, 4.12.96.

465 Jill Burger to Dr Wendy Orr, 16.4.96, Neil Aggett Papers.

466 As a newly qualified doctor, trained at the University of Cape Town, Wendy Orr had been so horrified by evidence of torture at the examiner's office in Port Elizabeth that, with legal support, she had successfully applied to the Supreme Court for an interdict against the police to halt further abuse of detainees. She had been the only doctor to take this step.

467 Dr Wendy Orr to Mr and Mrs Aubrey Aggett, 18.4.96, Neil Aggett Papers.

468 Johan Smit, TRC Final Report, 1998, Vol 5, Ch 9, p42.

469 Rokaya Saloojee, TRC Human Rights Violations Submissions, Johannesburg, Case: GO/0171, 29.4.96.

470 Hawa Timol, TRC Human Rights Violations Submissions, Johannesburg, Case: GO/0173, 30.4.96.

471 Elizabeth Floyd, TRC Human Rights Violations Submissions, Johannesburg, 2.5.96.

472 Tutu, *Ibid*.

CHAPTER 56 Truth and recognition

473 Truth and Reconciliation Commission of South Africa Report, Vol 3 Ch 6, pp579–80. Available from http://www.info.gov.za/otherdocs/2003/trc/.

474 Amnesty was refused to six of the seven applicants, citing the murder in June 1985 of the 'Cradock Four' – Matthew Goniwe, Sparrow Mkhonto, Fort Calata and Sicelo Mhlauli.

475 Howard Varney, Discussion Paper, 'Exploring a prosecutions' strategy in the aftermath of the South African Truth and Reconciliation Commission', 2010. Available from http://www.khulumani.net

476 TRC Report, Vol 1, Chairperson's Foreword, pp7–27.

477 Mam'Sylvia Dhlomo-Jele was the mother of student activist Sicelo Dhlomo, shot dead in 1988 a few days after he had appeared in the CBS television documentary 'Children of Apartheid'. Mam'Sylvia believed her 18-year-old son had been murdered by the police and dedicated herself to continue his struggle. She was devasted when four of his comrades applied for amnesty for his killing on the grounds that they believed he had become an informer. The evidence was insubstantial but they had acted in the heat of the moment. They received amnesty.

478 Constitutional Court, 2011, Case CCT 23/10, para 59. Available from http://www.saflii.org/za/cases/ZACC/2011/.

479 *Ibid*, para 61.

480 *Ibid*, para 102.

481 The Constitutional Court awarded Robert McBride R50 000 for this, reducing his previous damages from R150 000.

482 'Neil Aggett looked beyond symptoms', *Rand Daily Mail*, 16.2.82.

483 Siyaya: UDF West Coast Launch 20.8.83, Cape Town: Community Video Education Trust, http://www.cvet.org.za.

484 'Khulumani's perspective on the Robert McBride case against *The Citizen*

newspaper', 22.6.10, http://www.khulumani.net

485 Elizabeth Floyd, Neil Aggett Memorial Lecture, Kingswood College, Grahamstown, 12.3.10, http://www.kingswoodcollege.com.

486 In 2011, Kingswood College instituted a Neil Aggett Award through the support of the 'Class of 1970'. Non-monetary, it is symbolised by a Maureen Quinn bronze sculpture to be given annually to a young leader who places 'service above self'. The first Neil Aggett Award was presented to Luyolo Sijake by Neil's sister, Jill Burger, following the Memorial Lecture given by Jan Theron. See 'About Us', http://www.kingswoodcollege.com.

Select Bibliography

Anderson, David. *Histories of the Hanged*. London: Weidenfeld & Nicolson, 2005.

Barnett, Donald L & Karari Njama. *Mau Mau from Within*. New York and London: Modern Reader Paperbacks, 1966.

Barrell, Howard. 'Conscripts to their Age: African National Congress Operational Strategy, 1976–1986.' DPhil thesis in Politics, Faculty of Social Studies, University of Oxford, 1993.

Bell, Terry with Dumisa Ntsebeza. *Unfinished Business*. London: Verso, 2003.

Bernstein, Hilda. *No. 46 – Steve Biko*. London: International Defence and Aid Fund, 1978.

Biko, Steve. *I Write What I Like*. Edited by Aelred Stubbs CR. London: Penguin, 1978.

Bizos, George. *Odyssey to Freedom*. Johannesburg and Cape Town: Random House in association with Umuzi, 2007.

Bizos, George. *No One to Blame? In Pursuit of Justice in South Africa*. Cape Town: David Philip Publishers and Mayibuye Books, 1998.

Blundell, Michael. *So Rough a Wind*. London: Weidenfeld & Nicolson, 1964.

Boraine, Alex. *A Country Unmasked: Inside South Africa's Truth and Reconciliation Commission*. Oxford: Oxford University Press, 2000.

Dyzenhaus, David. *Judging the Judges, Judging Ourselves: Truth, Reconciliation and the Apartheid Legal Order*. Oxford: Hart, 1998.

Faulkner, William. *Go Down, Moses*. Harmondsworth: Penguin, 1960.

Frederikse, Julie. *South Africa: A Different Kind of War*. London: James Currey with Ravan Press (Johannesburg) and Mambo Press (Gweru), 1986.

Friedman, Steven. *Building Tomorrow Today: African Workers in Trade Unions 1970-1984*. Johannesburg: Ravan Press, 1987.

Goodman, David. *Fault Lines: Journeys into the New South Africa*. Berkeley: University of California Press, 1999.

Herbstein, Denis. *White Lies: Canon Collins and the Secret War Against Apartheid*. Oxford: James Currey, 2004.

Kariuki, Josiah Mwangi. *'Mau Mau' Detainee: The Account by a Kenya African of his Experiences in Detention Camps 1953-1960*. London: Oxford University Press, 1963.

Kazantzakis, Nikos. *Zorba the Greek*. London: Faber & Faber, 1961.

Kenyatta, Jomo. *Facing Mount Kenya*. Introduction by B Malinowski. London: Secker &

Warburg, 1938.

Krog, Antjie. *Country of My Skull*. London: Jonathan Cape, 1998.

Kuus, Juhan. *South Africa in Black and White*. With text by Trevor McDonald. London: Harrap, 1987.

Lelyveld, Joseph. *Move Your Shadow: South Africa, Black and White*. New York: Times Books, 1985.

Mandela, Nelson. *In His Own Words*. Edited by Kader Asmal, David Chidester and Wilmot James. London: Abacus, 2004.

Mashinini, Emma. *Strikes Have Followed Me All My Life*. London: The Women's Press, 1989.

Mtshali, Oswald Joseph. *Sounds of a Cowhide Drum*. Johannesburg: Renoster Books, 1971.

Murray, Martin. *South Africa: Time of Agony, Time of Destiny*. London: Verso, 1987.

Odhiambo, ES Atieno & J Lonsdale. *Mau Mau & Nationhood*. Oxford: James Currey, 2003.

O'Malley, Padraig. *Shades of Difference: Mac Maharaj and the Struggle for South Africa*. New York: Viking, 2007.

Russell, Diana EH. *Lives of Courage: Women for a New South Africa*. New York: Basic Books, 1989.

Sanders, James. *Apartheid's Friends: The Rise and Fall of South Africa's Secret Services*. London: John Murray, 2006.

South African Democracy Education Trust. *The Road to Democracy*, Volume 2 [1970-1980], Pretoria: University of South Africa, 2007.

Suttner, Raymond. *The ANC Underground in South Africa to 1976: A Social and Historical Study*. Johannesburg: Jacana, 2008.

Suzman, Helen. *In No Uncertain Terms*. Johannesburg: Jonathan Ball Publishers, 1993.

Truth and Reconciliation Commission of South Africa. Truth and Reconciliation Commission of South Africa Report. Available from http://www.info.gov.za/otherdocs/2003/trc/.

Van Wyk, Chris. *It is Time to Go Home*. Johannesburg: Ad Donker, 1979.

Wesley, John & Charles. *Selected Writings and Hymns*, 'The Nature, Design, and General Rules of the United Societies ... 1743'. Edited by Frank Whaling. Mahwah, NJ: Paulist Press, 1981.

List of Interviews

All interviews oral unless indicated otherwise.

Dr Rob Adam, correspondence, 6 September 2009, 18 June 2011.

Taffy Adler, Johannesburg, 7 August 1995.

Joy and Aubrey Aggett, Somerset West, 7 April 1995.

Dr Michael Aggett, Somerset West, 10 April 1995.

Dr Gavin Andersson, Johannesburg, 18 April 1995, 30 July to 8 August 1995, 9 August 2008 & correspondence.

George Bizos sc, Oxford, 25 February 2011.

Prof Phil Bonner, Johannesburg, 7 August 1995.

Yvette Breytenbach, correspondence from 15 November 2009.

Jill Burger, 6 June 2010; Jill & Paul Burger, Bournemouth, 26 to 27 August 2010 & correspondence/telephone.

Rev Frank Chikane, Cape Town, 24 July 1995.

Richard Cock, correspondence 9/11 October 2010.

Keith Coleman, London, 21 March 2010.

Clive Cope, Johannesburg, 8 August 1995.

Athalie Crawford, Cape Town, 22 July 1995.

David Dison, Johannesburg, 20 April 1995 & correspondence/Skype interviews.

Dr Elizabeth (Liz) Floyd, Johannesburg, 23 April 1995, 31 July 1995, 3 August 1995 and telephone interviews.

Dr Doug Hindson, via telephone, 7 February 2010.

Barbara Hogan, Cape Town, 20 & 30 July 1995.

Prof Trefor Jenkins, via telephone, 21 November 2011.

Bridget King, correspondence 15 February 2011.

Sipho Kubeka, Bournemouth, 6 & 8 May 1995 & correspondence.

Denis Kuny sc, via telephone, 11 September 2011.

Mac Maharaj, correspondence 20 March 2009.

Israel Mogoatlhe, Germiston, 5 August 1995.

Ismail Momoniat, Johannesburg, 8 August 1995.

Sisa Njikelana, Johannesburg, 31 July 1995.

Andrew Rein, correspondence from 30 July 2011.

Jane and David Rosenthal, Cape Town, 23 July 1995.

Dr Dennis Rubel, Johannesburg, 2 August 1995.

Brian Sandberg, correspondence from 25 February 2010.

Marius Schoon, Johannesburg, 8 August 1995.

Maurice Smithers, Johannesburg, 8 August 1995 & correspondence.

Annie Smyth, Johannesburg, 3 August 1995.

Jan Theron, Cape Town, 12 April 1995.

Dr Liz Thomson, Lentocow Mission Hospital, Creighton, 28 July 1995.

Auret van Heerden, correspondence 12 October 2009.

Edwin (Eddie) Wes, Johannesburg, 3 August 1995.

Joanne Yawitch, Johannesburg, 8 August 1995.

Note: Informal conversations also took place with Luli Callinicos and Prof Edward (Eddie) Webster, Johannesburg.

Acknowledgments

I owe thanks to many people who have trusted me to tell Neil's story, and, inevitably, part of their own. While searching for the sound of Neil's own voice, I have wanted the voices of those who knew him to be heard by the reader. His parents, Joy and Aubrey Aggett, spoke openly and bravely of their tragedy and were generous in giving me access to family papers, prior to these being lodged in the University of Cape Town archives. Neil's parents and his older brother Michael (who took me to Eagle's Nest) are no longer alive to read this biography, but I am deeply grateful to his sister, Jill Burger, for her steady support. In 1995, Aubrey Aggett authorised David Dison to give me a full set of the dockets submitted by the family's legal team to the inquest, so that I could bring them to England. David, who had been Neil's lawyer and his friend, provided me with my first bridge into Johannesburg's 'white left' in the 1970s. His outline of a network of activists, black and white, made me sense the bigger story, and I have much appreciated his ongoing assistance.

This book could not have been written without the unflagging support of Neil's close comrade Gavin Andersson. In 1995, Gavin took me on a tour of the landmarks of Neil's 'Jozi' and spent many hours explaining to me the fraught political landscape for activists in the late 1970s and early 1980s. Since my return five years ago to this earlier research, Gavin has been extraordinarily patient and prompt in responding to countless email questions. It has been a long journey.

I am very grateful to Liz Floyd, who, in April and July 1995, talked very frankly, both personally and politically. Special thanks go to Sipho Kubeka, who regarded Neil as a brother, for lengthy interviews given while in England, and to Jan Theron, Israel Mogoatlhe and Sisa Njikelana, for all their insights into Neil as a unionist. Israel's letters in the intervening years reminded me of his desire to see a book about his comrade.

Email offered new possibilities of seeking out those who knew Neil or who could add to his story. I have been touched by how his friends have generously opened up with memories, even when these were painful. My thanks for interviews – whether face to face or by correspondence – go to Rob Adam, Taffy Adler, Phil Bonner, Yvette Breytenbach, Frank Chikane, Richard Cock, Keith Coleman, Clive Cope, Athalie Crawford, Doug Hindson, Barbara Hogan, Trefor Jenkins, Bridget King, Denis Kuny, Mac Maharaj, Ismail Momoniat, Andrew Rein, Jane and David Rosenthal, Dennis Rubel, Brian Sandberg, Marius Schoon, Maurice Smithers, Annie Smyth, Liz Thomson, Auret van Heerden, Eddie Wes and Joanne Yawitch. Special thanks go to George Bizos for talking to me so passionately about the inquest, after almost 30 years, and for writing the Foreword.

I would like to thank Chris van Wyk for the use of his poem 'In Detention' and for an encouraging email that was a real fillip after I returned to this project in 2007. My thanks go to Jane Barrett for allowing me to use her vivid, poignant letter to Gavin Andersson, relaying events in the traumatic aftermath of Neil's death, and I appreciate use of the letters of condolence written to Neil's family.

I am indebted to all the photographers whose images appear here. In 1995, Eddie Wes gave me a number of prints, including his wonderfully spirited photographs of Neil among the Vegetable Gardeners. These have been a constant presence during my writing. My thanks go to Juhan Kuus, Lesley Lawson, Paul Weinberg and Omar Badsha for their particular assistance. I thank the makers of two documentary films that still speak volumes after 30 years: Cliff Bestall and Michael Gavshon, for *Passing the Message*, in which we glimpse Neil absorbed in listening at the Food and Canning Workers' Union conference in September 1981; and to Mark Newman, for his short, evocative film, made less than five months later, in the midst of mourners at Neil's funeral.

I have greatly valued the assistance received from Michelle Pickover and the excellent team at the Historical Papers Archive, University of the Witwatersrand, and from Lesley Hart at the University of Cape Town Libraries. I thank FAWU for permission to access AFCWU papers. My thanks also go to Fritz Schoon, formerly Co-ordinator of the Freedom of Information Programme at the South African History Archives, for his persistence in obtaining Neil's security files during a bizarre process of 'declassification'; Vino Reddy, Documentation Centre, University of KwaZulu-Natal; University of the Western Cape (UWC) – Robben Island Mayibuye Archive; Max and Audrey Coleman; Archbishop Desmond Tutu and his assistant; Carol Archibald, Anglican Church Provincial Archivist; Garrey Dennie for his paper on South African political funerals; Frances Suzman Jowell for a facsimile copy of Maurice Smithers' note and extracts from her mother Helen Suzman's letters; Kingswood College, Brian Sandberg and the 'Class of 1970' for inviting me and my husband Nandha to attend the 2011 Neil Aggett Memorial Lecture; Paul Trewhela, Ros Allison, Paul Burger and Mavis Aggett for digging into family memories and papers.

Very special thanks go to Luli Callinicos and Eddie Webster for providing me with a home while researching in Johannesburg. Many conversations helped me better understand the complex layers of perspectives and tensions as black unions emerged in the 1970s. I also thank Eddie Webster for reading and commenting on my first full draft. Steven Friedman's study, *Building Tomorrow Today: African Workers in Trade Unions 1970-1984*, provided a richly detailed source of information.

I thank my daughter Maya Naidoo for her assistance and companionship in my early research and for transcribing many of my 1995 interviews. I appreciate the generous assistance with translation given by Shereen Pandit and Hannchen Koornhof.

Olusola Oyeleye, Patsy Pillay and Phyllis Naidoo have all sustained me with their encouragement that I should tell this story. I am very grateful to Sharen Green, Maren Bodenstein, Sharon Muiruri and Jeanne Hromnik for their reading and comments. I thank Martin Coyne for his assistance with photos; John Aldridge and Margaret Ling for advice; and Lauren Jacobson for directing me to Jonathan Ball Publishers. I very much appreciate Jeremy Boraine's close involvement and am indebted to his reader, Finuala Dowling, for her astute advice on paring back an overlong manuscript. I am most grateful to my editor, Alfred LeMaitre, for his meticulous scrutiny and care and to Valda Strauss for proofreading. Should any errors exist, they are mine. My thanks go to Francine Blum, particularly for her good humour in helping track down old photographs, to Michiel Botha and Kevin Shenton for design, and to everyone at Jonathan Ball who has helped to bring this book to South African readers. I thank my agent Hilary Delamere, especially for her understanding as I put youth fiction plans on hold.

Finally, as ever, I thank my husband Nandha for his constant support during the long years of this project, offering me both sustenance and love.

Beverley Naidoo
BOURNEMOUTH, JULY 2012

Index

References to notes appear in italics

Beverley Naidoo was born in Johannesburg where she attended Parktown Convent and the University of Witwatersrand. She was detained under the General Law Amendment Act, dubbed the '90-Day Act', in 1964 before continuing her education at the University of York in England. She has worked as a teacher, educational adviser and writer, and holds a PhD from the University of Southampton for research into British teenagers' responses to literature and racism, published as *Through Whose Eyes?*

Naidoo began writing in exile. Her first two books, *Journey to Jo'burg* (children's fiction) and *Censoring Reality* (adult non-fiction) were banned in South Africa until 1991. She has also written novels, short stories, poetry and plays. Her many awards include the Carnegie Medal for *The Other Side of Truth* and honorary degrees from the The Open University and the Universities of Southampton and Exeter for a body of work. Naidoo and illustrator Piet Grobler, co-creators of a South African *Aesop's Fables*, were the 2008 South African nominees for the Hans Christian Andersen Award.

In *Burn My Heart*, Naidoo explored in fiction the colonial world into which her younger cousin Neil Aggett was born in Kenya during the Mau Mau resistance. *Death of an Idealist: In search of Neil Aggett* is a fully-referenced biography which examines his transformation into the militant yet gentle doctor-cum-union activist who became the 51st, and only white, detainee to die in security police custody.